PRAISE F
MODERN GENR

Like toddlers, we interpreters have been b̲e̲ ̲,̲ but Andrew Judd has given us a book that w̲ᵢₗₗ ̲ₕₑₗₚ us mature. This will soon be the go-to book for students and scholars on genre theory and its import for biblical studies. Engaging, informative, and accessible – highly recommended.

> **ANDREW T. ABERNETHY,** Wheaton College,
> professor of Old Testament

Forget what you think you know about biblical studies and genre! Dr. Andrew Judd shows us that genre theory is way more complicated than people think and yet he explains concisely and clearly how genres work, how they apply in biblical studies, and why we really need to know about literary genres if we want to understand Genesis 1 or Revelation 22. An outstanding book and a must-read for anyone who wants to know how to understand the Bible in its diverse literary expressions.

> **REV. DR. MICHAEL F. BIRD,** deputy principal
> at Ridley College, Melbourne, Australia

Andrew Judd argues that a robust genre theory has been woefully neglected in biblical studies. I agree and heartily commend his book to all scholars and students of the Bible. But don't be misdirected by its title. While the book does indeed address genre theory, it introduces theory in so captivating a way that you'll hardly recognize the genre. Judd deftly weaves theory – drawn from linguistic and rhetorical domains – with a multitude of illustrations, analogies, and practical applications to biblical genres. Judd's witty register, often humorous examples, and clear prose make this an enjoyable and essential read for biblical hermeneutics.

> **JEANNINE BROWN,** PhD, David Price Professor of Biblical and
> Theological Foundations, Bethel Seminary of Bethel University

Genre is at the heart of reading, and reading is at the heart of knowing and understanding the Scriptures. If you don't have a handle on genre, good luck with reading the Bible well. Andrew Judd's *Modern Genre Theory* is therefore a gift to students, professors, and, well, anyone who wants to read the Bible well. With a mix of flair, humour, scholarship, and immense clarity, this book is the most helpful introduction to genre theory for readers of the Bible. It is a great exemplar of its genre.

> **CONSTANTINE R. CAMPBELL,** research director,
> Sydney College of Divinity

This is a lively, engaging, and sometimes provocative review of modern genre theory and its relevance for biblical studies.

> **JOHN J. COLLINS**, Holmes Professor of Old Testament
> Criticism and Interpretation, Yale Divinity School

Reading this book is like being in the room with the best kind of teacher — learned but not stuffy, someone who knows the scholarly territory and its pitfalls and has a sure instinct for the right kind of questions to ask of a biblical text. Andrew Judd's book should be heavily used; it makes biblical studies as interesting, fun, and intellectually freeing as it should be.

> **ELLEN F. DAVIS**, Amos Ragan Kearns Distinguished
> Professor of Bible and Practical Theology,
> Duke Divinity School

Modern Genre Theory is not a dry or stuffy book about genre. Andrew Judd writes with such a delightfully friendly tone, making this highly informative book filled with not only clarity and insight but also wit and humor. I highly recommend this book, which you could expect from the genre of book endorsement, but I truly mean it because I derived so much enjoyment from learning more about genre.

> **JOHN ANTHONY DUNNE**, associate professor of New Testament,
> Bethel Seminary of Bethel University

Andrew Judd's exposition of contemporary genre theory is at once a lucid summary of the state of the art and an illuminating intervention in the field of biblical studies.

> **JOHN FROW**, emeritus professor, discipline of English
> and writing, University of Sydney

How human language works, particularly in its written form, is a concern that Bible readers cannot ignore. The analysis of the various genres of biblical literature is part and parcel of reading and understanding the Bible. Andrew Judd has done us a great service by identifying the issues that face us in dealing with biblical texts. Writing in engagingly accessible prose, he unravels some of the major genres and carefully lays out the ways and means that ordinary Christians can use to distinguish the various ways biblical texts convey God's word to us in our own time.

> **GRAEME GOLDSWORTHY**, PhD, former lecturer
> in biblical theology and hermeneutics,
> Moore Theological College, Sydney

Andrew Judd has written a profoundly helpful introduction on modern genre theory that will be a resource for both scholars and those just beginning their engagement with Scripture. With witty prose and scholarly rigour, Judd offers an insightful critique of how the field of biblical studies has disastrously misunderstood how genre works. The book offers a constructive way forward by pairing discussions on theory with engaging examples from biblical literature. Easily the best and most fun book on literary theory you will ever read.

BRANDON HURLBERT, PhD, lecturer in Hebrew Bible, Durham University

This witty, accessible introduction to genre is a delight to read. Although addressed to scholars in biblical studies, it richly deserves a wider readership – anyone who can draw on its scholarship and appreciate its pedagogic finesse. I can't think of a better guide to modern approaches to genre.

J. R. MARTIN, professor of linguistics, University of Sydney

In this remarkable and eye-opening book, Andrew Judd is both learned and accessible, scholarly and popular. Any and every student of the Bible should read it, as they will understand the whole Bible better as a result.

R. W. L. MOBERLY, emeritus professor, Durham University

The question of genre is a recurring and nagging problem of textual interpretation. Andrew Judd addresses the major issues head-on and provides a summary of the main theories, as well as an explication of key examples. One of the bonuses is a clear introduction to important recent theorizing about genre from a linguistic standpoint that appreciates situational context. This book should prove insightful and helpful for those who desire a timely introduction to the important field of genre studies.

STANLEY E. PORTER, PhD, president and professor of New Testament, and Roy A. Hope Chair in Christian Worldview, McMaster Divinity College

This book is as fun to read as it is precise. Too many scholars still work from outdated theories on genre. Andrew Judd helpfully moves the conversation forward by introducing the insights gained from modern genre theory. He does so in a way that is not reactive but measured; he not only speaks of theory but also applies theory to specific texts. I have now found my new favorite book on genre and will encourage all who study the Bible to read it and learn from it.

PATRICK SCHREINER, associate professor of New Testament and biblical theology, Midwestern Baptist Theological Seminary

MODERN GENRE THEORY

AN INTRODUCTION
FOR BIBLICAL STUDIES

ANDREW JUDD

ZONDERVAN
ACADEMIC

ZONDERVAN ACADEMIC

Modern Genre Theory
Copyright © 2024 by Andrew Judd

Zondervan is a registered trademark of The Zondervan Corporation, L.L.C., a wholly owned subsidary of HarperCollins Christian Publishing, Inc.

Requests for information should be addressed to customercare@harpercollins.com.

Zondervan titles may be purchased in bulk for educational, business, fundraising, or sales promotional use. For information, please email SpecialMarkets@Zondervan.com.

ISBN 978-0-310-14472-4 (audio)

Library of Congress Cataloging-in-Publication Data

Names: Judd, Andrew, author.
Title: Modern genre theory : an introduction for biblical studies / Andrew Judd.
Description: Grand Rapids, Michigan : Zondervan, [2024] | Includes bibliographical references and index.
Identifiers: LCCN 2023044344 (print) | LCCN 2023044345 (ebook) | ISBN 9780310144694 (paperback) | ISBN 9780310144700 (ebook)
Subjects: LCSH: Bible—Study and teaching. | Literature—History and criticism—Theory, etc. | Literary form. | BISAC: RELIGION / Biblical Criticism & Interpretation / General | LITERARY CRITICISM / Modern / General
Classification: LCC BS600.3 .J73 2024 (print) | LCC BS600.3 (ebook) | DDC 220.076—dc23/eng/20240119
LC record available at https://lccn.loc.gov/2023044344
LC ebook record available at https://lccn.loc.gov/2023044345

Cover design: Studio Gearbox
Cover image: © Normform / Shutterstock
Interior design: Kait Lamphere

Printed in the United States of America

24 25 26 27 28 LBC 5 4 3 2 1

{Dedication}
[To / ~~For~~] [~~the memory of~~] my
[~~beloved~~ / ~~long-suffering~~ / ~~estranged~~ / ~~famous~~ / ~~erstwhile~~ / ~~royal~~]
[~~patron~~ / ~~benefactor~~ / ~~wife~~ / teacher / ~~father~~ /
~~patron~~ / friend / ~~reader~~ / ~~acquaintance~~]
Liam Semler.

CONTENTS

ABBREVIATIONS

OLD TESTAMENT, NEW TESTAMENT

Gen	Genesis	Ezek	Ezekiel
Exod	Exodus	Dan	Daniel
Lev	Leviticus	Amos	Amos
Num	Numbers	Zech	Zechariah
Deut	Deuteronomy	Matt	Matthew
Josh	Joshua	Rom	Romans
Judg	Judges	1–2 Cor	1–2 Corinthians
1–2 Sam	1–2 Samuel	Gal	Galatians
1–2 Kgs	1–2 Kings	Eph	Ephesians
1–2 Chr	1–2 Chronicles	Phil	Philippians
Esth	Esther	Col	Colossians
Ps/PSS	Psalms	1–2 Thess	1–2 Thessalonians
Prov	Proverbs	1–2 Tim	1–Timothy
Eccl	Ecclesiastes	Titus	Titus
Song	Song of Songs	Phlm	Philemon
Isa	Isaiah	Heb	Hebrews
Jer	Jeremiah	1–2 Pet	1–2 Peter
Lam	Lamentations	Rev	Revelation

DEUTEROCANONICAL WORKS AND OLD TESTAMENT PSEUDEPIGRAPHA

1 En.	1 Enoch	Jub.	Jubilees
3 Bar	3 Baruch	T.Levi	Testament of Levi

JOURNALS, PERIODICALS, REFERENCE WORKS, SERIES

AB	Anchor Bible
ABR	*Australian Biblical Review*

ANEM   Ancient Near East Monographs
BAGL   *Biblical and Greek Linguistics*
BBR   *Bulletin for Biblical Research*
BECNT   Baker Exegetical Commentary on the New Testament
Beit. Gesch. Dtsch.   *Beiträge zur Geschichte der deutschen Sprache*
Sprache Lit.   *und Literatur*
Bib   *Biblica*
BibInt   *Biblical Interpretation*
BibInt   Biblical Interpretation Series
CBQ   *Catholic Biblical Quarterly*
CCEL   Christian Classics Ethereal Library
ConBNT   Conietctanea Biblica: New Testament Series
Crit. Inq.   *Critical Inquiry*
CTL   Cambridge Textbooks in Linguistics
CurBR   *Currents in Biblical Research*
DAPSAC   Discourse Approaches to Politics, Society and Culture
DSD   *Dead Sea Discoveries*
EEC   Evangelical Exegetical Commentary
EvQ   *Evangelical Quarterly*
FOTL   Forms of the Old Testament Literature
HS   *Hebrew Studies*
Int   *Interpretation*
JAAR   *Journal of the Academy of Religion*
JBL   *Journal of Biblical Literature*
JETS   *Journal of the Evangelical Theological Society*
JHebS   *Journal of Hebrew Scriptures*
JLS   *Journal of Literary Semantics*
JR   *Journal of Religion*
JSJSup   Supplements to the Journal for the Study of Judaism
JSNT   *Journal for the Study of the New Testament*
JSOT   *Journal for the Study of the Old Testament*
JSOTSup   Journal for the Study of the Old Testament Supplement Series
JSPSup   Journal for the Study of the Pseudepigrapha Supplement Series
JTISup   Journal of Theological Interpretation Supplements
Lang. Lit.   *Language and Literature*
LEC   Library of Early Christianity
LCL   Loeb Classical Library

LHBOTS	The Library of Hebrew Bible/Old Testament Studies
LHS	*Linguistics and the Human Sciences*
LNTS	The Library of New Testament Studies
NICOT	New International Commentary on the Old Testament
NLH	*New Literary History*
NovT	*Novum Testamentum*
NTS	*New Testament Studies*
PhT	*Philosophy Today*
Philos. Rhetor.	*Philosophy and Rhetoric*
PNTC	Pillar New Testament Commentary
ProEccl	*Pro Ecclesia*
Proof	*Prooftexts: A Journal of Jewish Literary History*
QJS	*Quarterly Journal of Speech*
RelSRev	*Religious Studies Review*
SBET	*Scottish Bulletin of Evangelical Theology*
SBLDS	Society of Biblical Literature Dissertation Series
SBLSBS	Society of Biblical Literature Sources for Biblical Study
SBL SymS	Society of Biblical Literature Symposium Series
SBT	Studies in Biblical Theology
SemeiaSt	Semeia Studies
STDJ	Studies on the Texts of the Desert of Judah
SydS	*Sydney Studies in English*
TQ	*TESOL Quarterly*
THL	*Theory and History of Literature*
TynBul	*Tyndale Bulletin*
VT	*Vetus Testamentum*
WAWSup	Writings from the Ancient World Supplement Series
WBC	Word Biblical Commentary
WC	*Written Communication*
WUNT	Wissenschaftliche Untersuchungen Zum Neuen Testament
ZECNT	Zondervan Exegetical Commentary on the New Testament

GENERAL AND TECHNICAL

AD	*anno Domini* (in the year of [our] Lord)
BC	before Christ
cf.	*confer*, compare
ed(s).	editor(s), edited by, edition

et al.	*et alia*, and others
i.e.	*id est*, that is
RGS	rhetorical genre studies
rev.	revised
SFL	systemic functional linguistics
trans.	translator, translated by
v(v).	verse(s)

INTRODUCTION

In 2018, Facebook came down hard on the Babylon Bee (a Christian satirical news site that used to be quite funny) for distributing misinformation. The Bee had shared one of its daily satirical posts ("CNN Purchases Industrial-Sized Washing Machine to Spin News Before Publication"), and while some people may have chuckled, not everyone was amused. An independent fact-checker (David Mikkelson of Snopes.com) was contracted by Facebook to investigate the claims, and he determined that the fake news article contained, well, fake news. The post was blocked, and the satirists warned that a repeat offence would result in the content industry equivalent of being summarily hung, drawn, and quartered (diminished reach and demonetization). There was no right of appeal.

The decision was ultimately reversed, and Snopes.com sensibly introduced a new category for labeling satire. But controversy over this and other satirical publications has continued. Serious money (and therefore lawyers) is involved. The satirists point out that punishing satirists for being factually incorrect would in itself be a good joke if it wasn't also threatening their livelihoods (they also claim a suspiciously partisan pattern to the "independent fact-checking"). In their defense, fact-checkers point out that – regardless of whether the articles are *intended* as satire – an alarming number of people share them *thinking* they are real news items. It can be hard to distinguish between a fake news-article and a fake-news article. You've probably got an uncle who struggles to tell the difference.

In fairness to everyone involved in this ridiculous kerfuffle, let's just acknowledge where responsibility for all this squarely falls. I don't blame the fact-checkers. I don't blame the satirists. (I don't even blame your uncle for sharing the article thinking it was real news.)

The true villain in this story is *genre*.

We will unpack what **genre**[1] means in the following chapters, but let's start with this: *Genres are relatively stable conventions that writers and readers use to make meaning in certain contexts but not others.*

---

1. When you see a word displayed in boldface, you will know to go to the glossary in the back of the book for a succinct definition.

This last bit ("certain contexts but not others") is what makes navigating genre so complex. The **conventions** of English grammar are tricky, but at least they apply whenever you are speaking English. The conventions of genre, in contrast, are far fickler. Sometimes they apply, but in other **situations** they don't. This means the same words can be taken in vastly different ways, depending on the reader's initial guess at which recurring situation we are dealing with and therefore which rules apply. In our Babylon Bee example, the reader is being asked to instantly distinguish between a real news article that is fake, and a fake news article that is trying to look real in its form and style but whose function is actually to make us laugh, not convey reliable information about current affairs. Genre expects a lot of us as readers.

And then there's the whole question of who gets to decide what the "correct" genre is. Sure, the owners of the Babylon Bee say on their website that it is "satirical" – but do they get the final word? If a significant number of our uncles share that article as if it were factual, at what point does that start to affect the genre? Can genre change from one social context to another?

And if you think it's only uncles on Facebook who stumble over questions of genre, allow me to reach for a whole other can of worms. (Wish me luck.)

GENESIS 1

Genesis 1 describes seven days in which God creates everything from light to trees to humans and then (in Gen 2:2) takes up rest. How would someone go about fact-checking this chapter? I can tell you. Some of my atheist friends will happily point out that (1) the sun is allegedly created on the *fourth* day, *after* plants appear on earth, but (2) plants require photosynthesis to live, and so (3) the biblical creation story is impossible. Case closed. Obvious misinformation.

The logic, I'll admit, is eminently watertight. But there is a massive missing step. Like the satirical fact-checkers, these folks are assuming an answer to these basic questions: What is this thing that I'm reading, and how does it work? Which conventions for communication apply in this situation? In other words, what *genre* is Genesis 1?

In fairness, though, even professional Bible scholars struggle to agree on which genre box Genesis 1 belongs in – which is surprising, or even a little embarrassing, given that it's page one of the Bible and already we can't even decide if what we are reading is poetry or narrative. Some say "elevated prose" or "narrative," others say "poetry," while still others say "poetic prose" or "prosaic poetry" (and that's before we consider options like "mytho-historical discourse" or "cosmic temple inauguration liturgy").

Whatever we decide about the genre of Genesis 1 will influence the way we read the **text**. What exactly does *create* mean? What significance should we put on the repetition of key words like *day*? What kinds of truth claims about the world are being made, and how do they relate to our scientific questions? Is the sequence of days determined by chronological or thematic concerns? And what does the text want us as readers to do with this information?

We are so used to making instant genre designations – satire, news article, novel, parking ticket – that we often jump to genre conclusions when reading old books. This is especially true with a great work of literature we are very familiar with, like the Bible. Reading the Bible a certain way just feels natural to us – it's the "plain reading of the text."[2] Perhaps we aren't even aware that we are reading it *as* something. But then something jumps out that just doesn't fit what we were expecting – we read that God made plants on day three and humans on day six (Gen 1:11, 26), but then we barely turn the page and read that God made humans before the plants (2:5–7). Perhaps the Bible *is* broken! Or, more likely, perhaps our assumptions about the genre of this text weren't quite right and we got off on the wrong foot in the beginning.

Complex, isn't it? We will return to Genesis 1 in chapter 8, but for the moment I just want to observe that genre has a lot to answer for. I think most of our big disagreements about the Bible begin as unconscious disagreements about genre. Genre is as vital to interpretation as it is tricky to nail down. Genre creates confusion and makes reading unpredictable as we struggle to read texts from long ago whose genres have disappeared from current usage.

THE GIFT OF GENRE

At the same time, genre is a gloriously productive gift. Genres offer us an endless variety of experiences as readers. Genre is the reason we can have poems as well as parking tickets. Genre is the reason we can be confronted with hard truths about ourselves in the fictional world of a novel, then pick up a scientific journal and marvel at entirely different kinds of truths.

Genre enriches our experience of literature. But it also enriches our knowledge of God. Genre is part of how God has revealed himself. We have in the Bible more than one kind of Scripture. It is too small a thing for God to reveal himself in one genre only. He has made his light shine through all manner of genres. Would we truly understand his faithfulness if we couldn't witness his

---

2. The "plain" or "literal" reading historically meant non-allegorical interpretations (basically the historical sense in Origen and Gregory the Great's model), but it has come to mean "what I thought the text meant before I thought about it much."

unwavering character and undivided commitment to humanity throughout the narratives? Could we feel the full force of his passionate love and indignant anger without the brutally vivid poetry of the prophets? Would monotheism and the abhorrence of idolatry have made it from head to stubborn heart without the creative repurposing of vassal treaty and marriage covenant? What would "love your neighbor" mean to us without the detailed case studies of Exodus or the parables of the Gospels?

(These, by the way, are rhetorical questions. But you knew that already. Why? That's right: genre!)

WHAT GENRE IS THIS BOOK?

Speaking of the genre of this book, you are currently reading an introduction to **modern genre theory** for biblical studies. I began with an illustration from recent events, which is your first clue that this is an introductory work aimed at an audience of graduate students and scholars who are not genre specialists (though it wasn't a story about climbing Mount Everest, so you know this isn't a "leadership self-help" book). And I'm writing in the first person, using contractions (like "I'm") and starting sentences with conjunctions, so you can tell that I'm aiming for an interpersonal dynamic between writer and reader on the friendly and accessible end of the spectrum, imitating an informal conversation.

That said, I've just used several Latin-derived words (*interpersonal, spectrum, nonspecialist, imitating,* and *conversation*) that, unlike homely Germanic words, tend to in English bump the **register** up from smart casual to dress boots and nice jacket territory. Also, in a couple pages, I'm going to drop some footnotes to intimidating-sounding technical works (something I try not to do in actual conversations), so while I'm aiming for friendly and accessible, I still want you to know that I have read the things and am qualified to guide you into this field of study (here's hoping!). The footnotes and annotated bibliography will also provide plenty for biblical studies professionals to follow up on as they are (again, here's hoping) emboldened to bring modern genre theory into their own area of specialization. I'll try to avoid unnecessary jargon, but there is a glossary at the end for any technical terms that slip through.

WHAT IS GENRE THEORY?

I hope you're not disappointed, but this isn't a general hermeneutics textbook telling you how I think you should go about interpreting the various genres in the Bible – at least, not primarily.[3] Sure, you could use it like that. Chapters 5 to 12 are full of practical examples of how genre theory might make a difference for the way we approach real-life biblical genres, from Old Testament narrative to apocalypse to letter. But these are offered as illustrations of something more fundamental. At its heart, this book is about *genre itself* – how it works, how we go about understanding biblical genres, and why subtly different understandings of a text's genre produce such different experiences and understandings of the biblical text. Specifically, I want to introduce modern genre theory and show why biblical studies urgently needs to take its tenets on board.

By genre *theory*, we mean more than thinking and talking about a particular genre (which happens all the time), but also a conscious reflection on what genre itself is and how genres work. And talking about *modern* genre theory implies that there are *ancient* or *classical* kinds of genre theories.

Classical Genre Theory

Classical genre theories try to make sense of all the different species of books in front of them by seeking to classify them within broadly applicable, mostly fixed categories. Each member belongs to a class, and classes generally don't overlap. This is cat. This is dog. Cats have four legs; dogs also have four legs. Dogs bark; cats do not bark. Sure, there are edge cases that test our ability to put everyone in the right box (for example, Australian wild dingoes look like dogs, but they don't bark and certainly don't play fetch or wait around for you to feed them). But with enough effort and definitional tweaking, we should be able to place even the hard cases into the right box (e.g., dingoes are an undomesticated relative of the dog).[4]

Classical genre theorists approach the different kinds of texts in a way similar to our classification of cats and dogs; in fact, they will often fall back on analogies from biological sciences, talking about classes, specimens, and **family resemblances**. There is some potential for the evolution of these genre species (through the careful genetic combination of two classes), but classical theories lean toward a static view, seeing genres as stable or fixed entities (at least once they reach maturity).

People often trace classical genre theory back to the Greek philosopher Aristotle (384–322 BC), who famously described three types of literature: lyric, epic, and drama (though his categories have probably been misunderstood in

---

3. There are some great books that do this already. My current favorite is Jeannine K. Brown, *Scripture as Communication: Introducing Biblical Hermeneutics*, 2nd ed. (Grand Rapids: Baker Academic, 2021).
4. My editor's cat both barks and plays fetch, which (1) is impressive and (2) illustrates why classification is a doomed enterprise.

modern times).[5] Ancient theorists had strong views on *the right way* to do a genre. The great Roman poet and genre policeman Horace (65–8 BC) was the one who laid down the law forbidding the mixing of genres. He looked down on poets mixing genres in the same way purists look down on pineapple on pizza or socks in sandals (though, like most Roman poets, he seems to have spent a lot of his time breaking his own rule – like that time he wrote a *letter* in *poetry* about how you definitely shouldn't mix genres).[6]

In terms of classical European genre theory, the person to see is Johann Wolfgang von Goethe (1749–1832), one of Germany's greatest writers, who spent a small part of his incredible life describing the different forms of German folk story. For Russian folk tales, you'll be wanting the literary critic Vladimir Propp (1895–1970). His *Morphology of the Folktale* (1927) was intended to approach genre as a "scientific" study: "as exact as the morphology of organic formations."[7] This kind of genre analysis can be described broadly as **structuralist**.[8] As the name implies the goal is to find the fundamental structures that work to create meaning in a genre like the folktale. If you like your genres precisely dissected and pinned to a laboratory table, then these are your people. Propp, for instance, worked out the thirty-one possible story functions and seven possible characters that make up a folktale. You can find websites online that will produce a folktale using his formula (watch enough kids movies and you'll start to suspect all the major studios are using it). More recent examples of this kind of structuralist approach to genre include the Canadian literary critic Northrop Frye (1912–1991). His *Anatomy of Criticism* (1957) divided the world of literature into four genres based on the way they are presented to us (drama, epos, lyric, and fiction), but also suggested other deep connections between works of literature, like the archetypal narrative shapes of romance, comedy, tragedy, and irony. This kind of genre analysis remains very common in film studies and is often used by screenwriters. When George Lucas wrote *Star Wars*, he consciously drew on a structuralist analysis of *The Hero's Journey* by Joseph Campbell.[9] From a structuralist viewpoint, the common textual functions and features

5. See Gérard Genette, "The Architext," in *Modern Genre Theory*, ed. David Duff (London: Routledge, 2014), 210–18; Paul Hernadi, *Beyond Genre: New Directions in Literary Classification* (Ithaca, NY: Cornell University Press, 1972), 153; Carolyn R. Miller, "Genre as Social Action," *QJS* 70 (May 1984): 152–53, 164.

6. Joseph Farrell, "Classical Genre in Theory and Practice," *NLH* 34.3 (Summer 2003): 394.

7. Vladimir Propp, *Morphology of the Folktale*, 2nd ed. (Austin: University of Texas Press, 1975), xxv, 19–21, 64, 79. On the evolution of genres: Vladimir Propp, "Fairy Tale Transformations," in *Modern Genre Theory*, ed. Duff, 50–67.

8. I'm simplifying things here a bit. Structuralist approaches to genre sometimes overlap substantially with more modern theories – for example, Jonathan Culler, *Structuralist Poetics: Structuralism, Linguistics and the Study of Literature*, classics ed. (London: Routledge, 2002), 149–59.

9. Joseph Campbell, *The Hero's Journey: Joseph Campbell on His Life and Work* (Novato, CA: New World Library, 1990). Thanks, Kane Lach, for this tip.

we encounter in a genre reflect something about how our human brains and societies work.

I'm going to pile all these ideas about genre together – from Aristotle to Northrop Frye – under the "classical genre theory" banner. There are less polite names people call them, such as "deductive" (because it seems like they're starting with predetermined theoretical categories), **essentialist** (because they believe the laws of genre are almost as hard-wired as the laws of geometry), or "normative" (because older theorists often insist that writers follow the rules of a genre). I think a more neutral way of describing them would be **synchronic**, as opposed to **diachronic** (because classical theorists are interested in how writers use genre systems rather than the historical development of those systems),[10] but not everyone is going to find that a friendly word to work with. So let's just call these approaches "classical."

This synchronic perspective is what sometimes makes it possible to compare and group texts across very different time periods and civilizations – turn your head a certain angle, and an ancient biblical narrative, an Icelandic folk tale, and *Star Wars* might actually belong to the same kind of story genre, sharing archetypes and character functions. These kinds of studies are looking for deep relationships between texts and aren't too bothered about proving any actual historical connections between the biblical scribe, Icelandic sage, and George Lucas. (This timeless perspective is why I describe it as a synchronic as opposed to diachronic way of looking at genre.)

While a faithful few still carry on this kind of classical genre theory, it went mostly out of fashion in the back half of the twentieth century. Some criticized these classical approaches for going in with predetermined categories, potentially shoehorning defenseless texts into their existing boxes rather than beginning with actual texts and working more inductively.[11] (For the record, I don't think this is a fair description of what classical genre theorists were doing, at least not always, but there you go.) Others from a more post-**romanticist** perspective have seen genre itself as irrelevant because all good literature defines its own genre (more on that in chapter 2). Most just moved on to other new and exciting critical

10. I'm borrowing these terms from semiotics. See Ferdinand de Saussure, *Course in General Linguistics*, trans. Wade Baskin (New York: Philosophical Library, 1959), 99–100; Terence Hawkes, *Structuralism and Semiotics*, 2nd ed., New Accents 1 (London: Routledge, 2003), 8–9. Hans Robert Jauss and Alastair Fowler sometimes use similar terms.

11. See Kathleen Hall Jamieson and Karlyn Kohrs Campbell, "Form and Genre in Rhetorical Criticism," in *Form and Genre: Shaping Rhetorical Action* (Falls Church, VA: Speech Communication Association, 1978), 22; Carolyn R. Miller, "Genre as Social Action," *QJS* 70 (May 1984): 153; Tzvetan Todorov, *The Fantastic: A Structural Approach to a Literary Genre* (Ithaca, NY: Cornell University Press, 1975), 8–23; Anis S. Bawarshi and Mary Jo Reiff, *Genre: An Introduction to History, Theory, Research, and Pedagogy* (West Lafayette, IN: Parlor, 2010), 22–24.

approaches, leaving genre theory to sit at the back of the kitchen cupboard along with your parents' fondue set and FM radio.

For a while, the study of genre looked like it was going out of fashion. But serious readers could hardly ignore the importance of genre for long. Even great texts are great, in part, because of the way they play with and redefine existing genres. What was needed was a way to talk about genre that was less concerned with strict classes and firm rules and more helpful in describing how genres work, how they relate to culture, and how they change over time.

Modern Genre Theory

Modern genre theory is a broad term, but what most modern approaches to genre have in common is a historical perspective.[12] In chapter 2, we'll go into some more detail about why this perspective is so important and what it means for how we think about genre. But the headline is that we begin to see genres, not as rules to be followed or categories set in stone, but as aspects of culture within history.[13] Modern genre theorists from all sorts of disciplines agree that genres change over time, but that the change is (mostly) slow enough that we can still find them useful. They are neither set in stone nor totally fluid, which is why we described genre above as "relatively stable."[14]

Recognizing that genres are always changing and breaking their own rules, we need to see genres as affected by – and in turn affecting – the history that we are all part of. I like the term *diachronic* (as opposed to *synchronic*) for this kind of historical perspective on genre.[15] I want to stress that I still see a place for the more classical ways of looking at how a given genre works (the synchronic approaches) too, just as long as we remember that the rules of a genre aren't eternal, like the laws of geometry are.[16] We can describe the apparent rules of a genre, but there is no guarantee they will stay that way forever.

In the first part of this book, I'm going to present a range of approaches from different disciplines under the modern genre theory banner. In chapter 2, I put

---

12. Genres reveal "an undercurrent of history" (Jamieson and Campbell, "Form and Genre," 26).

13. On genres as historically contingent systems of relations, see Hans Robert Jauss, *Toward an Aesthetic of Reception*, trans. Timothy Bahti, THL 2 (Minneapolis: University of Minnesota Press, 1982), 80; Alastair Fowler, *Kinds of Literature: An Introduction to the Theory of Genres and Modes* (Oxford: Oxford University Press, 1982), v, 221; Paul Ricoeur, "The Hermeneutical Function of Distanciation," *PhT* 17.2 (1973): 135; John Frow, *Genre*, 2nd ed. (New York: Routledge, 2015), 76–78; René Wellek, *Discriminations: Further Concepts of Criticism* (New Haven, CT: Yale University Press, 1970), 251.

14. M. M. Bakhtin, *Speech Genres and Other Late Essays*, ed. Caryl Emerson and Michael Holquist (Austin: University of Texas Press, 1986), 83.

15. See Fowler, *Kinds of Literature*, 221.

16. Michael Jensen sensibly argues for genres as "a factor *both* of universal human experience and of the contingent events of history" (*Theological Anthropology and the Great Literary Genres: Understanding the Human Story* [Lanham, MD: Lexington, 2019], 19, emphasis in original).

forward six tenets that emerge once we start looking at genre with a historical perspective, and that I think are relevant to biblical studies. My undergraduate and doctoral studies were in the English literature department at the University of Sydney, so I've naturally been influenced by literary approaches to genre, especially those of Liam Semler (my doctoral supervisor) and John Frow. But as literary theorists, we tend to be hopeless hoarders, and so in chapter 3, I consider what we can learn from approaches to genre in two more disciplines: **rhetorical genre studies** and **systemic functional linguistics**. These rhetorical and linguistic approaches to genre both look at genres within their particular social situations or contexts, and I believe this could be a game changer for biblical studies. Chapter 3's social perspective builds on the historical perspective of chapter 2, giving us six more tenets about how genres work. Armed with all twelve tenets about how genres work in their historical and social contexts, I go on in chapter 4 to suggest how we might go about identifying the genres we find in Scripture (as well as the genre of "Scripture" as a whole).

There's nothing worse, I think, than confidently pontificating about genre without actually doing any work on real live genres. So the second part of this book sets about seeing how useful these ideas might be for a range of real-life biblical genres – narrative (chapters 5 and 6), poetry (chapters 7 and 8), apocalypse (chapter 9), wisdom (chapter 10), gospel (chapter 11), and letter (chapter 12). Obviously I cannot pretend to be a specialist in every genre or book of the Bible, but I will do my best to illustrate what modern genre theory might look like in action. I hope that seeing powerful genre tools in my inexpert hands can inspire actual specialists to take on modern genre theory in their own research.

Before we get to any of this, however, we need to clear the air. Because biblical studies has its own home-brew genre theory. And as the next chapter argues, it's not very good.

PART 1

CHAPTER 1

GUNKEL'S HOME BREW

Form Criticism and Why It Needs to Die

Fifteen years ago, I drove up a narrow driveway with an old station wagon full of books and a bag of clothes to move into my new room on campus. It was a conservative seminary, and one of the rules in the single men's dorm was no alcohol. While we were welcome to share a beer with our professors and married students in their accommodation across the street, the singles' quarters were strictly alcohol-free. However, there was one loophole in the regulations. I checked. There was no rule against *brewing* beer in the dorm.

You can see where this is going. After a particularly inspiring lecture on Katharina von Bora – Luther's wife and legendary brewmaster – we recommissioned one of the upstairs bathtubs as a fermenter. When questioned by the dean, I explained, "We simply brought water, hops, and yeast into the house. What the Lord hath done since . . . well, it is surely a miracle!" Never one to quench the thirsty work of God, he gave us his blessing.

I cannot tell you how proud we were of our home brew. We printed up labels, complete with government warning labels ("may cause ordination difficulties"). We brought it with us to dinner and offered it to our hosts. I often named it as my favorite beer (my girlfriend subsequently had some difficulty finding it at the local liquor store). Eventually, a senior diocesan clergyman heard about our home brew and asked to try some. Like proud parents, we anxiously looked on as he took a sip of our beloved brew. After a thoughtful pause, he looked up with his wise pastoral eyes and declared his considered ecclesiastical judgment. "This is," he said, "without doubt the most disgusting thing I have ever tasted."

Biblical studies has its own home-brew genre theory. It is called **form criticism,** and many of its core assumptions about how genres work are wrong. This theory has led Bible scholars on a century-long wild goose chase after hypothetical preliterary genres rather than exploring how genres work to create meaning in the literary texts we have. The Bible deserves so much better.

GENRE AND BIBLE SCHOLARS

It's not that Bible scholars don't care about genre. The Bible is more like a library than a single book, and so the fact that it contains so many different genres weaved together forces us to think about genre all the time. Even secular scholars like Hans Robert Jauss have noticed this:

> The abundance of literary forms and genres ascertainable in the Old and New Testaments is astonishing. . . . The Bible contains worldly lyrics (songs of work, ridicule, drinking, burial, and war) as well as spiritual ones (the hymn or the lament). It developed the most varied forms of narrative prose: etiological, historical, and also heroic sagas (the legendary garland for Samson); legends of martyrs and novellas (the Kings novellas, but also the Book of Ruth). It contains the model for various forms of historiography (tribal legends, genealogy, royal chronicle), historical prose (documents, letters, contracts, war reports), and biography (the self-disclosures of the prophets). All imaginable forms of wisdom literature (proverb, riddle, parable, fable, debate, allegory) and religious instruction (sermon, exhortation, epistle) are also found in it.[1]

Open the Bible, and you will be struck by all these different genres at play. Read on, and you'll soon realize that these genres make a big difference for your interpretation of the text. Many of our most significant disagreements about what the Bible means start off as disagreements about genre. (Is Genesis 1 poetry or history or something else?)

Ancient Bible interpreters knew this, even if they didn't always talk explicitly about their genre theory. Some early church figures were very concerned about finding the right genre to understand a given passage.[2] Genre often came up in questions about the relationship between biblical texts and Greco-Roman genres. When Saint Jerome (AD 347–420) started studying the original Hebrew texts, he became encouraged to consider Old Testament texts and genres in light of their original cultural context rather than comparing them with Greek genres.[3] Later, when scholars shifted away from allegorical readings to focus more on the

---

1. Hans Robert Jauss, *Toward an Aesthetic of Reception*, trans. Timothy Bahti, THL 2 (Minneapolis: University of Minnesota Press, 1982), 102.
2. See Andrew T. Abernethy, "Genre and Theological Vision," in *Interpreting the Old Testament Theologically: Essays in Honor of Willem A. VanGemeren*, ed. Andrew T. Abernethy (Grand Rapids: Zondervan, 2018), 47; Martin J. Buss, *The Changing Shape of Form Criticism: A Relational Approach*, ed. Nickie M. Stipe, Hebrew Bible Monographs 18 (Sheffield: Sheffield Phoenix, 2010), 116–20.
3. See Michael Graves, "The Literary Quality of Scripture as Seen by the Early Church," *TynBul* 61.2 (2010): 179.

human author's intended meaning, this made the original literary genre of the text even more crucial to its interpretation.[4]

Today, it is pretty much universally agreed that genre is essential to good interpretation. Many modern statements of doctrine, both Catholic and Protestant, say something about the importance of genre. For many evangelicals, getting the genre right is an important way of ensuring that the meaning we get corresponds with the original author's intent. While the occasional jokester has wanted to declare that the Bible somehow transcends genre, everyone else has quickly pointed out that understanding genre is essential, given the dual nature of Scripture – divinely inspired, *human* literature. I defy you to find a hermeneutics textbook that doesn't talk about genre somewhere at the beginning of the exegetical process.

Given that genre is so central to our core business of reading the Bible, you'd expect that our genre *theory* – our working understanding of what genres are and how they work – would be highly developed, finely tuned, and well adapted to the sophisticated genres we find in Scripture.

I wish I had better news for you.

Gunkel's Home-Brew Recipe

The father of biblical studies' home-brew genre theory is Hermann Gunkel (1862–1932). Gunkel pioneered **form criticism** – a way of looking at the different genres we find in the Bible. He developed it mainly while working on Genesis and Psalms (with a little bit on the prophets), and so the genres he considers are mainly things like "folk legends" and "communal lament psalms." However, his method has been applied to just about every genre in the Bible. Form criticism still shapes how most biblical scholars think about genre today.[5]

The goal of form criticism was to get behind the written text of the Bible to its sources in oral tradition, isolating the pithy, pure, and preliterary genres preserved in the text and then trying as much as possible to reconstruct the recurring settings in which those genres originally developed.[6]

---

4. See A. J. Minnis, "Discussions of 'Authorial Role' and 'Literary Form' in Late-Medieval Scriptural Exegesis," *Beit. Gesch. Dtsch. Sprache Lit.* 99 (1977): 52.

5. The term "form criticism" is a bit of a mess. In Hermann Gunkel's original German terminology, *Form* meant the internal structures of the text, which combined with social setting to make the *Gattung* (genre). See Marvin A. Sweeney, "Form Criticism," in *To Each Its Own Meaning: An Introduction to Biblical Criticisms and Their Application*, ed. Steven L McKenzie and Stephen R. Haynes (Louisville, KY: Westminster John Knox, 1999), 59.

6. See further reading below for Gunkel's main works in English. A good overview is Hermann Gunkel, *What Remains of the Old Testament and Other Essays*, trans. A. K. Dallas (Eugene, OR: Wipf & Stock, 2016).

- The genres were *pithy* because Gunkel was mainly interested in looking at short passages of Scripture – a few verses, or paragraphs at most. He thought the longer chunks (sections or whole books of the Bible) were assembled much later, usually with only light editing and little creativity.[7]
- The genres he was interested in were *pure* because he thought that, as time went on, genres were increasingly mixed until they decayed and died out.[8] (Psalmists these days – always muddling up their thanksgiving songs and wisdom poems!)
- The genres were *preliterary* because he assumed that much of the biblical texts he was studying circulated orally as folk traditions long before anyone thought to write them down.
- The goal was to *place* these preliterary genres in their typical **life situation (*Sitz im Leben* in German)**. This technical term requires some unpacking. It is not that Gunkel was trying to work out the exact date and time when a particular text was written. Instead, he was trying to work out the recurring situation that *this kind* of oral text would originally have been used in. It's about the genre as a whole, not any one particular example. And it's about the genre's origins in oral tradition, not the written texts that preserve it for us. For example, Gunkel thought the communal lament genre of "psalm" was developed to accompany a particular liturgical event involving the whole nation and trumpets (the life situation). Modern examples of genres and their life situation might be eulogies (which are for funerals), soppy vows (for celebrity weddings), and insincere apologies (which are given after scandals go public).

For Gunkel, therefore, a genre was a two-sided coin. One side had its textual elements, including how the narrative is written and what it's about (its "treasury of thoughts and moods").[9] The other side was a recurring situation. Imagine you are trying to explain to Gunkel what country music is. On one side of the

---

7. Gunkel wrote, "The earliest story-tellers were not capable of constructing artistic works of any considerable extent. . . . Primitive times were satisfied with quite brief productions which required not much over half an hour. Then when the narrative is finished the imagination of the hearer is satisfied and his attention exhausted. . . . The brevity of legends is, as we have seen, a mark of the poverty of primitive literary art" (*The Legends of Genesis: The Biblical Saga and History*, trans. W. H. Carruth [Eugene, OR: Wipf & Stock, 2003], 47).

8. See Hermann Gunkel, *The Psalms: A Form-Critical Introduction*, trans. Thomas M. Horner (Philadelphia: Fortress, 1967), 39; see also "Problems of Hebrew Literary History," in Gunkel, *What Remains*, 65–66.

9. Hermann Gunkel and Joachim Begrich, *Introduction to Psalms: The Genres of the Religious Lyric of Israel*, trans. James D. Nogalski (Macon, GA: Mercer University Press, 1998), 16; see Buss, *Changing Shape*, 15; Erhard Blum, "Formgeschichte – A Misleading Category?," in *The Changing Face of Form Criticism for the Twenty-First Century*, ed. Marvin A. Sweeney and Ehud Ben Zvi (Grand Rapids: Eerdmans, 2003), 35.

country music coin, you might talk about banjos, catchy melodies, and stories about pickup trucks and young love. Flipping to the other side of the coin, you would then try to set the scene that caused this genre of music to be developed – America, Southern, Western, rural, cowboys, Republicans.

But if you are an American, you know all that already, because you are living in the culture (as an Australian city dweller I'm not, but we have Keith Urban and he told me all about it). How can we know about the life situation of the oral traditions preserved in ancient biblical texts, given that most of what we know about those times and places comes *through the very same texts*? It's a paradox, but luckily Gunkel had a time machine (or thought he did). Gunkel's time machine is built by using comparisons with ancient texts from other cultures, the folklore research of the brothers Grimm, and some heavy-duty presuppositions about how religions usually progress (for example, from "crass mythology to a belief in providence" or from cultic to noncultic stages).[10] Having isolated the roughly stitched seams of the oral sources behind the biblical text, he used these tools to make inferences about the relative ages of the preliterary genres. He could then reconstruct the recurring setting in which those preliterary genres arose.

Throughout the twentieth century, Hermann Gunkel's approach has grown and changed into a full-blown method for studying texts that has been applied to all kinds of Old Testament and New Testament literature.[11] Along the way, it has been intermingled with other literary methodologies, taking modern form criticism far beyond Gunkel's original project. In general, however, analyzing a passage using form criticism will involve three steps:

1. Observing the **structure** of the unit of text being studied.
2. Noticing what genre relationships seem to be relevant.
3. Situating the forms within their recurring social setting.[12]

---

10. See Gunkel, *Legends of Genesis*, 105; Gunkel, *Psalms*, 5. On Gunkel's intellectual context, see Martin J. Buss, *Biblical Form Criticism in Its Context*, JSOTSup 274 (Sheffield: Sheffield, 1999), 209–62.

11. Gunkel's students Sigmund Mowinckel and Albrecht Alt applied form criticism to poetry and law, using comparisons with ancient Near Eastern texts, while Martin Noth and Gerhard von Rad took on larger chunks of text. See Gene M. Tucker, *Form Criticism of the Old Testament* (Philadelphia: Fortress, 1971); Sweeney, "Form Criticism," 62–65; Sweeney and Ben Zvi, *Changing Face*, 2. For examples of the application to Old Testament genres, see Claus Westermann, *Basic Forms of Prophetic Speech*, trans. Hugh Clayton White (Louisville, KY: Westminster John Knox, 1991); George W. Coats, ed., *Saga, Legend, Tale, Novella, Fable: Narrative Forms in Old Testament Literature*, JSOTSup 5 (Sheffield: JSOT Press, 1985); Sweeney and Ben Zvi, *Changing Face*, 2–3. For a New Testament example, see Rudolf Bultmann, "The Study of the Synoptic Gospels," in *Form Criticism: Two Essays on New Testament Research*, trans. Frederick C. Grant (New York: Harper Torchbooks, 1962), 1.

12. See Sweeney, "Form Criticism," 59.

So What's Wrong with All This?

There are a lot of things to like about Hermann Gunkel's home brew. He was right to be interested in oral genres and was one of the first to look for comparisons with other ancient Near Eastern genres. His insight into the link between genres and a recurring social setting is brilliant. Even the heavy-hitting literary critic Hans Robert Jauss thought literary scholars could learn from Gunkel on this point.[13] (You may notice when we get to chapter 3 that form criticism's interest in a genre's life situation anticipates modern genre theory's interest in the social context of genres.[14])

Yet the problems in Gunkel's way of thinking about genre have been well known since the 1970s.[15] There are four main issues. First, Gunkel's approach was powered by many of the classical assumptions about the way genre works that modern genre theory has long left behind. The buckets into which texts are sorted tend to be quite rigid, and there is an element of what critics call an "Aristotelian essentialism" to Gunkel's approach.[16] *Essentialism* here is meant to be a slur (try using it in a tweet today!) and reveals that we are treating genres as almost set in stone, like the rules of geometry, rather than as relatively stable conventions.

In fairness, Gunkel didn't claim that genres are universal to humanity, but he did go into his study of the Old Testament with some pretty fixed genre categories, such as "myth," "legend," and "history," which he assumed applied across cultures from ancient Israel to Germany.[17] His method often relied on the assumption that genres start off pure, and only later do "mixed" genres emerge,[18] but this is not really how genres ever work, and "mixed genre" is about as tautologous as "mixed cocktail" (more on that in chapter 2). Gunkel generally assumed that each text belongs to one genre, whereas texts have complex relationships with multiple genres at the same time (again, more on that in chapter 2).

The second problem is that the "time machine" Gunkel used for identifying the earliest preliterary texts and reconstructing their social setting is broken, or at least should be used with extreme caution. Gunkel's method depended on assumptions about race, culture, religion, and history that few would accept today: "Legends," Gunkel confidently assumed, "come from ages and stages of civilisation

---

13. See Jauss, *Toward an Aesthetic of Reception*, 100.

14. *Sitz im Leben* also overlaps with "scene" in some genre pedagogies. See Anis S. Bawarshi and Mary Jo Reiff, *Genre: An Introduction to History, Theory, Research, and Pedagogy* (West Lafayette, IN: Parlor, 2010), 186.

15. An early critic of Gunkel's "monolithic conception" of genre was Rolf Knierim, "Old Testament Form Criticism Reconsidered," *Int* 27.4 (1973): 467. Knierim's alternative, however, involved dropping situation from genre. Chapter 3 suggests it should stay.

16. Buss, *Changing Shape*, xiv; see also Tremper Longman III, "Form Criticism, Recent Developments in Genre Theory, and the Evangelical," *WTJ* 47 (1985): 64.

17. See Gunkel, *Legends of Genesis*.

18. Gunkel, *Psalms*, 36.

which have not yet acquired the intellectual power to distinguish between poetry and reality."[19] His method also leaned heavily on a dated distinction between folk tradition and high literature. This was paired with assumptions about the relationship between oral and literary cultures that are now considered too simple.

Some of Gunkel's old-school assumptions we can simply leave behind, but other limbs of his approach are not so easy to amputate. This is because Gunkel's core method for isolating the earliest preliterary forms relied on those kinds of assumptions about the way cultures and religions evolve in history. Myths, "primitive legends," and sung poetry come first, then prose narratives, then finally objective history.[20] The earliest stories in Genesis can be identified by their "childlike" belief in a God who is active in history, which more advanced stages of civilization eventually grow out of. These assumptions are what allowed Gunkel to isolate the earliest forms preserved in the text and make inferences about the setting that gave rise to the oral genre that was later written down.

Even if we update the assumptions, any conclusions we reach about the preliterary forms using Gunkel's method will still come up against a third problem – lack of evidence. Our only access to these preliterary forms is through the literary texts in front of us. Yet Gunkel's reconstructions ended up being quite specific. He concluded that community laments, like Psalm 44, for example, were used on a national day of lament held at the sanctuary after crop failures that involved everyone tearing their clothes and blowing trumpets, with certain lines of the psalm allocated to the people and others to the priest.[21] Scholars using Gunkel's method have found themselves drawing quite firm conclusions about the connection between a genre and a particular recurring situation in life, dreaming up concrete historical groups or festivals behind genres for which there is very little, if any, evidence.[22]

Fourth, even if Gunkel's time machine worked as advertised, his method is still heavily geared toward understanding the preliterary genres behind the biblical text.[23] It has little to say about the final literary forms of the Bible (which a lot of people I know seem quite interested in).[24]

---

19. Gunkel, *Legends of Genesis*, 40.

20. Gunkel wrote, "Uncivilised races do not write history; they are incapable of reproducing their experiences objectively, and have no interest in leaving to posterity an authentic account of the events of their times" (*Legends of Genesis*, 1).

21. See Gunkel, *Psalms*, 13–15.

22. On "wisdom psalms" and form criticism, see Simon Chi-chung Cheung, *Wisdom Intoned: A Reappraisal of the Genre "Wisdom Psalms,"* LHBOTS 613 (London: Bloomsbury T&T Clark, 2015), 15–16. In fairness, Gunkel recognized that we can't always draw firm conclusions about the earliest oral traditions.

23. See Stuart Weeks, "The Limits of Form Criticism" (presented at the Society for Old Testament Study, Birmingham, January 2006), www.academia.edu/8782346/The_Limits_of_Form_Criticism_2006_.

24. Biblical texts might be more like compilations than works of a single genius auteur, but there is an art to a great playlist. It was left to redaction critics to appreciate the active compiling, framing, and shaping of traditions by the editors/compilers of the written text.

The Long Aftertaste of Gunkel's Home Brew

For all Gunkel's great insights, the home-brew genre theory he introduced into biblical studies was, as Tremper Longman observes, "already by his time an obsolete model of genre."[25] So why is it still so influential? It's important to understand that biblical studies and secular literary studies are a little like parallel universes. Occasionally an idea will be teleported over, but for much of its history, biblical studies has happily done its own thing. This sometimes leads to brilliant insights (like Gunkel's observations about social situation) but has also allowed substandard genre theory to survive way longer than it should have.

There are a lot of different modern form-critical methods.[26] Some newer versions have kept the focus on "situation" but mean something quite different from Gunkel's *Sitz im Leben* ("life situation") – not the situation in which the preliterary genre arose, but perhaps the actual historical circumstances of the text or even the general situations in which texts might be used by later readers. Others have given up on reconstructing the original preliterary forms and their settings entirely, pivoting toward analyzing passages' structure and final literary context (called *Sitz in der Literatur*, to give a nod to Gunkel and make it sound more *komplex* than it is). Sometimes what is described as "form criticism" today shows little continuity with Gunkel's approach (except perhaps his tradition of carefully ignoring modern genre theory).

In some areas, Gunkel and form criticism are still very much a big deal (for example, in Psalms studies, where Gerald Wilson developed Gunkel's approach substantially). Yet in many other fields, Gunkel's influence is felt in terms of a gaping hole. Seeing the problems in Gunkel's approach, hip scholars long ago jumped ship to other approaches, such as rhetorical criticism, leaving genre studies to drift dead in the water.[27] Some even decided, implicitly or explicitly, to move on and treat genre itself as irrelevant (which is a bit like deciding to break up with the alphabet).[28]

---

25. Tremper Longman III, "Israelite Genres in Their Ancient Near Eastern Context," in *Changing Face*, ed. Sweeney and Ben Zvi, 181.

26. See David L. Petersen, "Hebrew Bible Form Criticism," *RelSRev* 18.1 (1992): 29–33; Roy F. Melugin, "Recent Form Criticism Revisited in an Age of Reader Response," in *Changing Face*, ed. Sweeney and Ben Zvi, 58–59; Anthony F. Campbell, "Form Criticism's Future," in *Changing Face*, ed. Sweeney and Ben Zvi, 26–31; Blum, "Formgeschichte – A Misleading Category?," 44–45; Buss, *Changing Shape*, 191–96; Michael H. Floyd, "Basic Trends in the Form-Critical Study of Prophetic Texts," in *Changing Face*, ed. Sweeney and Ben Zvi, 302–3; Mark J. Boda, Michael H. Floyd, and Colin M. Toffelmire, eds., *The Book of the Twelve and the New Form Criticism*, ANEM 10 (Atlanta: SBL Press, 2015). See also the various methodologies in the Forms of the Old Testament Literature series (19 vols. [Grand Rapids: Eerdmans, 1981–2016]).

27. See James Muilenburg's watershed Society of Biblical Literature presidential address "Form Criticism and Beyond," *JBL* 88.1 (1969): 1–18. While not abandoning genre studies, he argued for greater flexibility and focus on individual texts. This was the beginning of "rhetorical criticism," which largely eclipsed form criticism.

28. Genre neglect in prophetic literature may be a reaction against form criticism's "dubious project of reconstructing the original words of the prophets" (Floyd, "Basic Trends," 301).

Don't get me wrong. I think there's much to love about form criticism's goals and many of its findings. It's the underlying home-brew *genre theory* that's the problem. Form criticism's most brilliant insights (that genres matter, and that they arise within social settings) are still bolted onto an awkward classical conception of how genres work. We keep trying new labels and new containers, but it's the same home-brew recipe, and it isn't tasting any better. Yet we keep drinking it anyway.

THE ALTERNATIVES

I'm going to call it. It's time to say goodbye to form criticism. What is there to replace it? Within the field of biblical studies, I would argue, not much.

That's not entirely fair. A huge amount of good work has continued *on genres* – Hebrew poetry, narrative art, epistolary form, and so on. Old Testament specialists working on narrative, poetry, and legal texts have developed sophisticated understandings of the way these ancient genres work and their relationship with other ancient texts. Comparisons to ancient Near Eastern texts have brought light to certain passages, especially the features of treaties, woe oracles, and lawsuits. What we need to support this work, however, is a sophisticated and robust account of *how genre itself works* – a workable genre theory. (Imagine, by analogy, trying to study infectious diseases without the help of modern germ theory.)

A little bit of this has been going on, but not nearly enough. Before we turn to modern genre theory in the next chapter, let's get up-to-date with a quick tour of some of the promising theoretical work on genre from within biblical studies.

Old Testament Genre Theory Developments

The rough story goes that after form criticism came redaction criticism, and after redaction criticism came literary approaches. This "literary turn" of the 1970s brought with it some strange new ideas about genre that had been bubbling away in literature departments. Two decades of enthusiasm about literary genre theory followed, much of it centered around the elusive genre of apocalypse.[29] In 1979, John J. Collins and the Society of Biblical Literature's Genres Project produced an influential definition of the apocalypse genre, and for their genre theory they drew on Alastair Fowler and E. D. Hirsch with the help of Mary Gerhart and William Doty.[30] It was more than an exercise in classification;

---

29. See Mary Gerhart, "Generic Competence in Biblical Hermeneutics," *Semeia* 43 (1988): 29–44; Roland Boer, ed., *Bakhtin and Genre Theory in Biblical Studies* (Atlanta: SBL Press, 2007).

30. John J. Collins, ed., *Apocalypse: The Morphology of a Genre*, Semeia 14 (Missoula, MT: Scholars Press, 1979).

they were trying to understand how the **formal features** and structures of the genre work together. In ditching form criticism and its emphasis on life situation, they explicitly left to one side the questions of social setting. We will consider some of this work on the apocalypse genre in chapter 9. (The apocalyptic genre also gets considered in relation to the book of Revelation, but that's jumping to the New Testament.[31])

The Russian literary theorist Mikhail Bakhtin and his buddies became all the rage in literary studies after their work was translated into English in the 1980s, and over the next few decades, all the most dapper Bible scholars got into it as well.[32] Bakhtin's genre theory and biblical form criticism have been described as a bit like long-lost siblings, bearing striking similarities despite very different upbringings.[33]

Bakhtin-induced discoveries of genres like "Menippean satire" or "polyphonic novel" in the Bible continue to keep presenters at academic Bible conferences busy.[34] His idea of the **chronotope** is very useful for talking about how genres bring together place, time, and ideology in their settings.[35]

Beyond Bakhtin, it is possible to find sporadic examples of explicit reflection on genre within Old Testament studies. In 1992, Mary Gerhart talked about the potential for experimenting with genres to produce new interpretations (and also called on biblical hermeneutics to examine the intersection of genre and gender).[36] In 2005, Carol Newsom published an influential chapter titled "Spying Out the Land" in which she identifies the out-of-date classificatory approach to genre being used in biblical studies and points toward some of the modern genre ideas we'll meet in the next chapter.[37] Several scholars have since picked up her

---

31. See, for example, Vern Sheridan Poythress, "Genre and Hermeneutics in Rev 20:1–6," *JETS* 36.1 (March 1993): 41–54. For more New Testament examples, see David E. Aune, *The New Testament in Its Literary Environment* (Philadelphia: Westminster, 1987).

32. For example, applied to apocalypse: Michael E. Vines, "The Apocalyptic Chronotope," in *Bakhtin and Genre Theory*, ed. Boer, 109–17. Finding heteroglossia and "prenovelistic Menippean satire" in Daniel: David M. Valeta, "Polyglossia and Parody: Language in Daniel 1–6," in *Bakhtin and Genre Theory*, ed. Boer, 91–108; David M. Valeta, *Lions and Ovens and Visions: A Satirical Reading of Daniel 1–6* (Sheffield: Sheffield Phoenix, 2008). On Song of Songs: Jennifer Pfenniger, "Bakhtin Reads the Song of Songs," *JSOT* 34.3 (2010): 331–49.

33. See Boer, *Bakhtin and Genre Theory*, 3.

34. Many discoveries of "Menippean satire" in the Bible often overemphasize formal features and might be aided by a more fulsome internalization of Bakhtin's genre theory; cf. M. M. Bakhtin, *The Dialogic Imagination* (Austin: University of Texas Press, 1981), 26. Only occasionally do we stop to marvel why Bakhtin himself (who, it's safe to assume, was aware of the Bible) failed to detect these genres in Scripture while we see them almost everywhere we look.

35. A brilliant use of Bakhtin to explore how the different genres in Job (narrative, philosophical dialogue, and wisdom text) are used to bring different ideological worlds into conversation is Carol A. Newsom, *The Book of Job: A Contest of Moral Imaginations* (New York: Oxford University Press, 2003).

36. See Mary Gerhart, *Genre Choices, Gender Questions* (Norman: University of Oklahoma Press, 1992), 69–96.

37. Carol A. Newsom, "Spying out the Land: A Report from Genology," in *Bakhtin and Genre Theory*, ed. Boer, 19–30. First published in 2005 in R. Troxel et al., eds. *Seeking Out the Wisdom of the Ancients* (Winona Lake, IN: Eisenbrauns, 2005). See also Carol A. Newsom, "Pairing Research Questions and Theories of Genre: A Case Study of the Hodayot," *DSD* 17.3 (2010): 270–88.

suggestion that cognitive linguistics might provide a way forward on questions of genre.[38]

Rather than endless debates over "the genre" of a biblical text, thankfully it is becoming more common in some regions of biblical studies land to talk about genres based on **prototypes** and perhaps even explore the "conceptual blending" that goes on when multiple genres come into collision in a text (more on this in chapter 2).[39] Colin Toffelmire suggests retrofitting a systemic functional linguistics approach to social context and function into the form-critical study of prophetic literature.[40]

The ongoing discovery and digestion of ancient texts from cultures around Israel has opened up a lot of interesting points of comparison with the biblical text and has inspired thoughtful reflection on what genre is – sometimes involving retiring Gunkel's form-critical methods in favor of more modern literary and rhetorical approaches to genre.[41] Scholars equipped with the tools of linguistic or discourse analysis have also managed to escape form criticism's pull.[42]

An important recent step in the right direction toward a modern genre theory is Will Kynes's provocative *An Obituary for "Wisdom Literature,"* which shows how

---

38. See Hindy Najman, "The Idea of Biblical Genre: From Discourse to Constellation," in *Prayer and Poetry in the Dead Sea Scrolls and Related Literature: Essays in Honor of Eileen Schuller on the Occasion of Her 65th Birthday*, ed. Jeremy Penner, Ken M. Penner, and Cecilia Wassén, STDJ 98 (Leiden: Brill, 2011), 307–22; B. G. Wright III, "Joining the Club: A Suggestion about Genre in Early Jewish Texts," *DSD* 17 (2010): 336–60; R. Williamson, "Pesher: A Cognitive Model of the Genre," *DSD* 17 (2010): 336–60; Cheung, *Wisdom Intoned*, 16–19; Beth M. Stovell, "'I Will Make Her Like a Desert': Intertextual Allusion and Feminine and Agricultural Metaphors in the Book of the Twelve," in *New Form Criticism*, ed. Boda, Floyd, and Toffelmire, 37–61.

39. See Colin M. Toffelmire, "Cohesion and Genre Blending in Prophetic Literature, Using Amos 5 as a Case Study," *JHebS* 21 (2021): 1–22. Thanks, Andrew Myers, for selling me on cognitive linguistics. On wisdom genres in New Testament epistles: Adam Ch'ng, "Assimilating Genre: Identifying Hebrews 12:4–14 as Proverbial Wisdom" (Master's Thesis, Ridley College, 2018).

40. Colin M. Toffelmire, "*Sitz im* What? Context and the Prophetic Book of Obadiah," in *New Form Criticism*, ed. Boda, Floyd, and Toffelmire, 221–44.

41. For comparative studies of Near Eastern genres: Tremper Longman III, *Fictional Akkadian Autobiography: A Generic and Comparative Study* (Winona Lake, IN: Eisenbrauns, 1991); F. W. Dobbs-Allsopp, *Weep, O Daughter of Zion: A Study of the City-Lament Genre in the Hebrew Bible* (Roma: Biblical Institute Press, 1993), 15–22; Longman, "Israelite Genres," 182. On the Babylonian building inscription genre: Margaret S. Odell, "Genre and Persona in Ezekiel 24:15–21," in *The Book of Ezekiel: Theological and Anthropological Perspectives*, ed. Margaret S. Odell and John T. Strong (Atlanta: SBL Press, 2000), 211. On comparisons between David's rise and the Hittite apology by a usurper king genre, using rhetorical genre studies (RGS): Andrew Knapp, "David and Hattushili III: The Impact of Genre and a Response to J. Randall Short," *VT* 63 (2013): 261–75; Andrew Knapp, *Royal Apologetic in the Ancient Near East*, WAWSup (Atlanta, GA: SBL Press, 2015). On scribal practice and whether "rewritten Scripture" is a genre, using RGS: Molly Zahn, *Genres of Rewriting in Second Temple Judaism: Scribal Composition and Transmission* (Cambridge: Cambridge University Press, 2020).

42. On the proverb (*mashal*) genre as "formal, rhythmic speech performed by characters" within a particular social context, using register analysis: Jacqueline Vayntrub, *Beyond Orality: Biblical Poetry on Its Own Terms*, The Ancient World (London: Routledge, 2019), 88. On woe, indictment, and hope oracle genres, using discourse analysis: JoAnna M. Hoyt, "Discourse Analysis of Prophetic Oracles: Woe, Indictment, and Hope," *HS* 60.1 (2019): 153–74. (I would query whether verb types can supply a more "objective" genre definition than form criticism's "subjective" criteria, as Hoyt claims.)

malnourished genre theory has run amok with the category of "wisdom literature," leading to something of a crisis in biblical studies. He draws on modern genre theory to redefine the wisdom genre as a "selective, self-reflective, and subjective" constellation of texts.[43] We will consider his argument in detail in chapter 10.

New Testament Genre Theory Developments

On the New Testament side of things, scholars have been more or less constantly debating "what is a gospel?" since the 1970s.[44] The basic question is whether the four canonical gospels are unique, or reflect the genre of something like an ancient Greco-Roman biography. The form critics were most interested in the pithy, pure, and preliterary traditions incorporated *into* the gospels, whereas a gospel as a *whole* they saw as "folk" literature – a compilation of shared oral tradition and not the work of an individual author. That meant they didn't go looking for parallels in Greco-Roman "high" literature (such as biographies or histories).

This focus changed with the move to redaction criticism and then again after World War II with the rise of more literary approaches. In his important 1992 work, Richard Burridge explicitly draws on Alastair Fowler's genre theory to advance the discussion over the genre of the four gospels. While this work helped to solidify the current consensus that the Gospels are indeed ancient biographies, a newer generation of scholars, often drawing on systemic functional linguistics (see chapter 3) or cognitive linguistics, have raised serious doubts about the theory, methodology, and conclusions supporting this consensus.[45] We will take this as a detailed case study in chapter 11. (Speaking of linguistics, much of this work using linguistics-based genre theory has happened under the influence of Stanley Porter, whose commentary on the letter to the Romans, for example, applies some of the insights we will see in chapter 3.) More broadly, Sean Adams has looked at the social context of genres in his study of Jewish authors using Greco-Roman genres and what that meant culturally.[46]

---

43. Will Kynes, *An Obituary for "Wisdom Literature": The Birth, Death, and Intertextual Reintegration of a Biblical Corpus* (Oxford: Oxford University Press, 2019), 12.

44. J. Arthur Baird, "Genre Analysis as a Method of Historical Criticism," in *SBL Book of Seminar Papers* (Atlanta: SBL Press, 1972), 385–411.

45. On Mark's gospel using Mikhail Bakhtin: Michael E. Vines, *The Problem of Markan Genre: The Gospel of Mark and the Jewish Novel* (Atlanta: SBL Press, 2002); Christopher C. Fuller, "Matthew's Genealogy as Eschatological Satire: Bakhtin Meets Form Criticism," in *Bakhtin and Genre Theory*, ed. Boer, 119–32. On Mark using John Frow: Helen K. Bond, *The First Biography of Jesus: Genre and Meaning in Mark's Gospel* (Grand Rapids: Eerdmans, 2020). On genres as cultural conventions: Jonathan Pennington, *Reading the Gospels Wisely: A Narrative and Theological Introduction* (Grand Rapids: Baker Academic, 2012), 19–22. On Mark using cognitive linguistics: Elizabeth E. Shively, "Recognizing Penguins: Audience Expectation, Cognitive Genre Theory, and the Ending of Mark's Gospel," *CBQ* 80, no. 2 (2018): 273–92.

46. Sean A. Adams, *Greek Genres and Jewish Authors: Negotiating Literary Culture in the Greco-Roman Era* (Waco, TX: Baylor University Press, 2020).

Most works of general hermeneutics recognize the importance of genre, but with a few exceptions, their engagement with modern genre theory tends to be limited. Jeannine Brown engaged with numerous modern genre theory scholars in a 2008 article and has an excellent treatment of genre in her hermeneutics textbook.[47] Kevin Vanhoozer uses Mikhail Bakhtin and speech act theory to highlight how literary forms are more than empty vessels for propositions. The biblical genres themselves bear theological freight.[48]

Despite such glimmers of hope, however, it's fair to say that New Testament scholars, like Old Testament scholars, are still in the "spying out the land" stage with regard to taking hold of modern genre theory's insights.[49]

So What?

We know that genre is vital to interpreting the Bible. We know more and more about the genres we meet in the Bible, thanks to an immeasurable volume of scholarly labor since Hermann Gunkel in fields such as linguistics, archaeology, and comparative ancient literature. But the home-brew genre theory we've been left with to support all this work is simply not up to scratch.

This matters because the Bible deserves better. More than a single book, it is an astonishing library of literature containing a treasury of diverse genres. Without an adequate genre theory, we cannot fully appreciate what is going on. Our scholarly discussions get tied up in circles arguing about whether a particular text is correctly categorized as this genre *or* that genre. We ignore how genres require different things of us as readers. We impose conceptions about genre from our culture on ancient texts and aren't even aware we are doing it. We lack the vocabulary to explain how genres are relating to each other within a single text – is this genre here being used, parodied, or adapted? We never wonder why *this* particular genre is chosen *here* and not there, and what that

47. Jeannine K. Brown, "Genre Criticism and the Bible," in *Words and the Word: Explorations in Biblical Interpretation and Literary Theory*, ed. Jamie A. Grant and David G. Firth (Nottingham, UK: Apollos, 2008), 111–50; Jeannine K. Brown, *Scripture as Communication: Introducing Biblical Hermeneutics*, 2nd ed. (Grand Rapids: Baker Academic, 2021), 135–62. See also James L. Bailey, "Genre Analysis," in *Hearing the New Testament: Strategies for Interpretation*, ed. Joel B. Green, 2nd ed. (Grand Rapids: Eerdmans, 2010), 141–65.

48. Kevin J. Vanhoozer, *The Drama of Doctrine: A Canonical Linguistic Approach to Christian Doctrine* (Louisville, KY: Westminster John Knox, 2005), 212–6; Kevin J. Vanhoozer, *Is There a Meaning in This Text? The Bible, the Reader and the Morality of Literary Knowledge* (Grand Rapids: Zondervan, 1998), 335–50. For application to Old Testament genres, see Abernethy, "Genre and Theological Vision," in *Interpreting the Old Testament Theologically*, 56.

49. While in a realm outside biblical studies, theologian Michael Jensen receives special mention for using modern genre theory to explore literary genres as theological sources of the self (*Theological Anthropology and the Great Literary Genres: Understanding the Human Story* [Lanham, MD: Lexington, 2019]).

might reveal about the social and power dynamics at play. We don't reflect on our genre assumptions or realize that our disagreements over what the Bible means often start off life as disagreements over genre.

In other words, we are worse off as readers without a workable theory of genre. Don't despair, though, because there is a thriving craft brew scene going on just over the page.

QUESTIONS FOR DISCUSSION AND REFLECTION

1. How much attention should we give to the final literary or canonical form of the Bible, and how much should we be concerned with recovering the original oral texts? Is that even possible?
2. How fair is the critique of Hermann Gunkel given in this chapter? Can form criticism be saved, or is a new approach to genre needed?
3. Why do you think biblical studies is so slow to take on board the insights of secular disciplines?

FURTHER READING

Introductory

Brown, Jeannine K. "Genre Criticism and the Bible." Pages 111–50 in *Words and the Word: Explorations in Biblical Interpretation and Literary Theory*. Edited by Jamie A. Grant and David G. Firth. Nottingham, UK: Apollos, 2008.

Judicious survey of biblical form criticism and modern genre theory.

Deep Dive

Boer, Roland, ed. *Bakhtin and Genre Theory in Biblical Studies*. Atlanta: SBL Press, 2007.
Collection of essays on genre in biblical studies, including Carol Newsom's important article "Spying Out the Land."

Buss, Martin J. *The Changing Shape of Form Criticism: A Relational Approach*. Edited by Nickie M. Stipe. Sheffield: Sheffield Phoenix, 2010.
A recent approach to form criticism.

Gunkel, Hermann. *The Legends of Genesis: The Biblical Saga and History*. Translated by W. H. Carruth. Eugene, OR: Wipf & Stock, 2003.
Gunkel's commentary on Genesis appeared in German in 1901, and its introduction is published here with an introduction by W. F. Albright.

——— *The Psalms: A Form-Critical Introduction*. Translated by Thomas M. Horner. Philadelphia: Fortress, 1967.
Reprint of an important encyclopedia article on Psalms summarizing his approach.

Gunkel, Hermann, and Joachim Begrich. *Introduction to Psalms: The Genres of the Religious Lyric of Israel*. Translated by James D. Nogalski. Macon, GA: Mercer University Press, 1998.

This introduction to Gunkel's Psalms commentary was published after his death (1932) with the help of his student.

Sweeney, Marvin A., and Ehud Ben Zvi, eds. *The Changing Face of Form Criticism for the Twenty-First Century*. Grand Rapids: Eerdmans, 2003.

Important collection of essays on the current state of form criticism.

Weeks, Stuart. "The Limits of Form Criticism in the Study of Literature, with Reflections on Psalm 34." Pages 15–25 in *Biblical Interpretation and Method: Essays in Honour of John Barton*. Edited by Katharine Dell and Paul Joyce. Oxford, UK: Oxford University Press, 2013.

Strikes more than a flesh wound against form criticism.

CHAPTER 2

DEATH AND TAXONOMIES

The Need for Historical Context

It's 1954, and Universal Pictures has a problem. As the undisputed home of horror, the studio has been churning out scary creatures for decades – *Dracula*, *The Mummy*, *Wolf Man*, and even *The Hunchback of Notre Dame*. The studio just spent good money filming their latest "creature film," *Creature from the Black Lagoon*, which features a prehistoric monster called "Gill Man." A group of scientists find the monster in the depths of the Amazon, only for the monster to fall in love with and kidnap the fiancée of the expedition leader. (In summary, *King Kong* underwater.)

The problem is that lately – as film genre theorist Rick Altman tells the story – horror films featuring scary creatures have been going out of fashion, with the 1950s box office glory going to new "science fiction" films.[1] Facing a shrinking audience for its wobbly creature costumes and the studio struggling financially, the publicity department comes up with the perfect solution. Leave the film exactly as is, they decide, but label it as a "science-fiction thriller." (It's a bit of a stretch, but the kidnapped woman is a scientist after all.) Henceforth, the film is now officially described as a "sci-fi" in radio advertisements and promotional pamphlets. Giddy with their new powers of re-genre-ing, the publicity department goes back through the vault and re-genres its entire catalog of creature films as "sci-fi."

As Altman observes, this is not how traditional genre textbooks tell you genre should work. In classical genre theory, a film or literary work "belongs" to categories the way animals belong to their species and genus (see introduction). Dog, mammal, vertebrate. Sonnet, love poem, literature. Such classifications, the theory goes, are intrinsic to the text and essential for understanding them properly. Finding the correct category may be hard sometimes (looking at you, platypus), but in principle, if you work hard enough, you should be able to chop up the world of literature neatly and file it away in the right boxes.

---

1. Rick Altman, *Film/Genre* (London: British Film Institute, 1999), 78.

The goal of a genre theorist is to develop a "taxonomy" of genres – defining each category, discerning the lines between them, and describing the rules of good taste that apply to them. This classification-heavy approach to genre often also involves determining where the genres sit in a hierarchy (e.g., epic poetry sits above airport novels, German art song above advertising jingles).

What happened with *Creature from the Black Lagoon* hints that this classical way of classifying genres the way we classify animals isn't quite right, and the analogy between genres and species might actually be more misleading than illuminating. To state the obvious, a marketing department can't suddenly decide to rebrand "cat" as "chicken" (at least I hope not). Yet Universal Pictures got away with reframing a "creature film" as a "sci-fi." And indeed they are not alone. Market forces mean that movie studios change the genres of their films like this all the time.[2] How?

To explain what's going on here we need to drop the classical approach to genres as rigid classes and normative rules and start seeing genres from a historical perspective – as conventions that writers and readers use to make meaning. The rest of the chapter will unpack what this means, making the case for six tenets of modern genre theory. To preview, the whole idea of texts belonging to a genre is misleading (actually, texts are promiscuous), as is the assumption that genres are unchanging categories (actually, genres are only relatively stable) and that they can be clearly distinguished from each other (actually, genres are fuzzy around the edges).

After unpacking these claims, I'll make some further observations about what genres do (genres invite us to play different games, offering different experiences, roles, goals, and resources), who is actively involved in genre (readers as much as writers), and what features of a text can be part of a genre (basically anything).

TENET 1: TEXTS ARE PROMISCUOUS

Universal Pictures was able to recategorize *Creature from the Black Lagoon* from creature film to sci-fi because the new genre, sci-fi, was there in the film all along. It wasn't an arbitrary choice. It's not like they tried to sell the film as a travel guide for the Amazon or as a forbidden interspecies love story.[3] The sci-fi elements of the film were present in the film already – to "change the genre,"

---

2. See Andrew James Myers, "From Scientific Romance to Disney Superhero," in *Superhero Synergies: Comic Book Characters Go Digital*, ed. James N. Gilmore and Matthias Stork (Lanham, MD: Rowman & Littlefield, 2014), 97–115.

3. For the interspecies love version, fans had to wait until Guillermo del Toro's *The Shape of Water* (2018).

the publicity department just had to bring to our attention one of the other genres the text was already participating in.

Films are never just one thing. *Star Wars: A New Hope* (1977), for example, could be categorized in all sorts of ways. At the most basic level, it is a film, not a book; drama, not stage show; science fiction, not history. Drilling down into its plot and themes, we find multiple overlapping genre designations – IMDB.com places it in the action, adventure, fantasy, and sci-fi genres.[4] But Han Solo's outfit and the shootout in the Mos Eisley cantina on Tatooine are straight out of a Western. When it comes to genre relationships, texts like *Star Wars* are unapologetically promiscuous. They have complex relationships with multiple genres. The same is true of the Bible.

Derrida and Participation without Belonging

One of the most significant essays in helping us understand how texts can belong to multiple genres is Jacques Derrida's "The Law of Genre." As soon as we talk about genre, Derrida complains, "a limit is drawn" and then normative rules soon follow – do this, don't do this.[5] One classic law of genre is:

> Genres are not to be mixed.
> I will not mix genres.
> I repeat: genres are not to be mixed. I will not mix them.

Derrida begins his essay with these three sentences, thereby ironically "breaking" the very law he is describing (by including this additional genre of "law" in his essay). His solution is to revisit what we mean when we say that a text belongs to a particular genre. It's not that we throw away genre in the way the romanticists suggested (see introduction), but we see the relationship between a text and a genre (or genres) as more like *participation* than membership or belonging:

> A text cannot belong to no genre, it cannot be without or less a genre. Every text participates in one or several genres, there is no genreless text; there is always a genre and genres, yet such participation never amounts to belonging.[6]

---

4. "Star Wars: Episode IV - A New Hope," IMDB, www.imdb.com/title/tt0076759.
5. Jacques Derrida, "The Law of Genre," *Crit. Inq.* 7.1 (1980): 56.
6. Derrida, "Law of Genre," 65; see Anis S. Bawarshi and Mary Jo Reiff, *Genre: An Introduction to History, Theory, Research, and Pedagogy* (West Lafayette, IN: Parlor, 2010), 26.

> Participation without belonging (or taking part without being part of) is logically necessary because texts can have complicated relationships with the genre they are meant to be a member of. How can the genre of "novel" be a closed set to which a definable number of texts belong, if half of those texts (usually the good ones) are actually challenging and reshaping what a novel is? One big takeaway is that a text can participate in multiple genres at the same time, and these can be almost anything – not just the standard labels on the front cover of books like *novel* or *drama*.[7]

The degree to which a text engages with a genre can vary, from full-on participation to subtle parody to complete subversion. Even when one genre is dominant, we can usually detect multiple generic relationships. We sometimes signal this when we describe something's genre by using an adjective – "*historical* fiction," "*fictional* autobiography," "*satirical* news," or "*graphic* novel." Usually, however, the generic labels just pile up on a text. You'll find John Milton's *Paradise Lost* categorized as "epic poem" (by most scholars and publishers), "Christian mythology" (by Wikipedia), and "British and Irish literature" (by Amazon.com, which also helpfully categorizes it as "book"). All this makes talking about "mixed genres" nearly as tautologous as talking about "mixed cocktails" or "multi-ingredient cakes."

People who like tidy stationary drawers find all these competing genre labels a little nauseating, and so we might want to be more specific about what we mean by *genre*. Depending on the methodology being used, theorists will often define genre narrowly and distinguish it from other regularities among groups of text.[8] One simple way of organizing texts is, at the most basic level, by the structure of presentation (or "radical of presentation"). This describes who is speaking to whom using which medium: a dramatic monologue, third-person story, song, film. (On this system a "horror film" and a "historical documentary" are different genres that share the same structure of presentation.) Another way to cut through the jungle is to arrange all the genres into a big master scheme, distinguishing between genres and subgenres: a psalm is a "genre"; a lament psalm is a "subgenre." An alternative approach is to distinguish between the main genre of a work and other thematic flavors using adjectives – so "novel" is

---

7. See Derrida, "Law of Genre," 64.

8. On the different kinds of genre: Northrop Frye, *Anatomy of Criticism: Four Essays* (New York: Atheneum, 1968). On genres and modes: Alastair Fowler, *Kinds of Literature: An Introduction to the Theory of Genres and Modes* (Oxford: Clarendon, 1982), 106–11; John Frow, *Genre*, 2nd ed., New Critical Idiom (New York: Routledge, 2015), 73.

a *genre*, but "gothic" is a ***mode***. In practice, however, genres rarely respect these lane markings, so in this book I'm going to use "genre" broadly to cover all levels of regularities and relationships between texts.

Conceptual Blending

A useful way to describe the effect of bringing two genres together is **conceptual blending**, which is borrowed from cognitive linguistics. Conceptual blending is often used to describe what happens when we run into a metaphor. Two different mental sets collide, and the result is often something new (see chapter 7 on poetic metaphors). But it can also be used to describe what happens when two genres are brought together in one text. Just as a metaphor brings together ideas that don't normally belong together, participating in two different genres brings together two sets of themes and social functions that normally live apart.

Have a think about what conceptual blending might be going on when these biblical genres are brought into collision:

- ☐ lawsuit and prophetic oracle (Amos 3)
- ☐ funeral dirge and prophetic oracle (Amos 5)[9]
- ☐ air-raid alarm and disputation (Jeremiah 6)[10]
- ☐ disputation and hymn of praise (Job 12)
- ☐ sermon and international treaty (Deuteronomy)
- ☐ biography and creation story (John 1)

What ideas are normally tied up in each genre, and what is the effect of bringing them together?

Genre promiscuity is also seen in another slightly different way in **complex genres**, which are genres that allow other genres to be **embedded** within them. Think of the famous gothic novel *Frankenstein* by Mary Shelley. The book opens with four letters from Captain Robert Walton, an adventurer exploring the arctic, to his sister:

---

9. See Colin M. Toffelmire, "Cohesion and Genre Blending in Prophetic Literature, Using Amos 5 as a Case Study," *JHebS* 21 (2021): 12–13.

10. Thanks, Andrew Myers, for this example.

Letter 3

To Mrs. Saville, England.
July 7th, 17 – .

My dear Sister,
    I write a few lines in haste to say that I am safe – and well advanced on my voyage.[11]

He goes on to describe finding a man called Victor Frankenstein, who shares his incredible life story. Walton then relays that life story to his sister in the chapters that follow, and so the letters provide a frame for Victor Frankenstein's first-person narration. While Shelley's book as a whole can be described in a few different ways (novel, gothic, even early science fiction), we can also identify the first four chapters as participating in the genre of "private letter" or "travel update."

Genres that can include other genres within them in this way are often called "secondary genres" or "macro-genres" (the novel is a classic example of a secondary genre).[12] The smaller texts (for example, a letter or a speech) contained within them are called "primary genres."[13] I prefer to use the terms "complex genres" for the novel, and "embedded genres" for the mini-texts, because even secondary genres can be embedded within another genre. For example those letters from Walton at the start of *Frankenstein* are a primary genre within the secondary genre of the novel, but his letters in turn could easily have included a little poem, which would give us three levels of genre: a poem within a letter within a novel. (And yes, this kind of "genre within a genre within a genre" thing is starting to sound like a Christopher Nolan movie.)

A text is never just one thing. It can be described in different ways, depending on what level you are looking at it (a book could be described as prose, novel, fiction, or gothic).[14] Wherever you look there is bound to be genre mixing

---

11. Mary W. Shelley, *Frankenstein; or, The Modern Prometheus* (Cambridge, UK: Sever, Francis, 1869), 20.

12. On embedding genres by extension, elaboration or "projection": J. R. Martin and David Rose, *Working with Discourse*, 2nd ed. (London: Bloomsbury, 2007), 262. On macro-genres or mixed texts: J. R. Martin and David Rose, *Genre Relations: Mapping Culture* (London: Equinox, 2008), 88, 242.

13. M. M. Bakhtin, *Speech Genres and Other Late Essays*, ed. Caryl Emerson and Michael Holquist (Austin: University of Texas Press, 1986), 85; M. M. Bakhtin, *The Dialogic Imagination* (Austin: University of Texas Press, 1981), 33.

14. Some prefer to call "book" a medium or format of presentation rather than genre. But now that we "read" the same "book" in ebook, braille, or audio format, does medium still define what a book is?

(a gothic text might also be adventure, epic, or sci-fi). Some genres can even embed additional genres within it (an apology within a speech, within a letter, within a novel). This illustrates our first modern genre theory insight: texts do not belong to a genre; they are promiscuous and can have complex relationships with multiple genres.

TENET 2: GENRES ARE RELATIVELY STABLE CONVENTIONS, LIKE GAMES

The second thing we learn from *Creature from the Black Lagoon* has to do with what genres themselves are. Classical genre theory tended to see genres almost as immutable categories – in other words, they don't change much (at least in their purest forms they shouldn't). Aristotle, Cicero, and Horace all famously discouraged the mixing of genres.[15] Aristotle, for example, says poets writing a tragedy must be careful not to bring in the many plotlines of an epic: "As noted several times, the poet must remember to avoid turning a tragedy into an epic structure . . . by dramatizing the entire plot of the *Iliad*."[16] Now, to state the obvious, Aristotle was no fool. He knew that a genre like tragedy didn't always exist and so must have undergone development in the past. But once it had reached its perfect form, he figured it had no reason to change.[17] Mixing of genres might sometimes occur, but on the whole it is to be avoided (at least in theory).[18] In the dog/cat view of genres as species there is some room for evolution, though mostly dogs and cats keep their paws off each other.

In contrast, modern genre theory recognizes that real genres, unlike species of animals, are much more fluid. Even the labels we use are constantly changing. We don't really talk about "creature films" today. We would more readily describe *Creature from the Black Lagoon* as an example of early "sci-fi" or "horror." Even then, what "horror film" meant in the 1950s or 1960s is very different from the genre today. Consider Alfred Hitchcock's *Psycho*. Many people who write about horror films point to this as one of the defining moments in the evolution of the genre, and yet on some modern definitions of horror film, it doesn't even count as one (you'll usually find it listed under "psychological thriller"). We try in vain to find a genre label or definition that will stick for one film within one film industry over a matter of decades – let alone across cultures and centuries.

15. On ancient genre theory: Sean A. Adams, *The Genre of Acts and Collected Biography* (New York: Cambridge University Press, 2013), 26–56.

16. Aristotle, *Poetics*, LCL 199, 93.

17. "After going through many changes tragedy ceased to evolve, since it had achieved its own nature": Aristotle, *Poetics*, LCL 199, 42–43.

18. See Joseph Farrell, "Classical Genre in Theory and Practice," *NLH* 34.3 (2003): 394.

Somehow, in amongst this constant change, genres hold together and are meaningful. I recently went to see a movie with my pastor, and after the trailers he turned to me anxiously: "Wait, is this a horror film we're seeing?" Despite the diverse array of horror genres on offer, from slasher to supernatural to satire, it was clear to him that what he was about to see was not a romantic comedy – and that he should have paid more attention when we booked the tickets. Genres are constantly changing, but they are just stable enough for us to know what to expect when we sit down to see a horror film.

This illustrates the second observation of modern genre theory: genres are *relatively stable*.

Bakhtin and the Relatively Stable Speech Genres

Mikhail Bakhtin observes that we use language in particular ways within each area of human activity. So between the global rules of a national language (like English, Russian, or Hebrew) and the words we say or write on particular **occasions**, there is a diverse range of "speech genres," which are **realized** in the content, style, and structure of whole utterances:

> Each separate utterance is individual, of course, but each sphere in which language is used develops its own relatively stable types of these utterances. These we may call speech genres.[19]

It is important to give weight to both sides of the "relatively stable" equation. Genres are not totally stable, but nor are they totally unstable. The rules of a genre aren't written on two stone tablets for all time: they change over time. But, equally, genres aren't totally ephemeral: they change just slowly enough that you can recognize them and know what to do with them. Catherine Schryer writes, "Genres can be described as stabilized-for-now or stabilized-enough sites of social and ideological action."[20]

We have seen already that genres cannot be perfect, eternal, and unchanging categories handed down on stone tablets. Lyric, epic, and drama may have been the three main genres in Aristotle's day, but there is nothing magical or essential

---

19. Mikhail Bakhtin, "The Problem of Speech Genres," in Bakhtin, *Speech Genres*, 60. Literary forms are a "dynamic phenomenon": Yuri Tynianov, *The Problem of Verse Language*, trans. Michael Sosa and Brent Harvey (Ann Arbor, MI: Ardis, 1981), 33.

20. Catherine F. Schryer, "Records as Genre," *WC* 10.2 (1993): 204; Catherine F. Schryer, "Genre and Power: A Chronotopic Analysis," in *The Rhetoric and Ideology of Genre: Strategies for Stability and Change*, ed. Richard Coe, Lorelei Lingard, and Tatiana Teslenko (Cresskill, NJ: Hampton, 2002), 77.

about those three. We might find similarities between them and modern genres, but then again, there might also be a lot of differences. Aristotle never read a novel or watched a soap opera (as far as we know).

But at the same time, genres are not arbitrary or subjective. Universal Pictures couldn't just say, "This is a romantic comedy," or "This is a heavy metal Martian cooking show opera." Nor could they say, "This is a whole new genre called black lagoon film." Creators and audiences need to have some shared conception of what that genre is – this is the "enough" in Schryer's "stabilized-enough" description. Genres can and do change over time, and at any given time, different people will have something different in mind when you say "sci-fi."

To try to capture this relative stability, people often try out a variety of metaphors. Some run with the metaphor of stargazing, conceiving genre as a "constellation of substantive, stylistic, and situational characteristics."[21] I don't mind this metaphor, as long as we remember that, unlike stars, the elements of a genre have a functional relationship. A more rigorous but perhaps less inspiring metaphor is that genres are *institutions*.[22] This metaphor tends to be popular amongst those with a background in semiotics and linguistics. Genres are seen as realities that exist in the way a school or a national government exists.

A related idea is that genres work like *contracts*.[23] This captures the social nature of a genre, but it can be misleading. We need to be clear here that we are not talking about some kind of explicit bilateral agreement between reader and writer. Genres aren't prearranged by individuals like some secret code.

For this reason I think the best metaphor to use is not a metaphor at all but the well-established philosophical and linguistic concept of **convention**. Genres (like other aspects of communication) are conventions that give rise to shared expectations. Conventions help us play nicely with others. Technically, conventions are "regularities in behavior, sustained by an interest in coordination and an expectation that others will do their part."[24] In Australia we have

---

21. Kathleen Hall Jamieson and Karlyn Kohrs Campbell, "Form and Genre in Rhetorical Criticism: An Introduction," in *Form and Genre: Shaping Rhetorical Action* (Falls Church, VA: Speech Communication Association, 1978), 17–26. See also introduction to *Rhetoric and Ideology of Genre*, ed. Coe, Lingard, and Teslenko, 3; Alastair Fowler, *Kinds of Literature: An Introduction to the Theory of Genres and Modes* (Oxford: Clarendon, 1982), 106–11; Frow, *Genre*, 14. The "constellation" metaphor was used earlier by M. A. K. Halliday, Walter Benjamin, and Roland Barthes to make slightly different points: Thomas O. BeeBee, *The Ideology of Genre: A Comparative Study of Generic Instability* (University Park: Pennsylvania State University Press, 1994), 282.

22. See René Wellek and Austin Warren, *Theory of Literature* (New York: Harcourt, Brace, 1942), 235; Frow, *Genre*, 13.

23. Jonathan Culler, *Structuralist Poetics: Structuralism, Linguistics and the Study of Literature*, classics ed. (London: Routledge, 2002), 172.

24. David K. Lewis, *Convention: A Philosophical Study* (Cambridge, MA: Harvard University Press, 1969), 208.

lots of conventions you might find strange if you come from somewhere else. I know this because Jess, our admissions officer at Ridley College, is originally from North Carolina, and she often finds things that are very normal to me highly amusing. Like the way we pronounce "as," which to her sounds like "ass" (making very common phrases like "sweet as" just a little bit funny). She thinks it's weird when a guy she has just met asks to "catch up" for coffee. We wear "thongs" on our feet in public (unless we are walking around barefoot). We shorten every word we can (afternoon is "arvo," cup of tea is "cuppa," service station is "servo"). "Yeah, nah" means you disagree, and "Nah, yeah" means you agree. The way we pronounce "scones" sounds like we ingest light fixtures with our morning coffee. She could go on.

If you want to be understood in this country, you quickly pick up these local quirks. There is no law about these things, nor is there a Central Office for the Creation of Confusing Aussie Conventions. Conventions like these are stabilized and sustained purely by our mutual interest in understanding and being understood. Likewise, genres arise in situations where people have a shared interest in communication. Neither authors nor readers are entirely in control of genre. I can't just make up my own private idea about how a thank-you letter or an invitation should work. We all play by the rules because if we didn't, we wouldn't be able to get things done together.

Speaking of "playing by the rules," there is one metaphor I do find useful for talking about genres: genres tell us *which game we are playing*. Just as games are about more than one individual, communication is bigger than just what's in the head of the author or reader. Communication is governed by conventions, or rules of play, which are bigger than any individual – though within those boundaries players also have a lot of freedom. Usually, though not necessarily, the goal of reading is to play along with the writer – to create meaning in **coordination** with them – and genres help us do that by specifying which rules we can expect everyone to be playing by. (More on this under tenets 4 and 5 below.)

Conventions are stable enough, but they do change over time. We will return to the "social and ideological action" part of Catherine Schryer's definition in chapter 3, but for now it's worth observing that the impetus behind the change in *Creature from the Black Lagoon*'s genre from creature film to sci-fi was tied up in economic and social factors – the declining popularity of one genre, a competitive film industry, and a strong ideological commitment to making money. Genres change over time, and these changes often have as much to do with what's happening outside the cinema as within.

Many changes in a genre are driven by the generic promiscuity we discussed above (tenet 1). If texts can engage with multiple genres at the same time, then there is much more potential for mixing genres to create new genres. From the 1950s to today, we see constant genre-based creativity within the horror film industry. Creature films, sci-fi, film noir, melodrama, gothic, and satire constantly combine and recombine to create something new. Star Wars created something new by taking themes often explored in comic books and putting them on the big screen (a change in the structure of presentation). Mary Shelley's *Frankenstein* is another great example. At one level it is so brilliantly unlike anything before that we rightly credit her with starting a whole new genre (and indeed an entire mythology). But her new genre emerged out of old ones. Shelley famously wrote the first version as part of a competition to write the best ghost story. Its published form delighted audiences of the gothic novel while offering something new. The novel is framed by the unembedded (disembodied?) letters of an explorer named Robert Walton, who tells the story on his way to the North Pole (casting Dr. Frankenstein as a kind of adventurer). The subtitle of the first edition ("The Modern Prometheus") invites us to read it alongside the tragic hero of Greek mythology. Shelley is about as close to creative genius as you get. And yet, like her tragic hero, she assembles her new genre out of the severed limbs of other genres.

The most important way genres change is through being combined with other genres.[25] There are, of course, other creative forces to look out for:

- Technology can provide new forms of presentation; for example, gothic novels eventually become horror films.
- Genres can be shifted from one form to another; for example, a novel is made into a musical.
- Existing genres can be combined within another larger work; for example, religious texts are combined in a hymnal or prayerbook, or speeches are incorporated into a literary work.
- An established form can take on new topics; for example, an epic poem is used to tell the Christian story as in John Milton's *Paradise Lost*, or a comic book format and fable-like animal characters are used to tell a Holocaust survivor's autobiography as in Art Spiegelman's *Maus*.
- The scale of the work can be changed; for example, the forty-six-minute LP (long playing) vinyl format redefines the modern album, or a social media network turns fifteen-second videos into an artform.
- Shifts in the broader genre ecosystem can transform a genre; for example, the development of sci-fi alters how old creature films are perceived.

---

25. See Fowler, *Kinds of Literature*, 178–88.

- Genres can be influenced by other cultures; for example, the genres of dominant Greek culture are borrowed and adapted by ancient Jewish authors.[26]
- A genre can be used for a new rhetorical or social function; for example, a shopping list is used as part of an advertising campaign, or a political message is made through a mock children's story.
- An existing genre can be satirized; for example, the film *Scream* deploys familiar horror tropes to make us laugh.

All these factors push genres to change over time, which explains why genres are only *relatively* stable – stabilized for now.

Todorov and the Constant Transformation of Genre

In answer to the question, "Where do genres come from?" Todorov gives this straightforward answer:

> Quite simply, from other genres. A new genre is always the transformation of an earlier one, or of several: by inversion, by displacement, by combination. . . . There has never been a literature without genres; it is a system in constant transformation.[27]

Genre conventions are a bit like flooring the accelerator, but with the hand-brake on at the same time. Genre mixing, borrowing, technology, and social factors push change, but the need for mutual understanding puts on the brakes. The result is neither rapid instability nor immoveable stability, but somewhere in the middle – stabilized-for-now.

TENET 3: GENRES ARE FUZZY AROUND THE EDGES AND SOLID AT THE CORE

The third thing we learn from *Creature from the Black Lagoon* is that the difference between the genre called "creature film" and the genre called "sci-fi" is not clear-cut, which gave the marketing department at Universal Pictures the wiggle room they needed.

---

26. See Sean A. Adams, *Greek Genres and Jewish Authors* (Waco, TX: Baylor University Press, 2020).

27. Tzvetan Todorov, *Genres in Discourse*, trans. Catherine Porter (Cambridge: Cambridge University Press, 1990), 15. See also Tzvetan Todorov, "The Origin of Genres," *NLH* 8.1 (1976): 159–70.

Classical genre theory was always looking to clarify precisely where the line was between genres, because logically a thing cannot belong to two classes at once. The same animal cannot be a snake *and* a lizard, so we need to work out where to draw that line (and fast usually). I might struggle with an odd example, like Australia's legless lizards – but even in this case, if I ask the right people, they can tell me which species they belong to.[28]

Modern genre theory sees things differently. Genres are not logically discrete classes like species. As Alastair Fowler observes, genres are "types, rather than fixed categories with borders."[29] Where does creature film end and sci-fi begin? What makes something a horror film and not a psychological thriller? Unlike snakes and lizards, the lines are blurry, and so a text might actually fall in the overlap between two categories. The lines are so blurry, in fact, that it might be better to ditch talk of lines and categories completely.

No More Biological Metaphors, Please

To help steer us away from seeing genres as rigid categories, various metaphors get a workout.[30] Some talk about genres as a kind of **family resemblance**. The advantage of this metaphor is that it is broad enough to cover almost anything; the problem is that it is broad enough to cover almost anything.[31]

Family resemblance is one of several biological metaphors you may come across, alongside "genus" and "evolution" of genres. As tempting as it is to place genres on the great family tree of literature, modern genre theorists tend to be a little allergic to these metaphors. As John Frow points out, these metaphors offer a reassuring sheen of scientific rigor, but in reality, genres are far fuzzier.[32] To state the obvious, genres do not work the way species do. Texts participate in multiple genres, whereas you cannot be both horse and human. Nor, as Zachary Dawson reminds us, can dogs be bred with dolphins or dinosaurs – whereas genres from any time period can be combined.[33]

---

28. Snakes don't have eyelids, I'm reliably informed.
29. Fowler, *Kinds of Literature*, 249. He means "hard borders": cf. Fowler, *Kinds of Literature*, 74.
30. See David Fishelov, *Metaphors of Genre: The Role of Analogies in Genre Theory* (University Park: Pennsylvania State University Press, 1993).
31. See John Swales, *Genre Analysis: English in Academic and Research Settings* (Cambridge: Cambridge University Press, 1990), 51. The metaphor is often hastily borrowed from Ludwig Wittgenstein. Cognitive linguistics employs it in a more developed way (see note 34).
32. Frow, *Genre*, 57–59.
33. Zachary K. Dawson, "The Problem of Gospel Genres: Unmasking a Flawed Consensus and Providing a Fresh Way Forward with Systemic Functional Linguistics Genre Theory," *BAGL* 8 (2019): 45.

Genres are conventions (see tenet 2 above) that arise and are stabilized by our mutual desire to be understood. They are stabilized as conventions through recurring interactions, but these genres need to be organized in our heads somehow. One popular way to think about how this works is to see genres as overlapping groups of texts centered on **prototypes**. On this way of looking at genre, the strength of a text's relationship with a genre depends on how closely it compares to one or more prototypes. This shifts our focus from the edges of a genre to the center – it's no longer about finding a firm line to divide sci-fi and creature film, but about identifying what is at the core of each of those genres.

This idea of prototypes is borrowed from cognitive linguistics.[34] It helpfully observes that when humans think of a concept, we don't bring up a definition in our minds and tick off the necessary and sufficient criteria one by one. Instead, we start with a couple of indisputable examples and compare to those. What do you think of as a "pet"? Probably a dog or a cat. I suppose you could have a pet mouse or turtle. I would be very surprised to learn you have a pet whale. The same process happens when we think about a genre. To explain what a "1960s horror film" is, I will probably make you watch *Psycho* or *Night of the Living Dead*. If I want to work out what an "epic poem" is, I should start with *Paradise Lost* or the *Iliad*. If you claim that James Joyce's *Ulysses* is an "epic," I'm going to mentally compare it to one of those prototypes and see how closely it is related (admittedly, it's not written in heroic verse, but it is attempting to tell the all-encompassing story of a nation . . . sort of). Importantly, these prototypes are personal realizations of culturally relative terrain – ask people in different parts of the world to think of a "fruit," and whether their prototype is "apple" or "date" depends on whether you live in Sydney or Jordan.[35]

The prototype model is very useful for talking about how language users think about genre. It gives us a handle on the fuzziness of genres, and how we know what a "novel" is, even if it's surprisingly difficult to define it and mark out its firm borders. But while prototype theory and cognitive linguistics provide another useful angle on genre, I don't find it sufficient as a model for what

---

34. The prototype model was pioneered by psychologist Eleanor Rosch (1938–), developing Ludwig Wittgenstein's semantic model of family resemblances and earlier work by Karl Erdmann and others: see William Croft and D. Alan Cruse, *Cognitive Linguistics* (New York: Cambridge University Press, 2004), 77–106. On its use in genre studies: Brian Paltridge, *Genre, Frames and Writings in Research Settings* (Philadelphia: John Benjamins, 1997), 53; Frow, *Genre*, 59–60; Anis S. Bawarshi and Mary Jo Reiff, *Genre: An Introduction to History, Theory, Research, and Pedagogy* (West Lafayette, IN: Parlor, 2010), 43. On its use in literature: Michael Sinding, "A Sermon in the Midst of a Smutty Tale: Blending in Genres of Speech, Writing and Literature," in *Cognitive Literary Studies: Current Themes and New Directions*, ed. Isabel Jaén and Julien Jacques Simon (Austin: University of Texas Press, 2012), 145–62; Barbara Dancygier, "What Can Blending Do for You?," *Lang. Lit.* 15.1 (2006): 5. Thanks, Andrew Myers, for selling me on cognitive linguistics and for suggesting many of these resources.

35. See Croft and Cruse, *Cognitive Linguistics*, 78.

genres are.[36] That's why I define genres not *as* prototypes but as conventions organized in our heads *around* prototypes.

Whichever metaphors we use – or indeed if we choose not to use any metaphor! – the shift to modern genre theory frees us from the need to define clear edges between genres. If texts (unlike animals) can belong to multiple genres (unlike species), then there is no logical need to have hard borders. That doesn't make the borders nonexistent. As Alastair Fowler points out, the "boundaries [between genres] may not be hard-edged, but they can nonetheless exclude."[37] But rather than focus on the edges, it is more useful to think about genres by comparing texts to the central, quintessential examples and seeing how they relate. Genres may be a little fuzzy around the edges, but they all have more or less solid examples at the core.

We have so far explored three ways that modern genre theory corrects some of the unhelpful assumptions of classical genre theory, using our trusty B-grade case study, *Creature from the Black Lagoon*, as an illustration of what genre is. It's now time to look at what genre *does*.

TENET 4: EACH GENRE INVITES US TO PLAY A DIFFERENT READING-GAME, WITH DIFFERENT EXPERIENCES, ROLES, GOALS, AND RESOURCES

We have seen that texts have complex relationships with multiple overlapping and stable-enough genres. But why? What's the point of genre? What's in it for writers – and readers – to participate in a genre? I like to think of each genre as inviting us to play a different **reading-game**.[38] Participating in a genre offers us distinctive experiences, roles, goals, and resources to play with as we make meaning together.

In classical genre theories, the point of genre classification is often normative – to give rules for authors and criteria for readers to judge the quality of a work. In response, some literary critics complained that no good author ever really plays by these rules. If that's the case, then maybe we would be better off scrapping the concept of genre completely.

---

36. Cognitive linguistics is handy for describing how we hold genres in our heads and the cognitive frames (or networks of ideas) that come to mind when using a genre. However, genres are *social* conventions, not just mental categories. Prototype theory therefore can't provide a full account of how a genre arises historically, functions socially, or is realized literarily. Just as there's more to football than sports psychology, there's more to genre than cognitive linguistics.

37. Fowler, *Kinds of Literature*, 74.

38. On genres as reading-games using Hans-Georg Gadamer's hermeneutics, see my *Playing with Scripture: Reading Contested Biblical Texts with Gadamer and Genre Theory*, Routledge Interdisciplinary Perspectives on Biblical Criticism (Abingdon, UK: Routledge, 2024).

Croce, Ever the Romantic

One of the leading anti-genre campaigners was the Italian Benedetto Croce (1866–1952). As a **romanticist** (which is a reference to the literary movement, not a comment on his love life), he thought every true work was unique:

> Every true work of art has violated some established kind and upset the ideas of the critics, who have thus been obliged to broaden the kinds, until finally even the broadened kind has proved too narrow, owing to the appearance of new works of art, naturally followed by new scandals, new upsettings and – new broadenings.[39]

He argued that seeking the laws or definitions of a genre was no more useful to hermeneutics than attempting to discern the "laws" guiding all the books shelved under "A" in the library.[40] To put it bluntly, literary critics should leave the job of classifying books to librarians.

This kind of distaste for the whole idea of genres is often associated with romanticism, a movement that tends to put a high value on the creative genius of the writer. This is seen in Friedrich Schlegel in the eighteenth century, in Maurice Blanchot in 1959, and in the 1980s with Jacques Derrida's new law of genre.[41] Genre seems like too much of a constraint for a true genius; all true works of art are their own genre, sui generis.

The romanticists had a point. Genres are best not seen as normative or used to judge the value of a work. But we shouldn't throw the baby of genre out with the bathwater of classic prescriptive genre theory. Great authors aren't constrained by genre; they are powered by it. Take Shakespeare for instance. In some ways his plays are hard to nail down to a single genre. But is popular literary critic Harold Bloom right to claim that Shakespeare therefore transcends genre, has no genre, or that genre is almost irrelevant for understanding his plays?[42]

39. Benedetto Croce, "Aesthetic as Science of Expression and General Linguistic," in *Modern Genre Theory*, ed. David Duff (London: Routledge, 2014), 27.

40. Croce, "Aesthetic," 28; René Wellek, *Concepts of Criticism*, ed. Stephen G. Nichols (New Haven, CT: Yale University Press, 1963), 46; Bawarshi and Reiff, *Genre*, 27.

41. See Michel Beaujour, "Genus Universum," *Glyph* 7 (1980): 16; Philippe Lacoue-Labarthe and Jean-Luc Nancy, "Genre," *Glyph* 7 (1980): 1–14; Frow, *Genre*, 29.

42. Harold Bloom, *The Anatomy of Influence: Literature as a Way of Life* (New Haven, CT: Yale University Press, 2011), 42, 46–47. Bloom makes similar claims about the Bible: Mary Gerhart, *Genre Choices, Gender Questions* (Norman: University of Oklahoma Press, 1992), 93.

Er, no.

The technical term for this perspective is NRN, or "Neo-Romanticist Nonsense."[43] Genre is never irrelevant for understanding a work of literature. Shakespeare is great, but not because he has somehow "transcended genre." That claim is a bit like watching the ski jumpers at the Winter Olympics flying through the air for 350 feet and saying that they have "transcended gravity." In fact, gravity is what makes their jumps possible, as they accelerate on the downhill to over 65 miles per hour. Likewise, genre is essential to genius. As literary theorist Rosalie Colie points out, much of Shakespeare's creativity in his plays comes from playing *with genre*. He mixes genres together to make something new, uses classical genres to invoke ancient subcultures, and surprises and delights us by upsetting the norms of genre.[44] Bob Dylan was awarded a Nobel Prize for creating "new poetic expressions" and forever changing the song genre, but his work was still "rooted in the rich tradition of American folk music" and influenced by "the poets of modernism and the beatnik movement."[45]

Let's put it simply. You can't break all the rules if there aren't any rules.[46] As Mikhail Bakhtin insists, speech genres are very flexible (much more so than other language forms), but they still "have a normative significance for the speaking individuum, and they are not created by him but are given to him."[47] That's why I think it's helpful to see genre conventions like different reading-games we are invited to play. The rules of a game don't constrain play; they make it possible.

Far from stifling creativity, genres offer writers *and readers* a shared treasury of resources to draw on as they create meaning.[48] Genres open up possibilities for creativity and help authors get things done. A horror film invites us to explore behind the surface of orderly society, embodying our anxieties in a monster.

---

43. Just to be clear, before you go citing NRN in a paper, this is not a real thing.

44. See Rosalie L. Colie, *The Resources of Kind: Genre-Theory in the Renaissance*, ed. Barbara K. Lewalski (Berkeley: University of California Press, 1973).

45. "Bob Dylan: Facts," The Nobel Prize in Literature 2016, www.nobelprize.org/prizes/literature/2016 /dylan/facts, accessed August 31, 2023.

46. Almost everyone makes this point: Tzvetan Todorov, *The Fantastic: A Structural Approach to a Literary Genre* (Ithaca, NY: Cornell University Press, 1975), 8; Hans Robert Jauss, *Toward an Aesthetic of Reception*, trans. Timothy Bahti, THL 2 (Minneapolis: University of Minnesota Press, 1982), 78–79; Frow, *Genre*, 30; Hayden White, "Anomalies of Genre: The Utility of Theory and History for the Study of Literary Genres," *NLH* 34.3 (2003): 605; Beaujour, "Genus Universum," 16, 30; Yuri Tynianov, "The Literary Fact," in *Modern Genre Theory*, ed. Duff, 35.

47. Bakhtin, *Speech Genres*, 80–81. Speech genres sit snugly between *langue* and *parole* in Ferdinand de Saussure's model – more flexible than the rules of English grammar but still binding within their context.

48. Fowler, *Kinds of Literature*, 22; Frow, *Genre*, 2; Paul Ricoeur, "The Hermeneutical Function of Distanciation," *PhT* 17.2 (1973): 135; Lloyd F. Bitzer, "Aristotle's Enthymeme Revisited," *QJS* 45.4 (1959): 408. Genres work as "a set of conventional and highly organized constraints on the production and interpretation of meaning": Frow, *Genre*, 30. On writing and reading biblical texts: Gerhart, "Generic Competence," 34.

It gives us permission to depart from the studied realism of, say, a historical novel, and because we all agree to accept impossible things as real and threatening, we can explore different kinds of truths about ourselves and the world we live in. The genre also provides a tool kit of settings, characters, tropes, and themes – the graveyard at dusk, the slow-moving zombie, and the arrogant idiot (who we all know will be first to go).

Creators can draw on these resources, or even subvert them. Agatha Christie is the master of the genre of murder mystery because of the way she plays with the genre's expectations. In *Murder on the Orient Express*, she subverts the convention that the true murderer will be revealed when the other suspects are excluded (spoiler alert: they were all in it together!). Likewise in *The Murder of Robert Ackroyd*, it turns out (spoiler alert) that the narrator was the murderer all along. Even though the rules of the genre are broken, the reader's experience hinges on these shared expectations. For authors to break the rules in interesting ways, everyone has to know them first. Genre expectations are like handrails – some authors hold on to them tightly, others skateboard off them. Either way, genre is an indispensable resource for creativity.

Modern genre theory sees genres as more than classifications for classification's sake or rigid norms for aspiring writers to be judged by; they are functional. Each genre invites us to play a different *reading-game*. They offer different *experiences*. They invite us to take up different hermeneutical *roles* and pursue particular *goals*. They equip us as writers and readers with different *resources* to play with as we make meaning together.

TENET 5: GENRES ARE ABOUT READERS AS MUCH AS WRITERS

I mentioned above that genres offer writers *and readers* shared resources for making meaning. One of the most important things genre does is tell the reader what game they are meant to be playing. A murder mystery is not a biography; a poem is not a parking ticket. Different genres expect very different things from us as readers.

Identifying a genre helps readers create meaning by giving them clues about what to expect. In Bakhtin's speech genres model, the existence of typical utterances in typical situations provides a heuristic tool that makes understanding possible by enabling us to predict, for example, the length of the utterance from its very first words.[49] Hans Robert Jauss puts it like this:

---

49. See Bakhtin, "Problem of Speech Genres," in Bakhtin, *Speech Genres*, 90.

> Every work belongs to a genre – whereby I mean neither more nor less than that
> for each work a preconstituted horizon of expectations must be ready at hand
> (this can also be understood as a relationship of "rules of the game" . . .) to orient
> the reader's (public's) understanding and to enable a qualifying reception.[50]

If reading is like a game, then it helps at the outset to know the rules: what counts as a goal, what equipment we should bring, and what potential moves we can expect from the other players (especially the writer).

Our expectations might not be met, but at least we can narrow down the possibilities. If we are reading John Donne's holy sonnets, we expect him to throw some interesting metaphors around – "One short sleep past, we wake eternally"[51] – and so can rule out interpretations of the poem that make it into an extended discussion about the benefits of a good night's sleep or the proper pre-op procedures for anesthesia. Jauss's language of "ready at hand" is helpful. When doing a DIY project around the home, I have certain tools out next to me and the rest stay in the tools cupboard. In a similar way, genres tell us what tools we should get out of the shed. Across all human cultures and writing there are an incalculable number of ways to use words to make meaning, and readers can't have all of them in their back pocket at every moment. But as soon as we read, "Once upon a time," we know what to expect – faraway locations, talking animals, giants, princesses, and simple moral lessons are all on the table. Genres help make the possibilities manageable and make it more likely that writer and readers will end up on the same page.

Not only do genres tell us readers what to expect; they also give us a *job* to do. Returning to the murder mystery for a moment, it is assumed that our job in a "whodunit" is to work out . . . well . . . who done it.[52] We expect the crime fiction writer to put in some red herrings, and we get great satisfaction from winning the battle of the wits: I knew it was the butler all along! You *could* try to read Luke's gospel this way, but ideally the job of the gospel genre reader is not to guess who ends up betraying and killing Jesus (we will explore precisely what this readerly role is when we look at the gospel genre in chapter 11). These jobs can vary significantly between genres. A riddle is designed to be solved, whereas a good poem lets readers puzzle over things without ever reaching closure.

---

50. Jauss, *Toward an Aesthetic of Reception*, 79. Similarly: Grant R. Osborne, *The Hermeneutical Spiral: A Comprehensive Introduction to Biblical Interpretation*, 2nd ed. (Downers Grove, IL: InterVarsity, 2006), 183, 510; E. D. Hirsch, Jr., *Validity in Interpretation* (New Haven, CT: Yale University Press, 1967), 70–71; Anis Bawarshi, *Genre and the Invention of the Writer: Reconsidering the Place of Invention in Composition* (Logan: Utah State University Press, 2003), 23.

51. John Donne, "Sonnet X: Death Be Not Proud."

52. This example is borrowed from Alastair Fowler who borrowed it from Frank Kermode: Fowler, *Kinds of Literature*, 72.

We cannot understand a political cartoon unless we correctly identify who is being satirized, whereas a love song works better if we don't try to guess which former partner of the pop star is behind which lines. Different genres mean different roles for readers.

This raises our next point, which is that the job assigned to the reader also informs the amount of *creative freedom* granted to them in interpretation. Some texts anticipate a high degree of coordination between the writer and the reader. The literary and nonliterary payoffs of such "high-coordination genres" will encourage the reader to strive to understand what kinds of things a speaker might have intended in the original situation. (A royal edict backed by immediate capital punishment has a way of focusing the mind on likely authorial intent.) But to strive for this degree of coordination with the speaking situation when reading other kinds of texts is to miss the point. For example, there are a lot of theories about what was happening behind the scenes of *Hamlet*, yet the play continues to delight audiences who have no idea about the exact political situation Shakespeare had in mind. This isn't a problem – its independence from Shakespeare is part of the enduring allure of the play! The reason people still want to see *Hamlet*, long after the original situation has passed, is the way that the play invites and inspires seemingly endless recontextualization: "*Hamlet* is a fertile realm in which to get lost and find versions of oneself."[53] The royal edict and Shakespearean drama each invite very different degrees of coordination with the original speaking situation and likely intention, and so each provide vastly different scope for the reader's creativity.

Genres offer different experiences, roles, and resources that are used by both *writers* and *readers* to make meaning.

TENET 6: GENRES CAN REGULATE ALL SORTS OF THINGS ABOUT A TEXT (INCLUDING FORMAL FEATURES, CONTENT, AND SOCIAL CONTEXT)

When describing a genre, what features of a text can we look at? For Aristotle, genres are defined by three criteria: the media used, the objects being represented, and the mode of presentation.[54] In modern genre theory, however, the kinds of resources that a genre can supply are virtually unlimited.[55] Let's return

---

53. Liam Semler, "A Proximate Prince: The Gooey Business of 'Hamlet' Criticism," *SydS* 32 (2006): 98.

54. Aristotle, *Poetics*, LCL 199, 34–35

55. Rhetorical genre studies theorists tend to identify genres by looking for regularities in three general dimensions: the way a text is composed, the way readers engage with the text, and the broader social situation of the genre's participants: Anthony Paré and Graham Smart, "Observing Genres in Action: Towards a Research Methodology," in *Genre and the New Rhetoric*, ed. Aviva Freedman and Peter Medway (London: Taylor & Francis, 1994), 122.

to the country music example from the previous chapter. How would you explain to someone from another planet what country music is? To me, a good definition of this musical genre would need to cover three aspects of the genre.

First, there are the **formal features** (sometimes called the "external features") of the country music genre. Here "formal" refers to the form or shape of the genre, not how casual or formal the language is. It is how the song is written. As a musician, I would start with the common song structures – the ballad form and the potential it offers to tell a story; the verse, chorus, bridge structure; the rhythmic potentials of 2/4-, 4/4-, and 6/8-time signatures. I might also talk about the distinctive instrumentation (guitars, banjos, fiddles).

None of these features are exclusive to country music, of course, so we need to look beyond the form to what is going on *inside* a country music song. The second sort of things to look out for, therefore, are to do with *content* (sometimes called the "internal features") of a genre. We think of this as the "treasury of thoughts and moods" that a particular genre offers us.[56] For country music, this treasury might include certain recurring themes (young love, hard work), moods (brave optimism, deep nostalgia), and images (pickup trucks). Johnny Cash famously defined it using exactly those kinds of internal features: "Of emotions, of love, of breakup, of love and hate and death and dying, mama, apple pie, and the whole thing. It covers a lot of territory, country music does."[57]

However, even this is not quite enough. Understanding a genre like country music probably also requires us to know something of its *social context*. You could talk about its historical origins in the rural populations of the southern and western USA. If you're brave, you might venture to mention the predominantly White American audiences, the link with conservative politics, and the shared cultural and ideological assumptions you might expect to find at a country music festival. There are notable exceptions, of course, but they are notable precisely because they break with genre expectations. Think of the backlash when Natalie Maines of the Dixie Chicks made comments onstage about George W. Bush that were "practically punk rock."[58] Genres are historical creatures, so they cannot be fully understood without an eye on their broader historical and social context. (This third aspect sounds a bit like the life-situation of Hermann Gunkel's form criticism, but as we will see in chapter 3 there are important differences.)

Under these headings – formal, thematic, and social – the range of possible

---

56. Despite the horrible things I said earlier about form criticism, I gratefully borrow this phrase from Hermann Gunkel, *An Introduction to the Psalms* (Macon, GA: Mercer University Press, 1998), 16.

57. Johnny Cash, "Larry King Live," 26 November 2002, https://transcripts.cnn.com/show/lkl/date/2002 -11-26/segment/00.

58. Quoted in Betty Clarke, "Review: The Dixie Chicks," *The Guardian*, 13 March 2003, www .theguardian.com/music/2003/mar/12/artsfeatures.popandrock.

genre distinctives is vast. I've included a table below in which I list some of the common features of genres to be on the lookout for (with a focus on literary texts). Before you read this list, I want you to promise that you won't take it as definitive. Deal? The reason is that a list like this is always highly selective and really just reflects my own culture and literary preferences. I've included "meter" on this list, but there is nothing immutable or essential about that as a feature of poetry. Some literary cultures make a big deal of meter (patterns of long and short syllables), others do meter in a different way (patterns of stressed and unstressed syllables), while still others don't have meter like this at all (a notable example, especially for biblical studies purposes, is Hebrew poetry, which has rhythm but not meter). There are enough similarities across cultures and throughout history that we can try to generalize, but really there is nothing stopping a particular literary culture from inventing entirely new techniques and assigning them to a genre. Imagine trying to explain to a first-century Roman poet why "typeface," "camera angles," or "use of emojis" are important markers of genre!

Another word of warning before you read this table is that features of a genre will often bleed over these neat categories. For example, I've put register under "social context," but register overlaps with lots of other items. (Don't worry if these terms are unfamiliar. I'll define them as we go, and you can always check the glossary.)

A Totally Inadequate List of Things a Genre Might Regulate

Social Context

- recurring **situations** and functions: recounting events, teaching a student, substituting for physical presence
- **register variables: field, tenor, mode**
- interpersonal dynamic: private/public, specific/general addressee, narrow/wide audience
- negotiation of roles and moves within dialog: commands, interrogatives, responses, exchanges of objects or information
- relative power dynamics of writer/speaker and audience: pleading, instructing, commanding
- negotiation of attitudes: feelings, appraisals, engagement with other voices, strength of stance
- values shared (or assumed) by the speaker and community
- social grouping: addressed to an in-group or wider audience
- **uptake** system: preceding and anticipated genres

Paratext
- title
- typeface
- accompanying text: marginal notes, foreword, back cover endorsements
- material: binding, production techniques
- page layout

Formal Features (or "External Features")
- means (or "radical") of presentation: oral, written, written but read aloud, visual, sculpture, film
- **staging structure**: the expected sequence of compulsory elements (**stages**) and optional elements (**phases**)
- structural markers: divisions, signposting, macrosyntactic markers
- embedded genres
- dialog: direct or indirect reported speech
- voice: narrator's voice, point of view, grammatically first person, second person, third person
- word choices: technical, colloquial, loanwords
- tone and mood: formal or informal, degree of amplification, concession or evaluation
- meter or prose type
- grammatical choices: passive or active, subordinate sentences, presence or absence of syntactical markers
- length
- music: lyrics, songs – the old walking song in *The Hobbit* or the songs performed in Shakespeare's plays

Content (Internal Features)
- opening, stock phrases: "once upon a time"
- subject matter: scope, focus, space allocated
- characters and participants: number, kind, social class or grouping, moral quality, human/divine, quality, method of characterization, specific/generic people
- intertextuality: use of sources, references, quotation conventions
- setting, **chronotope**: place, time, and value
- event and time management: historical/ahistorical, specific/generic, chronological scope, cycles, plot arrangement, narrative time, or logical sequence
- information flow: when and how themes and new ideas are introduced

- **truth effects**: abstract truths, scientific truths, poetic license
- image and metaphors: stock images, type-scenes, tropes
- lexical resources: expected or inappropriate vocabulary, formulas
- devices: wordplay, repetition, parallelism
- activities and objects

Readerly Experience
- expectations
- task or hermeneutical game: solve the murder mystery, be convinced, reflect on one's life
- goal: creative freedom or strict coordination
- anticipated **uptake** or genre of response: RSVP, call for papers, film review

SUMMARY

Modern genre theory invites us to leave behind the essentialist approach of classical genre theory and see the relationship between texts and genres in a more historical light. We have covered a fair amount of ground so far in this chapter, so let's check back in on our working understanding of texts and genre. We began with this definition:

> Genres are relatively stable conventions that writers and readers use to make meaning in certain contexts but not others.

To this we can add the following six tenets of modern genre theory:

> Texts do not "belong" to a genre but are promiscuous (tenet 1) and have complex relationships with multiple genres.
> Genres are relatively stable and overlapping conventions or games (tenet 2), fuzzy around the edges but centered around prototypes (tenet 3).
> Genres tell us what game we are playing. They offer different experiences, roles, goals, and resources (tenet 4) for both writers and readers (tenet 5) to play with as they make meaning. Genres can regulate all sorts of features of a text (tenet 6).

But this definition of genre is incomplete. We are missing perhaps the biggest contribution that modern genre theory makes to our understanding of genre

– namely, that seeing genres in their *historical* context raises questions about their *social* context as well. In the next chapter we are going to explore how, as a social phenomenon, genre is power.

QUESTIONS FOR DISCUSSION AND REFLECTION

1. How does a historical perspective change how we approach genres?
2. Which tenets laid out in this chapter do you find easiest to accept? Do you want to push back on any of them?
3. If genres are constantly changing, how can we hope to understand a historical text from another culture?
4. Our working definition of what counts as a "genre" is very broad. Is it too broad? Can *any* similarities we see between texts be considered a genre? Is "Bible" a genre? Is "anthology" a genre? Is "Agatha Christie novel" a genre?

FURTHER READING

Introductory

Duff, David. *Modern Genre Theory*. Longman Critical Readers. New York: Routledge, 2000.
   Handy anthology of major twentieth-century theorists.
Frow, John. *Genre*. Second edition. New Critical Idiom. New York: Routledge, 2015.
   Gold-standard account of modern literary genre theory.

Deep Dive

Bakhtin, M. M. *Speech Genres and Other Late Essays*. Edited by Caryl Emerson and Michael Holquist. Austin: University of Texas Press, 1986.
   Establishes a historical perspective on genres and their social situations.
Derrida, Jacques. "The Law of Genre." *Critical Inquiry* 7.1 (1980): 55–81.
   As always with Derrida, irritatingly written and insightful.
Fowler, Alastair. *Kinds of Literature: An Introduction to the Theory of Genres and Modes*. Oxford, UK: Clarendon, 1982.
   Influential work well on the way to modern genre theory.
Frye, Northrop. *Anatomy of Criticism: Four Essays*. New York: Atheneum, 1968.
   A classic structuralist masterpiece, improbable in interesting ways.
Todorov, Tzvetan. *Genres in Discourse*. Translated by Catherine Porter. Cambridge, UK: Cambridge University Press, 1990.
   Deep insights that build on his earlier structuralist analysis of the fantastic.

CHAPTER 3

GENRE IS POWER

The Need for Social Context

Back when I was a college student, I earned money for buying books by selling my (musical) soul as a pianist in a wedding covers band. I remember one Saturday evening we were at a fancy venue on Sydney Harbour when my bass player Pete decided to play a "hilarious" trick on me. He found a piece of paper that looked exactly like a parking ticket. Then while I wasn't looking, he put it on my car, which was parked outside. When we all came out for a break, he stood back and watched with tasteless satisfaction as I fell for it – I absolutely thought I'd just lost my entire night's pay on a parking violation. As soon as he saw the devastation on my face, he and the rest of the band quickly confessed: "Haha, don't worry, it's not real!" I don't think I punched him, but I might have cut short his bass solo.

The "parking ticket" (or "traffic violation" or "infringement notice") genre is much feared because of its power to drain bank accounts and ruin whole days. Genre is power. What Pete put on my car, however, was not a parking ticket. No matter how much it looked like one – no matter how accurately he mimicked the genre's structure, rhetorical forms, language, and even paper weight and color – something was missing. That "something" is all to do with the social situation – and this is the final piece in the modern genre theory puzzle.

Two of the main contributions to modern genre theory discussion come from the fields of linguistics and rhetoric: **systemic functional linguistics (SFL)** and **rhetorical genre studies (RGS)**.[1] While each approach to genre has developed in its own distinct discipline, they both, in their own way, contribute to our understanding of genre by inviting us to step back and examine genres in their social situation. If genres are historical conventions, then they must exist within a

---

1. See Sunny Hyon, "Genre in Three Traditions: Implications for ESL," *TQ* 30.4 (1996): 693–722. Other traditions not dealt with here include English for Special Purposes (giving disadvantaged students access to technical genres, such as university essay writing) and the "Brazilian school" (using a range of approaches to similar ends): see Anis S. Bawarshi and Mary Jo Reiff, *Genre: An Introduction to History, Theory, Research, and Pedagogy* (West Lafayette, IN: Parlor, 2010), 162–66.

social context. It's not enough to talk about what a particular genre looks like; we also need to understand who uses it, and what for. We need to bring genre to life.

SYSTEMIC FUNCTIONAL LINGUISTICS

SFL is an approach to language based on the pioneering work of a British linguist named M. A. K. Halliday. If you've done any study in linguistics, you'll probably know SFL already,[2] but many Bible scholars have never heard of it. For example, in an extraordinary book review of an SFL-based approach to the gospel genre, a leading scholar dismissed it as an "approach from educating schoolchildren" in Australia that not even his Australian biblical scholar friends "had even heard of."[3] Let's fix that right now.

To be clear, SFL is not only a theory about genre; it's a much broader discipline covering everything from grammar to the power dynamic between speakers. In fact, Halliday himself had little to say about genre, so originally SFL was light on genre theory. But in the 1980s, J. R. Martin and his students developed an approach to genre from within the SFL framework, separating out context into two levels: register and genre.[4]

There is now a solid community of researchers who have applied this SFL framework to various practical questions having to do with genre.[5] Some of the most famous and fruitful applications have been to do with primary school literacy programs – exploring how children gain competency in particular genres. But alongside this important practical pedagogical question, their work is driven by a more fundamental interest in the power of genres, and particularly in "redistributing the literacy resources of Western culture to the people

---

2. See Constantine R. Campbell, *Advances in the Study of Greek: New Insights for Reading the New Testament* (Grand Rapids: Zondervan, 2015), 62–68.

3. Richard A. Burridge, "Review of *History, Biography, and the Genre of Luke-Acts* by Andrew Pitts," *JETS* 64.1 (2021): 191–95. While Michael Halliday ended up at Sydney University, he was born in England and held positions everywhere from Cambridge to Stanford (I mention this in case being from Australia is a dealbreaker).

4. Genres regulate or predict these register variables within different contexts. See J. R. Martin and David Rose, *Working with Discourse: Meaning beyond the Clause*, 2nd ed. (New York: Bloomsbury Academic, 2007), 296–309; Douglas Biber and Susan Conrad, *Register, Genre, and Style*, 2nd ed., CTL (Cambridge: Cambridge University Press, 2019), 1–2.

5. SFL genre theory is sometimes called the "Sydney School." Some non-SFL scholars used the term in papers from a 1992 conference in Ottawa to refer to what J. R. Martin and others at the University of Sydney were doing: J. R. Martin, "Looking Out: Functional Linguistics and Genre," *LHS* 9.3 (2014): 307–21. I would avoid the term. It conflates a theory (SFL) with one application of that theory (genre pedagogy research): J. R. Martin, "One of Three Traditions: Genre, Functional Linguistics, and the 'Sydney School,'" in *Genre around the Globe: Beyond the Three Traditions*, ed. N. Artemeva and Aviva Freedman (Edmonton, AB: Trafford, 2016), 66. Also, Sydney University has produced two influential genre schools – one in the discipline of English literature (John Frow and Liam Semler) and the other in linguistics (Jim Martin).

who have historically been subjugated by them."[6] It's never been solely about educating schoolchildren. Early SFL work on genre focused on negotiations between buyers and sellers in a Libyan marketplace, narratives, the sociology of dog breeders, nursery stories, gossip, environmental discourse, and administrative paperwork (to name a few), and their work has continued across all sorts of social contexts.[7]

SFL's deep theoretical insights into how genres work in context are useful for any researcher thinking about genre. At the heart of SFL is the insight that something only means something in context.[8] To understand a word or a text we need to look to two levels of context: the **context of situation** and the **context of culture**.

Think about the context of situation for a parking ticket. You park illegally; the parking inspector writes the ticket, and so you must pay the fine (or write a letter to the magistrate begging for mercy). When SFL analyzes this kind of recurring situation, it looks at something called **register**, which is made up of three variables: **field, tenor,** and **mode**.[9]

Register Analysis

In SFL, we analyze the register or context of a text using three variables:

- Field is *what* is happening (the kinds of social activity and typical topics).
- Tenor is *who* is taking part (the kinds of participants, their typical actions, and their typical relationships and roles, including power dynamics and affinity).
- Mode is *how* language is involved (what part words play in the situation as opposed to nonverbal factors, what medium is used, how language is organized in texts).

We can keep zooming in and see how these "register variables" are reflected in language choices within the texts themselves. For example, if you're begging the magistrate for mercy, you will choose language that is formal and

---

6. Martin and Rose, *Working with Discourse*, 332.

7. Martin, "Looking Out," 312; Martin, "One of Three," 34.

8. "Context of situation" comes from Bronisław Malinowski's anthropological research (1923–1935), developed by J. R. Firth (1957), then Michael Halliday and Ruqaiya Hasan: Martin, "One of Three," 36. Malinowski may have been influenced by Hermann Gunkel: Martin J. Buss, *The Changing Shape of Form Criticism: A Relational Approach*, Hebrew Bible Monographs (Sheffield: Sheffield Phoenix, 2010), 152–56.

9. See Martin and Rose, *Working with Discourse*, 297.

deferential. (If you want to sound like a linguist, you could say that "the regis-ter variable of tenor in a given situation is an emergent complex pattern at the level of register, **realized** in the interpersonal metafunction at the discourse semantic and lexicogrammatical levels" – try that in an essay today!) These choices help construct communities by including some people and excluding others, and studying them can help us guess, for example, the social relation-ships between the apostle Paul and the recipients of his letters (more on this in chapter 12).

SFL is a systemic and linguistic approach, which means we are interested in the system of contrasting choices that enable language users to make meaning within these situations. We are also interested in how language is being used to get things done, which often means asking about the sequential structure or "staging" that goes on in situational encounters: what things must you say (or can you say) in what order, to negotiate the desired outcome? These **stages** of a genre organize our discourse in predictable sequences.[10] (Within those stages there might also be a sequence of more optional **phases**.)

That's the context of situation, and it helps make sense of the features of the text in front of us. But let's step back for a moment. Situations like these, and the texts we use in them, are not invented from scratch for each occa-sion (this is not the first illegally parked car the inspector has come across!). An important insight of SFL is that the situations we find ourselves in are recurring, and so we develop conventional ways of using language to navi-gate them.[11] Our culture supplies us with a ready-made system of genres that we can use (and adapt, or transform). Genres live outside the particular situa-tion, at the higher level of context of culture. From there, they are realized in patterns at every other level. The parking ticket genre predicts a distinctive configuration of field, tenor, and mode that governs the recurring situation of "parking fine ruining your day." Genres thus give us a kind of handle to pick up what is going on in discourse within particular situations and the culture more broadly.

Genres live at the context of culture level, so the genres available within twentieth-century Australian culture will be different from those available to a first-century Jewish author. That's why when we study the Bible, we spend so much time trying to understand the cultural context.

---

10. See Martin and Rose, *Working with Discourse*, 10. Where you're up to in the sequence of stages will predict (or regulate) other aspects of language. In the "evaluation" stage of a report, you might be expected to use more appraisal-type words.

11. See M. A. K. Halliday, *Language as Social Semiotic* (London: Edward Arnold, 1978), 144–45; John Frow, "Discourse Genres," *JLS* 9.2 (2009): 73; Bawarshi and Reiff, *Genre*, 36.

SFL Definition of Genre

J. R. Martin and David Rose define a genre as:

> a recurrent configuration of meaning that matters in the culture.[12]

Or, more technically:

> a recurrent configuration of meaning, selecting appropriate field, tenor and mode variables and staging them as unfolding phases of meaningful discourse.[13]

Practically speaking, this way of looking at genre sees text and context as two sides of the one genre coin:

> We use the term *genre* in this book to refer to different types of texts that enact various types of social context. . . .
>
> For us genre is a staged, goal-oriented social process. Social because we participate in genres with other people; goal-oriented because we use genres to get things done; staged because it usually takes us a few steps to reach our goals.[14]

All this SFL terminology is powerful, but I realize it can be quite daunting for newcomers. The important thing to take away from all this is that, from an SFL point of view, genres are about more than what's written on the page; they're about who is trying to achieve what with the piece of paper. Returning to the parking ticket example, we can see that genre is about more than just patterns at the level of the text itself (date, time, plate number, amount); writing a parking ticket is not simply about repeating certain words in the right order. To explain what a parking ticket is, we need to zoom out a little and explain the familiar social situation of a car parked next to a sign that reads, "No Parking," and a notice put under the windscreen wipers specifying a dollar penalty. The parking ticket has a purpose within that situation, namely, to inform the bad driver (which I'm not!) that they have parked illegally (which I didn't!) and requiring them to pay a fine (which I haven't!) or face serious consequences.

---

12. Martin and Rose, *Working with Discourse*, 256.
13. Martin, "One of Three," 37.
14. Martin and Rose, *Working with Discourse*, 8.

But even this situation is not the full picture. Why are some people (parking inspectors) and not other people (say, bass players) able to write parking tickets? To explain this, we need to zoom out again and consider the culture. Australia is a high-compliance culture, with very strict road rules and a government that is able to appoint certain people to enforce those rules and punish those who don't pay their fines. Not every culture that has existed or could exist will necessarily have a place for the "parking fine" genre – I don't think a hundred years ago they were sticking these things on horses. Our culture supplies us with certain genres and not others.

When we zoom back in, we see that these genres impact what happens at all levels of discourse, including the level of text and situation. A genre like a parking ticket strictly regulates the interpersonal relationship between the officer and the vehicle owner. It's clear that this is a formal relationship, with a certain mood and tone. It's also clear what our roles are and who has the power. This is reflected all the way down to the clause and how many adverbs you can use. One difference between the "parking ticket" genre and the "nasty note left by your neighbor for blocking their driveway" genre is the expected use of intensifiers and other kinds of grammatical and lexical amplifiers ("extremely," "stupid," "selfish").

All this means that genres don't just reflect pre-existing social relations; they help create and sustain them. When you speak or write, you are making a thousand choices about tone and mood, and these together create a voice and set up expectations about the kind of community you think you are taking part in. That's why genre is so powerful. Genres regulate what we can and cannot do in certain situations (try reading a eulogy at a wedding and you'll see what I mean). They tell us what kinds of purposes we can have, and the right words to accomplish them. They shape the communities we belong to by establishing the things we can take for granted, the values we share, and who is in charge. In other words, the path between text and situation, and situation and culture, is not a one-way street, but rather the relationships go both ways.

Confessions of a Late Convert to SFL

Coming from an English literature background, I was initially a little skeptical of SFL and how beneficial it would be for studying literary texts like the Bible. Let me explain my two main reservations, and why I changed my mind.

First, all the linguistics jargon can be a little daunting at first (it was made up by linguists, after all). That's one reason it can be a hard sell to get people in other fields to take on board the insights of SFL. But I've come to appreciate having a few tightly defined technical terms when trying to get a handle on something as slippery as genre. In this book, I'm going to use terms like **context of situation, staging, register,** and **realization** and occasionally draw on SFL genre models like the **exemplum** (I'll explain when we get to them, and you can always refer to the glossary). Besides, even if you don't end up using any of the SFL jargon, the central insight about texts within a context is definitely worth holding on to.

Second, I used to think that SFL was fine for parking tickets but the wrong tool for studying *literary* texts – like trying to use a fountain pen to paint a fence. SFL genre theory's origins in primary school education means that many studies focus on the relatively simple texts that we use to get things done in everyday life (like letters, reports, and biographies). It doesn't usually get used for complex literary genres like novels or epic poems – or Scripture.[15] It also tends to focus on the typical structure or staging of texts, which makes total sense for teaching kids how to write a letter but seems less relevant when studying literary genres (what's the correct way to start a novel?).

I've come to appreciate, however, that even complex literature is made up of the kind of building blocks that SFL researchers routinely study. And besides, many of the genres we study in the Bible are the genres of everyday life that SFL studies: letters, speeches, songs, farewells, promises, blessings, and so on. We will look at a good example of this in chapter 12 on letters.

RHETORICAL GENRE STUDIES

Rhetorical genre studies (RGS) arrives at a similar interest in recurring social situations as SFL but comes at it via a different path. As the name implies, this is genre theory for people who study rhetoric rather than linguistics. Arguably, RGS got there before SFL. Kenneth Burke connected situation and rhetoric as early as 1945, and the idea was developed by Edwin Black in 1965 and Lloyd Bitzer in 1968.[16] Rhetoricians noticed that similar rhetorical situations tend to call for similar rhetorical forms.

---

15. SFL often describes complex genres like novels as "macro-genres," "meta-genres," or "mixed texts": see Martin and Rose, *Working with Discourse*, 261; J. R. Martin and David Rose, *Genre Relations: Mapping Culture* (London: Equinox, 2008), 88, 242.

16. See Kathleen Hall Jamieson and Karlyn Kohrs Campbell, "Form and Genre in Rhetorical Criticism," in *Form and Genre: Shaping Rhetorical Action* (Falls Church, VA: Speech Communication Association, 1978), 14; Lloyd F. Bitzer, "The Rhetorical Situation," *Philos. Rhetor.* 1.1 (1968): 13.

RGS Definition of Genre

Setting the course for the RGS tradition, Kathleen Hall Jamieson and Karlyn Kohrs Campbell define genre in light of the situation it responds to:

> If the recurrence of similar forms establishes a genre, then genres are groups of discourses which share substantive, stylistic, and situational characteristics. Or, put differently, in the discourses that form a genre, similar substantive and stylistic strategies are used to encompass situations perceived as similar by the responding rhetors. A genre is a group of acts unified by a constellation of forms that recurs in each of its members. These forms, *in isolation*, appear in other discourses. What is distinctive about the acts in a genre is the recurrence of the forms *together* in constellation.[17]

It's important to understand how the features of a genre function together:

> A genre does not consist merely of a series of acts in which certain rhetorical forms recur; for example, it is conceivable that parallelism and antithesis might recur jointly without establishing a generic similarity. Instead, a genre is composed of a constellation of recognizable forms bound together by an internal dynamic.[18]

One of the most important essays for RGS was written by Carolyn Miller, and in it she argues that genre is best understood as a kind of "social action." For her, genres are not merely communicative tools, but also "typified rhetorical actions based in recurrent situations."[19]

These situations aren't pre-existing situations that exist externally to the genre or that "recur" in an objective, materialist sense. (How do you know it is "Christmas"? Or that you are at a "funeral"? These are intersubjective, or social phenomena.[20]) Part of the job of a genre is to *create* that situation,

---

17. Jamieson and Campbell, "Form and Genre," 20, emphasis in original. See also "Genre as Action, Strategy, and *Difference:* An Introduction," in Catherine F. Schryer, "Records as Genre," *WC* 10.2 (1993): 204; Catherine F. Schryer, "Genre and Power: A Chronotopic Analysis," in *The Rhetoric and Ideology of Genre: Strategies for Stability and Change*, ed. Richard Coe, Lorelei Lingard, and Tatiana Teslenko (Cresskill, NJ: Hampton, 2002), 3; John Frow, *Genre*, 2nd ed. (New York: Routledge, 2015), 14. The "constellation" metaphor appears in the same year in Halliday, *Language as Social Semiotic.*

18. Jamieson and Campbell, "Form and Genre," 21.

19. Carolyn R. Miller, "Genre as Social Action," *QJS* 70 (May 1984): 159.

20. Compare this with Hans-Georg Gadamer's analysis of the "festival" in *Truth and Method*, trans. Joel Weinsheimer and Donald G. Marshall, 2nd ed. (New York: Continuum, 1994), 123.

helping us recognize two separate events as somehow the same recurring action. Within these recurring situations, there are certain things that genres allow us to get done. You or I might have any number of personal goals, motives, or purposes, but genres offer us a finite number of typified responses to the situations we find ourselves in.[21] As Miller observes, "We learn that we may eulogize, apologize, recommend one person to another, instruct customers on behalf of a manufacturer, take on an official role, account for progress in achieving goals."[22]

RGS therefore helps us see that genres are not just tools we pick up and put down at will. We are to a large degree shaped by them. As Catherine Schryer explains, we are being "genred all the time."[23] Genres work to reproduce, and reconstruct, the rhetorical communities we take part in.[24] They aren't doing all this neutrally. They inevitably have an ideological edge, both serving and indeed creating power structures.

What Is the Difference between RGS and SFL?

There is obvious overlap between SFL and RGS, with both focusing on the situation in which texts and genres operate. But SFL analyzes these situations *through the texts* themselves, whereas RGS looks beyond the texts to the social situation itself. Catherine Schryer helpfully sums up the difference: SFL is about "exploring *genres* in their contexts," whereas RGS is about "exploring genres in their *context*."[25] In her famous study of medical record keeping within a veterinary college, for example, Schryer shifted the focus from individual texts to the surrounding context, observing how seemingly straightforward genres like "medical report" participate as social actions in decisions about treatment, funding, and the clash of values within a professional community.[26]

This shift from text to context does not leave behind close study of the texts themselves, but opens up a broader scope for study. It also leans on slightly different methods. Schryer's study was ethnographic, meaning she spent six months

---

21. Genres help to mediate between our private individual motives and more general social exigencies: Miller, "Genre as Social Action," 162–63; Carolyn R. Miller, "Rhetorical Community: The Cultural Basis of Genre," in *Genre and the New Rhetoric*, ed. Aviva Freedman and Peter Medway (London: Taylor & Francis, 1994), 62.

22. Miller, "Genre as Social Action," 165. On genres as "habitats" within which we perform actions using structuration theory and speech act theory: Charles Bazerman, "The Life of Genre, the Life in the Classroom," in *Genre and Writing: Issues, Arguments, Alternatives*, ed. Wendy Bishop and Hans Ostrom (Portsmouth, NH: Boynton/Cook, 1997), 22.

23. Schryer, "Genre and Power," 95. Children develop language one situation at a time: Miller, "Genre as Social Action," 157.

24. Miller, "Rhetorical Community," 64.

25. Schryer, "Genre and Power," 78.

26. See Schryer, "Records as Genre."

in the veterinary college conducting interviews and making observations to give extralinguistic context to the texts being studied.[27]

RGS has a special interest in examining the connection between genre and power. "Genres survive," after all, "because they work for someone (however egregiously or oppressively for others)."[28] Genres don't just reflect the existing power imbalances in society; they also actively create and preserve them by reinforcing ideologies, protecting certain interests, and helping us construct reality.

In another study, Schryer looked at letters written by insurance companies to their clients rejecting their claims. The genre of "rejection letter" obviously shapes reality for the unfortunate recipient, but it even constrains what strategies are available to the person writing the letter.[29] It's interesting to compare SFL and RGS on this point. SFL researchers are often motivated by a desire to give access to the power of elite genres to disadvantaged students; RGS seeks to uncover and perhaps even deconstruct those systems of power.

But Wait, Is All This Relevant to Literary Texts, or the Bible?

Before we move on, I need to deal with an objection that sometimes gets raised to bringing all this social genre theory stuff into the study of literature like the Bible.[30] Sure, they say, recurring social situations might be relevant for an everyday rhetorical genre like "rejection letter," but literary texts are something else entirely. The whole point of great novels and poems is that they are liberated from an identifiable speaking situation and take on a semi-autonomous life of their own. We all know what a parking ticket is for, but what on earth is the "social situation" or "function" of a poem?

There are lots of things to say about this. First, the hard and fast division between "literary" and "everyday" texts is notoriously tricky and needs a lot more thought. But the very existence of such distinctions can only be explained by looking at the social context, which rather proves the point, I think.[31] This is

---

27. SFL points out that this "extralinguistic" context is invariably studied using words: Martin, "Looking Out."

28. Editors' introduction in Coe, Lingard, and Teslenko, *Rhetoric and Ideology*, 3. Similarly, Richard Coe, "'Rhetoric 2001' in 2001," *Composition Studies* 29.2 (2001): 29–30.

29. Schryer, "Genre and Power," 95.

30. On the compatibility of rhetorical and literary genre theory: Amy J. Devitt, *Writing Genres*, Rhetorical Philosophy & Theory (Carbondale: Southern Illinois University Press, 2004), 163–90; Molly Zahn, *Genres of Rewriting in Second Temple Judaism: Scribal Composition and Transmission* (Cambridge: Cambridge University Press, 2020), 63.

31. What counts as a "literary genre" is often a value judgment, which rather proves the point that social power dynamics determine the status of genres. See Adena Rosmarin, *The Power of Genre* (Minneapolis: University of Minnesota Press, 1985); Thomas O. BeeBee, *The Ideology of Genre: A Comparative Study of Generic Instability* (University Park: Pennsylvania State University Press, 1994); Frow, *Genre*, 77.

even more obvious when we think of biblical literature. The difference between reading a text as literature and reading it as Scripture is hard to explain without talking about the function that text is (or is not) playing within a community.

Second, social setting doesn't have to be super specific. Part of being a literary genre seems to be that it anticipates a broad social situation. Even if function is hard to pin down, that in itself is still worth thinking about.

Finally, even if you don't think social situation and function are relevant to complex literary genres themselves, remember that even complex literary texts participate in everyday genres. A farewell speech embedded within a novel will project that typical social setting (even if only within the world of the story). A novel written in letter form may never have been anywhere near a postbox in real life, but that is beside the point – simply using the form is enough to invoke the familiar social function of a letter as part of the effect of the text.

When biblical studies turned off form criticism in the 1970s, it was mainly for good reasons. However, there was a significant baby-in-the-bathwater casualty. We decided to ignore social setting when trying to work out what makes up a genre. This was a real shame, because just about the only thing about Hermann Gunkel's genre theory that was ahead of its time was his idea that form was linked to a life-situation (*Sitz im Leben*). Hans Robert Jauss thought that romance philology could actually learn a thing or two from Gunkel, particularly in his attention to the needs of the life of the community, which is expressed in genre:

> Literary forms and genres are thus neither subjective creations of the author, nor merely retrospective ordering-concepts, but rather primary social phenomena, which means that they depend on functions in the lived world. The Bible is also a *literary* monument that bears witness to the life of a community; it can no longer remain withdrawn from historical understanding.[32]

As we've seen, there were problems with the specifics of Gunkel's version of life-situation, and I'm not suggesting we try to revive the home-brew version and start speculating about the original setting of the preliterary forms. But it is time, I think, that we take on board the insights of SFL and RGS and think about what genres are for in context.

Having introduced these two overlapping approaches, I want to propose some principles to do with the social side of genre that we can use in biblical studies.

---

32. Hans Robert Jauss, *Toward an Aesthetic of Reception*, trans. Timothy Bahti, THL 2 (Minneapolis: University of Minneapolis Press, 1982), 100. He was a fan of Rudolf Bultmann too.

TENET 7: GENRES ARE RECURRING
RESPONSES TO RECURRING SITUATIONS

SFL and RGS both recognize that genres are more than their formal features; they are social creatures. They need to be understood in context as recurring responses to recurring situations. This observation dovetails with Mikhail Bakhtin's work on speech genres. While every utterance is unique, language users within a given sphere of human activity will cluster around "relatively stable types" of utterances, which Bakhtin calls speech genres.[33]

Hermann Gunkel's interest in the life-situations (*Sitz im Leben*) of the biblical forms looks like a long-lost ancestor of Carolyn Miller's understanding of genre as "typified rhetorical actions based on recurrent situations"[34] and the way teachers try to place genres within the "scene" they come from.[35] Where modern genre theory's interest in situation is different, however, is that form criticism took "life-situation" way too narrowly. Form critics wanted to know about the specific historical contexts that gave rise to the early oral genres preserved within a text – and if you don't know, just make it up. SFL and RGS differ a little on this point, but both take "situation" in a much broader sense (encompassing the whole work, not just the preliterary forms, and sometimes in quite general terms). Their analyses are typically far more anchored in the situations anticipated or constructed by the texts themselves (especially in cases where we don't have access to much ethnographic information about the culture the text is from). For example, SFL might be used to study the recurring situation and function of the "wedding invitation" genre without delving too far into the historical context of the weddings involved; form criticism would probably end up in a decades-long scholarly debate about rival wedding planning groups and how each felt about birthday parties.

The emphasis on genre as a response to a recurring situation is an important starting point, but we shouldn't imagine that language users are constrained to only use certain genres in certain situations. It can be powerful when a writer takes a genre out of its normal situation.[36] Think, for example, of the use of the funeral dirge in Amos 5. There is something chilling about hearing someone sing your funeral dirge while you're still alive![37] In this case, the actual *occasion* on which the text is performed contrasts the typical recurring *situation* that the genre anticipates.

---

33. M. M. Bakhtin, *Speech Genres and Other Late Essays*, ed. Caryl Emerson and Michael Holquist (Austin: University of Texas Press, 1986), 83.

34. Miller, "Genre as Social Action," 159.

35. Bawarshi and Reiff, *Genre*, 186.

36. See Anne Freadman, "Uptake," in *Rhetoric and Ideology of Genre*, ed. Coe, Lingard, and Teslenko, 146.

37. This complex relationship with multiple genres is hard to squeeze into Hermann Gunkel's classical genre theory: see Hermann Gunkel, *The Psalms: A Form-Critical Introduction*, trans. Thomas M. Horner (Philadelphia: Fortress, 1967), 3.

TENET 8: GENRES ARE REGULAR WAYS OF GETTING STUFF DONE WITH WORDS

The social side of genre exposed by SFL and RGS has significant implications for how we analyze a genre. Classical genre theory tended to explore a genre by asking, "How is it written?" We look for recurring stylistic features and group texts together that look similar in their openings, structure, meter, mood, themes, and so on. But SFL and RGS, each in their own way, challenge us to take a step back and ask a different question – not only, "How is it written?" but also, "What is it for?" and "What does it do?" John Frow summarizes genre as "a form of symbolic action: the generic organization of language, images, gestures, and sound makes things happen by actively shaping the way we understand the world."[38] To understand what a genre is, therefore, we need to know what its function is within the system of recurring social situations that make up a culture.

Note that in genre studies we are not asking about the specific purpose behind the writing of an individual text; it's more general than that.[39] We are asking about what types of socially recognized things this genre can get done – not, "Why did you write this eulogy?" but "What is a eulogy typically used for?" (Scholars sometimes use the RGS term "exigence" to make clear we're talking about something more social, systemic, and recurring than just the individual author's private "purpose."[40])

SFL starts with *why*. I would love to see biblical studies pick up this habit of approaching genres with a view to function.[41]

Genres are about getting stuff done. That's why SFL researchers will often label a particular genre as "a genre *for*" something.[42] The kinds of functions that genres perform can vary. Some genres are fairly practical, like a phone book, which was a twentieth-century device for finding the phone numbers of every resident in a city (and/or for propping open doors). Other texts have more complex purposes, such as a letter or a novel.

When a text is embedded within a different genre (as in the case of complex genres like novels), the social purpose of the text changes. The purpose of a letter between family members is normally to strengthen interpersonal relations, but when a letter is embedded in a novel (such as in Frankenstein's opening frame

---

38. Frow, *Genre*, 2. See also Devitt, *Writing Genres*, 31.

39. Of course, discovering an author's intention in writing a particular text might be our ultimate goal. But genre analysis is concerned with regularities at the level of social convention that precede any individual act of communication.

40. See Miller, "Genre as Social Action," 158.

41. This could build on existing applications of speech act theory. See Kit Barker, *Imprecation as Divine Discourse: Speech-Act Theory, Dual Authorship, and Theological Interpretation*, JTISup 16 (Winona Lake, IN: Eisenbrauns, 2016), 85–88.

42. See Martin and Rose, *Working with Discourse*, 260.

– see tenet 2), the primary purpose is to give the reader an insight into the events from the point of view of the writer.

This is a significant insight for biblical studies, because the Bible is a layer cake of genres. Speech genres are embedded within narratives, which are themselves worked together to make books (like prophetic works or gospels), which are collated together as part of the genre of "Scripture."

TENET 9: GENRES REFLECT AND CREATE THE WORLD WE TAKE FOR GRANTED

I just said that genres are recurring responses to situations that help us get stuff done, but as we learnt from RGS, that's not quite true. Genres are also part of *creating* those situations for us to experience. This is because genres don't just arise within situations; genres help create them. A genre is more than literary conventions. Rosalie Colie describes how genres give us a "frame" or "fix" on the world.[43]

Genres both reflect and help create and sustain the cultures around them. Catherine Schryer points us here to Mikhail Bakhtin's idea of the chronotope, which combines time, place, and values.[44] When we load into our brains the setting of a Western film, we are not just importing particular formal or thematic features, but a whole worldview including a set of values. The same is true of biblical genres, as we will discuss when we look at narrative in chapter 5. Michael Jensen even argues that genres are "ideologically 'thick,'" with even apparently secular genres presenting their own distinctive theology.[45] Genres "orient human beings to certain accounts of transcendence, purpose, and identity" and present the relationship between humans and the world "by appeal to *metaphysical* concepts like 'fate' or 'destiny,' or 'providence.'"[46] He illustrates this with Roald Dahl's *Charlie and the Chocolate Factory*, a children's story that expects retributive justice behind every door and sees humans as basically creatures of desire.

The **truth effects** of a genre refer to the relationship the text seeks to have with the world. John Frow observes that "far from being merely 'stylistic' devices, genres create effects of reality and truth, authority and plausibility, which are central to the different ways the world is understood in the writing of history or of philosophy or

---

43. Rosalie L. Colie, *The Resources of Kind: Genre-Theory in the Renaissance*, ed. Barbara K. Lewalski (Berkeley: University of California Press, 1973), 8; Frow, *Genre*, 20. Genre "is a way of creating order in the ever-fluid symbolic world": Charles Bazerman, *Shaping Written Knowledge: The Genre and Activity of the Experimental Article in Science* (Madison: University of Wisconsin Press, 1988), 319.

44. Schryer, "Genre and Power," 75–76, 85. See "Epic and Novel," in M. M. Bakhtin, *The Dialogic Imagination* (Austin: University of Texas Press, 1981), 13–14.

45. Michael Jensen, *Theological Anthropology and the Great Literary Genres: Understanding the Human Story* (Lanham, MD: Lexington, 2019), 20.

46. Jensen, *Theological Anthropology*, 13, 21.

of science, or in painting, or in everyday talk."[47] A cartoon and a portrait both seek to represent a historical person, but they are used to show different aspects of their personhood and permit different degrees of exaggeration to achieve that function.

We need to separate the question of *whether* a text is true from *what type of truth* is being presented. A forged student ID is untrue if it fails to accurately represent the person whose name is on it, whereas to call Edvard Munch's *The Scream* inaccurate is to miss the point. The truth effects of a genre are part of the social convention (you can't just claim your tax return was intended as fantasy, or your marriage vows as parody). It's important not to import the wrong standards of accuracy into a genre (which is what the Snopes.com fact-checkers did to the *Babylon Bee* article in the introduction).

The relationship between genre and social action within a particular situation has an interesting implication. It may be that by studying genres we can open a window on other worlds – perhaps even worlds that are otherwise lost to history. A problem we often have in biblical studies is there is so much we would like to know but can't know. What's the point of a theory of genre that leans so heavily into social situation when we know almost nothing about the setting for most biblical texts, and what little we do know is highly contested anyway? Maybe it's best, at least within biblical studies, to ignore questions of social setting and just consider recurring patterns within the text itself.

Modern genre theory, however, gives us reason to hope that we can recover something of the social setting from the text itself. We saw above that the relationships between the text, the context of situation, and the context of culture are two-way streets. The culture we are in gives us certain genres to work with, but also the choices we make linguistically help form our communities of shared values. Compared to the intentions of an individual, a genre is relatively stable, so Paul Ricoeur thinks it is easier for two people to hold them in common.[48] Hans Robert Jauss believes that even where the social function and norms of a text are lost to history, something can "still be reconstructed through the horizon of expectations of a genre system that pre-constituted the intention of the works as well as the understanding of the audience."[49] In a similar way, SFL researchers use genre as a window on culture, and culture is modelled as a system of genres.[50]

---

47. Frow, *Genre*, 2. The importance of genre for understanding truth claims is recognized by Article XIII of "The Chicago Statement on Biblical Inerrancy," 1978, www.etsjets.org/files/documents/Chicago_Statement.pdf.

48. Paul Ricoeur, "The Hermeneutical Function of Distanciation," *PT* 17.2 (1973): 137.

49. Jauss, *Toward an Aesthetic of Reception*, 108. See also Hans Robert Jauss, "Literary History as a Challenge to Literary Theory," trans. Elizabeth Benzinger, *NLH* 2.1 (1970): 19; James Muilenburg, "Form Criticism and Beyond," *JBL* 88.1 (1969): 7. Devitt shows how genres can provide access to contexts that are off-limits for legal reasons: Amy J. Devitt, "Uncovering Occluded Publics: Untangling Public, Personal, and Technical Spheres in Jury Deliberations," in *Genre and the Performance of Publics*, ed. Mary Jo Reiff and Anis S. Bawarshi (Logan: Utah State University Press, 2016), 139–56.

50. Martin and Rose, *Working with Discourse*, 296.

Maybe our two cultures share a similar situation, and so have recurring forms that are comparable. We might think of the way puzzling features of the book of Esther have driven modern interpreters to "try it out" as different kinds of thing – a "diaspora tale," or a dark satire.[51] If these modern genres "fit" the text, that might be a clue that postexilic Jews in the Persian period were dealing with situations that might have been familiar to modern post-Holocaust novelists.

Or maybe there are clues in the discourse itself about the social situations it is constructing. Even if we know nothing of what a suzerain-vassal relationship entailed in the Assyrian period, something of the interpersonal power dynamic will be reflected in the way they talk to each other – it will be clear who is the boss! There are well-established tools for this kind of analysis, because unlike the more ethnographic approach of RGS, SFL researchers do not tend to conduct field studies with video cameras in hand; they carefully study the texts produced by the culture and use them to understand situations and cultures anticipated by the text.

In chapter 9 we will consider how this insight might apply to the apocalyptic genre, and in chapter 11 we will come across some attempts to use SFL to describe the social function of a gospel.

The gap between the culture and context of the writers and our own situation is most daunting when reading old books like the Bible. But I would argue that genres help humans in different times and places communicate, despite that gap in history and culture.[52]

TENET 10: GENRES ALWAYS WORK FOR SOMEONE

Genres are about enacting purposes within a social situation, so social questions of relationships and power dynamics will often take center stage in our analysis. There is a lot of power in a genre, because we don't usually question the situations we find ourselves in. Things just go without saying, and as Catherine Schryer argues whatever we take as "common sense" will constrain what actions we think are possible.[53]

One thing that just goes without saying within the context of culture is who is, and who isn't, allowed to use a genre. I could practice writing parking

---

51. See Ellen F. Davis, *Opening Israel's Scriptures* (New York: Oxford University Press, 2019), 380.

52. See my *Playing with Scripture: Reading Contested Biblical Texts with Gadamer and Genre Theory*, Routledge Interdisciplinary Perspectives on Biblical Criticism (Abingdon, UK: Routledge, 2024).

53. Schryer, "Genre and Power," 75–76, 85. Frow calls this "the ideological second nature, which constitutes the real": Frow, "Discourse Genres," 79.

tickets all day, but I could never write a "parking ticket." Why? Because of my social role. I am not a city of Melbourne parking officer, and so authoring that genre (of "parking ticket") is not available to me.

That's a simple example. But genres can create and sustain power relations in much more subtle ways. As John Frow puts it, "Discursive competence is a symbolic capital acquired in the process of socialisation, and the class structure determines relations of possession or dispossession of this capital."[54] In other words, your class and educational background make a big difference – not just to the balance in your bank account, but also to the contents of your genre tool kit.

Marxism and Genre

Some scholars draw on Marxist theories to study genres in their social context. John Frow's comments about the possession of symbolic capital (above) reflect his Marxist background.[55] SFL's interest in power dynamics goes back to its origins in the British Communist Party.[56] However, you don't need to share a Marxist worldview to recognize that power dynamics are relevant to understanding the social context of speech (see Eccl 8:4).

A while back, my wife, Steph, and I received our very own letter from an insurer rejecting a recent claim. The letter was written with a sympathetic but firm message, making clear that there was no other possible outcome and certainly nothing we could do. Challenge accepted. I wrote a "rejection letter rejection letter" back to them, briefly laying out the errors in their decision-making process, and advising them of the steps we would take to pursue our desired outcome. Within a week, our claim was paid out in full. In one sense, anyone can send this genre of "rejection letter rejection letter." But my wife and I reflected afterward how different our experience would have been if we were from a non-English speaking background, or if I hadn't trained as a lawyer before becoming a Bible scholar. You see, I knew exactly the right words and

54. Frow, "Discourse Genres," 78. See also BeeBee, *Ideology of Genre*; J. R. Martin, "Writing History: Construing Time and Value in Discourses of the Past," in *Developing Advanced Literacy in First and Second Languages: Meaning with Power*, ed. Mary J. Schleppegrell and M. Cecilia Colombi (London: Lawrence Erlbaum, 2002), 87–118.

55. See preface to John Frow, *Marxism and Literary History* (Cambridge, MA: Harvard University Press, 1986).

56. See J. R. Martin and Ruth Wodak, eds., "Introduction," in *Re/Reading the Past: Critical and Functional Perspectives on Discourses of History*, DAPSAC (Amsterdam: Benjamins, 2003), 3.

staging structure to make sure the genre worked and our claim escalated to the right department. In Frow's terms, my discursive competence in the rejection-letter-rejection-letter genre reflects my symbolic capital (I know some big words and have a law degree in my back pocket) and further determines my possession of capital (we now have $1,000 in our bank account thanks to that letter). Genre can be lucrative.

The sneaky thing about the power of genre is that it is so invisible. The way that genres work together seem so natural to us when we are using them that we don't stop to question them – even when we are being disadvantaged by them![57] But genres are not natural; they are actually human-made structures that work to keep us all in line (Schryer calls them "structured structures that structure"[58]). The task of RGS is to disassemble these structures and see who they are really working for – who is made more powerful by them?[59]

The Social Side of Genre

Richard Coe and Aviva Freedman propose some critical questions to ask about any genre, including:

What sorts of communication does the genre encourage and, what sorts does it constrain against?

Who can – and who cannot – use this genre? Does it empower some people while silencing others? . . .

What values and beliefs are instantiated within this set of practices?

What are the political and ethical implications of the rhetorical situation constructed, persona embodied, audience invoked, and context of situation assumed by a particular genre?[60]

These questions are helpful because they encourage us to step back and ask not only about the textual features on the page, but also about how those features define recurring situations and regulate our relationships within society.

---

57. Schryer, "Genre and Power," 76.

58. Schryer, "Genre and Power," 95.

59. Aviva Freedman and Peter Medway, "Introduction. Locating Genre Studies: Antecedents and Prospects," in *Genre and the New Rhetoric*, ed. Freedman and Medway, 10.

60. Richard M. Coe and Aviva Freedman, "Genre Theory: Australian and North American Approaches," in *Theorizing Composition: A Critical Sourcebook of Theory and Scholarship in Contemporary Composition Studies*, ed. Mary Lynch Kennedy (Westport, CT: Greenwood, 1998), 139.

TENET 11: GENRES DON'T LIVE ALONE

RGS encourages us to take a step back from analyzing genres in isolation to see genres as part of broader ecosystems. It has become common for RGS scholars to analyze, not individual genres, but whole "genre systems" or "economies of genres."[61] As John Frow puts it:

> Texts – even the simplest and most formulaic – do not "belong" to genres but are, rather, uses of them; they refer not to "a" genre but to a field or economy of genres, and their complexity derives from the complexity of that relation. Uses of texts ("readings") similarly refer, and similarly construct a position in relation to that economy.[62]

To understand a genre, we need to look at more than just the similarities between texts: we also need to think about the *differences* between genres, and indeed the way they function together. Think of the complex activity systems involved in running, say, a seminary – enrolling students, borrowing books, delivering lectures, grading essays, granting extension requests, and so on. These recurring activities are not isolated events; they work together as part of a system. Now imagine all the paperwork that accompanies these systems: the enrolment form, the subject bibliography, the lecture timetable, the grading and feedback form, the extension request form, and more. These genres help us navigate all these interconnected systems, but they also construct and maintain them by constructing our subject positions and setting our expectations.[63] Being a student or professor is partly about the genres available to you – one sets essay questions, while the other answers them.

Anne Freadman captures this shift in focus from isolated texts to the interaction *between* texts, using the term **uptake** (which she borrows from J. L. Austin and speech act theory).[64] Part of understanding a genre is understanding what it responds to and what response it occasions within the system. Returning to our seminary example, the genre of "grading sheet" is an uptake of the genre "essay," which is, in turn, an uptake of "essay question" and so on. This means

---

61. Charles Bazerman, "Systems of Genres and Enactment of Social Intentions," in *Genre and the New Rhetoric*, ed. Freedman and Medway, 82; Tzvetan Todorov, *Genres in Discourse*, trans. Catherine Porter (Cambridge: Cambridge University Press, 1990), 10.

62. Frow, *Genre*, 2.

63. Bawarshi and Reiff, *Genre*, 95; Anis Bawarshi, *Genre and the Invention of the Writer: Reconsidering the Place of Invention in Composition* (Logan: Utah State University Press, 2003), 45.

64. Anne Freadman, "Anyone for Tennis?," in *Genre and the New Rhetoric*, ed. Freedman and Medway, 37–56; Freadman, "Uptake," in *Rhetoric and Ideology of Genre*, ed. Coe, Lingard, and Teslenko.

an exam question requires you to respond in essay form, not compose a limerick. (I know of someone who wrote his whole final theology paper in rhyme – his professor was not amused.) A film review is (ideally) a response to a film you have previously seen. A parking ticket invites payment, not a poem. You don't really understand what a genre is unless you step back and see how it fits in a system like this – that certain genres of text invite a particular kind of response or uptake genre.

It is possible, however, to refuse the uptake that is expected . . .

TENET 12: THE BALL IS ALWAYS IN THE READER'S COURT

To state the obvious, texts don't read themselves. You don't need to go all "death of the author" to recognize that most human authors are, as it happens, dead (and the rest don't want to help you with your homework). That leaves you. The meaning of a text can only come together inside the mind of the reader.

Once the other person has played their shot, the ball is in the reader's court. The text arrives in their lap, and it's up to them to decide what to do with it. Readers might have a good idea of what they are meant to do with the text (pay the parking ticket!). Or they may choose to play out a few different genres with the texts they are given to see what works best. Writers will inevitably leave strategically placed signals as to the genre they anticipate their texts will participate in. But whether the reader picks up on those clues – or chooses to follow them – is up to them.

The shift to seeing genres as moves that readers enact raises the possibility of different kinds of uptakes or responses to the genre. As a reader, I might choose to respond in an unexpected way. Instead of paying the parking fine, I could analyze it and respond by writing a book on genre. Or I might choose to read the text deliberately as something else – "This is a terrible love letter!" (We will explore such **tactical** genre uptakes further in chapter 4 and try one out on Judges in chapter 6.)

Before you worry that I've jumped off the deep end into an entirely reader-centric reading, it's important to clarify what this doesn't mean. I'm not saying that all readings are equally good or that readers should make the text mean whatever they like. I happen to think that coordinating our understanding with a writer's intention is both possible and the basis for most forms of communication.[65] Genres are resources used by writers as well as readers (tenet 5). Genres are also social conventions, not subjective decisions, and both writers and readers

---

65. See my *Playing with Scripture*.

need to play along if they want favorable payoffs (tenet 2). You can interpret a parking ticket as a love letter all you like, but it won't be a good one, and it's not going to stop them from towing your car away.

There is a stream of postmodern thinking about genre that sees genre as entirely something that readers and critics choose to do to texts.[66] But seeing genre in its social context actually walks us back from this extreme. As intellectual fashions have shifted from modernism to structuralism to poststructuralism, literary criticism has tended to focus almost exclusively on either author or text or reader; social models of genre, in contrast, tend to find a place for everybody. When we participate in a genre – whether as writers or readers – we are participating in something bigger than ourselves. Genre is like a game, a type of conventional social action, whose rules are evolving but nevertheless stable-for-now. Now, nothing is stopping you from being a bad sport, but as we'll see in the next chapter, don't expect the text to play along nicely.

SUMMARY

A historical perspective on genre requires us to consider genres in their social context. While SFL and RGS are different approaches, they both see genres as responses to recurring situations (tenet 7). We need to ask not just *how* a genre is written, but *why* – what is its function (tenet 8)? Genres reflect and indeed help create the world we experience (tenet 9), including the power dynamics between language users (tenet 10). Genres don't live alone, but function within systems of genres (tenet 11). While genres anticipate certain responses or uptakes, the ball is always in the reader's court (tenet 12).

QUESTIONS FOR DISCUSSION AND REFLECTION

1. How far do you think we can take a historical approach to genre without considering genres in their cultural and situational contexts? Can you think of any reasons why we might want to accept tenets 1–6 but ignore tenets 7–12?
2. How is this social approach to genre both similar and different to Hermann Gunkel's form-critical method explained in chapter 1?
3. How worthwhile is it to talk about the situation and function of a genre if we can't know who wrote a text or what their purpose was? List some potential benefits and drawbacks of putting social context aside and focusing exclusively on the formal features of a genre.

---

66. For example: Rosmarin, *Power of Genre*; Devitt, *Writing Genres*, 163–90.

4. Can you think of reasons why the SFL approach (starting with the text itself) or the RGS approach (starting with the context around the text) might be more or less useful for biblical studies?
5. How is recognizing that the ball is in the reader's court any different from accepting a reader-response or subjectivist account of meaning?

FURTHER READING

Introductory

Bawarshi, Anis S., and Mary Jo Reiff. *Genre: An Introduction to History, Theory, Research, and Pedagogy.* West Lafayette, IN: Parlor, 2010.
> Surveys linguistic, rhetorical, and special purpose genre approaches.

Martin, J. R., and David Rose. *Genre Relations: Mapping Culture.* London: Equinox, 2008.
> Introduction to genre theory from an SFL perspective.

Miller, Carolyn R., and Amy J. Devitt, eds. *Landmark Essays on Rhetorical Genre Studies.* New York: Routledge, 2019.
> Anthology of significant essays from an RGS perspective.

Deep Dive

Coe, Richard, Lorelei Lingard, and Tatiana Teslenko. *The Rhetoric and Ideology of Genre: Strategies for Stability and Change.* Cresskill, NJ: Hampton, 2002.
> Essays from RGS practitioners and theorists.

Devitt, Amy J. *Writing Genres.* Rhetorical Philosophy and Theory. Carbondale: Southern Illinois University Press, 2004.
> Genre theory from an RGS perspective.

Freedman, Aviva, and Peter Medway, eds. *Genre and the New Rhetoric.* London: Taylor & Francis, 1994.
> Essays from RGS practitioners and theorists.

Martin, J. R., and David Rose. *Working with Discourse.* Second edition. London: Bloomsbury, 2007.
> Demonstrates SFL in action using texts on reconciliation in post-apartheid South Africa.

Toffelmire, Colin M. "*Sitz im* What? Context and the Prophetic Book of Obadiah." Pages 221–44 in *The Book of the Twelve and the New Form Criticism.* Edited by Mark J. Boda, Michael H. Floyd, and Colin M. Toffelmire. Ancient Near East Monographs, Volume 10. Atlanta: SBL Press, 2015.
> Proposal for SFL-style register analysis of Obadiah's context of situation.

CHAPTER 4

THE BOOMERANG TEST

Playing the Right Game with Scripture

One of the most awkward sermon videos I've ever watched featured John Piper speaking on September 16, 2009, to a meeting of Christian counsellors in Nashville.[1] His message was titled "Beholding Glory and Becoming Whole," and reading the sermon text, it seems like exactly what you'd expect from that genre of Reformed Protestant preaching – earnest in delivery, vulnerable about his own sin, and unapologetically focused on God's glory.

Yet right from the start, something perplexing starts happening, and keeps happening, to the point that it becomes painful to watch. Piper begins by declaring, "I'm a sinner." Immediately, the audience laughs.

Slightly taken aback, he continues to confess his weaknesses: "I'm a man who, to be more specific, must crucify the love of praise every day. . . . A man who struggles with the same fifteen-year-old adolescent fears at sixty-three, namely, the fear of looking foolish." [*more laughter*]

He pushes on with a litany of besetting sins – his feelings of guilt, lack of compassion, and even problems in his marriage. Each time, eight thousand counsellors laugh at him. This continues for three long minutes, until eventually he breaks from his script and acknowledges that something strange is going on:

> You're a very strange audience [*laughter*] because I totally did not expect laughter [*laughter*] and I'm continually perplexed. . . . I guess I'd better just get used to it . . . This is a serious talk in case you're wondering, but . . .

At this point the poor preacher is finally overtaken by an ovation of laughter and applause.

What on earth is going on here? It's hard to imagine that these thousands of trained counsellors would respond with laughter to a client who confessed these

---

1. John Piper, "Beholding Glory and Becoming Whole," Desiring God, September 16, 2009, www.desiringgod.org/messages/beholding-glory-and-becoming-whole. Thanks, Matt Capps and the Ridley research seminar, for sharing this excruciating video.

flaws. Yet something about *this situation* and *this sermon* created a mismatch of expectations – is this a confession or a comedy routine?

Their lack of coordination over expectations of the "sermon" genre makes more sense when we know two things. The first is that, according to Piper, "In fifty years, I have never told a joke in a sermon." For him, that kind of "clowning" in sermons reflects a culture of entertainment that he doesn't fit.[2] On the other hand, as he realizes mid-sermon, "You've been set up for an hour and a half maybe a little differently." The staging structure of the typical conference talk expects "opening self-deprecating jokes," not a sincere and honest confession from the first minute.

What's salutary to consider too is how little control the speaker has over the genre decisions made by an audience – even one in the same room as them. After all, genres are a game (tenet 2), and the ball is in the interpreter's court (tenet 12). The more John Piper tries to convince his audience that he is being serious, the more determinedly they parse his earnestness as dead-pan irony:

> I list those absolutely true, absolutely serious [sins], and though they make you laugh, they make me cry, and I mean that, so you've *got to stop laughing like that* [*more laughter*].
>
> I just don't understand you folks.

In fact, *they* don't understand *him* either. These are not strange folks who find sin funny. The reason they are laughing at his earnest confession is that their genre expectations have been misaligned right from the start. Modern genre theory tells us that more is at stake in decisions about genre than correctly sorting the right text into the appropriate class.[3] If you classify a book in the wrong section of a bookstore, it may be harder to find (or make for an amusing juxtaposition, as when "travel" books were mischievously reshelved under "fantasy" during COVID-19 lockdowns[4]), but the book still works despite the misclassification. But genres are about more than classification; they provide functional resources and roles for writers and readers (tenet 4). It doesn't matter how carefully you interpret the syntax or historical context; every level of meaning can be turned upside down by genre. The genre tells us what game we are playing – are we confessing our sin or just clowning around?

---

2. "John Piper's Most Bizarre Moment in Preaching," Desiring God, September 27, 2019, www.desiringgod.org/interviews/john-pipers-most-bizarre-moment-in-preaching.

3. Genre informs purpose, which is usually considered when assessing the success of a work. See C. S. Lewis's famous "corkscrew to a cathedral" analogy: C. S. Lewis, *A Preface to Paradise Lost* (London: Oxford University Press, 1960), 1.

4. See Megan Herbert's cartoon, "We've Moved a Few Things Around," Megan Herbert: Cartoons, November 2020, https://meganherbert.com/cartoons.

This chapter begins by looking at the problem of identifying the many genres at play in Scripture. I introduce what I think is our most useful and underappreciated tool for working out whether we have got the genre of a text right – "the boomerang test." Next we briefly survey some of the clues that can guide our initial guess about the genre of a text. We also revisit an idea from the last chapter – if the ball is in the reader's court (tenet 12), then that raises the possibility of genre decisions that are more tactical, or even resistant, to the game that the writer is playing. Finally we think a little about the most significant genre choice that we make when reading the Bible – the decision to take the text, in all its different genres, as Scripture.

THE BOOK OF GENRES

Working out the genre is important in any field where careful reading matters, but in biblical studies especially so. Part of the grandeur of Scripture is its wealth of genres. Zooming in all the way, we find representations of the basic genres of everyday speech, like the "question," "promise," "prohibition," and "request." Zoom out a little, and we can identify dialogs, songs, parables, treaties, lawsuits, and proverbs. Pull back some more, and whole books seem to be framed with the use of the complex genres of narrative, biography, instruction, and letter. And for all this, genre is never spent. Running through all these genres is a continuum from everyday speech at one end to the language games of poetry at the other. If we look beyond formal features, more conceptual or situational genres like wisdom literature and apocalyptic start to come into focus. Throw in comparisons with ancient Near Eastern genres, as well as vexing questions about parody, and the question of "what kind of Scripture is this?" starts to look wonderfully more complex than we could have imagined. There's a reason they say that the three most important things to consider when interpreting any text in the Bible are genre, genre, and genre.

Chicken and the Egg

Genre is important, but it's also difficult – especially when dealing with old books. It's hard enough when writer and reader are both part of the same context of culture (just ask John Piper and the eight thousand counsellors), but when you throw in a few thousand years of time and a solid dose of culture shock, things get quite tricky.

Given how powerful genre is in creating meaning, it's surprising how little thought often goes into the process by which writers invoke, and readers decide, the genre of a text like the Bible. Genre presents readers with a bit of a chicken-and-egg question.[5] We need to know the genre to interpret the text. Mikhail Bakhtin observes that "we guess its genre from the very first words," and this enables us to make predictions – for example, about the work's length – without which speech communication would be "almost impossible."[6] But many of the clues about genre can only be found by interpreting the text. So which comes first, the egg of genre designation or the chicken of text interpretation?

If you are the sort of person who likes clear criteria and logically watertight premises *before* you start interpreting, this whole situation might seem like playing golf in the dark (how would you even know if you've scored a hole in one?).

Don't lose heart – identifying genre is not as hopeless as it might seem. Back in chapter 2, I recommended we think of genres as social conventions, or as games we play with words. While a contract requires explicit prior collusion, conventions arise and are sustained by repeated interactions and mutual payoffs for coordination.[7] For example, each country has a convention about what side of the road to drive on. In Australia you drive on the left, whereas in the United States you drive on the right. Now, there is probably a law somewhere that established this convention, but I've never read it, nor do other people seem to need traffic cops to force them to conform to it. The convention just exists in the fact that every day everyone else is driving on one side, and the payoffs for "you do you" in this matter are very negative. Even if nobody told me what the convention was when visiting the USA, repeated encounters with other vehicles would soon help me reach coordination with everyone else (assuming I survived the first few iterations).

Language in general is a social convention, which is why inductive language education works and children can master complex rules of language without a weak verb paradigm table in sight. Like semantics or syntax, genres are conventions that regulate language use at a particular level (though genres are particularly complex aspects of language and tend to be far more niche in their usage, which is why SFL developed an approach to help disadvantaged students gain competence in them; see chapter 3).

---

5. Hans-Georg Gadamer, the father of modern hermeneutics, sees this circularity as unavoidable whenever we try to understand something. We can't read without making assumptions, but we can't know in advance which assumptions are right or wrong. All we can do is be open to revising our assumptions and have another go when something in the text doesn't fit our expectations.

6. M. M. Bakhtin, *Speech Genres and Other Late Essays*, ed. Caryl Emerson and Michael Holquist (Austin: University of Texas Press, 1986), 90.

7. I'm drawing here from the fields of philosophy of language and economic game theory. See especially David K. Lewis, *Convention: A Philosophical Study* (Cambridge, MA: Harvard University Press, 1969); Hans-Georg Gadamer, *Truth and Method*, trans. Joel Weinsheimer and Donald G. Marshall, 2nd ed. (New York: Continuum, 1994); Robin Clark, *Meaningful Games: Exploring Language with Game Theory* (Cambridge, MA: MIT Press, 2012); my *Playing with Scripture: Reading Contested Biblical Texts with Gadamer and Genre Theory*, Routledge Interdisciplinary Perspectives on Biblical Criticism (Abingdon, UK: Routledge, 2024).

Our understanding of a text's genre starts with an educated guess and an open mind. But how do we know we are on the right track? It comes down to whether our guess at the genre of the text "works." In everyday conversations, the payoffs come naturally (get your genres mixed up when ordering a pizza and you'll go hungry). But when studying an ancient text, we need something a little more artificial, which I like to call "the boomerang test."[8]

THE BOOMERANG TEST

A boomerang (known as a *wonguim* by the Wurundjeri people on whose land I live and work[9]) is an elegantly crafted tool made from wattle wood and shaped over fire into its distinctive bend shape. Its aerodynamics means if you throw it just right, it will return to you. Question is, how do you know that the stick you are holding is a boomerang and not a baseball bat? There are lots of clues, but ultimately your best bet is to give it a throw and see what comes back.

This is a deceptively powerful principle, and it applies nicely to genre analysis for ancient texts. How do you know that your guess about a text's genre works? Take it up as a particular genre and see if it works – see if the text gives you back something meaningful.

The Boomerang Test

Take up your guess about the kind of genre your text falls into, give it a throw, see what comes back. If the payoffs suggest it doesn't work, try again.

Mary Gerhart is onto something similar when she describes how a reader forms a genre hypothesis and then "tests alternative readings of the text *as* different genres."[10] Discussions around genre identification often focus on the data that goes into our initial educated guess, and that's important (we'll talk about these below). But by far the most useful guidance comes from the feedback we get from the text itself. Genre designations work best as a kind of heuristic – a messy combination involving educated guess, trial and error,

---

8. Thanks, Brandon Hurlbert, for reminding me about this phrase.

9. "Wurundjeri Tools and Technology," Deadly Story, https://deadlystory.com/page/aboriginal-country-map/Aboriginal_Country_Completed/Wurundjeri/Wurundjeri_Tools_Technology, accessed 31 August 2023.

10. Mary Gerhart, "Generic Competence in Biblical Hermeneutics," *Semeia* 43 (1988): 36; Mary Gerhart, "Generic Studies: Their Renewed Importance in Religious and Literary Interpretation," *JAAR* 45.3 (1977): 316.

and a fair bit of going back to the drawing board. A beautiful way of describing the interplay of expectations and payoffs in a genre hypothesis is as an "arousing and fulfilment of desires."[11] When a text invokes (or seems to invoke) a genre, this raises desires within us as readers that most texts aim to satisfy in one way or another. If a text fulfils nothing that we think we have been promised, it may be that our initial genre hypothesis was off the mark and we need to make another guess.

To make this genre hypothesis–testing process work, we need just two things – feedback and multiple guesses. We start interpreting a text in relation to a particular genre, but for whatever reason it just doesn't quite work. To borrow an idea from economic game theory, the payoffs for our choice of genre are not good. We then tweak our genre hypothesis and see if our second guess is any closer to the mark. This time we get all the way through the text and think, *Ah, so* that's *what this is.* Or perhaps we try again with something else. As long as we are sensitive to the payoffs and willing to try out different genres, eventually (probably) we will reach a better guess at the kind of thing we are reading. The payoffs we are looking for will vary, but I often look for things like the fit between the assumed function and all the various stages. The reading of the whole that accounts for most of the parts is probably a better one. I tend to assume that writers know something that might be true, and so if the text seems moronic, I might be misunderstanding it.[12]

Literary and biblical scholars don't normally talk explicitly about evaluating payoffs for reading a text as a certain genre, but this is something we do (implicitly at least) all the time in our everyday genre experiences. My church rents a movie theatre for our Sunday services, and it's always funny when people turn up in cinema 11 by accident, expecting a romantic comedy. One time, I was in the front preaching and a couple walked in holding popcorn, took their seats, and watched me – slightly confused – for about ten minutes before they got up and left. I'm not sure what movie genre they were expecting, or why it took them ten minutes to realize I was a real person, but eventually they decided my preaching wasn't the genre experience they were expecting. They picked up their popcorn and shuffled awkwardly away. I'll never know what they made of my sermon, but I hope at least they found the genre they were looking for. Before they start trying cinemas at random, of course, they might consider some of the clues that will guide them toward the right genre.

---

11. Quoted in Richard Coe, "'An Arousing and Fulfillment of Desires': The Rhetoric of Genre in the Process Era – and Beyond," in *Genre and the New Rhetoric*, ed. Aviva Freedman and Peter Medway (London: Taylor and Francis, 1994), 153.

12. See Hans-Georg Gadamer's "prejudice of completeness": *Truth and Method*, 293–94.

CLUES

Before we put a genre to the boomerang test, we have already made an informed guess about what the genre of the text might be. There are several clues that can feed into this initial genre hypothesis.

Recurring Social Situations and Function

An awareness of the social situation to which the text belongs will often help narrow things down. SFL (see chapter 3) encourages us to ask questions about the field, tenor, and mode of the text (i.e., its "register") first when determining genre. Genres don't usually jump into our heads out of nowhere; they come to us in certain recurring situations and with certain kinds of people involved. Sometimes the social situation is instantly recognizable and essential to the genre – a parking ticket comes stuck to your windshield when you're least expecting it. Walking back from the shops, I know what a parking ticket says before I am close enough to even read it.

Unlike a parking ticket, however, we don't always have first-hand experience with the social situation of an ancient text (unless the genre we are studying is embedded in narrative that describes the situation). Comparisons with other ancient Near Eastern texts and historical information should inform our hunches, though we certainly don't want to repeat the mistakes of form criticism in going beyond the historical evidence we have. Sometimes the evidence available is very limited.

However, we can usually still make inferences about the situation from the functions realized in language itself. SFL explains how the texts themselves help construct the social situations we find ourselves in. Without language, and the system of texts that makes up our legal system, I would not know what a "parking inspector" was, nor would I recognize my unpleasant interactions with them as recurring.[13]

These recurring functions are realized by concrete recurring language forms, so it may sometimes be possible to recover what the speaker or writer was trying to do by creating this text. A lament psalm is best identified by its function – expressing complaint and asking God to do something about it. A prayer communicates our commitment to and dependence upon God.[14] Of course, particular texts can have more than one aim, and precisely what a writer wants

---

13. The physical events involved in a "recurring" situation never actually repeat. It's a different car, different officer, different day. What repeats is the understanding of those events based on genre.

14. See Zachary K. Dawson, "The Problem of Gospel Genres: Unmasking a Flawed Consensus and Providing a Fresh Way Forward with Systemic Functional Linguistics Genre Theory," *BAGL* 8 (2019): 69.

to achieve is unique to each work. But what we are looking for are the recurring functions that a genre makes possible. Genres help us get certain things done and not others.

In making our first guess about genre, therefore, we should consider everything we know or can infer about the situation the text functions in.

Embedded Dinosaur DNA

One of the saving graces for biblical studies is that so much of the Bible is presented as narrative, and inside those narratives we have other embedded genres. This is extremely helpful for genre studies because we can tell a lot about how those embedded genres work by looking at how they are framed by the surrounding narrative. Like the dinosaur DNA preserved in amber in *Jurassic Park*, these embedded genres allow us to recover the typical recurring situation they anticipate. For example, we can tell a lot about what psalms are for by looking at all the occasions when a character in narrative sings one (see chapter 7).

Paratexts and External Factors

"Paratexts" are everything that is around the text – the title of the work, the name of the author, the publishing house logo, and so on. I don't know what you expected when you picked up this book, but Zondervan Academic's editors, book designers, and marketing team have worked hard to make it clear to you that this is a nonfiction book on literary genres (my apologies if you were expecting a cooking book[15]). This paratextual information is not always a lot to go on. I could guess that a book with "P. D. James" on the cover is a detective story – she is a renowned crime fiction author. But in 1992, she published *Children of Men*, which is a very different kind of story (some of the newer cover designs actually say "dystopian thriller" just to clear that up). Biblical texts sometimes come with such paratextual labels attached: psalm headings, proverb collections, or words like "gospel" and "apocalypse." However it is important to note that these are almost always added later in the history of the text by editors, scribes, or modern publishers.

---

15. To ease your disappointment, I offer this scone recipe from Timmy, chef at Ridley College: Place 3 cups of self-rising flour and a pinch of salt in a bowl. Using light hands incorporate 1 cup of milk and 3/4 cup of full cream until just combined. Lightly roll out 1 inch thick on a lightly dusted board and cut to size. Brush with milk and bake in 356-degree oven for 10–12 minutes or until risen and slightly toasted. I recommend serving with jam (on the bottom) and whipped cream (on the top).

Taking a step back, the whole process of canonization is relevant to how texts function within communities as Scripture. The fact that a book like Song of Songs or Esther is in the Bible forces us to consider in what respect they are "religious" texts, even though neither can be accused of being overly explicit about God in the book (they might be interpreted quite differently if they were dug up on separate scrolls outside of the religious context of the Bible). The placement of the book of Daniel in the "Prophetic Books" in the English canon might lead us to different assumptions than if we read it in the Hebrew canon, where it is placed with the "Writings." When someone stands up and reads a passage of the Old Testament as part of a nine-lessons-and-carols Advent service, it is hard not to understand the text as a messianic prophecy.

External or contextual clues are essential to our guess about genre, but they are not always conscious. Assumptions about what kind of stories we *should* find in a book with "Holy Bible" printed on the front, for example, has made a big difference for how people have read the ancestral narratives on the issue of slavery (see chapter 5).

Strategic Genre Signals

Writers tend to be strategic in signaling genre early on in the work. The first few sentences are often critical because they subtly push the reader's guesses about genre in a certain direction, and bring certain generic conventions to mind right from the start.[16] The movie *Shrek* (2001) begins, "Once upon a time there was a lovely princess," and this is obviously intended to situate the film in relation to the fairy-tale genre. The book of Proverbs begins with a reference to King Solomon and a cluster of "wisdom" words (Prov 1:1–6).

Openings can be more subtle too. By framing her narrative within letters from an arctic explorer, Mary Shelley encourages us to read *Frankenstein* as a kind of tragic adventure story, while the first four words of the *Star Trek* (1966) voiceover – "Space: the final frontier" – places what follows somewhere between a Western and a sci-fi. The book of Ecclesiastes invokes the Solomonic wisdom genre more subtly than Proverbs with a reference to "the Teacher, son of David, king in Jerusalem" (Eccl 1:1).

It's worth noting, however, that as with paratexts these explicit strategic genre signals within the text are not always determinative. Orson Welles's radio drama adaptation of *The War of the Worlds* was aired on Halloween 1938 as a series of progressively more startling news bulletins interrupting a standard night of

---

16. See Alastair Fowler, *Kinds of Literature: An Introduction to the Theory of Genres and Modes* (Oxford: Oxford University Press, 1982), 88; Coe, "Arousing and Fulfillment," 153; Bakhtin, *Speech Genres*, 90.

music programming. The clear genre signals of "news bulletin" are relevant only to the embedded texts, not the show as a whole, so if listeners missed the introduction to the radio drama and assumed the news bulletins were real, they might have had an exciting night.[17] Likewise, the Coen brothers' film *Fargo* (1996) was labelled as a "true story" in its opening titles, and even in subsequent press interviews. But this was all part of the effect – as Ethan Coen later revealed: "We wanted to make a movie just in the genre of a true story movie. You don't have to have a true story to make a true story movie."[18] (Like me, you may need to read that last sentence a few times.)

The point is this: explicit genre signals early on are important, but they aren't the only thing we need to pay attention to. Job introduces itself as a narrative, but very quickly becomes something else entirely. Esther starts off like a historical account of the reign of Xerxes (Esth 1:1), but ends up being focused on Esther herself (which is why some take it as novella, resistance literature, or even satire). Daniel begins much the same way as 2 Kings ends, but I don't think anyone would read them as the same genre.

Staging Structure

SFL genre theorists place particular emphasis on the "staging structures" of the text – that is, what elements are supposed to come at you, and in what order. Not all genres have strict staging structures, but some do.

We can see this illustrated nicely in the four covenantal lawsuits in Amos. Chapters 3, 4, 5, and 8 each begin with a call to "hear this" addressed to an accused, a recount of events, and then a description of judgment to come. This reflects the staging structure of a genre (let's call it "lawsuit") that might have been used in the ancient world when a vassal king had double-crossed their suzerain, bringing inevitable retaliation. Here, however, the genre has been framed within a prophetic oracle (Amos 1–2), which is a genre for recording the messages of authorized people who spoke to and from God. The normal social situation anticipated by the lawsuit genre (the exclusivity and power dynamic of the suzerain–vassal relationship) is adapted to make the terrifying point that God's people have wronged God himself, and this lack of exclusivity and obedience in their relationship with him should be seen as treason on a cosmic scale.

---

17. Contrary to folklore, there is little evidence that listeners really thought they were being invaded by aliens from Mars: see Michael J. Socolow, "The Hyped Panic Over 'War of the Worlds,'" *Chronicle of Higher Education* 55.9 (2008).

18. Gavin Scott, "How Much of 'Fargo' Is Actually Based on a True Story?," *SBS Guide*, 23 May 2017, www.sbs.com.au/guide/article/2017/05/23/how-much-fargo-actually-based-true-story. Thanks, Brandon Hurlbert, for this example.

Formal Features

The next clues are in the formal features of the text themselves. Almost anything can become associated with a genre (tenet 6). A genre has certain features, so if the text has those certain features, then, *voilà*, we have identified the genre. For example, the length of a text might be a clue as to its genre. For example, a novel is not a haiku. If the text matches enough of these features of a novel and doesn't match any other genre's features quite so well, we might be confident declaring it to be a novel.

Any feature of language can become associated with a genre, but a genre need not be interested in every feature of language. The use of the second-person address is pretty standard for a prayer, and so when a third-person narrative in the Bible switches to second person, it is one of the clues we can use to work out where the prayer starts and ends. But a recount genre like a narrative can be told in first, second, or third person – it's a matter of style and intended effect rather than the genre itself. Some genres are as much about a vibe – its tone and worldview – than anything else, which makes defining them in terms of formal features quite tricky; for example, see the discussion of wisdom psalms in chapter 10. This is why it's important to understand the functional connection between features of a genre, not just tick features off a list.[19]

Content and Subject Matter

Some genres are more commonly associated with certain subject matter. A wedding speech is usually about the virtuous qualities in the bride or groom; a twenty-first birthday speech in Australian culture is normally about all the stupid things they've ever done – it can be quite awkward and embarrassing for everyone when somebody ignores this subtle but important distinction! SFL approaches will sometimes look to analyze the "field" of discourse by looking at the grammatical participants – who are typically the subject and object of each clause? The Lord's Prayer, for example, is about requesting God to do something, and this is reflected in the grammatical fact that God is the usual agent of the processes involved.[20] Wisdom literature is often identified by its distinctive vocabulary (see chapter 10).

We need to be careful here, however. For complex literary texts a less lexicogrammatical and more literary analysis may be required. *Frankenstein* is "about" something deeper than the monster that dominates the story. Likewise,

---

19. There is an inescapable (but not necessarily vicious) circularity here. Identifying the genre tells you what features to expect; noticing features is the best way to identify the genre.

20. See Zachary K. Dawson, "The Problem of Gospel Genres: Unmasking a Flawed Consensus and Providing a Fresh Way Forward with Systemic Functional Linguistics Genre Theory," *BAGL* 8 (2019): 65.

the parable of the sower seems to be about seeds and soil (Matt 13:1–9), until Jesus explains to his disciples what it is really about (13:18–23). The significance of subject matter, therefore, depends on its functional relationship with the other features of the genre.

Scales and Disambiguation

The task of identification based on the features of the text is complicated by our awareness that texts have multiple genres (tenet 1), and that genres are only relatively stable (tenet 2), are overlapping and fuzzy around the edges (tenet 3), and can involve almost any feature you can think of (tenet 6). Taking length into account, for instance, some caution is required. Yes, a novel is not a haiku. But other genres can combine in ways that alter the length substantially (like when folk ghost story becomes a gothic novel, or classical aria becomes a three-minute pop-opera track). The letters we have in the New Testament, for instance, tend to be longer than most ancient personal letters, perhaps because they also participate in a didactic genre and, unlike most letters, are intended to be read to a church community (see chapter 12).

Rather than list the distinctive features of a genre, some genre studies locate texts on a series of spectrums. Based on where a text falls on these spectrums (or **clines**[21]), we can conclude that it is more like one genre than another. This approach has the benefit of providing disambiguation criteria – telling us what a genre *is not*. For example, if we analyze the way different texts deal with participants, we might propose a scale where on one end a biography tends to focus on individual participants, whereas history is more interested in groups. In chapter 11, we will explore this in some more detail when we look at the debate over the genre of the Gospels and Acts. Ultimately, of course, such genre disambiguation is only as good as the scales you've chosen to focus on. It still relies on decisions such as which prototypical texts to include for each genre, and where the text being analyzed fits on the scale. And if a text participates in multiple genres, our disambiguation criteria may need to go out the window.

---

21. See J. R. Martin, "Analysing Genre: Functional Parameters," in *Genre and Institutions: Social Processes in the Workplace and School*, ed. Frances Christie and J. R. Martin (London: Continuum, 1997), 15; J. R. Martin, "One of Three Traditions: Genre, Functional Linguistics, and the 'Sydney School,'" in *Genre Studies around the Globe: Beyond the Three Traditions*, ed. N. Artemeva and Aviva Freedman (Edmonton, AB: Trafford, 2016), 51; Anis S. Bawarshi and Mary Jo Reiff, *Genre: An Introduction to History, Theory, Research, and Pedagogy* (West Lafayette, IN: Parlor, 2010), 43.

Identifying genre remains, despite our best efforts, more art than science. These clues give us a starting point, and running the boomerang test can help confirm the payoffs for taking up the text as a certain genre (or help us tweak our understanding of that genre). We might need to try out a couple of genres before we start getting a sense from the payoffs that the genres are coordinating. Often, more than one genre will offer good payoffs, so we may conclude that the text participates in a handful of genres to different degrees.

TACIT AND TACTICAL UPTAKES

The assumption so far has been that our goal as readers is to correctly diagnose the genre of a text. E. D. Hirsch, for example, makes identifying the true genre of a text one basis for determining the meaning of a text: "Valid interpretation is always governed by a valid inference about genre."[22] Our job as genre detectives is to zero in on what Hirsch calls the "intrinsic genre" of each text – *"that sense of the whole by means of which an interpreter can correctly understand any part in its determinacy."*[23]

I think Hirsch's idea of a determinate "intrinsic genre" for each text is a mirage (especially given the instability and fuzziness of real genres, as well as our lack of access to them except through the texts themselves). But he is right that most of the time it is in everyone's interests to coordinate genre designations between writer and reader.[24] Normally writers and readers share an interest in communication that gives incentives and payoffs for agreeing on genre. Let's call such genre designations, which implicitly aim for coordination between writer and reader, **tacit** uptakes.

But what if readers are feeling uncooperative? Genres provide guidelines for reading, but as John Frow points out, "This is not to say that these guidelines must be respected."[25] Neither authors nor readers have total control over the shared structures of genre; they must "negotiate the generic status of particular texts" without having "the power to make their ascriptions an inherent property of those texts."[26] We might imagine a range of circumstances in which readers decide to interpret something regardless of the genre intentions of the writer

---

22. E. D. Hirsch, Jr., *Validity in Interpretation* (New Haven, CT: Yale University Press, 1967), 113. On the origins of Hirsch's normative approach: David Duff, ed., *Modern Genre Theory* (London: Routledge, 2014), 15.

23. Hirsch, *Validity*, 86.

24. That is, the genre realized by the writer's strategic decisions in the text reaches a cooperative equilibrium with the genre assumed in the strategic decisions of the reader, generating mutually beneficial payoffs.

25. John Frow, *Genre*, 2nd ed. (New York: Routledge, 2015), 118.

26. Frow, *Genre*, 119.

– that is, to "productively ignore" (in Frow's expression) the strategic intentions of a writer.[27]

I call these conscious decisions about genre **tactical** uptakes.[28]

Some tactical uptakes aim to better understanding the text. We might follow Kathleen Jamieson's practice of using creative genre identification as a "productive critical ploy" to spotlight features of the text that are there but may have been obscured, and so ultimately "better" understand the text.[29] Unlike a tacit decision about genre, we are not just picking up and instinctively reading it the way we would any story, because we recognize the gap between our culture and the culture that produced the text. The hope is often still to arrive at a reading that has a greater degree of **coordination** with what someone who produced the text in that situation likely intended.

A simple tactical move I like to make is to try experiencing the ancient story *as* something else – for example, a film. This genre decision might look a little creative at first – after all, film was not invented until a couple thousand years after these stories were written. But the goal is not a resistant posture towards the text, but ultimately one of better coordination. I will give this a go in my reading of Judges 19 – first as horror film (chapter 6) and then as wisdom (chapter 10).

In contrast, Mary Gerhart raises the possibility that we might test out different genres not only to better understand the author's intention but in fact to find "alternative versions and visions of the text" as well.[30] Going even further, a reader might decide that the text is immoral or part of an unhealthy power dynamic, and so deliberately go against what the author is trying to do.

These examples illustrate that tactical uptakes can be on a spectrum from coordination to resistance – depending on whether the goal is to respect the strategic decisions of the writer, produce a creative new interpretation, or subvert the author's likely intention.

THE SCRIPTURE GENRE

The most important genre decision we have to make, however, is whether or not to read the Bible as Scripture. It is possible to take up the Bible simply as a work of literature or for purely historical interest. But to take up a book of the

---

27. Frow, *Genre*, 4.

28. I adapt this idea of "tactical uptakes" from Dylan B. Dryer, "Disambiguating Uptake: Toward a Tactical Research Agenda on Citizens' Writing," in *Genre and the Performance of Publics*, ed. Mary Jo Reiff and Anis S. Bawarshi (Logan: Utah State University Press, 2016), 60–79.

29. Kathleen Hall Jamieson, "Generic Constraints and the Rhetorical Situation," *PhR* 6.3 (1973): 169. She tried reading papal encyclicals as if they were Roman imperial decrees to better understand them.

30. Gerhart, "Generic Competence," 41.

Bible as Scripture is to make assumptions about a social situation and function that affects every level of meaning. This doesn't make what we've been saying about the smaller genres in the Bible irrelevant, but it is an additional layer of complexity we need to consider.

The Scripture genre affects the interpersonal dimension of the text – who we think the text is speaking from and to. A letter's audience is normally taken to be those people mentioned in the opening (for example, from Paul to Timothy). Yet taking the letter of 1 Timothy as Scripture complicates this picture, because we also believe – while not doubting the human origins of the text – that the text is nevertheless in a truer sense "from God" and "for us." (We will explore the complexities of this in chapter 12.)

The Scripture genre affects the scope for intertextual readings. If we believe that the Bible is God's word, we may expect a degree of coherence across the canon. It becomes much more important to consider how a book like Amos not only reflects the communicative intent of an eighth-century prophet but also how it speaks within the book of the Twelve, the Prophets, the Old Testament, and (as Christians) the New Testament as well.

The Scripture genre shapes what we think the text is for. It means that these ancient stories are not just historical information but God's word to his people today, "useful for teaching, rebuking, correcting and training in righteousness, so that the servant of God may be thoroughly equipped for every good work" (2 Tim 3:16–17). We assume that the text continues to be relevant (able to say something into new contexts), but somehow also stable and authoritative (it doesn't mean whatever we want it to mean).

To read the Bible as Scripture is a theological presupposition, but it is also a fundamental decision about genre.

SUMMARY

Genres are like games (tenet 2), and while writers have the power to realize genres through the staging structures and textual features of the text itself, the power to play out a genre lies with the reader. The author has played their only shot, and from now on, the ball is in the reader's court (tenet 12).

When it comes to recognizing and responding to a genre (what RGS calls "uptake"), we can imagine different kinds of responses from readers. Genre recognition is often tacit. If I'm part of the same culture (or think I am), I don't think twice about what game we are playing, I just return the shot. Everyday communication relies on tacit genre decisions that aim for coordination. But uptakes in an academic sphere tend to be less tacit and more tactical. If I am reading an Assyrian treaty document in an academic context, I will think carefully about the genres and what rules might guide my interpretation. I might even decide on tactical resistance rather than compliance with the writer's goals and expectations.

Having described twelve tenets of modern genre theory and introduced a boomerang test for evaluating our decisions about genre, we are ready to start trying out these ideas on actual texts. The next six chapters will sketch out what modern genre theory can do for biblical studies.

QUESTIONS FOR DISCUSSION AND REFLECTION

1. Is it legitimate to disagree with the writer of a text about the genre of the text they created?
2. What would some examples of "tactical" genre decisions be? Where are they on the spectrum of coordination to resistance?
3. What kind of feedback do we get when we run the boomerang test on a biblical text? What are some of the payoffs for getting it right? What are some of the obvious signs we have got it wrong?
4. Why is it helpful to recognize "Scripture" as a genre? What do we assume when we take up a text as Scripture?

FURTHER READING

Introductory

Fowler, Alastair. *Kinds of Literature: An Introduction to the Theory of Genres and Modes.* Oxford: Clarendon, 1982.

> Chapter 6 is a classic answer to the problem of identifying genres.

Deep Dive

Gerhart, Mary. "Generic Competence in Biblical Hermeneutics." *Semeia* 43 (1988): 29–44.

> Sketches out different decisions about genre from a biblical studies perspective.

Jamieson, Kathleen M. Hall. "Generic Constraints and the Rhetorical Situation." *Philosophy & Rhetoric* 6.3 (1973): 162–70.

> Uses genre tactically to "better" understand a text.

Judd, Andrew. *Playing with Scripture: Reading Contested Biblical Texts with Gadamer and Genre Theory*, Routledge Interdisciplinary Perspectives on Biblical Criticism (Abingdon, UK: Routledge, 2024). andyjudd.com/playing.

> My philosophical argument for how this works, using Hans-Georg Gadamer and game theory.

PART 2

CHAPTER 5

GOOD OLD SLAVEOWNERS

Reading Narratives, Not Fairy Tales, in Genesis

Perhaps it wasn't the ideal week to invite my aunt to church, but she was in town and I was rostered on to preach, so she came along with my dad. Our church was – and I probably should have warned her about this – doing a series on a fairly violent section of Old Testament narrative, and that week's Bible reading contained a particularly graphic narration of some very questionable behavior from the main characters. As the reading ended and I got up to preach, she turned to my dad: "I can't believe in a god who endorses this!" She's not alone in this. I remember a taxi driver once telling me they couldn't believe the Bible is a good book of "holy men" because of all the immoral things going on in it.

I'm fascinated by these wonderfully honest responses because I think they reveal some very common assumptions we make about the genre of the Bible. We expect to read tales of holy heroes and their exemplary deeds, and assume that our job is to be inspired by their faith and go forth and do likewise. But is this really how stories work in the Bible?

In this chapter, I want to put our modern genre theory insights to work on the common biblical genre of narrative. We will begin by describing some of the distinctive features that contribute to the experience of biblical narrative, often using analogies to film. We will explore not just how narratives are written but what they are for – the types of social functions that different kinds of narratives have. Finally we will look at how slightly different understandings of genre, and the function of the genre, have produced wildly different interpretations and applications of a biblical narrative.

The main case study for this chapter will be Hagar's story in Genesis 16. Historically, some interpreters have used this chapter to support the institution of slavery, whereas others have seen it as an example of God's care for enslaved people. I want to show how this disagreement over how to interpret the chapter actually boils down to (you guessed it!) a disagreement over genre: *What kind of narrative is Genesis 16?* This might sound like a funny question to ask. Surely all sides can agree that it is narrative! And using a classical understanding of genres, that's right. Almost everyone can agree that it has the formal features of a narrative. But modern genre theory encourages us to look beyond classifications. We need to also ask what this genre is *for*. What role does it call on readers to perform? How are characters developed and evaluated, and what does this reveal about the ideology reflected in, and constructed by, the text?

Stories can transport us to distant places and times. Yet we must be thoughtful travelers, because every culture has its own way of talking about its past. In fact, even within one culture, there may be many different kinds of stories, each with a subtly different purpose. How do we know we are reading biblical stories the way they were probably intended to be read?[1]

EXPERIENCING A STORY

Different genres offer readers different experiences (tenet 4), and the experience of being drawn into a story is one of the most universal pleasures across human cultures. As the campfire is lit and the story begins, it's as if past becomes present, and hours can pass before we remember where and who we are. Children are often drawn in by Bible stories from a very early age (in contrast, I've had trouble getting my kids as entranced by the Old Testament genealogies, which offer a slightly different experience of the past).

To illustrate how Hebrew narrative genres work their particular magic, and why genre is the key to our interpretive disagreements, we will take Hagar's story (Gen 16) as our main example. The basic story goes like this: Despite the promises of innumerable offspring (Gen 15:5), Sarai still hasn't had any children, so she decides to give the Lord a running start at fulfilling his promises. She offers her Egyptian slave Hagar to Abram as a second wife, so he can sleep with her and start building a family (this kind of surrogacy arrangement was recognized in ancient law codes). But when Hagar becomes pregnant, Hagar starts looking down on her childless mistress, who then puts her back in her place by abusing her. It gets so bad that Hagar runs away, taking Abram's only heir with her in her womb. In the desert, she meets the angel of the Lord, who speaks to her, assures her that the Lord has seen what's been happening, and sends her back with a name for the child (Ishmael) and a promise of numerous descendants of her own.

That's the basic story, but the way the Hebrew narrator works to tell the story is much more sophisticated (and enjoyable) than my brief recount of events. To understand why, let's consider some of the main features of Hebrew narrative: staging structures, characters, dialog, camera, ideology, social function, and devices.

---

1. Assuming that coordination is our goal (see tenet 12).

Stages

There is more to telling a great story than just recounting what happened. The best storytellers are masters of the information flow. They think carefully about how much to share, in what order, and how quickly, so that they can keep their audience on the edge of their seats.

The way the story is structured and unfolds is at the core of what makes a narrative a narrative. Recount and **exemplum** are two similar genres for describing past events (whether real or imaginary), but they differ from narrative in their purpose and therefore their staging structure. An exemplum describes the actions of a character and gives assessment, whereas a recount simply records events in sequence.[2]

Recount	Narrative	Exemplum
A genre for recounting events in sequence	A genre for resolving a complication in a story	A genre for judging character or behavior in a story
Orientation Record of Events	Orientation / Exposition Complication Change / Quest Unravelling / Denouement Ending	Orientation Incident Evaluation

All three kinds of stories can be found in the Bible, but the most significant and memorable stories are usually told as narrative.

The engine room of a narrative is tension and release. Early on in the story, complications are introduced that wind up the spring that holds our attention until eventually we find resolution (Odysseus returns home; Esther's people are saved). This dynamic is reflected in the staging structure of the narrative. Yairah Amit describes the staging of a biblical narrative as Exposition > Complication > Change > Unravelling > Ending.[3] In Hagar's story, we could identify the stages roughly like this: Sarai is childless so they use Hagar as a surrogate (Exposition), but mistreatment leads Hagar to escape with Abram's only heir (Complication), yet the angel meets her and blesses her (Change), and so Abram can name the

---

2. These terms and the table are SFL terms adapted from J. R. Martin and David Rose, *Working with Discourse*, 2nd ed. (London: Bloomsbury, 2007), 344. I've tweaked the staging structure for narrative based on Yairah Amit's analysis.

3. Yairah Amit, *Reading Biblical Narratives*, trans. Yael Lotan (Minneapolis: Fortress, 2001). Compare Amit's analysis to Northrop Frye's narrative circle: *The Great Code: The Bible and Literature* (San Diego, CA: Harvest, 1982), 175.

child Hagar gives birth to (Unravelling), leaving Abram finally a father at eighty-six years old (Ending).

Plot Wheel

When analyzing narratives, I like to borrow a tool used by screenwriters called the "plot wheel" or "story circle."[4] At the top of the circle is the "Orientation" stage, and the scenes in the narrative are placed clockwise around the circle until we get back to the "Ending."

Read the book of Esther aloud (if you are in a group, have one person be the narrator and invite different people to speak for the different characters). As you go, take note of the main scenes and events and draw them on a plot wheel.

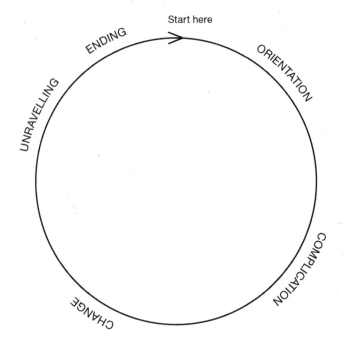

- Where is the tension and release in the story? See if you can label the five stages of the main narrative. (There may be subplots with their own resolutions.)

---

4. See Dan Harmon, "Story Structure 101," Channel 101 Wiki, https://channel101.fandom.com/wiki /Category:Dan_Harmon; Christopher Vogler, *The Writer's Journey: Mythic Structure for Writers* (Studio City, CA: Wiese, 1992). These contemporary methods often adapt Joseph Campbell's hero's journey, Gustav Freytag's pyramid, or Jungian psychology.

- Draw a line through the center of the circle connecting related events together (for example, if a thread left hanging early on is picked up in a later scene).

Within the general narrative staging, there is a great deal of freedom. Biblical narratives draw on "type-scenes" to help tell the story.[5] A classic type-scene is the "marriage negotiation at water source" – for example, in Genesis 24 where Abraham's servants go to find a wife for Isaac and meet Rebekah. In Genesis 16, we have a classic "theophany" or "divine annunciation of VIP birth" type-scene where a divine being appears to a woman, beginning with "behold!" to announce a future birth of a son, naming him and giving a poetic preview of what he will become (Gen 16:11–12).[6]

Leaving Us Hanging

We find an interesting staging structure at work in the book of Jonah, which ends with the Lord's pointed question hanging in the air: "And should I not have concern for the great city of Nineveh, in which there are more than a hundred and twenty thousand people who cannot tell their right hand from their left – and also many animals?" (Jonah 4:11).[7] This seems like an abrupt way to leave the story if we are expecting the normal staging structure of a narrative with a clear Ending (". . . realizing that God was right after all, Jonah returned to Gath Hepher and lived happily ever after.").

To leave us with a question hanging in the air instead of the expected Resolution or Ending stages makes the staging structure of Jonah more like a parable than a classic narrative arc. In both Old Testament and New Testament parables, the story usually ends on a cliffhanger, with the complication unresolved and a question or statement hanging in the air: Jesus's parable of the lost sons ends with the father's speech hanging in the air, and we never find out whether the elder son (like Jonah) comes around.[8]

---

5. See Robert Alter, *The Art of Biblical Narrative* (New York: Basic Books, 2011), 59–78.

6. Matitiahu Tsevat, "Hagar and the Birth of Ishmael," in *The Meaning of the Book of Job and Other Biblical Studies: Essays on the Literature and Religion of the Hebrew Bible* (New York: Ktav, 1980), 61.

7. On alternative translations: JoAnna M. Hoyt, *Amos, Jonah, and Micah*, EEC (Bellingham, WA: Lexham, 2019), 520.

8. After the hanging speech, Jesus sometimes asks what will happen next, or explains the principle: Matthew 13:30; 18:33; 20:15; 21:31; 21:40; 22:13; 25:12; 25:30; Mark 12:9; Luke 12:20; 14:23; 15:6, 9, 31; 16:7; 18:5, 13; 19:27; 20:15. Old Testament examples include Judges 9:7–15 and Ezekiel 17:9–10. The "short story plus pithy saying" genre is sometimes called an *apophthegm* or *chreia*: N. T. Wright, *The New Testament and the People of God* (London: SPCK, 1992), 443.

Characters

There's an old playwriting motto that goes like this: "Show – not tell!"[9] In a good play or film, you don't usually make your mind up about a character based on a voiceover's explicit evaluations. There's nothing worse than laborious exposition! Instead, we form a picture of the characters by observing their actions and overhearing their dialog.

Biblical narrative offers an experience that in many ways is more like watching a film or a play than reading a novel. We don't get long descriptions and explanations like we might find in a novel. Instead, the biblical narrators are masters at showing, not telling. While the form critic Hermann Gunkel attributed the lack of explicit characterization in biblical narratives to a primitive writing style, Yairah Amit observes that the narrators in biblical narratives often develop characters subtly and indirectly.[10] Rather than being told things directly ("Sarai was in the wrong and Abram should never have listened to her") we are meant to form an impression of a character by watching their words and deeds. Robert Neff likens the ancestral narratives to an Icelandic saga cycle, which gives very little explicit description of the characters: "One of the main charms of the sagas is precisely how much one can and must read there between the lines."[11]

Biblical narratives are, in this respect, nothing like fairy tales. In a fairy tale, you often can tell all you need to know about a character by their name – the "Wicked Witch of the West" tells you her moral status, occupation, and postcode. But Shimon Bar-Efrat points out that biblical characters only ever get epithets based on their origin, never their character – we must judge that for ourselves by their actions.[12]

The great benefit of this non-fairy-tale style of characterization is that it leaves us with a three-dimensional picture of characters – in all their complexities and contradictions.[13] Focusing on their deeds and words means that biblical characters can often end up quite complex. Like real people, their actions from one moment to the next can be ambivalent or unpredictable: a "center of surprise."[14] The Bible loves presenting us with complex characters[15] like this.

---

9. Arthur Edwin Krows, *Playwriting for Profit* (New York: Longmans, 1928), 28.

10. See Amit, *Reading Biblical Narratives*, 74–82; see also Menahem Perry and Meir Sternberg, "The King through Ironic Eyes: Biblical Narrative and the Literary Reading Process," *Poetics Today* 7 (1986): 282.

11. Robert W. Neff, "Saga," in *Saga, Legend, Tale, Novella, Fable: Narrative Forms in Old Testament Literature*, ed. George W. Coats, JSOTSup 5 (Sheffield: JSOT Press, 1985), 25. The saga characterization goes back to Hermann Gunkel.

12. Shimon Bar-Efrat, *Narrative Art in the Bible*, trans. Dorothea Shefer-Vanson (Sheffield: Almond Press, 1989), 90.

13. On the "narrative technique of studied reticences," see Alter, *Art of Biblical Narrative*, 126.

14. Alter, *Art of Biblical Narrative*, 126.

15. Analyzing "characterization" in no way denies that Abram and Sarai were real people: even real people need to be drawn. There's art to telling a true story.

Abram is a great example of a complex character. He can be a model of faith one moment (Gen 15) but make very questionable decisions the next (Gen 16).[16] Hagar suffers terribly from Sarai's mistreatment (Gen 16:6), but it's also true that she belittled Sarai (Gen 16:4).

Alongside primary characters who are complex and dynamic, the narrative will also sketch out secondary characters (and a crowd of extras). These other characters often help reflect back on the primary characters.[17]

Dialog

When a novel is made into a film, all the author's descriptions of characters, with their backstory and motives, need to be conveyed using different techniques. Dialog is one of the most important tools a screenwriter has at their disposal, and the same is true of biblical narrators.

The narrator is under no compulsion to relay every word spoken by every figure in the biblical narratives, so when dialog is included, it is always there for a reason.[18] As in a screenplay, dialog is the main way we get access to the inner lives of the characters. Sometimes biblical narrators use embedded speech to make the motivations behind characters' actions explicit.[19] In Genesis 16, we overhear Sarai explaining why Abram should sleep with her servant ("perhaps I can build a family through her") and why she mistreats her ("now that she knows she is pregnant she despises me").

Dialog changes the pace of the narrative. At this point, narrative time slows down – in direct reported speech, the time it takes to tell the story (narrative time) is almost the same as the time passing in the story (narrated time).[20] This throws the spotlight on a crucial moment.

Hagar's story contains six speeches – three between Sarai and Abram and three between the angel and Hagar. The conversation with the angel is heavily spotlighted and takes up almost half the story (whereas her actual return back

---

16. I find several characters fascinatingly complex: Gideon tears down his father's Baal altar (Judg 6:27) but also creates an ephod that Israel worships (8:27); David is clearly God's choice to succeed Saul (1 Sam 16), but his behavior is often just as questionable (1 Chr 21:1).

17. Bar-Efrat, *Narrative Art*, 48–64.

18. Whether dialog is meant to be taken as a full, unedited transcript of a single conversation depends entirely on the genre. Modern historiography seeks to evaluate external sources, which requires quotations to be verbatim and quarantined from the historian's perspective by using quotation marks. Biblical narrative has a different function, so narrators may be allowed more poetic license – perhaps condensing or combining conversations, or even representing characters' implicit understanding using explicit dialog so we can overhear it.

19. Some dialog seems as much for our benefit as the other characters. When Jacob is preparing to meet Esau, his anxieties are made explicit by words said to nobody in particular (Gen 32:8, 20).

20. For example, the book of Ruth races over Naomi's whole life in Moab in a few mainline verbs, but the crucial conversations over a few days involving her future with Boaz are narrated almost in real time.

to Canaan is implied but never narrated). If we are looking for the main point of the narrative, the angel's speech is the place we are probably going to find it.

Camera

We don't often think about it while we are enjoying a film, but the positioning of the camera makes a big difference for the way in which the director wants us to understand characters and events. Are we following one character around and seeing the world through their perspective? Or are we getting a bird's-eye view of the whole scene all at once? Every shot contributes to the overall point of view we are getting.

Likewise, in biblical narrative, the point of view of the narration is crucial to understanding what is going on and what we should be paying attention to. The narrator of the story is usually omniscient (with some exceptions – for example, in narratives embedded in speeches, letters, or the "we" passages of Acts), giving a God's-eye view on what's happening. But even in omniscient narration, there is a point of view – which is implied by the narrator's decisions about which events and thoughts to tell us about.

When experiencing a biblical narrative, then, it's helpful to ask, "Where is the 'camera' positioned, and whose perspective are we getting most strongly here?"[21] In Genesis 16, the camera follows Hagar into the desert and back, reporting an experience that only she could have testified to. Crucially, her perspective is assumed to be true – there is no question about whether she made up the whole angel encounter. So when Abram names the child Ishmael, it is a confirmation of the name given to Hagar in the desert, and the meaning of his name ("God hears") is a vindication of her own experience of being seen by God (Gen 16:11, 15).

Ideology

Modern genre theory tells us that these formal and stylistic features are not just window dressing. A genre reflects, sustains, and helps develop the worldview of the culture it belongs to. The techniques that biblical narrators use to paint their characters, as Robert Alter observes, reflect a biblical view of humanity – after all, "art does not develop in a vacuum."[22] It is a style of narration fit for theological purpose. Every human carries the image and likeness of God but also (since Gen 3) the tragic potential of sin, which we see expressed in every

---

21. Job has some great camera work. Initially, an omniscient narrator gives us access to the heavenly council (Job 1:6–12), but after that, the camera is almost in Job's head. Tragedies are reported to him by a succession of breathless messengers all arriving at once (1:13–19); anyone could have observed him tear his robes, but we hear his prayers (1:21) and inner resolve (1:22).

22. Alter, *Art of Biblical Narrative*, 115.

generation. We are haunted by the consequences of this great and terrible potential. Nobody, not even a righteous person like Noah or a faithful person like Abram, is beyond being pulled back in. They are all, in Alter's words, a "bundle of paradoxes." The Bible is no fairy tale – and I mean this as an observation about its *genre*. Its characters cannot easily be separated into cartoon heroes and villains. There is no place in this story for a two-dimensional "Wicked Witch of the West." Not even Satan himself is a simple character in the Bible (compare Job 1–2 and Zech 3). When it comes to an ancestral narrative like Genesis 16, we must be prepared for Abram and Sarai to sometimes profoundly inspire and sometimes deeply disappoint us.[23]

All this can lead to some culture shock when we pick up a biblical narrative. I described in the beginning of this chapter how my aunt and my taxi driver both struggled with the Bible's unblushing portrayal of poorly behaved major characters. I've noticed that the newspaper articles and social media I consume tend to divide the world into the famous and the infamous – even putting "disgraced" or "controversial" in front of people's names to warn us who is who. Biblical narrators, in contrast, tend not to divide the world so cleanly down the middle. They seem happy presenting their ancestors as they find them – the good, the bad, and the ugly. Genres reflect their context of culture in the way characters are presented.[24]

Another way the biblical narrative genre reflects a biblical take on the world is in the settings. The setting of any story invokes what Mikhail Bakhtin calls the chronotope – an intersection of time and value. This means that the setting is more than a blank set on which the drama plays. A cowboy Western like *The Magnificent Seven* invokes a certain cultural milieu, along with its physical location and time. In biblical stories, so much history and theology become tied up in geography. Hagar encounters the Lord's messenger in the desert – a potent place for a life-changing theophany, at least for those who have read ahead in the Bible.

Social Function

People tell lots of different kinds of stories. Each culture will have its own set or system (tenet 11) of overlapping and fuzzy-bordered (tenet 3) genres for talking about events in the past. In terms of their formal features, they might look quite similar, but the function they serve (tenet 8) might be very different. That's why

---

23. Indeed, "there is often a tension, sometimes perhaps even an absolute contradiction, between election and moral character": Alter, *Art of Biblical Narrative*, 117.

24. See Arthur Keefer, "But Was Abraham *Good*? Ethical Complexity and Moral Reasoning in Genesis," The Biblical Mind, 19 May 2022, https://hebraicthought.org/was-abraham-good-moral-psychology-in-genesis.

it is essential to take up modern genre theory's invitation to look beyond formal features to the social context: what is this kind of story *for*? We will see in the next part of this chapter, when we compare proslavery and abolitionist readings of Hagar's story, that different understandings of function can produce very different interpretations.

Nathan and the Genre Trap

The prophet Nathan masterfully exploits the subtle differences between narrative genres in his confrontation with King David.[25] When Nathan tells David the story of the rich man and the poor man's sheep (2 Sam 12), it is presented as a recount of events with little indication as to why the story is being told. I think he leaves it deliberately ambiguous as to what kind of story he is telling. David apparently assumes it is a historical report of a recent scenario, or perhaps a legal statement of claim inviting his royal evaluation (he burns with anger against the man and condemns him). But it's a trap, of course. It turns out the story is actually a kind of parable or allegory for David's *own* crimes against Uriah and Bathsheba. This genre-based sleight of hand turns David's uptake of condemnation towards what he thinks is a real man into a striking self-assessment.

Some types of stories are designed to bring about moral formation. An exemplum, for example, describes the actions of a character and gives an assessment.[26] Examples of the exemplum might be a medieval morality play or water-cooler gossip complaining about a colleague. The moral assessment can be simplistic ("be like Abraham!"), but it also can be more nuanced, and the example can be positive or negative. Exempla aren't usually the most sophisticated in terms of storytelling technique because, unlike in a saga, there's often little tension driving the narrative forward. Events are recounted and then evaluated. But they do succeed in creating and sustaining a moral community (having heard the gossip, you will think twice about repeating whatever Ben from accounting did!). An example of a biblical exemplum might be the story of Nadab and Abihu in Leviticus 10. They offered unauthorized fire before the Lord and were killed on the spot. This is followed by two poetic verses making clear the moral of the story – only authorized professionals who follow the right protocols can safely approach God's high-voltage holiness.

---

25. This example is borrowed from Kyle Greenwood, *Scripture and Cosmology: Reading the Bible between the Ancient World and Modern Science* (Downers Grove, IL: IVP Academic, 2015), 21.

26. See Martin and Rose, *Working with Discourse*, appendix 2.

Is Genesis 16 meant to be taken as an exemplum like this? There is no explicit evaluation stage in Genesis 16, but then again, explicit moral evaluation of an individual character is less common than you might think in Hebrew narrative.[27] Taken as an exemplum, Genesis 16 might be read as a cautionary tale against surrogate arrangements or as a rebuke to slaves thinking of running away (hold that thought).

Another more explicit type of story is an **etiology**, which explains why something is the way it is through the use of a story from the past. After Hagar names God as "the God who sees me," we are told that "this is why the well was called Beer Lahai Roi" (Gen 16:13–14), though this probably doesn't explain the function of the chapter as a whole.[28]

Etiology and the Origins of Marriage

Genesis 2:24 makes clear that the story about Adam and Eve is more than just a "how I met your mother" story to satisfy humanity's curiosity. "This is why," the story concludes, "a man leaves his father and mother and is united to his wife, and they become one flesh." Accordingly, when asked to weigh in on an ethical debate about marriage, Jesus refers back to Adam and Eve's story as an authority (Matt 19:4–6). In Genesis, etiological stories explain why the Sabbath is the Sabbath, why snakes have no legs, why there are different languages, and how certain places got their names (Gen 2:3; 3:14; 11:9; 19:22; 33:16).

The social function of biblical genres can be hard to pin down. Great stories like Esther can certainly be told to entertain, but their inclusion in the canon and participation in the Scripture genre suggest a broader purpose than that.[29]

The type of truth (truth effects) that different kinds of stories give rise to will vary. In a novella, it is "the truth we find, even if it did not happen."[30] Some would want to read Jonah, Esther, or even the Joseph stories as kinds of novellas that tell truths about the world in general, if not historical events in

---

27. Examples include 1 Samuel 15:19; 2 Samuel 11:27. More common are corporate evaluations (Judg 2:10–12) and evaluation summaries of reigns in histories (1 Kgs 16:30).

28. Texts that participate in the etiological genre can also participate in these more complex story genres as well. Esther 9:26 explains the origin of Purim while telling Esther's story.

29. On the Moses narratives as entertaining, and God-glorifying "heroic saga": George W. Coats, "The Moses Narratives as Heroic Saga," in *Saga, Legend, Tale*, ed. Coats, 33–44.

30. W. Lee Humphreys, "Novella," in *Saga, Legend, Tale*, ed. Coats, 83 (adapting Ken Kesey's phrase in *One Flew over the Cuckoo's Nest*). For Humphreys, a novella depicts "what happens" in general, if not "what happened" in history (86).

particular. My caution here would be that literary sophistication does not rule out a historical referent. A powerful painting can still be a portrait.

Devices

While film directors use techniques like lighting, set design, costume, sound effects, and music, biblical narrators use a different array of devices to feed our imaginations and shape our experiences of the story. Often these work like a spotlight, drawing our attention to things they want us to notice and inviting us to tarry with certain ideas long after story time is over.

- *Repetition* of events, words, and phrases can be used to shine a spotlight on particular themes or highlight contrasts. We are twice told that Hagar is Egyptian (Gen 16:1, 3). Repeated phrases are a common way of suggesting intertextual links – Abram "listened to the voice" of his wife and slept with Hagar (16:2 NRSVue), which reminds us of another time a husband made bad choices (3:17).
- Clever *word choice* lets the narrator add a dash of color. Names are often significant – for example, Ishmael is so named because "God hears" (Gen 16:11). A rare or memorable word can suggest subtle intertextual links to other stories, and a double meaning (pun) sometimes makes us think twice about a certain character or event.[31] When Sarai "afflicts" the Egyptian slave Hagar, who then "flees" (16:6), they are the same words used for the Egyptian mistreatment of the Israelites (15:13, Exod 1:12) and their escape (Exod 2:15; 14:5). Does this parallel raise doubts about Abram and Sarai's behavior, and whose side God is really on?
- *Irony* can help highlight discontinuities in a way that serves the ideology of the story. There is a certain irony to Sarai oppressing an Egyptian slave, given that we have just found out her descendants will be slaves in Egypt (Gen 15:13).
- Similarly, *humor* does more than make the story entertaining. Once you've found something funny, you're already seeing things from the narrator's perspective. However, humor is very contextual, so it can be difficult to tell if something was meant to be funny or not. As Brandon Hurlbert cautions, "Too often readers find comedy within the biblical text that mirrors their own sense of humour."[32] For example, in Judges 3:22,

---

31. Such intertextual connections may work for one audience and not another, raising the thorny question of which audience's perspective we are talking about.

32. See Brandon Hurlbert, "Sanctioning Sacrilege: Towards Rereading Judges as Christian Scripture" (PhD thesis, Durham University, 2022), 54.

Ehud stabs King Eglon and the blade sinks into his fat, and this could be read as hilarious satire or horrific gore, depending largely on the reader's prejudices.

- *Props* are reasonably rare in biblical narrative, so if the narrator describes an inanimate object, it's significant – the bones of Joseph, Moses's staff, the ark, the linen ephod, the sword of Goliath. We might invoke here a variation on the rule of "Chekhov's gun." The Russian playwright insisted that if a gun appears on stage, it has to go off by the end of the play. For example, the description of Absalom's hair takes longer than that of many northern kings' whole reigns, including how much it weighed when he cut it (2 Sam 14:26). It isn't until later that we find out why (18:9).

- *Geography* plays an underappreciated role in biblical storytelling. Hagar is on the road to "Shur," which is on the northeastern border of Egypt. Her geographical movement from Canaan to Egypt and back again is a motif that anticipates the forced migration of Isaac's descendants later on in Genesis and their return in Exodus.

- *Gaps* and *discontinuities* in the narrative are things that are left unexplained – for example, apparent contradictions in a character's motivations. They ensure that the experience of the story keeps going as we walk away. It's no accident that the stories we remember are the ones with the biggest unanswered questions: Where did the snake come from, and was he right after all (Gen 3:4)? Why *did* God prefer Abel's offering (4:5)? Is Lot *tricking* the men of Sodom (19:8)? *What* did Abraham and Isaac talk about on the way home from the test on the mountain in Moriah (22:19)? What's with God *wrestling* Jacob (32:24)?[33]

  In Hagar's story, there are similarly thought-provoking discontinuities. Why doesn't Abram intervene to protect Hagar? Hagar "returns," but does she "repent" (the word can have that connotation)? Why is Hagar sent home only to be cast out again (Gen 16:9, 21:10)? While scholars love to put these down to incompetent editors, my general life rule is to trust editors. They are often better at their job than we are at ours.

These devices are worth paying attention to. They not only contribute to the narrative experience by engaging and delighting the audience; they also guide us towards the meaning of the narrative by spotlighting certain elements and not others.

---

33. Similarly for many New Testament stories – for example, what *did* Jesus write on the ground (John 8:6)?

The Ball Is in the Reader's Court

While writers can strategically signal the genres they anticipate their texts will participate in, once their shot is played and the text is released into the world, the ball is in the reader's court (tenet 12). While the various types of stories share many of the same formal features, they can have very different social and ideological functions and invite their readers to take up quite different roles (tenet 4).

Satire and Parody

Perhaps the most dramatic shift a reader can make is to choose to read a story as satire or parody. For example, it's become common to read Jonah as a satire or parody, perhaps targeting Assyria or even the Deuteronomistic theodicies of the biblical postexilic prophets themselves.[34] Doing so will often completely flip the meaning of the story. You might have thought the point of Jonah was that God can have mercy on anyone – even Assyria – but actually, read as a satire, Jonah could be mocking that view.

My rule of thumb is this: "It's probably not satire." By this I mean that the communities that first produced and treasured these texts would probably be startled to find themselves participating in satire. Admittedly, there is very little that any text can do to dissuade someone who is determined to read it as satire (as John Piper experienced in the last chapter). But the historical evidence for ancient satire within the Bible's context of culture is unconvincing.

Often biblical scholars draw on Mikhail Bakhtin's description of ancient Menippean satires and then go looking for the (mainly formal) features Bakhtin lists as being "Menippean." For example, using Bakhtin's analysis, David Valeta reads Daniel 1–6 as Menippean satires.[35] Menippus was a third-century BC satirist, and while we don't have any of his writings, he shows up as a character in later works by Lucian. Read a "Menippean satire" (for example, the "Pumpkinification of Claudius," which is attributed to Seneca the Younger),[36] and you soon get the vibe; it's much more like Ricky Gervais's *The Office* or Monty Python's *Life of Brian* than anything in the Bible. This is not to deny, of course, that there is irony, exaggeration, or humor in the biblical narratives.

---

34. Stephen Derek Cook, "'Who Knows?' Reading the Book of Jonah as a Satirical Challenge to Theodicy of the Exile" (PhD thesis, University of Sydney, 2019).

35. David M. Valeta, "Polyglossia and Parody: Language in Daniel 1–6," in *Bakhtin and Genre Theory in Biblical Studies*, ed. Roland Boer, SemeiaSt 63 (Atlanta: Scholars Press, 2007), 91–108; David M. Valeta, *Lions and Ovens and Visions: A Satirical Reading of Daniel 1–6* (Sheffield: Sheffield Phoenix, 2008). Compare M. M. Bakhtin, *The Dialogic Imagination* (Austin: University of Texas Press, 1981), 26.

36. See Petronius, *Satyrica*, ed. R. Bracht Branham and Daniel Kinney (Berkeley: University of California Press, 1996), xvii–xviii. Thanks, Dirk Buursma, for this reference.

But satire is not the only genre that is funny, and a handful of ironic moments does not a Menippean satire make. Sean Adams observes that Jewish authors mostly avoided adapting Greek comedy genres, including parody.[37]

Of course, the ball is in the reader's court (tenet 12), and the fact that biblical texts were probably never intended as Greek satires or parodies is not a problem necessarily for tactical readings. It may be there are similarities between the Greek satirical genres and the biblical narratives that a tactical reading can reveal. Or modern biblical interpreters may even be doing resistant uptakes, and so aren't interested in coordinating their understanding with the tradition. In pursuing such tactical readings, however, we must take additional responsibility for the ethics of our uptake. Satirical readings involve weaponizing the text's comic elements against some kind of target, and such readings can tend all too easily towards anti-Judaism.[38]

So far in this chapter, I've made assertions about how Hebrew narrative works – the staging structures, characters, dialog, camera, ideology, social function, and devices. I'm reasonably confident in this understanding of the genre. I'm drawing on some of the best readers of biblical narrative, as well as years of experience reading and teaching these texts. But ultimately, it's up to you as a reader whether you take these observations on board. It is entirely possible to ignore what we've discussed about, for example, how characters are drawn. You might decide to use the story for a completely different social function. In fact, you wouldn't be alone.

In the final part of this chapter, I want to show how different understandings of the genre of Genesis 16 have led to some fundamental disagreements about what the story means.

THE MORAL OF HAGAR'S STORY

Let me share a couple different interpretations of Hagar's story.[39] Historically, Christians have read this story in lots of different ways, but we're going to focus on two. The big point of disagreement in these interpretations is over the

---

37. Sean A. Adams, *Greek Genres and Jewish Authors: Negotiating Literary Culture in the Greco-Roman Era* (Waco, TX: Baylor University Press, 2020), 295–96.

38. See Yvonne Sherwood, "Cross-Currents in the Book of Jonah: Some Jewish and Cultural Midrashim on a Traditional Text," *BibInt* 6.1 (1998): 49–79. Thanks, Brandon Hurlbert, for this tip.

39. For the more detailed version, see my "Hagar, Uncle Tom's Cabin, and Why We Cannot Agree on What the Bible Says about Slavery," *BBR* 31.1 (2021): 1–15. Seeing how people across different times, places, and traditions have interpreted a text is called "reception history," or "history of effects" (*Wirkungsgeschichte*, if you want to show off some German).

significance of slavery in the story. Hagar is, after all, an Egyptian slave. She escapes Sarai's oppression but then is sent back by the angel. So can we take the moral of the story as "God approves of slavery and disapproves of slaves running away"? It's possible – but it all depends on the genre.

The Proslavery Reading

One common way to read the story is as a kind of exemplum, a story genre whose function is to judge the behavior of a character. The stages in a typical exemplum are Orientation > Incident > Interpretation. On this reading, Hagar's story goes like this: the unhappy family dynamic is introduced (Orientation); Hagar runs away (Incident); the angel condemns her flight by sending her back (Interpretation). The moral of the story is that slaves shouldn't run away from their masters, no matter how difficult the circumstances. This reading of the story might never have occurred to you. But in the nineteenth century, it was quite common in proslavery pulpits and tracts.

The decision to take up Genesis 16 as an exemplum affects how the characters' actions are interpreted. After all, the function of an exemplum is to present the behavior of characters and evaluate it: do this, or do not do this. There is no question, on this reading, that Abram is the hero to be emulated, and so the lack of censure indicates we should emulate him. A South Carolinian presbytery called on "good old slaveholders and patriarchs" like Abram as alibis for their system of enslavement.[40] There is little nuance in such readings of Abram's character. Here is a "friend of God" and a "holy" man, so if he owned slaves, then slavery as a whole must be acceptable to God.[41] Such arguments even made it to the United States Congress. In 1820, South Carolinian congressman Charles Pinckney made a speech arguing that for the "father of the faithful, and the beloved servant of the Most High," to buy an "African slave" like Hagar proves God is in favor of the institution.[42]

The exemplum genre also affects the understanding of the plot, so what happens in the story makes clear where God stands on the issue of enslaved people seeking to escape. In a speech to the Synod of Cincinnati, George Junkin pointed to Hagar's story as "a simple case of a runaway slave," seeing the angel's command to return as God's command to all enslaved people in his day.[43]

40. Harmony Presbytery, South Carolina – quoted in Albert Barnes, *An Inquiry into the Scriptural Views of Slavery* (Philadelphia: Perkins & Purves, 1846), 30.

41. Presbytery of Tombecbee and Dr. Richard Fuller – both quoted in Barnes, *Inquiry*, 58–59.

42. Charles Cotesworth Pinckney, "Missouri Question: Speech of Mr. Pinckney, of S. Carolina, in the House of Representatives (14 February 1820)," in *Niles' Weekly Register*, ed. Hezekiah Niles (Baltimore: Franklin, 15 July 1820), 355.

43. George Junkin, *Integrity of Our National Union, vs. Abolitionism: An Argument from the Bible* (Cincinnati, OH: Donogh, 1843), 40.

In 1847, a proslavery catechism from Wisconsin was republished in a Washington newspaper that puts it even more starkly:

> How do you know that Abraham's servants were slaves? *Because he whipped Hagar.*
>
> How do you know that? *Because she ran away.*
>
> How do you know that it is right to flog slaves? *Because God sent Hagar back.*[44]

John Henry Hopkins was bishop of Vermont (and father of the guy who wrote the Christmas Carol "We Three Kings"). Hopkins wrote a defense of slavery in 1864 in which he uses Abram and Sarai's ownership of a slave as "proof that slavery was sanctioned by the Deity."[45] Taking the story as a kind of exemplum, he interprets the Incident (Hagar running away) through using the Interpretation (the angel's conversation in the desert) to provide the moral of the story: slaves should not try to escape. For Hopkins, the story casts Hagar as a "fugitive." On this basis, he argues, the Fugitive Slave Act of 1850 (which required people in free states to return escaped enslaved people to states where slavery was legal) is in line with God's will: "If the philanthropists of our age, who profess to believe the Bible, had been willing to take the counsel of that angel for their guide, it would have preserved the peace and welfare of the Union."[46]

These nineteenth-century proslavery interpreters are by no means out on a limb in interpreting the story as an exemplum concerning "runaway" slaves. The sixteenth-century theologian John Calvin concludes from the story that "liberty is not to be obtained by stealth, nor by flight, but by manumission."[47] The twentieth-century theologian Gerhard von Rad is also sympathetic to Hagar, but the unavoidable moral of the story is that "Yahweh will not condone the breach of legal regulations."[48] Even when they don't support slavery, in general the tradition is quick to award Abram hero status. The early church father John Chrysostom calls Abram a "man of steel, God's noble athlete," whom husbands would do well to emulate.[49]

Interestingly, Harriet Beecher Stowe observes that this tendency to take up

---

44. "A Pro-Slavery Catechism," *The National Era*, vol. 1, no. 27 (8 July 1847).

45. John Henry Hopkins, *A Scriptural, Ecclesiastical, and Historical View of Slavery* (New York: Pooley, 1864).

46. Hopkins, *Scriptural, Ecclesiastical, and Historical View*, 7–8.

47. John Calvin, *Commentary on the First Book of Moses Called Genesis*, trans. John King (Bellingham, WA: Logos, 2010), 430–31.

48. Gerhard von Rad, *Genesis: A Commentary*, rev. ed. (London: SCM, 1972), 194.

49. Chrysostom, "Homily 38," 366. Augustine, Philo, Josephus, and Martin Luther likewise all praise his behavior with regard to Hagar.

the story as an exemplum is in part conditioned by the social function ascribed to the genre as it is read in contemporary worship:

> We have been so long in the habit of hearing the Bible read in solemn, measured tones, in the hush of churches, that we are apt to forget that these men and women were really flesh and blood, of the same human nature with ourselves. A factitious solemnity invests a Bible name, and some good people seem to feel embarrassed by the obligation to justify all the proceedings of patriarchs and prophets by the advanced rules of Christian morality.[50]

In contrast, the abolitionists (including Stowe) feel no such embarrassment.

The Abolitionist Reading

The abolitionists were writing at the same time as the proslavery interpreters, asking the same questions, with access to the same literary and historical insights into the text. Yet they come to radically different conclusions. There are many abolitionist sermons and pamphlets that refute the proslavery reading of Hagar's story.[51] Sometimes the abolitionist interpreters do this by pointing out the differences between the situation of ancient Israelite bondservants like Hagar and contemporary African slaves.[52] But more often, the difference comes down to the fact that they are reading the story as a narrative, not as an exemplum.

Where we see genre most strongly at play is in the assumptions about the social function of the genre. Unlike the proslavery interpreters, the abolitionists don't assume that the text is an exemplum designed for putting forward an example to be judged and emulated. For example, Albert Barnes, a New Jersey theologian, considers the mention of Abram's slaves as "the record of a mere *fact*. There is no command to buy servants or sell them or to hold them as property – any more than there was a command to the brethren of Joseph to enter into a negotiation for the sale of their brother."[53] So for Barnes, it comes down to the social function of the genre. He thinks the commands around slavery in Deuteronomy *are* to be taken as normative, but not the actions of characters in narratives like Genesis 16. William Morris considers Abram's many failings as simply historic facts that "are not recorded for the *imitation* of

---

50. Harriet Beecher Stowe, *Woman in Sacred History: A Series of Sketches* (New York: Ford, 1873), 18.

51. For example, Samuel Sewall (1700), the younger Jonathan Edwards (1791), George Cheever (1860), Isaac Allen (1860), and Reuben Hatch (1862). These abolitionist readings build upon a tradition that is sympathetic to Hagar, going back to Philo, Rabbi Moshe ben Nahman, John Chrysostom, Hilary of Poitiers, and some Islamic texts. See the Further Reading section at the end of the chapter.

52. See Stowe, *Woman in Sacred History*, 41–43.

53. Barnes, *Inquiry*, 71.

Christians."[54] Jonathan Edwards (not *that* Jonathan Edwards – his son) makes a similar point: the passage no more endorses Abram's possession of slaves than the surrogacy arrangements (preachers presumably weren't encouraging good Christian men to sleep with their slaves).[55]

The choice not to read Genesis 16 as exemplum influences how the abolitionists interpret the narrative's subtle characterization. We have observed already that biblical narrative is subtle in its drawing of characters and rarely gives explicit moral evaluation. If this is an exemplum, with clear goodies and baddies to emulate and avoid, then it makes sense to assume that Abram is the flawless hero and to take the narrator's lack of censure as tacit approval. In an exemplum, we expect to find exemplary behavior. The abolitionists, in contrast, look around at the behavior of the ancestors and point out that nobody in their right mind would suggest everything they did was God's will.

It's not that narratives are devoid of ethical lessons. You just have to work a little harder with the text to discern them. As a preacher, Orpheus T. Lanphear thinks you only need to look at God's care towards Hagar and his liberation of Israel from slavery in Egypt later on to work out that God is on Hagar's side, and that her suffering was the result of Sarai's "lack of faith and disobedience."[56]

Read in this way, Hagar's story becomes something quite different. Twentieth-century feminist, womanist, and African-American interpretations sometimes find in Hagar a representation of their own suffering, a model of survival, and an example of God's concern for the oppressed.[57]

RESULTS OF THE BOOMERANG TEST

When it comes to genre, the ball is in the reader's court (tenet 12). That means if proslavery preachers decide that this story is an exemplum, then that's the meaning they'll take away from it. But that doesn't mean all readings are equal. I would suggest that one of them does much better on the boomerang test.

First, taken as an exemplum, the story comes back at us with a strangely

54. William Morris, *Ancient Slavery Disapproved of God* (Philadelphia: Scriptural Knowledge Society, 1862), 6, emphasis in original.

55. Jonathan Edwards, *The Injustice and Impolicy of the Slave Trade* (Boston: Wells and Lilly, 1822), 18.

56. O. T. Lanphear, *A Discourse Delivered at the United Service of the Congregational Churches in Lowell, on Fast Day, April 10th, 1856* (Lowell, MA: Brown & Morey, 1856), 13.

57. See Elaine James, "Sarah, Hagar, and Their Interpreters," in *Women's Bible Commentary*, ed. C. A. Newsom, S. H. Ringe, and J. E. Lapsley (Louisville, KY: Westminster John Knox, 2012), 54; Phyllis Trible, "Ominous Beginnings for a Promise of Blessing," in *Hagar, Sarah, and Their Children: Jewish, Christian and Muslim Perspectives*, ed. Phyllis Trible and Letty M. Russell (Louisville, KY: Westminster John Knox, 2006), 33–70; Delores S. Williams, "Hagar in African American Biblical Appropriation," in *Hagar, Sarah, and Their Children*, ed. Trible and Russell, 183; Nyasha Junior, *Reimagining Hagar: Blackness and Bible* (Oxford: Oxford University Press, 2019), 46–62.

unbalanced staging structure. The purported Evaluation stage takes up barely five words of verse 9 ("Go back to your mistress and submit to her"), leaving almost half the chapter with the angel as extraneous to the function of the story. Curiously, of all the things the angel does say, the central bit about it being wrong to escape oppressive enslavement is completely overlooked. In fact, the angel overall shows so much sympathy for Hagar that critical scholars sometimes want to get the scissors out and put the command down to the work of a later redactor.

When taken up as a narrative, however, it makes much more sense why the focus of the chapter is on the revelation to Hagar, not on her return (which is never narrated). The complication being resolved is not about whether escaping enslavement is wrong; it's about Hagar's place in the family of promise. Taken this way, the text comes back to us with no contradiction between the angel's command to return and the promise of blessing. She returns in order for Ishmael to be named and therefore legitimized as an heir to the promises to Abram.[58]

Second, the narrative techniques of point of view, characterization, setting, and type-scenes observed above have much better payoff on the abolitionist reading. The camera is with Hagar most of the time, and her experience of the angel in the desert and his "seeing" of her misery is vindicated in the end by the naming of Ishmael ("God hears"). As the abolitionists all point out, assuming that the narrator's silence can be taken as tacit approval of Abram and Sarai's actions would lead to absurd conclusions across the ancestral narratives.

The setting of the story in Shur, on the northeastern border of Egypt, invokes a chronotope that includes themes of deliverance out of Egypt. The type-scene of the angel appearing to Hagar places her in a category not of rebuke but of God's reassurance and blessing. While there is an instruction to return, the register of a theophany and birth annunciation does not fit easily with the idea that this is all about rebuking a runaway slave. In fact, God seems to be on her side in the conflict. He makes promises to her descendants in a way that mirrors the blessings to Abram (Gen 15:4). Hagar is the first recipient of an angel annunciation, the only woman to be promised innumerable descendants, and the only person to name God.[59] The name given to Ishmael reflects the fact that the Lord has "heard of your misery" (Gen 16:11), which is normally a sign that God is about to

---

58. David W. Cotter, *Genesis*, Berit Olam (Collegeville, MN: Liturgical Press, 2003), 105; Matitiahu Tsevat, "Hagar and the Birth of Ishmael," in *The Meaning of the Book of Job and Other Biblical Studies: Essays on the Literature and Religion of the Hebrew Bible* (New York: Ktav, 1980), 58–59.

59. See John L. Thompson, *Writing the Wrongs: Women of the Old Testament among Biblical Commentators from Philo through the Reformation* (Oxford: Oxford University Press, 2001), 18; Phyllis Trible, "Ominous Beginnings for a Promise of Blessing," in *Hagar, Sarah, and their Children*, ed. Trible and Russell, 33–70.

intervene (Exod 3:7). And her response, naming God "*el roi*" ("God of seeing") would be an odd comeback for someone who has just been rebuked.

Third, the abolitionist view of Abram and Sarai as imperfect people fits much more easily with the theology of humanity seen so far in the book of Genesis – that this side of the fall, nobody is perfect. Making Abram beyond critique introduces a foreign ideology into a story where the only flawless hero is God.

Fourth, to function as Scripture for a community, we expect there to be coherence across the canon. The intertextual connections to the rest of the canon all point towards a position that is sympathetic to Hagar. Reading the story as an exemplum against slavery contradicts what we see in God's character in his dealings with a nation of runaway slaves, Israel, in the exodus, and his commands not to return foreign slaves to their masters (Deut 23:15–16).

In summary, for me it's 4–nil on the boomerang test. Taking up the story as an exemplum justifying slavery returns to us a strangely incoherent text, whereas taking it up as a biblical narrative with complex characters hits us in the head with a powerful and thought-provoking story.

SUMMARY

There are different kinds of story genres that cultures can use to recount past events, and these provide readers with distinctive experiences, roles, and resources (tenet 4). We observed that in many ways, biblical narrative works more like a film than a novel. We looked at the staging structures, characterization, dialog, camera angles, ideology, social function, and devices. We also observed that the ball is in the reader's court (tenet 12), so when it comes to a story like Hagar's, it is possible to read it in multiple ways – with the slavery apologists as an exemplum on why slaves shouldn't run away, or with the abolitionists as a narrative where even heroes do bad things. Putting both uptakes through the boomerang test, however, the latter comes back as a better reading with better payoffs.

Suggested Workflow for Interpreting Narratives

For each genre, I will offer some basic questions I find useful to guide interpretation. The headings reflect my own tradition's reception of the Bible in three broad genres – as historical, literary, and scriptural texts within a Christian community. They're not meant to be taken as a sequential process, because things you discover in one part may force you to go back and reconsider another.

History

☐ Where and when is the narrative set? What values and cultural beliefs are assumed? Are there references to particular people, geography, customs, or events? (If so, what is the potential significance of these?) Do we know anything about when it was written?

☐ What truth effect or relationship to reality is the narrative seeking to offer? For example, is it a parable, or a sequential recount of a king's reign?

☐ What is the wider context of the narrative? Are these events told as part of a bigger story? Are there questions hanging over us from previous episodes?

☐ What is this kind of narrative for? What function and recurring social situation does it anticipate? What about the function of the genre that the narrative is embedded in? (How do these functions interact?)

☐ How have communities in different times, places, and cultures approached the narrative? Given your own tradition, what assumptions are you likely to make about the story?

Literature

☐ Place the main scenes on a plot wheel and identify the stages. Where is tension built and released? Do earlier scenes set things up that are returned to later? Are there parallels, contrasts, or ironic reversals between scenes?

☐ Identify the primary characters in the narrative. How are they depicted through their actions and words? Is there any explicit description or evaluation? How do contrasts with secondary characters shed light on them?

☐ Where is the camera throughout the different parts of the story? Whose perspective, knowledge, and thoughts are we getting access to?

☐ What devices are used in the narrative? What key words or phrases stick out? How do they contribute to the experience of the narrative?

☐ What themes or motifs emerge from the story? Are there echoes from earlier episodes?

☐ What gaps or puzzles are there in the text? What do these encourage the reader to go away and think about?

☐ What other genre relationships can you identify in or around this text (including embedded genres)? Why are they there, and what do they each bring to the table? What new ideas or effects emerge from combining the different genres?

Scripture

- ☐ What perspective on God, people, life, history, suffering, justice, the world (and so on) is being assumed or developed? How might this feed into our systematic theology (anthropology, soteriology, ecology, and the like)?
- ☐ What potential connections can we identify between the characters, events, and themes of this story and the rest of the Bible? How does this story contribute to the big story of the Bible, and vice versa?
- ☐ Is there a strong ethical teaching in the story or is it more subtle? How might this story help calibrate our moral compass? Are there necessary or possible implications for our lives? How *shouldn't* we apply this story?
- ☐ What would be missing from our understanding of God, people, and salvation history if this narrative were missing or overlooked? What ideas does it develop, or balance, or complicate?

QUESTIONS FOR DISCUSSION AND REFLECTION

1. How do people tend to read biblical narratives in the tradition you are most familiar with?
2. Do narratives in the Bible always have implications for our ethics? How do we discern what the story means for us today?
3. Is every speech reported in biblical narrative a transcript of a historical conversation? How much poetic license should narrators be given to put words in the mouth of a historical figure?

FURTHER READING

Introductory

Amit, Yairah. *Reading Biblical Narratives.* Translated by Yael Lotan. Minneapolis: Fortress, 2001.
    Introduces how Hebrew narrative works.
Thompson, John L. *Reading the Bible with the Dead: What You Can Learn from the History of Exegesis That You Can't Learn from Exegesis Alone.* Grand Rapids: Eerdmans, 2007.
    Invitation to reception history from one of the best.

Deep Dive

Alter, Robert. *The Art of Biblical Narrative.* New York: Basic Books, 1981.
    A classic on biblical narrative.

Bar-Efrat, Shimon. *Narrative Art in the Bible*. Translated by Dorothea Shefer-Vanson. Sheffield: Almond Press, 1989.

Another classic on biblical narrative.

Berlin, Adele. *Poetics and Interpretation of Biblical Narrative*. Sheffield: Almond Press, 1983.

A third classic on biblical narrative, particularly methods of characterization.

Perry, Menahem, and Meir Sternberg. "The King through Ironic Eyes: Biblical Narrative and the Literary Reading Process." *Poetics Today* 7.2 (1986): 275–322.

Masterful reading of the David and Bathsheba story.

Thompson, John L. *Writing the Wrongs: Women of the Old Testament among Biblical Commentators from Philo through the Reformation*. Oxford: Oxford University Press, 2001.

Judicious reception history on Genesis 16 up to the Reformation (chapter 1).

Trible, Phyllis and Letty M. Russell, eds. *Hagar, Sarah, and Their Children: Jewish, Christian and Muslim Perspectives*. Louisville, KY: Westminster John Knox, 2006.

Reception history including more contemporary womanist and feminist approaches.

CHAPTER 6

LET'S GET TACTICAL

Judges as Horror Film

We saw in the previous chapter how two ways of reading Hagar's story begin with a different understanding of the story's genre: Is it an exemplum, or a more complex kind of narrative? In that example, the decision about genre is implicit and automatic, as both sides assume what the story is for and run with it. But this gets me thinking, *What if we could use a decision about genre to see if a biblical text works in different ways?* Back in chapter 4, we raised the possibility of "tactical" genre uptakes in which the reader ignores some of the clues as to genre and takes up the text in an unexpected way (perhaps to subvert the intended meaning). Here my goal is not subversion, but it is tactical. I want to use a different genre to try to get a different angle on what the text might be doing.[1]

I'll warn you now that the text I'm going to choose, Judges 19, is a dark one – a young woman tries to escape an unhappy marriage, only to be betrayed by her husband, raped, murdered, and dismembered. Even by the standard of Judges, it's a disturbing story. What I find even more disturbing is the way that commentators throughout history have read the story and blamed the young woman for what happened to her. The story often becomes, like Hagar's story, a kind of exemplum on the dangers of breaching sexual norms. Commentators have consistently failed to respond to this young woman's story with fairness and compassion. She is only a whore, they say, who got what she had coming for her.[2] It's an old variation on the "what was she wearing?" trope in discourse around

---

1. For a more technical version of this example, see my *Playing with Scripture: Reading Contested Biblical Texts with Gadamer and Genre Theory*, Routledge Interdisciplinary Perspectives on Biblical Criticism (Abingdon, UK: Routledge, 2024), 153–98.

2. On the passage's reception history, see my *Playing With Scripture*; John L. Thompson, *Writing the Wrongs: Women of the Old Testament among Biblical Commentators from Philo through the Reformation* (Oxford: Oxford University Press, 2001); Joy A. Schroeder, "Dismembering the Adulteress: Sixteenth-Century Commentary on the Narrative of the Concubine (Judges 19–21)," *Seminary Ridge Review* 9.2 (2007): 5–24; David M. Gunn, "Judges," in *The Oxford Handbook of the Reception History of the Bible*, ed. Michael Lieb, Emma Mason, and Jonathan Roberts (Oxford: Oxford University Press, 2011), 89–103; Marion Taylor, ed., *Women of War, Women of Woe: Joshua and Judges through the Eyes of Nineteenth-Century Female Biblical Interpreters* (Grand Rapids: Eerdmans, 2016).

sexual assault, and I think it's important to resist this kind of reading, which is not only horrific and harmful, but also (I strongly believe) not what the story is meant to be taken as.

Justifiably outraged by this treatment, commentators since the late-nineteenth century have fought back. Many have concluded that the story itself, not just its history of effects, is deeply immoral.[3] Interestingly, though, this resistance often shares with the tradition it is opposing an unspoken agreement about the genre of the text and how the reader is meant to respond to it. Both sides assume that this is the kind of Bible story in which characters are held up as examples for imitation. The narrator never explicitly condemns what happened to the young woman, and so, the assumption is, the actions of the men are implicitly condoned by the text. The men, narrator, the text – and perhaps God himself – are all in it together in their abuse of the poor young woman.

But is it possible to hold on to her story while resisting the tradition of its effects? If we are to escape the history of this text's effects, we are going to need a new understanding of "what kind of thing" it *is*. How does this kind of story work, and what are we supposed to do with it?

Maybe a tactical genre move can help? What happens when we take literally Phyllis Trible's description of this story as a "text of terror"[4] – that is, what if we experience and respond to Judges 19 *as if it were a horror film*? By choosing to experience the text on the basis of a deliberately anachronistic (mis)identification of the text's genre, my hope is to avoid the traditional uptakes of Judges 19 as an exemplum and suggest a different kind of narrative experience. This heuristic method may suggest different responses, which might come less naturally to the standard Bible commentary or sermon, and which might allow us to hold tightly to the text, and loosely to the tradition of its reception.

THE HORROR GENRE

What, then, do we mean by a "horror film"? One common definition focuses on the feeling of agitation that monsters have on us as an audience.[5] Monsters are metaphors for what we find threatening and impure, and these metaphors hit a deep nerve with our personal or cultural anxieties. However modern genre theory has already cautioned us about relying too heavily on theoretical definitions, preferring

---

3. See, for example, Elizabeth Cady Stanton et al., *The Woman's Bible: Comments on the Old and New Testaments from Joshua to Revelation* (New York: European Publishing Company, 1898), 2:17.

4. See Phyllis Trible, *Texts of Terror: Literary-Feminist Readings of Biblical Narratives* (Philadelphia: Fortress, 1984), 65–91.

5. Noël Carroll, *The Philosophy of Horror, or, Paradoxes of the Heart* (New York: Routledge, 1990), 27.

to begin with prototypes when thinking about a genre (tenet 3). My reading is going to be mainly based around some classic horror film prototypes – Alfred Hitchcock's *Psycho* (1960) and George A. Romero's *Night of the Living Dead* (1968).

Psycho is an important early prototype of the horror genre (though today we would probably call it a "psychological thriller" because the genre has moved on, just as tenet 2 expects). The central character is Marion Crane, a young woman from Phoenix, Arizona. She runs away with $40,000 in cash stolen from her employer, hoping to meet her boyfriend in California and use the money to get married and start a new life together. But heavy rain forces her to take a detour on her journey, and she stays overnight at a small motel off the highway. The motel is run by a seemingly nice young man called Norman Bates and his mysterious mother. By morning, the young woman is dead.

Night of the Living Dead is the original slow-moving zombie film. Barbra and her brother are visiting a cemetery when a pandemic of mass murder breaks out across America, with recently dead bodies coming to life to feast on human flesh. Her brother is mauled to death, but Barbra escapes and runs to a nearby farmhouse, where she meets Ben, who is also fleeing the zombies. There are actually five others hiding in the house, including a sick child and a hotheaded fool called Mr. Cooper. They fend off the zombies outside throughout the night, but the threat from inside the house only keeps growing.

What happens if we ignore the fact that Judges 19 is an ancient narrative and pretend for a moment that we are watching a horror film like *Psycho* or *Night of the Living Dead*?

Let's see.

Orientation (Ordinary People)

In the first scenes of a horror film, things are often quite normal. We begin in the everyday reality we are used to. The opening of *Psycho* zooms in on a single anonymous window in a city apartment block, where we meet an ordinary young woman called Marion. *Night of the Living Dead* also begins in the daylight with a very ordinary brother and sister having a very uneventful day – so far! Likewise, in Judges 19, the woman and man are unnamed, and this anonymity suits the horror genre well:

In those days Israel had no king. Now a Levite who lived in a remote area in the hill country of Ephraim took a concubine from Bethlehem in Judah. (Judg 19:1)

Here are some nameless, ordinary people. They have no idea they are about to star in a horror film.

The woman is described somewhat ambiguously as a "concubine." People have read into her description as a concubine in ways that have biased the tradition against her. The English word *concubine* makes her sound like a royal sex slave, but that's way off. It's *pilegesh* in Hebrew, which could mean a second wife, except there is no mention of a first wife in this story. If I were writing a Bible commentary, I'd have to nail down this ambiguity. But the horror film genre allows us to sit with this ambiguity a little while, so for now I'm just going to call her the "young woman" (Judg 19:3, my translation) because that's what she is called for the brief period in the story when she is safe in her father's house. It's the perfect way to describe the first victim in a horror film – young, sexually aware, and in a precarious social position.

The one thing we are told about the man is that he is a Levite – a member of the priestly tribe who is meant to be close to the spiritual heart of the nation. Hold that thought because we will soon see that the heart is rotten to the core.

We are also reminded in this opening that there is no king – and that setting is also significant, since it explains the religious chaos that is to come in the following chapters. It also foregrounds some of the social anxieties of the historical setting. Part of a king's job is to keep Israel on track spiritually. But without such central leadership at this stage in Israel's history, there is constant worry that Israel will be infected by the impure moral and religious practices of the nations all around it. You can tell a lot about a historical period by its monsters. The zombies in *Night of the Living Dead* embody 1960s fears about radiation, race, and government; the monsters in Judges 19 embody fears about religious and moral corruption in pre-monarchical Israel.

Complication (Perfect Victims)

The complication that sets the plot in motion is introduced in Judges 19:2. The young woman did something – most translations read, "she was unfaithful to him."

Historically, commentators go two ways on this. The majority take her unfaithfulness as central to the moral of the story. For them, what happens to her later in Gibeah is God's justice on her adultery: "As she sinned by her own lust, so she paid the penalty with the lust of another."[6] More recent commentators have tried to resist this awful conclusion by turning the young woman into the perfect victim – translating away any hint of scandal from her past (on this view, verse 2 becomes "she was angry with him"). But hang on – does this imply that if she *had* been guilty of adultery, her fate would be justified? To me, the revisionist

---

6. Martin Bucer, *Commentary on Judges*, 19:29.

approach is just as unsatisfactory, because in trying to create her into the perfect victim, the same assumptions are at work.

Taking up the story as a horror film gives us more options here. The monster's first victims often have a socially transgressive edge. In *Psycho*, Marion is introduced as an unmarried woman having sex on her lunch break, and the whole thing starts when she runs away with $40,000 of her boss's money. But there is, in the end, neither rhyme nor reason to their fate – a serial killer like Bates has no interest in proportionate justice, and in fact he goes on to kill the very detective who is chasing Marion! This is no exemplum about what happens to thieves or liberated young women in an ordered moral world. It is a terrifying exposé of a more unpredictable and monstrous reality in which anyone could be next.

Whereas the exemplum invites us to moralize about the young woman's backstory in Judges 19:2, or turn her into the perfect victim, the horror film lets us acknowledge the possibility of her sin without finding any justice in her fate. It allows us to respond to the horrifying madness that follows, not with calm explanation, but with deep anxiety. If this is the real world, then who is next?

Quest (Journey into Darkness)

After the incident (whatever it was), the young woman leaves and goes back to her father's house in Bethlehem. After waiting four months (maybe to check that she wasn't pregnant?), the Levite goes after her to try to "speak to her heart" (Judg 19:3, my translation) and persuade her to come back with him. This so far looks like it's going to be a classic quest, with the Levite graciously resolving the complication of their broken marriage by travelling to get her. Is this not wonderfully exemplary behavior from the Levite? Again, watch this space.

The journey into darkness is a classic horror film trope. As the sun sets, the world is revealed for what it truly is, as all our suppressed monsters come out to terrorize us. It is in the darkness that we find out who our neighbors really are. Just as Marion's journey to Bates Motel takes place in the evening, so the transition from day to night is a constant feature of the Levite's journey – it's mentioned four times. When he arrives in Bethlehem, he ends up spending five days enjoying lavish hospitality from his father-in-law (there's no mention of the young woman taking part in the food, or in the discussion). The Levite keeps trying to leave, and the host keeps insisting he stay longer. Eventually he does leave, but by then, it's the afternoon, and he has nowhere near enough time to make it back to his home in the remote hill country of Ephraim. It reminds me of *Night of the Living Dead* when Johnny and Barbra leave too late to get home from the cemetery and thus are in the worst possible place when the zombies emerge.

The Levite and the young woman make it part of the way back home, and his servant suggests they stop overnight in Jebus, which is a non-Israelite town. In a classic horror film bad decision (don't go in there!), the Levite ignores this advice and suggests they try to make it to Gibeah, which is two hours further. He doesn't want to risk staying overnight in a non-Israelite town and reckons that he will find better treatment amongst his fellow Israelites (once more, watch this space).

They make it just before sunset to Gibeah and are a little perturbed that nobody takes them in for the night – a massive breach of hospitality norms in the ancient world, where travel depended on strangers taking you in at each stop. Eventually an old man comes in from working in the fields and takes him into his house.

Rule number one for people in horror films: never let your guard down. It's just when you think you've made it to safety that the monsters come out. Marion is relieved to escape the storm and the police when she arrives at Bates Motel and is greeted by a nice young host. Likewise, having survived a risky journey, avoided staying with foreigners, and been rescued from the town square, the Levite and the young woman are finally relaxing and enjoying the nice old man's hospitality. Sure enough, right at this moment, the horrors of the night show themselves:

> While they were enjoying themselves, some of the wicked men of the city surrounded the house. Pounding on the door, they shouted to the old man who owned the house, "Bring out the man who came to your house so we can have sex with him." (Judg 19:22)

When I hear of the wicked men pounding on the door, I can't help but think of the classic scene in *Night of the Living Dead* when the zombies are banging on the door and Ben and the others are stuck inside trying to keep them out. Even better, "wicked men" here is literally "sons of *belial*," which is a way of describing those who threaten social order, and in later Jewish and Christian texts, Belial is personified as a demonic force. In other words, they are monsters.

Adding to the horror is that these wicked men are demanding to violate the man – insisting that the old man bring out the Levite so they can "know him." There is a history of debating what this means. Some have seen this as an example of homosexual lust, and others have tried to remove the sexual element almost completely and interpret the story as simply about inhospitality to strangers. Neither fits the text very well for a variety of reasons. Here once more I find that the horror film genre helpfully shifts our focus from trying to understand the motivations of the mob (is it about satisfying homosexual lust, or is it about humiliation of strangers?) to what their demand represents. In Noël Carroll's definition, monsters typically represent something threatening and impure, often by crossing boundaries. Here that threatening and impure element is represented by the idea of male-male sexual assault carried out by Israelites on a Levite, which crosses all sorts of boundaries. The Israelites are behaving like Canaanites in their lack of hospitality and oppression of outsiders. For the Levite, who is meant to be ceremonially pure (Exod 32:25–29; Deut 33:8–11), the male-male sexual activity being threatened is especially boundary-crossing (see Lev 18:22). All the social boundaries are being threatened by this mob, and the ambiguity about what they want serves to heighten the anxiety of those inside the house.[7]

But we haven't had the twist yet.

The Twist: The Calls Are Coming from Inside the House!

One important phase in a horror narrative is the twist – or the jump scare. In *Psycho*, it is when we finally meet Mother, and she turns around and . . . oh my!

The old man has so far impressed us as the one friendly resident of Gibeah who keeps the norms of hospitality – but now he shocks us. He gives up on appealing to their better judgment and proceeds to offer them a sickening compromise:

Look, here is my virgin daughter, and his concubine. I will bring them out to you now, and you can use them and do to them whatever you wish. But as for this man, don't do such an outrageous thing. (Judg 19:24)

This is an unthinkable offer, of course – two women offered to save one man. But before we have a chance to think about it, the jump scare comes without warning. The Levite takes the young woman, and he himself throws her outside to the mob.

The classic horror twist is that the monster was within all along – the calls are coming from inside the house! In *Night of the Living Dead*, they are so busy keeping the zombies outside at bay they don't realize (spoiler alert!) that the greatest threats are inside – first in Mr. Cooper's fatal stupidity, then in the little, sick girl downstairs who wakes up and devours her own mother. The zombies of Romero's film have no respect for sacred family relationships. Likewise in

---

7. Scholars have struggled to explain why the mob refuses the old man's offer of two women and yet settles for one woman a moment later. Seeing the mob like zombies outside the farmhouse door means we don't have to explain. Zombies are nonrational, chaotic evil. Don't be surprised that their negotiating position and actions are inconsistent.

Judges, it turns out that the true monsters were in the house all along – the old man who offers his own daughter, and the Levite who goes after the young woman to "speak to her heart" but then throws her to the mob to save himself and then at daybreak dismembers her body (alive or dead, we aren't told) and lies about what happened.

We thought the monsters of this story were outside the house, but they were inside all along. At daybreak, the monsters don't go away, because what appeared that night in Gibeah turns out to be true of life in general in Israel. Those charged with purity and protection of the nation are corrupt. This one appalling rape and murder in Gibeah is escalated again and again, until eventually we are witnessing scenes of mass murder and mass forced marriages (Judg 20–21).

The Boomerang Test: The Payoffs for a Tactical Reading

The ending of the narrative invites us to respond in a particular genre uptake (see tenet 11): "Just imagine! We must do something! So speak up!" (Judg 19:30). This is a call to remember and speak up about the horror of what we have seen. Sadly, traditional interpretations have responded in a very different way, trying to make sense of senseless violence, or even trying to explain away what happened as somehow an example of providential justice.

These awful interpretations start off life as a decision about the genre of the story. Readers assume this is the kind of Bible story where characters are held up as examples for imitation (an exemplum). In contrast, our tactical decision to take up the story as a horror film is one way to challenge these automatic reflexes, retraining us to see alternative ways of experiencing the story. Taken as a horror film, the text comes back with a very different meaning and, I think, better payoffs. We no longer expect the narrator to say out loud that the horrific things we are seeing are horrific (or assume that if actions aren't explicitly condemned, they must be condoned by God). We stop trying to fill the gaps and explain away the ambiguities, and instead experience the tensions in the story as part of the chaos of the night.

Most helpfully, the horror film genre suggests there might be appropriate responses to Scripture you won't find in any commentary – anxiety, outrage, or perhaps even silence. Are we left with unanswered and unsettling questions at the end of Judges 19? Absolutely. That's exactly what a great horror film director like Hitchcock or Romero would want. You don't experience a horror film as an objective commentator. It's meant to get under your skin. You're meant to feel something and take it with you. All this to say, for me, Judges 19 works much better as a horror film than as the traditional cautionary tale against "playing the harlot."

SUMMARY

In this chapter we considered whether a tactical misreading of the genre of a text can produce new and better understandings of an ancient text. Reading Judges 19 as "horror film" does a better job explaining some of the puzzling features of the story and helps us escape a history of interpretation that has not done justice to the young woman.

QUESTIONS FOR DISCUSSION AND REFLECTION

1. What assumptions about genre have influenced how Judges 19 is traditionally interpreted? Can you think of other narrative passages in the Bible that have been taken up in similar ways?
2. Thinking about your own context, what do people tend to assume about a story as soon as they know it is from the Bible?
3. Can a tactical decision about genre like the one in this chapter bring us closer to coordination with the genre the storyteller is participating in? Should that be the goal?
4. Based on the boomerang test, what are the positive and negative payoffs of the horror film reading?

FURTHER READING

Introductory

Block, Daniel I. *Judges, Ruth*. Volume 6 of The New American Commentary. Nashville: Broadman & Holman, 1999.

A standard and mostly reliable introduction to Judges.

Overstreet, Jeffrey. *Through a Screen Darkly: Looking Closer at Beauty, Truth and Evil in the Movies*. Ventura, CA: Regal, 2007.

Why we should watch more films.

Deep Dive

Hamley, Isabelle M. *Unspeakable Things Unspoken: An Irigarayan Reading of Otherness and Victimization in Judges 19–21*. Eugene, OR: Pickwick, 2019.

Creative and sensitive reading of the passage.

Hurlbert, Brandon M. "Cut & Splice: Reading Judges 19 Cinematically." *Biblical Interpretation* (2020): 1–25.

Uses Quentin Tarantino's *Django Unchained* to highlight the text's "cinematic sensibilities."

Lapsley, Jacqueline E. *Whispering the Word: Hearing Women's Stories in the Old Testament*. Louisville, KY: Westminster John Knox, 2005.

Subtle analysis of the narrator's perspective.

Taylor, Marion, ed. *Women of War, Women of Woe: Joshua and Judges through the Eyes of Nineteenth-Century Female Biblical Interpreters*. Grand Rapids: Eerdmans, 2016.
   The best nineteenth-century commentators on Judges 19 did not write traditional Bible commentaries.
Thompson, John L. *Writing the Wrongs: Women of the Old Testament among Biblical Commentators from Philo through the Reformation*. Oxford: Oxford University Press, 2001.
   Judicious survey of the text's reception up to the Reformation (chapter 3).

CHAPTER 7

WHY CAN'T YOU JUST SAY WHAT YOU MEAN?

Reading Poetry without Ruining Poetry

In 1974, United States President Richard Nixon had dinner with President Ephraim Katzir of Israel. As he proposed a toast, President Katzir retold the story of the Jewish nation's return to Zion. In the aftermath of World War II, he said, "a battered people emerged from the valley of the shadow of death into the light of liberty."[1] It's hard to miss the reference to Psalm 23. President Katzir takes King David's words about YHWH shepherding his people Israel through danger and into abundance in the late Bronze Age and uses them to speak of the twentieth-century establishment of the nation of Israel and the construction of the parliament in which the two presidents were standing.

This was not the first time, nor the last, that Psalm 23 has been used to speak into a significant moment like this. President George W. Bush quoted Psalm 23 in 2001 after the September 11 attacks. President Barack Obama quoted Psalm 23 after a mining accident in West Virginia. Coolio quoted Psalm 23 in his 1995 smash hit "Gangsta's Paradise" to talk about street violence. And you may have heard the psalm at a funeral (or in a movie) as part of the Church of England burial rites.

This practice of reaching for a psalm to give the words we need in a moment of crisis goes back to the Bible. In significant moments, both good and bad, participants in the drama of the New Testament will often speak out loud in the words of a psalm. Take Peter in Acts. When Peter stands up to address the disciples in the wake of Judas's betrayal (Acts 1:16–22), he quotes Psalms 69:25 and 109:8 out loud. In doing so, he applies the words of these psalms in ways

---

1. "Toasts of the President and President Ephraim Katzir of Israel at a State Dinner in Jerusalem. June 16, 1974," in *Richard Nixon: January 1 to August 9, 1974*, Public Papers of the Presidents of the United States (Washington: Government Printing Office, 1975), 518–25. Responding to the toast, President Nixon praised the contribution of Jewish immigrants to America, saying that their "names are legion" – an unfortunate choice of biblical allusion, if you think about it.

that go far beyond the specific situations of David's psalms.[2] He even changes the wording ("their dwelling place" becomes "*his* dwelling place") to make the psalm more appropriate to talk about Judas's betrayal.

It's not just Peter either. In John 15:25, Jesus quotes from Psalm 69 to talk about his enemies. In fact, as we'll see, as a general rule, when a psalm is quoted in the Gospels and Acts, it is spoken aloud by a character in the narrative, with the function of marking a critical moment of God's salvation, and using the hermeneutical move of typology to make a Christological point.

Why is it that the characters in the New Testament so often reach for a psalm to speak out loud in a significant moment? And what is it about a psalm that lends itself to being applied, using a typological and Christological hermeneutic, to a situation that goes far beyond the original historical context, even to the point of changing certain words to fit that occasion? I think it has a lot to do with what a psalm is – with its genre. And the first thing we need to talk about is the fact that a psalm is on the poetry spectrum. Then we will look at some of the other features that contribute to the experience of poetry, before finally addressing why psalms get applied the way they do.

THE POETRY SPECTRUM

The great American poet Robert Frost had a saying he often repeated to his friends: "Poetry is what is lost in translation."[3] I'm not so sure about that. In the hands of a great translator, not all is lost. For example, collections of English poetry will often include translated poems from the King James Bible – because even in translation, it's hard not to be struck by the power of the poetry of Song of Songs:

> Set me as a seal upon thine heart,
> as a seal upon thine arm:
> for love is strong as death;
> jealousy is cruel as the grave.[4]

Just sit with those words for a moment. Whatever was lost in translation, there sure is plenty left over.

---

2. For more technical versions of examples in this chapter, see my *Playing with Scripture: Reading Contested Biblical Texts with Gadamer and Genre Theory*, Routledge Interdisciplinary Perspectives on Biblical Criticism (Abingdon, UK: Routledge, 2024); "Gadamer, *Wirkungsgeschichtliches Bewusstsein*, and What To Do about Judas (Acts 1:12–22)," *ABR* 66 (2018): 43–58; "Do the Speakers in Acts Use Different Hermeneutics for Different OT Genres?," *JETS* 64, no. 1 (2021): 109–27.

3. Quoted in Louis Untermeyer, *The Letters of Robert Frost to Louis Untermeyer* (New York: Holt, Rinehart and Winston, 1963), 301, 386.

4. Song of Songs 8:6 KJV.

At the same time, I know what Robert Frost is getting at. The subtle connotations – even the very sound of those words in Hebrew (eleven words in total!) – is part of what this remarkable poem is. It's not enough for me to tell you that the Hebrew words for *strong* and *love* and *jealousy* and *cruel* start with similar sounds. Nor is it fun to enumerate the myriad connotations of the words translated "cruel" or "jealousy." That's like having a joke explained to you. You have to hear it for yourself. No – *feel* it for yourself.

Yet there is a persistent power, a deep translatable truth, to the simile between love and death that still resonates in any language. The words *love* and *death* are such opposing ideas that to bring them together at first seems like a reckless choice – but it works. There is something uncompromising, consuming, dangerous about love that this poem reminds us of.

When I think of my favorite English poetry, there are many images like these that I find hard to shake: John Milton's fallen angels strewn across the plains of hell "thick as autumnal leaves," or Eve's "wanton ringlets" with all their risky connotations[5]; T. S. Eliot's evening spread out against the sky "like a patient etherized upon a table"[6]; Gerard Manley Hopkins's glimpse of the grandeur of God flaming out "like shining from shook foil."[7]

A great poem is like an art installation made out of words. Take Lewis Carroll's word for it:

> 'Twas brillig, and the slithy toves
> Did gyre and gimble in the wabe:
> All mimsy were the borogoves,
> And the mome raths outgrabe.[8]

Carroll evokes such a fantastic feeling of childlike wonder – even though (or perhaps because) the words themselves are mostly nonsense. The very sound of the words is part of the meaning. Even the very feel of the words in your mouth can be part of the experience: as when Wilfred Owen describes the suffering of a dying soldier "gargling from the froth-corrupted lungs . . . bitter as the cud."[9]

It's hard to say exactly what these words mean – and yet they *mean* so

---

5. John Milton, *Paradise Lost* I.302, IV.304.

6. T. S. Eliot, "The Love Song of J. Alfred Prufrock," *Collected Poems 1909–1962* (London: Faber & Faber, 1963), 11. Used by permission.

7. Gerard Manley Hopkins, "God's Grandeur," Poetry Foundation, www.poetryfoundation.org/poems/44395/gods-grandeur, accessed 31 August 2023. Thanks, Steph Kate Judd.

8. Lewis Carroll, "Jabberwocky," in *Through the Looking-Glass* (London: Macmillan, 1872), 21.

9. Wilfred Owen, "Dulce et Decorum Est," Poetry Foundation, www.poetryfoundation.org/poems/46560/dulce-et-decorum-est, accessed 31 August 2023. Thanks, Alice Fraser.

powerfully. As Chris Lawn puts it, poetry is "language at its most playful."[10] I knew someone who was doing a thesis on the work of a living poet, and the temptation was to call up the poet and ask what the words mean – but of course, if the poet could tell them that in a phone call they wouldn't have needed to write a poem. To tweak Frost's epigram, poetry is what is lost when we try to simmer poetry down to proposition, or decode the wild metaphors into something cold, tame, and domesticated.

There is no one genre of "poetry." The dangerous and playful potential of language we've been describing can show up in various degrees and different forms, across diverse genres in disparate contexts of culture. I remember at school a friend of mine declaring that poetry wasn't poetry unless it rhymed (I think John Milton would have something to say about that). In fact, the way language is being used – its relationship to the world and to truth – is far more important in understanding poetry than particular structural or formal devices. Rather than define "poetry" in a rigid way, modern genre theory recognizes that genres like "poetry" are fuzzy around the edges (tenet 3). We shouldn't try to place texts definitively inside or outside a class called "poetry." Instead, we can place texts on a poetry spectrum (or cline), which we can sketch using a few clear prototypes. At one end is the prototype of a traffic signpost, which describes specific concrete things with maximum efficiency and accuracy (technically, language as *representation*). At the other end we find written performance art, which creates abstract experiences with maximum evocativeness and abundance of meaning (technically, language as *presentation*).[11] There is skill in producing a good street sign, but the artistry is in the background and the focus is on the world outside the text; in written performance art, the power of language itself is being foregrounded.

This spectrum raises some confronting questions for Bible scholars. Ben Witherington III observes that poetry is a "risky thing – it can mean more than you realize when first you create it."[12] What do we think about the fact that so much of God's word to us comes from the poetic end of the spectrum? How would our faith be different if God had given us a more tamable text in numbered propositions, enlisting the genre of legal drafting rather than poetry?

---

10. Chris Lawn, *Wittgenstein and Gadamer: Towards a Post-Analytic Philosophy of Language* (New York: Bloomsbury, 2004), 130.

11. See Hans-Georg Gadamer, *The Relevance of the Beautiful and Other Essays*, ed. Robert Bernasconi, trans. Nicholas Walker (Cambridge: Cambridge University Press, 1986), 142–46; Tzvetan Todorov, *Genres in Discourse*, trans. Catherine Porter (Cambridge: Cambridge University Press, 1990), 71. On Hebrew poetry's continuum of formality and "heightening effects": James L. Kugel, *The Idea of Biblical Poetry: Parallelism and Its History* (New Haven, CT: Yale University Press, 1981), 94–95.

12. Ben Witherington III, *Psalms Old and New: Exegesis, Intertextuality and Hermeneutics* (Minneapolis: Fortress, 2017), 326–27.

BIBLICAL POETRY GENRES

Before we start talking about how Hebrew poetry works, we need to get something straight. There is no "poetry" in the Hebrew Bible – if by "poetry" we mean a single genre with that name. When we talk about biblical poetry, we are attempting a comparison between the English genre (or mode) we call "poetry" (or "poetic") and a number of genres we find in the Old Testament that seem to have a similar impulse and sit on a similar end of the poetry spectrum – curses, prayers, songs, proverbs, laments, riddles, prophetic oracles, and so on.[13]

These poetic genres are often embedded within the narrative as characters respond to significant moments – for example, David's lament for Jonathan and Saul in the "Lament of the Bow" (2 Sam 1:17–27). This text, we are told, appears in something called the "Book of Jashar," and indeed many poetic texts have been curated for us in collections such as the songs of Asaph (Psalms 73–83) or the proverbs collected by Hezekiah's men (Prov 25:1). These in turn have been brought together into the three "song books" (Psalms, Song of Songs, and Lamentations) and the three "wisdom books" (Proverbs, Job, and Ecclesiastes).[14] Prophetic books will often embed various poetic genres, from hard-hitting oracles against the nations to funeral songs.

Formal Features

In English (as in Greek and Latin), a pretty safe bet that you're reading poetry is meter – a regular rhythm of stressed and unstressed (or long and short) syllables. Here is a silly thing I wrote with alternating lines of four and then three iambic feet (da-DUMs):

> I <u>want</u> to <u>be</u> a <u>syllable</u>
> with <u>emphasis</u> on <u>two</u>
> But <u>if</u> you <u>put</u> the <u>stress</u> on <u>one</u>
> the <u>lines</u> will <u>sound</u> like . . .

Try saying it out loud. It is almost impossible to say it any other way. You may also notice the strong urge to complete the final line with a word that rhymes with "shoe." Not all English poetry rhymes (Milton thought it was tasteless),

---

13. See Kugel, *Idea of Biblical Poetry*, 69–70. Jacqueline Vayntrub cautions that our conceptions of Hebrew poetry often reflect modern Greek-influenced intellectual categories and doubtful form-critical assumptions: *Beyond Orality: Biblical Poetry on Its Own Terms* (New York: Routledge, 2019), 23.

14. The framing of these books differs between canons, and the whole wisdom literature category is troublesome (see chapter 10).

but often there is a pattern in which the end vowel and consonant are the same or close (for example, in lines two and four).

Here's the thing though: Hebrew poetry works quite differently. While often rhythmic, it isn't characterized by a consistent "meter."[15] There are poetic lines, but they vary in exact length and number of stressed syllables (the line breaks you see in English Bibles are added by the translators).

There is little point looking for end rhymes, given that Hebrew nouns and verbs often attract similar sounding suffixes. What we see in Hebrew poetry is often described as "parallelism" or a kind of "thought rhyme."[16] Look at this from Psalm 33:6–9:

> [6]By the word of the LORD the heavens were made,
>   their starry host by the breath of his mouth.
> [7]He gathers the waters of the sea into jars;
>   he puts the deep into storehouses.
> [8]Let all the earth fear the LORD;
>   let all the people of the world revere him.
> [9]For he spoke, and it came to be;
>   he commanded, and it stood firm.

You may have noticed that each verse presents the one thought two ways, in slightly different words. The "word of the LORD" is answered or "seconded" by "the breath of his mouth"; the "heavens" by "their starry host." The second line takes the form and idea of the first, but develops or extends it in some way, taking it to the next level. Older textbooks describe this classic marker of Hebrew poetry as "synonymous parallelism" (one of three types invented by eighteenth-century scholar Robert Lowth), but that terminology is now recognized as misleading.[17] It's best to think of it as a syntactic choice between two options: each new line can either develop the same idea ("apposition") or move on to something else ("non-apposition").[18] This syntactic choice allows the poet to shape

---

15. See Tremper Longman III, "A Critique of Two Recent Metrical Systems," *Bib* 63, no. 2 (1982): 230–54; Michael Wade Martin, "Does Hebrew Poetry Have Meter?," *JBL* 140, no. 3 (2021): 503–29. A possible exception is the *qinah*, or lament, which is often said to be characterized by a 3–2 stressed syllable pattern, but even these are irregular by Greek, Roman, or English meter standards.

16. A "mounting semantic pressure . . . a structure of intensification": Robert Alter, *The Art of Biblical Poetry* (New York: Basic Books, 1985), 3–84.

17. See Kugel, *Idea of Biblical Poetry*, 12–13; Alter, *Art of Biblical Poetry*, 9; Robert D. Holmstedt, "Hebrew Poetry and the Appositive Style," *VT* 69 (2019): 617–48; F. W. Dobbs-Allsopp, *On Biblical Poetry* (New York: Oxford University Press, 2015); Adele Berlin, *Dynamics of Biblical Parallelism*, rev. ed. (Grand Rapids: Eerdmans, 2008), 64–65.

18. See Holmstedt, "Hebrew Poetry and the Appositive Style," 623.

the flow of information, either slowing us down to really dwell on an image or moving us on to something new. A chain of appositional lines (or versets) can go on as long as the poet thinks the idea or image has more to give – usually two lines, but sometimes three or even more lines can be "in parallel." Some psalms are very regular, consisting of a regular sequence of pairs of lines in apposition, but others, such as Psalm 137, use apposition sparingly to great effect.

The relation between these lines is more subtle than the old "synonymous" or "antithetical" categories imply. Having chosen to stay with an idea for another line, the poet has a great deal of freedom in how they play around with it. The movement is often what Robert Alter describes as "heightening or intensification . . . of focusing, specification, concretization, even what could be called dramatization."[19] James Kugel describes it as "A is so, and what's more, B."[20] This can be as simple as an increase in number ("one thing God has spoken / two things I have heard," Ps 62:11). More subtly, perhaps the poet will choose different words that give a slightly different color; move from general to specific, literal to metaphorical; or even flip things around and say something the complete opposite.[21] This overlaying of images – stereometry – reflects a way of thinking about the world.[22] To completely understand you need to see both sides of the coin.

This parallelism or appositional structure is the most distinctive feature found in most Hebrew poetry. You'll see it in sentence proverbs too (see Prov 10–31).[23] Some caution is required, though, as not every line of poetry in the Bible is part of a pair, and narrative can use apposition as well (for example, Gen 21:1).

The flexibility of Hebrew word order often allows poets to shape their parallel lines into chiasms, where matching elements of the two lines will be arranged in reverse order (i.e., A B / B A). You can see from this awkward half-translation of Psalm 19:1 how the seven words of Hebrew form an X shape (which in Greek is chi (χ), hence the name "chiasm"):

The-heavens	*declaring*	*God's-glory*
And-the-work of-his-hands	*reporting*	*the-firmament*

---

19. Alter, *Art of Biblical Poetry*, 19.

20. Kugel, *Idea of Biblical Poetry*, 23.

21. Two lines in parallel like this is technically called a "bicola," and you sometimes find three or more lines in parallel too ("tricola," etc.). The second line will sometimes be missing a verb (ellipsis), which is supplied from the first (sometimes this is reversed in a kind of enjambment, one of the many surprises biblical poets pull on us: see Alter, *Art of Biblical Poetry*, 56, 213).

22. See Bernd Janowski, *Arguing with God: A Theological Anthropology of the Psalms* (Louisville, KY: Westminster John Knox, 2013), 14–35.

23. Lines that break the expected flow of parallels often serve to spotlight something (see Ps 23:3).

Alongside apposition, another distinctive formal feature of biblical poetry is that it is notoriously laconic. Color is splashed on the canvas with an elegant economy of paint. Many of the grammatical handrails you find in narrative are left out – the Hebrew equivalents of words like "the" or "because."[24]

Playing with Words

Poetry gives permission to be especially playful with words. Here are some favorite games that biblical poets like to play.

- *Acrostic* poems are where each line starts with the next consonant of the Hebrew alphabet (Psalm 119 and Lamentations 1–4 are the classic examples). The exact effect is unclear. Did it help memorization? Do the partial acrostics of Lamentations give a sense of order in chaos, or of total destruction from A-Z? Or is it a purely aesthetic constraint to test creativity?
- *Alliteration* is where consonants are repeated for effect – such as Psalm 147:13, where "he-blesses your-sons within-you" is *berak banayk beqirbek*.
- *Assonance* is the same as alliteration but with a vowel sound – such as Psalm 102:6, where the two lines begin with words that sound similar: *damiti* (I am like) and *hayiti* (I become).
- *Diction* or *word choice* is the careful selection of words poets make, perhaps for their sound, their rarity, their connotations, or intertextual links. In Song of Songs 7:10, the "desire" of the man for the woman is a word used only one other time – in the curse on the woman in Genesis 3:16! Proper nouns like places or people can invoke all sorts of connotations for people who know the stories. For example, "Zion" in Psalm 137:1 connotes Jerusalem the city, its capture by David, a theology of God's commitment and protection, and prophetic hope for a restored future.
- *Ellipsis* or *verb gapping* is where a word is left out of the second clause but the sense is supplied or carried over from the first clause – such as Psalm 33:6, where only the first line has a <u>verb</u> ("By the word of the LORD the heavens <u>were made</u> / their starry host by the breath of his mouth").
- *Hyperbole* is where something is expressed in extreme or absolute terms to make a striking point: "No one is faithful . . . everyone lies" (Ps 12:1–2), "there is no one who does good" (14:1), "from the womb they are wayward, spreading lies" (58:3).

---

24. Though these are pointers, not proofs: see Wilfred G. E. Watson, *Classical Hebrew Poetry: A Guide to Its Techniques*, JSOTSup 26 (Sheffield: JSOT Press, 1984), 44–62.

- *Synecdoche* is the use of a part of something to represent the whole – the Lord "trains my hands for war, my fingers for battle" (Ps 144:1), which doesn't mean he missed leg day. A similar technique is merism, which identifies the two extremes to talk about everything in between – Psalm 74:17 says the Lord made "summer and winter," which doesn't mean autumn and spring are the devil's work. More generally, metonymy is where something is referred to through using something closely associated – some trust in chariots, we trust in the Lord's name, says Psalm 20:7.
- *Voice* is who is speaking to whom, and it can be shifted for effect, perhaps by shifting from second (you) to third (he) person address of God (Ps 138) or swapping grammatical gender (as in the he/she parts of the Song of Songs).
- *Word order* can be varied to put the spotlight on something – for example, when a word is moved unexpectedly to the start of a line to put the spotlight on it.
- *Wordplay*, *puns*, or *paronomasia* is when a word is used because it sounds a lot like something else (think "Dad jokes"). In Psalm 136:24, God freed us from "our enemies" (*mitzareinu*), which sounds a bit like "Egypt" (*mitzraim*).

Imagery and Metaphor

As a seasoned songwriter, Pat Pattison knows what metaphor is: "A collision between ideas that don't belong together. It jams them together and leaves us to struggle with the consequences."[25] He offers "decaffeinated rainbow" as a whimsical example of how thought-provoking this collision of ideas can be. We see a similarly evocative set of collisions in the psalms – take Psalm 102, for instance:

> My days are like the evening shadow;
>   I wither away like grass.
>
> But you, LORD, sit enthroned forever;
>   your renown endures through all generations. (Ps 102:11–12)

---

25. Pat Pattison, *Writing Better Lyrics*, 2nd ed. (Cincinnati, OH: Writer's Digest Books, 2009), 23. For a more rigorous theory of metaphor: Erin M. Heim, *Adoption in Galatians and Romans: Contemporary Metaphor Theories and the Pauline* Huiothesia *Metaphors* (Leiden: Brill, 2017), 24–112.

I normally think about my life as quite distinct from shadows and grasses, but comparing them here in a simile forces me to struggle with a confronting truth – we are temporary. And yet while God obviously doesn't need to sit down, the metaphor in the next verse contrasts my flimsiness with the stability and power of a king who is never getting off his throne.

The psalms are full of metaphors and similes (a type of metaphor introduced with "like") that bring together two ideas from different fields. The wicked and chaff in the wind (Ps 1:4). God's judgment and shattering pottery (2:9). Throats and open graves (5:9). Death and a rope (18:4). Wickedness and childbirth (7:14). Words and refined silver (12:6). Mistreating people and eating bread (14:4). People and the pupil of an eye (17:8). Defeating enemies and trampling dust in the street (18:42). God's protection and a rock, fortress, mountain, shield, horn, stronghold, furnace (18:2, 30; 21:9). The sun and a bridegroom (19:4–5).

God is often described using anthropomorphic images – sharpening his sword (Ps 7:12), working with his fingers (8:3), placing his feet (18:9), gathering water in a pile (33:7). God, and people, are also often described as animals – lions (7:2; 10:9; 17:12), worms (22:6), and winged creatures (17:8).[26] The heavens speak (19:1–4), and doors lift their heads (24:9).

Much of the power of psalms comes from their use of extended visual metaphors or "images." A tree planted by still waters (Ps 1). A bed so drenched in tears that it floats (6:6). A man getting trapped in his own hole, or net (7:15; 9:15). An angry mob, or dogs ambushing an innocent person (17:9–12; 22:16). Drowning in deep waters (18:16). A sticky mouth and bones you can count (22:15, 17). A shepherd leading his sheep through a valley, or a table prepared before enemies (23).

Some images take on special significance and can be described as "symbols" – a horn of power (Ps 18:2; 89:17, 24; 92:10; 112:9; 132:17; 148:14), a cup of blessing or judgment (16:5; 23:5; 75:8; 116:13), the parting of the heavens (18:9). Recurring motifs like fire and smoke instantly remind us of the exodus and the giving of the law at Sinai (104:32).

It can be tempting for people who study the Bible in an academic context to immediately parse the metaphors and images into something more propositional – for instance, the Lord is my shepherd = the Lord cares for us. But metaphors cannot be decoded in this way without tragic loss. What they mean is what they are – a collision of worlds that makes us see something from new and challenging angles.

---

26. God as a lion can have opposite connotations. For Joel, it's a comforting image of protection (Joel 3:16); over the page in Amos, it's a terrifying image of judgment (Amos 1:2).

The Lord and a Shepherd

In Psalm 23, we are invited to think about the Lord as "my shepherd." When processing an image, it can be helpful to slow down and ask some questions in stages:

- *See the image.* What field of activity does the image come from in its ancient context? In this case, nomadic animal herding.
- *Feel the image.* What is the emotional charge of the image? What potential connotations come with it? What unintended connotations are being left behind? A shepherd has connotations of persistent benevolence and protection against predators. We are probably not meant to wonder if the shepherd enjoys mutton.
- *Think the image.* How does this image connect with other images in Scripture? What would the logic of the poem be missing without this image? Lots of connections spring to mind – notably with David, the shepherd boy who became king. In this psalm, it complements the image of a feast and an anointing (vv. 5–6) with a sense of God's daily presence and leading through life.

Try this same process with Psalm 144. How many images can you find? Choose one, and work through these stages with it.

Staging Structure

You can instantly tell the difference between a jazz standard and a worship tune by the structure. "I Got Rhythm" alternates between the main "A" section melody ("I got rhythm . . .") and a "B" section ("old man trouble . . .") in a typical AABA structure; "How Great Is Our God" has a typical verse, chorus, verse, chorus, bridge, chorus (. . . chorus, chorus, chorus) structure. In a similar way, one of Hermann Gunkel's headline form-critical insights was that different types of psalms typically have different structures.[27]

While form critics differ on the exact categories they use, the main choices are between praise and lament psalms, and between individual and community psalms.[28] The most common form in the Psalter is individual lament – prayers

---

27. Gunkel's five main forms (hymn, community lament, royal psalm, individual lament, and individual thanksgiving) were developed substantially by Sigmund Mowinckel, Erhard Gerstenberger, and Claus Westermann.

28. Other categories are about subject matter: kings (Ps 2), wisdom (Ps 1), Torah (Ps 119), etc. Walter

for deliverance from enemies, illness, or accusation (e.g., Ps 6) – but we have a bunch of communal laments – the same but for a national crisis like the destruction of Jerusalem (e.g., Ps 74, or Lam 3). Thanksgivings tend to be individual praise declaring what God has just done for me (e.g., Ps 30; 32) or a hymn of praise describing who God is and what he's done in general (e.g., Ps 117).

The Stages of Lament

Psalm 54 demonstrates clearly the stages of an individual lament psalm. It begins with an *invocation stage* asking God for help:

¹Save me, O God, by your name;
    vindicate me by your might.
²Hear my prayer, O God;
    listen to the words of my mouth.

Then the individual names their complaint in a *lament stage*:

³Arrogant foes are attacking me;
    ruthless people are trying to kill me –
    people without regard for God.

Then there is an expression of confidence:

⁴Surely God is my help;
    the Lord is the one who sustains me.

The singer then makes clear what he wants God to do in the *petition stage*:

⁵Let evil recoil on those who slander me;
    in your faithfulness destroy them.

And in the final stage the psalmist *makes a vow* to praise God if God comes through and gets him out of this situation:

Brueggemann even groups psalms by psychological phases (orientation, disorientation, and new orientation): *The Message of the Psalms: A Theological Commentary*, Augsburg Old Testament Studies (Minneapolis: Augsburg Fortress, 1984), 19–23. Various schemes can work because psalms participate in multiple genres (tenet 1).

> [6]I will sacrifice a freewill offering to you;
>   I will praise your name, LORD, for it is good.
> [7]You have delivered me from all my troubles,
>   and my eyes have looked in triumph on my foes.
>
> See if you can identify similar stages in Psalms 3, 6, 13, and 74.

Form criticism's attention to the typical staging structure of psalm types is very much in line with modern genre theory's insights into genres as staged activities (see chapter 3). The problem, however, is when we combine this insight with a rigid classical view of genres as pithy, pure, and preliterary (see chapter 1). Inevitably, Hermann Gunkel and his mates would come across a psalm that didn't quite fit so neatly into the stages they were expecting. Psalm 40 seems to begin as a thanksgiving but quickly becomes a lament.[29] Psalm 19 starts off talking about creation but soon becomes about the law.[30] The temptation for form criticism is to "fix" a psalm to make it fit the expected staging structure – for example, by declaring that the two halves of a psalm are really independent compositions. Of course, they may well be right that the two halves of Psalm 40 or Psalm 19 started off independently (we just don't know). But one thing I'm sure of is that these psalms work just fine as they are. More than that – I think they're stunning. By getting the scissors out, we may keep Gunkel's system intact, but we deface a work of art. It's far better, I think, to expect that sometimes a psalm will break with the expected staging structure and then to see that as part of the experience – psalms are art, and art is meant to surprise us.

This allows room for poets to use other staging features. A shift in voice gets our attention. The strategic repetition of a phrase puts a spotlight on an idea – "his steadfast love endures forever" (Ps 136 NRSVue) – or fills it with content so we return to it as from a new direction (for example, the "inclusio" at the beginning and end of Ps 8).

Social Function

While form criticism fixed scholarly attention on the hypothetical institutional setting in the preexilic cult (for example in a "covenant festival"), modern genre theory invites us to consider the social function of the psalms in a new way. Why would someone *do* a psalm?

---

29. See Peter C. Craigie and Marvin E. Tate, *Psalms 1–50*, 2nd ed., WBC 19 (Nashville: Nelson, 2004), 314.

30. Artur Weiser, *The Psalms: A Commentary* (Philadelphia: Westminster, 1962), 201.

One way to understand the social situation anticipated by a psalm is to see how songs more broadly are used within the biblical narrative. Often they are in response to significant moments when God has acted in creation or salvation history. In Genesis, we have Adam's exultation over Eve ("bone of my bones and flesh of my flesh," Gen 2:23) – which is met ominously after the fall with Lamech's violent boast to his wives (Gen 4:23–24). After the Lord brings Israel out of Egypt, Moses, the Israelites, and Miriam sing songs of praise to the Lord (Exod 15:1–18, 21). When God gives the people water in the desert, they sing the song of the well (Num 21:17–18). As Moses prepares to leave the Israelites at the edge of the promised land, he reminds them of their history by teaching them a song (Deut 31:19–30). When God gives Joshua victory over the Amorites, there is another song from the Book of Jashar (Josh 10:12–14). Deborah and Barak celebrate God's deliverance with a long song (Judg 5). The more complex judge Samson even gives himself a little ditty when he slays a thousand men with a donkey's jawbone, for some reason (Judg 15:16). David's story ends with a song about how God delivered him from Saul (2 Sam 22), followed by his final poetic reflections (2 Sam 23).

Shlomo Goitein observes that women seem to have participated prominently in public life through the social action of poetic genres:

> She sang in times of love and during the days of mourning, expressed the joy of victory and the agony of defeat, words of wisdom and whispers of prayer. . . . Her poetry or her lament, her mockery or her blessing, were not only an expression of feeling or opinion; they *performed an action*.[31]

The women of Israel celebrate David's victories in a song that drives Saul mad (1 Sam 18:7; 29:5). In the books of Samuel, Hannah's prayer celebrating God's deliverance (1 Sam 2:1–10) frames the narrative that follows and introduces the criteria by which we will assess Saul and David.

Songs of salvation give way eventually to more songs of lament. David laments the deaths of Jonathan and Saul (2 Sam 1:17–27) and Abner (2 Sam 3:33). Ezekiel and Amos take up several laments against Israel and the nations (Ezek 19; 26; 27; 28; 32; Amos 5). Isaiah has songs of judgment as well as hope (Isaiah 5; 23:16; 26).

They're not songs, as such, but we might add to these the blessings in the ancestral narratives that link each generation together back to God's promise to

---

31. S. D. Goitein, "Women as Creators of Biblical Genres," trans. Michael Carasik, *Proof* 8, no. 1 (1988): 30, emphasis in original.

Abraham in Genesis 12 and are typically expressed in poetic form – Rebekah's (Gen 24:60), Jacob's and Esau's (27:27–30, 39–40), Joseph's (48:15–16), and Jacob's sons' (49). The Aaronic blessing ensures this continues indefinitely (Num 6:24–27), as does the blessing of the tribes (Deut 33). On the other hand, there are also a couple of curses – the Lord's judgments on the serpent, Eve, and Adam (Gen 3:14–19); Joshua's curse on Jericho (Josh 6:26).

Certain poetic texts have a more liturgical flavor. When moving the ark, Moses has special words to go and stop (Num 10:35–36). David equips Asaph with a standard song to extol, thank, and praise before the ark of the Lord (1 Chr 16:7). The same song is sung when the ark arrives at Solomon's temple (2 Chr 5:13), at the head of the army (20:21), and when the second temple's foundation is laid (Ezra 3:11).

To summarize, then, a defining feature of much Hebrew poetry is that it is an oral performance in response to particular events.[32] Songs and other poetic speeches in the Old Testament provide the soundtrack to significant moments. Almost always they are sung or spoken by characters within the narrative, underlining the emotional and theological weight of recent events – normally God's acts of salvation or judgment in history. They are rare moments of insight and reflection within Hebrew narrative's characteristically sparse narratorial style (see chapter 5). They do more than communicate what is happening, though; they provide words with just the right weight for the moment. Through songs, characters can express what is really going on – sounding the depths of human emotional life – from the birth of a child in Hannah's song to the death of a friend in David's lament for Jonathan.

The way characters in the New Testament speak in poetry to mark significant moments is something they pick up from their predecessors in the Old Testament. The tradition of unpacking great moments of salvation in poetry carries on in Mary's song (Luke 1:46–55), Zechariah's prophecy (Luke 1:68–79), and the praise of God in Revelation (especially Rev 4:11; 5:9–10; 15:3–4).

When Songs Become Psalms

Unlike the songs of characters embedded in narrative, however, the book of Psalms is a compilation of songs abstracted from a particular social setting. For example, the song Asaph and his priestly party sang before the ark after David brought it to Jerusalem in 1 Chronicles 16 appears as Psalm 105 without a frame.[33] This requires us to rethink the psalm genre's anticipated social function within

---

32. These register variables are arguably more crucial for identifying biblical poetry than formal features like apposition or imagery. Narratives, after all, can be beautifully written.

33. Whereas David's praise in 2 Samuel 22 shows up in Psalm 18 *with* a historical superscription.

the biblical canon, and indeed within the life of subsequent communities. What is a psalm for when it is no longer anchored to a particular character's speech in a particular moment in time?

Part of the nature of poetry is that it is about as far removed from the immediacy of speech as you can get.[34] A negotiation between buyer and seller in a market has a very clear interpersonal relationship and definite referents. If you don't know what the other person is talking about, you can ask them to point. In contrast, the words of poetry are meant to take on a life of their own. You don't need to know who Sting was married to when he wrote a love song like "Fields of Gold" – in fact, it works better for everyone if you don't think about the songwriter's personal life at all.[35]

In this respect, a psalm is the opposite of a letter (see chapter 12). The original situation of a letter is key to understanding its meaning, whereas much biblical poetry is given to us without a clear historical context. Only fourteen superscriptions in the book of Psalms identify the psalm with an event in David's story.[36] Even when they do – for example, in Psalm 51, which links to David's crime with Bathsheba (2 Sam 12) – the themes are universal enough that even garden-variety sinners can use the words in liturgical confession.[37] Jacqueline Vayntrub points out that while Hebrew poetry is, at its heart, character speech, much of it has been recontextualized in the canon into anthologies:

> The anthology shifts voice away from a singular performance captured by the story and its characters to a perpetual one, unmediated by an audience in the story-world. It would be as if Lamech speaks directly to the text's readers instead of imploring his two wives to listen in the story.[38]

The relative autonomy of a psalm and loose tethering to the original author's situation make a psalm able to be recontextualized for generations to come. Psalm 102 is a "prayer of an afflicted person who has grown weak and pours out a lament before the Lord." That could be anyone – and that is the point.

In becoming a psalm, canonical context becomes significant too. Reframed and received as part of the Writings, a collection within the Tanak or Old

---

34. See Gadamer, *Relevance of the Beautiful*, 142–46.

35. Northrup Frye describes how in verse (unlike, say, drama), the thematic takes priority over the internal narrative: *Anatomy of Criticism: Four Essays* (New York: Atheneum, 1968) 52.

36. Jamie A. Grant, "Singing the Cover Versions: Psalms, Reinterpretation and Biblical Theology in Acts 1–4," *SBET* 25.1 (2001): 34.

37. In other psalms, the superscription serves perhaps more as an illustration. For example, David in the desert introduces the theme of spiritual thirst in Psalm 63.

38. Vayntrub, *Beyond Orality*, 218.

Testament, in the Hebrew or Christian Bible, the situation that the psalm genre anticipates shifts towards the ongoing spiritual life of a community.[39] I like how Ben Witherington III locates the psalm genre in the recurring situation of synagogue and church:

> When the poetry is often as generic and universal as the Psalms, speaking to the general human conditions (the fears, the hopes, the dreams, the foibles, the prayers of humans hoping for divine help), then the door is left wide open for later meaningful appropriation in ways that go beyond, but not against, the original meaning of the poetry . . .
>
> The Psalms, in short, speak not only "for us" but if we read them and embrace them they speak "as us" . . . for they become our words in the sincere recital of them. Indeed, total immersion in the Psalms happened because they were sung, they were heard, they were responsively read, they were taught, they were memorized, they were preached to a degree unlike any other form of the OT.[40]

Being unmoored from the immediate historical situation means a psalm can be applied by future generations in new ways without being captive to the original historical context. They not only communicate a revelation of what God has done, but also give us words to respond to him, expressing the full range of our emotions – from praise to lament, and everything in between. That's what a psalm is *for*.

Types of Truth

Part of the "truth effects" of a genre is what relationship the text seeks to have with the world. Our question here is not *whether* a text is true, but *what type of truth* is presented by a text and *how* (tenet 9).

Here's something we need to get out of the way right now: Poetry in the Bible is not just pretty wallpaper; it is just as much about communicating truth as historical narrative is. For starters, it is entirely possible to use a poetic genre to describe historical or even scientific truths. The Roman writer Lucretius wrote his most famous didactic work of Epicurean philosophy (*De rerum natura*, often seen as an early source for atomic theory) in hexameter. Wilfred Owen's poems are not historical recounts, but they do reflect his real experiences as a soldier in the First World War. In a similar way, Psalms 78, 106, and 136 all recount

---

39. Which genre(s) and which situation(s) are relevant to which readers or community of readers? I'm not suggesting that a psalm's genre is subjective, but reframing the text within the canon does shift our focus from the solo speech acts of the psalmist to the team sport of the Scripture genre.

40. Witherington, *Psalms Old and New*, 324–25. He goes on to observe that this is even more relevant to a psalm than a prophetic oracle, as a psalm gives voice to the human side of the conversation (p. 330).

victories that are also narrated in prose in other places. As Og, king of Bashan, could testify, these are not metaphorical victories.

But that doesn't mean that poetry tells the truth in precisely the same way. While it can be used to recount historical events, poetry is more commonly used to embody other kinds of truths.[41] In Exodus 15, we have the Song of the Sea, which presents the same event we just had narrated for us in Exodus 14: Moses and the Israelites escape from Egypt via the sea, and Pharaoh's army is destroyed. But there are subtle differences. In the narrative version, Moses is actively involved, and the parting of the seas is the result of a strong wind (Exod 14:21–22). But in the poetry version in the next chapter, different agents are involved: the Lord himself hurls the horse and driver into the sea (Exod 15:1); the enemy is shattered by his "right hand" (v. 6); and the waters are piled up "by the blast of your nostrils" (v. 8). These anthropomorphic images focus our attention away from what intermediate personal and physical forces you would have seen if you were there on the day (Moses and the wind) and towards a more significant but invisible truth – the incomparable power of the God who saved Israel from its enemies, and the contrasting responses of his people and his enemies. The narrative and poetry are different, but not contradictory, ways of getting at the same truth.

THE USE OF PSALMS IN THE NEW TESTAMENT

We began by asking what it is about psalms that lend themselves to being quoted in significant situations in the New Testament, like when Peter stands to address the disciples in Acts 1. It turns out that responding to significant moments in salvation history is pretty much exactly what poetry in general, and psalms in particular, are for.

The way Peter recontextualizes Psalms 89 and 109 in Acts 1 can be startling if we have been trained to prioritize historical context in the application of texts – surely he has failed the first rule of responsible exegesis! But actually, good exegesis requires us to remember the genre. Peter's recontextualization of psalms in Acts 1 to reflect on a significant moment of God's salvation is entirely appropriate, because that is what psalms are for.

Different genres invite us to play different games, responding to texts with different interpretive moves (tenet 5). It is no accident that almost always when a psalm is quoted in the narrative texts of the New Testament, it is spoken aloud by a character, with the function of marking a critical moment of God's salvation

---

41. On poetry and truth, see Gadamer, *Truth and Method*, trans. Joel Weinsheimer and Donald G. Marshall, 2nd ed. (New York: Continuum, 1994), 446.

and using the hermeneutical move of typology to make a Christological point.[42] Nine times out of ten in the book of Acts, psalms are applied by using typology to make a Christological point, whereas other genres receive a range of hermeneutical treatments.[43] In the first volume of that work, Luke quotes seven psalms, all of which are spoken aloud (by Jesus, Satan, or the crowd) to make a typological and Christological point.[44] This pattern continues in the other gospels, where psalms are almost always spoken aloud by Jesus or the crowd to make a Christological point using typology.[45]

At every level we look at it, the psalms participate in genres that push in those directions. The psalms are poetry, speaking of common human experiences that are easy to relate to new situations. In the Old Testament, their social function is marking significant moments in God's salvation or judgment. The psalms are songs abstracted from historical narrative by being compiled in the Psalter, a songbook, inviting use by future communities. The psalms are part of a broader genre of Scripture that invites us to find new relevance in God's future works of salvation. Many of the psalms are framed by Davidic superscriptions, which strongly encourages a Christological hermeneutic.

To read psalms as Christian Scripture is to recognize the texts as participating in at least two genres – the psalm genre and the Scripture genre. It means having a sensitive ear to the immediate literary context of the Psalter, including the shaping of the Psalter as a whole. It means appreciating an ancient artform on its own terms – the formal features, imagery, staging, anticipated social function, and kind of truth that is being communicated. But it also means following in the hermeneutical footsteps of the apostles in Acts, and recontextualizing them in the wake of the death and resurrection of Christ Jesus. This is a two-way hermeneutical street. For Peter, experiencing the death and resurrection of Jesus leaves him in no doubt as to the ultimate meaning of the messianic psalms – we

---

42. Typology is when a significant person, place, or thing (usually in the Old Testament) is picked up and applied in a bigger way to something new (usually in the New Testament): Jesus is the ultimate David; the church is the temple. We are considering narrative texts here, but a quick look at the epistles shows that psalms are still often used in a typological way, though they are also sometimes used to support general theological, ethical, or historical points (especially in the books of 1 Peter and Hebrews).

43. See my "Do the Speakers in Acts Use Different Hermeneutics for Different OT Genres?"

44. Luke 4:10–11 (Ps 91:11–12); 13:27 (Ps 6:8); 13:35 (Ps 118:26); 19:38 (Ps 118:26); 20:17 (Ps 118:22); 20:42–3 (Ps 110:1); 23:46 (Ps 31:5–6). There is one other possible allusion by the narrator (Luke 23:34; Ps 22:18). We might add to this the songs of Mary and Zechariah (Luke 1), which, though distinct compositions, make strong use of the psalm genre.

45. Matthew 4:6 (Ps 91:11–12), 7:23 (Ps 6:8?), 13:35 (Ps 78:2), 21:9 (Ps 118:25–26), 21:16 (Ps 8:2), 21:42 (Ps 118:22–23), 22:44 (Ps 110:1), 23:39 (Ps 118:26), 27:46 (Ps 22:1). Mark 11:9–10 (Ps 118:25–26), 12:10–11 (Ps 118:22–23), 12:36 (Ps 110:1), 15:34 (Ps 22:1). John 2:17 (Ps 69:9), 10:34 (Ps 82:6), 12:13 (Ps 118:25–26), 13:18 (Ps 41:9), and 15:25 (Ps 69:4; cf. 35:19). I say "almost always" because another two psalms are quoted by the narrator in John 19:24 (Ps 22:18) and 19:36 (Ps 34:20). There are many poetic texts from the prophets we could add to this list: for example, Isaiah 6:9–10 in Matthew 13.

know Jesus is the Christ because God raised him from the dead. At the same time, the psalms help Peter know how to think and feel when the close friend of the Christ turns out to be his betrayer.

SUMMARY

Whatever you do, don't ask a psalmist, "What do you really mean?" If God wanted to speak only in prose, he could have. But as it happens, he has chosen to put a significant amount of poetry in the Bible. Personally, I'm deeply grateful.

To take up a psalm for what it is, we need to pay attention to its function within a recurring social situation (tenet 7). There are lots of poetic genres in the Bible, but one of the most significant is the psalm. While formal features like parallelism and imagery are important aspects of this genre, modern genre theory encourages us to look deeper into the social situation and function. Why would someone *do* a psalm? Looking at how psalm-like poetry is embedded within the narrative texts gives us a strong clue. Biblical poetry is often an oral performance in response to significant situations of God's justice or salvation.

When we get to the New Testament, this understanding clarifies what is going on when characters use Old Testament psalms. Good exegesis, then as now, requires us to pay attention to genre. The apostles don't apply psalms by using the same hermeneutic as legal or narrative passages; they recontextualize it, almost always using typological hermeneutical moves to make a Christological point. This flows naturally from our understanding of what psalms are for.

Taken up as Christian Scripture, therefore, a psalm participates in multiple genres (tenet 1). We must appreciate the original literary context of this ancient artform. But we also recognize psalms as Scripture – texts that speak within a canonical context and continue to be authoritative and relevant in our community today. Living in the wake of the resurrection, we take them on our lips as songs of salvation brought through Jesus Christ.

Suggested Workflow for Interpreting Poetry

History

☐ Is the poetry framed within a specific situation or context – for example, by being embedded in a narrative or introduced by a superscription? Are there clues that point to a specific time or place? What people, places, things, cultural concepts, or events are portrayed? Does it take on the voice of a particular figure or group? What beliefs and values are assumed?

☐ Is there a parallel description of similar events in a different genre somewhere else in the Bible?

☐ What is this genre of poetry for? What is the probable function and recurring social situation that this kind of poetry responds to? What is the function of the genre that the poetry is embedded in? How do these two functions interact?

☐ How have communities in different times, places, and cultures understood and applied this poetry to themselves? Given your own tradition, what assumptions are you likely to make about the poetry?

Literature

☐ Where on the poetry spectrum does the language usage seem to belong? Is it trying to represent its subject matter transparently (like a sign warning you about "Ice on Road" ahead), or does it present itself as an artwork to be focused on (like Samuel Taylor Coleridge's poem "Frost at Midnight")?

☐ Read through the work carefully a few times. Can you identify clear stages – paying attention to changes of content, voice, or vibe?

☐ Is the staging structure familiar, meeting your expectations for a particular genre of poetry – for example, individual lament, thanksgiving psalm, and so on? Or does it depart from the expected staging structure? Either way, how does each stage contribute to the experience of the poem and serve the function of the genre? What journey does it take you on?

☐ What images or metaphors are being used? See each image, feel each image, and think through each image. What would be missing if these images were not used?

☐ Mark out the lines that are in apposition. How do they reinforce each other?

☐ What other ways does the poet play with words?

Scripture

☐ What types of truth are being portrayed in this poetry? For example, is it recounting specific events, or describing a general human experience?

☐ What perspective on God, people, life, history, suffering, justice, the world, and so on is being assumed or developed? How might this develop, or balance, or complicate our systematic theology? What would be missing from our understanding of God and ourselves if this poetry were missing or overlooked?

☐ Does the poetry pick up motifs from other parts of the Bible? Are there any loaded symbols (people, places, things, and so on) that might be picked up typologically and reapplied in light of the death and resurrection of Jesus?

☐ Where might the poetry's theological assumptions or emotional charge come into contact with your life, or that of your community? How might this poetry help calibrate our moral compass? Are there necessary or possible implications for our lives? How *shouldn't* we apply this text?

QUESTIONS FOR DISCUSSION AND REFLECTION

1. What are some of your favorite poems, and why are they meaningful to you? If you don't like poetry, can you explain why not?

2. Pick a few of your favorite Bible verses. Where might you place them on the poetry spectrum? What are some potential benefits of seeing poetry as a spectrum rather than as a single genre?

3. What happens to the meaning of a song when it is taken out of a particular situation in a narrative and placed in a collection like the Psalms?

4. Compare the descriptions of Joshua's victory over the Amorite kings in Joshua 10:9–11 and 10:12–14. How would you describe the genre and truth effects of each description? Are they describing separate events, or the same event in different ways?

5. How might this chapter's description of the poetry genre sit with Christian beliefs about the clarity and authority of Scripture? What points of tension can you see?

FURTHER READING

Introductory

Longman, Tremper, III. *How to Read the Psalms*. Downers Grove, IL: InterVarsity Press, 1988.

> Perceptive guide for reading poetry.

Deep Dive

Alter, Robert. *The Art of Biblical Poetry*. New York: Basic Books, 1985.

> Classic on poetry in the Bible.

Holmstedt, Robert D. "Hebrew Poetry and the Appositive Style." *Vetus Testamentum* 69 (2019): 617–48.

> Recent article on apposition.

Kugel, James L. *The Idea of Biblical Poetry: Parallelism and Its History.* New Haven, CT: Yale University Press, 1981.

    Classic on biblical poetry as a spectrum.

Vayntrub, Jacqueline. *Beyond Orality: Biblical Poetry on Its Own Terms.* The Ancient World. London: Routledge, 2019.

    Understanding poetry in its biblical narrative frame.

CHAPTER 8

BUT WHAT KIND OF TRUE?

Genesis 1 and the Poetry Spectrum

It's Christmas Eve 1968, and the Apollo 8 crew are sixty-eight hours into their mission, orbiting the moon. They are the first three humans to see the earth rise on the horizon of the moon. Back home, a billion people – a quarter of everyone alive on earth – are watching. NASA and the astronauts had thought long and hard about what they should say to mark this moment. In the end, they decide to begin their message with these words:

> For all the people on Earth, the crew of Apollo 8 has a message we would like to send you:
>
> In the beginning God created the heaven and the earth.
> And the earth was without form, and void; and darkness was upon the face of the deep.
> And the Spirit of God moved upon the face of the waters.
> And God said, Let there be light: and there was light.
> And God saw the light, that it was good: and God divided the light from the darkness.[1]

These, of course, are the first few verses of Genesis 1 from the King James Version. They are some of the most recognizable words in human history, shaping how billions of people see the earth and their place in the universe. But the familiarity of the text can also, paradoxically, make it harder to hear what it says. We bring to it all sorts of preunderstandings, including the fundamental question of what the text *is* – its genre. And here, as much as anywhere, genre makes a huge difference.

Way back in the introduction to this book, I raised the problem of nailing down the genre of Genesis 1. Some call it simple "prose narrative," part of the

---

1. William Anders, Jim Lovell, and Frank Borman, "Apollo 8 Christmas Eve Broadcast, " ed. David R. Williams, NASA, 24 December 1968, https://nssdc.gsfc.nasa.gov/planetary/lunar/apollo8_xmas.html.

continuous temporal development from Genesis to 2 Kings (and any doubt about its status as "nonfiction" is put down to modern critical skepticism about its truth claims).[2] We might split the difference and call it "elevated prose,"[3] or perhaps "poetic prose or prosaic poetry."[4] Karl Barth called it "'non-historical' history"; Bill Arnold calls it "mytho-historical" discourse.[5] John Goldingay suggests that Westerners need to read it as "verse" in order to remind us not to read it as straightforward narrative.

Of course, there is much more at stake in this whole poetry/prose debate than just about verb forms, object markers, and poetic parallelism. Start talking about the genre of Genesis 1 and you are walking right into a long-running and passionate proxy war about whether the Bible is inerrant, whether Genesis is fiction or nonfiction, and what we should do about science and evolution.[6] Readers will often jump from a vague genre designation (poetry or prose narrative) to equally blunt terms taken from our own literary culture (fiction or nonfiction). But my question here is not primarily about the truth of the Bible or scientific accounts of the earth's origins. I'm confident it is telling the truth – but what is it trying to say?

IS IT POETRY?

Having loaded our tasting plate with twelve insights from modern genre theory (chapters 2 and 3), and considered some of the dynamics of biblical narrative (chapter 5) and poetry (chapter 7), we are in a better position to understand what's going on and what would be required to decide what Genesis 1 is. Modern genre theory complicates the simplistic binaries of poetry/narrative, myth/history, and fact/fiction that are assumed in many of our tacit uptakes of Genesis 1. The ancient text refuses to fit into our modern genre categories – what we mean by "history" is nothing like what the ancient author is doing, but that doesn't mean they are doing "make-believe" either. We must take up modern genre theory's invitation to a historical (diachronic) perspective on genre, recognizing that what "poetry" or "history" is for us will be very different than what it was for those in the ancient world.

The problem is, however, that it's hard to find points of comparison for

---

2. See Vern S. Poythress, "Dealing with the Genre of Genesis and Its Opening Chapters," *WTJ* 78.2 (2016): 217–30.

3. Gordon J. Wenham, *Genesis 1–15*, WBC 1 (Waco, TX: Word, 1987), 10.

4. John Goldingay, *Genesis*, Baker Commentary on the Old Testament: Pentateuch (Grand Rapids: Baker Academic, 2020), 21.

5. Bill T. Arnold, "Genesis and the Challenges of a 21st-Century Reading," *ProEccl* 29.4 (2020): 403.

6. See Poythress, "Dealing with the Genre of Genesis." To test this out, I recently asked Twitter, "What genre is Genesis 1?" I don't recommend you do the same.

Genesis 1. The closest texts to it in the Old Testament are the creation psalms (Pss 8; 104; Job 38–41), and as we will see, ancient Near Eastern creation accounts give us as much to contrast as to compare. Let's start with some of the observations we made about poetry in the Bible and see how well this genre fits with Genesis 1.

Formal Features

The text of Genesis 1 doesn't exactly jump out at us as Hebrew poetry, as it lacks the telltale sign of consistent parallelism or apposition.[7] The exception is verse 27, which seems to have three lines in apposition, and perhaps the spoken blessing in verse 28.[8]

Apart from this, the formal features are mostly that of prose. From verse 3, the verb forms are anchored around a string of *wayyiqtols* (a type of Hebrew verb that marks out the mainline events), which is often indicative of prose narrative, although psalms can use *wayyiqtols* to narrate events too (Pss 78; 105–6).

But even prose genres might be placed somewhere on the poetry spectrum. Just as Psalm 148 tours the heavens and earth with the repeated call to "praise him," so in Genesis 1, there is an undeniably rhythmic quality. The repetition of structural markers ("there was evening, and there was morning, the second day," "saw that it was good . . . it was good . . . it was very good") must be more than merely functional information flow (we know that morning follows evening – that's what "day" means – we don't need to be told six times!). The orderliness of the words reflects the orderliness of creation itself, and the grand register reflects the grandeur of the transcendent creator (in contrast to the next creation account, which is down-to-earth, stressing God's immanence).

This kind of self-conscious use of language, the fusion of form with message, is one of the hallmarks of the poetry end of the spectrum. The rhythmic quality, numbered sequence, and elevated style would make this chapter much easier to learn and recite liturgically than the parallel account in Genesis 2. This could suggest a text designed with an ear for performance, again perhaps pushing us slightly further down the spectrum towards poetry.[9]

Imagery and Metaphor

It is interesting to compare Genesis 1 to Psalm 8, which depicts the same creation using anthropomorphic images ("the work of your fingers," v. 3), or Psalm 104 ("he stretches out the heavens like a tent," v. 2).

---

7. Though narrative occasionally uses parallelism to mark a point (Gen 21:1) and poetry doesn't always use parallelism.

8. See Wenham, *Genesis*, 32.

9. Thanks, Andrew Shead, for the stream of consciousness on a train that inspired this paragraph.

In contrast, it's not clear how many (if any) images are being employed in Genesis 1, as most of the language can be taken as colorful but direct descriptions. Here the waters don't "flee" (Ps 104:7 NRSVue); they are "separated" (Gen 1:7). The spirit "hovering" over the waters in verse 2 may be an image. The descriptions of the sky as a "vault" (v. 6) sounds like a metaphor to us, but in the ancient world it just reflects common cosmological assumptions (just as we describe a "sunrise" without thinking of it as a metaphor). Apart from these, everything is representing itself. The animals are real animals; the humans are real humans.

Staging Structures

Genesis 1 is tightly structured. Verses 1–2 provide an introduction to an inhospitable landscape ("the earth was formless and empty"). Then we get a sequence of six "days" recounted with recurring phases: (1) what God says, (2) what then happens, (3) an assessment, and (4) a time marker:

(1) And God said, "Let there be light,"
(2) and there was light.
(3) God saw that the light was good, and he separated the light from the darkness. God called the light "day," and the darkness he called "night."
(4) And there was evening, and there was morning – the first day.

The pattern is extended on the sixth day, when God creates humanity, with a poetic apposition (v. 27) and a blessing and commission (vv. 28–29). The seventh day contains no speech or creation, but just a completion statement (Gen 2:1), and a statement that God blessed the day and rested (2:3).

A further structural observation about the six days is that the first three seem to create spaces by separating things (light and water), perhaps reversing the "formlessness" of the landscape. The last three put things in those spaces, perhaps reversing the "emptiness" of the landscape.

1	Day and night	4	Sun, moon, and stars
2	Sky and oceans	5	Birds and fish
3	Land and seas	6	Animals and humans

This pattern seems to explain why day and night is created on day one, when the light-bearers themselves are not created until day four. Rather than a strictly chronological sequence of activities as in a narrative, the information flow is organized according to more abstract principles. Within the Pentateuch, the use of tight structuring and repetitive forms to recount an origins story reminds me a little of a census (Num 1:20–54), camping layout (2:1–34), or a land allocation (34:1–29). But perhaps the strongest parallel is with the recount of the building of the tabernacle in Exodus 35–40. God speaks (40:6–15), then Moses makes it happen (40:16–33). So "all the work on the tabernacle, the tent of meeting, was completed" (39:32) just as "the heavens and the earth were completed in all their vast array" (Gen 2:1). Long before books could be printed with full-color graphics, this kind of highly structured prose can function a bit like a spoken-word diagram or an audiobook tour of the temple or cosmos.[10]

Whether the temporal markers are transparently recounting a sequence of events or are themselves part of the artwork being presented will depend on where we locate the text on the poetry spectrum. The further down the poetry end of the spectrum, the more imaginatively we need to approach the use of language. In this case, perhaps Genesis 1 is best experienced as a theological infographic, a seven-panel praise mural, or a spoken-word worship diorama.

One possibility we can exclude is that Genesis 1 is a straight narrative genre in the sense we described in chapter 5. While recount genres are used to relay events in chronological order (e.g., the making of the tabernacle), a narrative is driven forward in time by the dynamics of tension and a resolution. While Genesis 2 has tension (the lack of a worker, the lack of a suitable helper), in Genesis 1 there is none – man and woman are created at the same time, and it is no problem that the garden is created before the gardener. Genesis 1 may be prose recounting of creation, but it is not crafted as a typical narrative.[11]

Social Function

While Genesis 1 embeds oral performances (the deliberation and blessing of vv. 26–28), there is no indication that Genesis 1 anticipates the kind of oral performance register that we've seen above in psalms. This doesn't rule out Genesis 1 as a kind of poetry, but it would be a different kind of poetry from what we see embedded throughout the Old Testament.

It was fashionable once to describe Genesis 1 as a Priestly reworking of ancient Near Eastern creation texts like Enuma Elish.[12] This is doubtful, as the picture of God that Genesis presents – one unrivalled God creating everything

---

10. Thanks, George Athas, for the analogy of a diagram.

11. What follows after Genesis 1, however, is narrative. As Bill Arnold observes, the mythology of ancient Near Eastern cosmogonies has been dragged into a narrative to serve a different function.

12. See, for example, John B. Gabel et al., *The Bible as Literature: An Introduction*, 5th ed. (New York: Oxford University Press, 2006), 49.

by his effortless word – is just so different from the bloody conflicts and sexual exploits of polytheistic creation accounts. Nor are there enough direct parallels of form or style to suggest a conscious polemic.

More likely what we are dealing with here are texts with similar social functions and perhaps a shared cosmological understanding. Within the literature of the ancient world, etiological narratives and poems provide obvious parallels for understanding the social function of Genesis 1. Etiological narratives explain something about the world by giving the backstory. To read the function of Genesis 1 as similar to an etiology or cosmogony is surely not far off the mark. Through it we get a clear picture of the purposeful origins and order of the world we experience, the dignified place of humans in it, and the reason why the seventh day is a day of special rest.[13] However it is important to remember that these are parallels not proformas, and genres exist within social contexts. The way the ancient Babylonians imagined the universe to fit together and the stories they told about its origins (their "cosmology" and "cosmogony") might be quite different from the worldview of ancient Israelites. Polytheism makes a difference in how you see the world.

Types of Truth

I am committed to the truth of the Bible, but I am not committed to my preconceptions about what *kind* of truth is being communicated.[14] Genesis 1 is true – Amen! – but what type of truth are we talking about?

It is possible to read Genesis 1 as presenting astronomical truths. However, this reading raises some questions. In John Calvin's day, there was a big debate over why the moon is listed as the second greatest light when astronomers know that the other stars and planets actually are much bigger. Read as an astronomy textbook, Genesis is not very reliable – but, says Calvin, this misses the point of what Genesis is trying to communicate:

> If the astronomer inquires respecting the actual dimensions of the stars, he will find the moon to be less than Saturn; but this is something abstruse, for to the sight it appears differently. Moses, therefore, rather adapts his discourse to common usage. . . . There is therefore no reason why janglers should deride the unskilfulness of Moses in making the moon the second luminary; for he does not call us up into heaven, he only proposes things which lie open before our eyes. Let the astronomers possess their more exalted knowledge; but, in the meantime,

---

13. On etiology and the function of Genesis, see Arnold, "Genesis and the Challenges."
14. Thanks, Andrew Shead, for this precious insight.

they who perceive by the moon the splendor of night, are convicted by its use of perverse ingratitude unless they acknowledge the beneficence of God.[15]

Don't be a "jangler"! Similar issues arise for us today when we try to mine the text for what it says about evolution, or ask how it is possible for the plants to photosynthesize if the sun isn't made until the fourth day. I would humbly suggest that a reading of the text as communicating chronological truths about the sequence in which life on earth emerged fails the boomerang test (see chapter 4). The simple reason is that Genesis 2 presents the same creation in a different order. In Genesis 1, humans are made on day six after everything else. But in Genesis 2, the earthling is created before the garden (2:8) and the animals (2:19). And whereas in Genesis 1, man and woman are both described together, in Genesis 2, woman is made after man, not at the same time.

Now what do we make of this? People have tried valiantly to massage the two accounts to fit them both into the same timeline, but for me the boomerang just isn't coming back. The different orders, I think, are our best clue that we're not dealing with a linear recounting of events, but something more. The purpose and focus of each account are slightly different – with a different but complementary emphasis leading to a different sequence.

Reading Genesis 1 with Apollo 8

In terms of formal features like apposition and verbal forms, Genesis 1 reads comfortably as prose. Yet poetry is a spectrum that is about more than formal features. The rhythm of Genesis 1 lends itself to performance, and the apparent social function suggests it might belong further down the poetry end of the spectrum than other parts of Genesis. For me, the best illustration of the poetic genre of Genesis 1 comes from the crew of Apollo 8 when they read Genesis 1 to humanity on Christmas Eve 1968 as they glimpsed the earth rise on their horizon. With the Vietnam War on everyone's mind, nobody knew how to mark the moment for all humankind without sounding crass. In the end, Christine Laitin, who was married to someone on the Apollo project, suggested they read from Genesis 1.

It's a striking choice of text. Here are three people viewing the earth from space, demonstrating the heights of humanity's scientific power. What could an ancient cosmogony like Genesis possibly teach such clever people? What could it tell them about the world that they couldn't already see in greater clarity than

---

15. John Calvin, *Commentary on Genesis*, vol. 1, CCEL, on Genesis 1:16, www.ccel.org/ccel/calvin/calcom01.vii.i.html.

anyone who has ever lived, glimpsing the whole earth for the first time from space? In that moment, I think the astronauts were reaching for more than information about the earth. Just as the characters in the New Testament so often reach for a psalm to speak out loud in a significant moment, they were reaching for poetry to express the emotional and spiritual depth of their experience.

Genesis 1 gave them what they were reaching for because, like a psalm, its genre is well down the poetry end of the spectrum when it comes to social function. Here are words to perform – or perhaps even recite as an act of worship. It is a fitting response to glimpsing God's sublime creation and our small but precious place within it. Bill Arnold suggests that the function of Genesis 1 as Scripture for the church is not to know things about how the world was made, but to know God through an individual and corporate experience of his salvation.[16] This might suggest the ultimate boomerang test of our chosen genre uptake: If we seek answers to scientific curiosities in Genesis, all we get are more difficulties. But if we take up Genesis to help us wonder at the created order, understand the meaning of our existence, and get a sense of our place in the universe, then – like the Apollo 8 astronauts and billions of other readers over the millennia – we will get what we came for and more. We might even start getting to know our creator.

SUMMARY

When it comes to Genesis 1, modern genre theory again invites us to consider not just what it is but what it does for us (tenet 8). We find a text that is written in highly structured prose, beautifully arranged to lead our imagination on a tour of creation. It uses language in ways that are towards the poetry end of the spectrum but without the parallelism or heavy-lifting imagery of typical biblical poetry.

In terms of social setting, there is no indication that it is meant to be taken as the kind of oral performance we see in Psalms. What it does do is fulfil a similar function to other ancient Near Eastern cosmogonies, though with a very different theological message. It's a genre for more than merely satisfying our curiosity about how the world was put together. One way to think of the experience of Genesis 1 is as a kind of theological infographic, a seven-panel praise mural, or a spoken-word worship diorama. It presents the true origins of the world in a way that still today leads to wonder and worship. As a chronological recounting of events, it fails the boomerang test (see chapter 4), but as an introduction to the origins and orderliness of the world we live in, there's nothing like it.

---

16. Arnold, "Genesis and the Challenges," 406.

QUESTIONS FOR DISCUSSION AND REFLECTION

1. What genre(s) do you think Genesis 1 participates in most strongly? Would your answer change if Genesis 1 were its own book of the Bible and not the introduction to the narrative history of Genesis 2–50?
2. How does the creation account in Genesis 2 complement that of Genesis 1? Is this complementariness reflected in their respective genres?

FURTHER READING

Introductory

Charles, J. Daryl, ed. *Reading Genesis 1–2: An Evangelical Conversation*. Peabody, MA: Hendrickson, 2013.

    Useful conversation between five evangelical views.

Collins, C. John. *Reading Genesis Well: Navigating History, Poetry, Science, and Truth in Genesis 1–11*. Grand Rapids: Zondervan, 2018.

    Introduces some of the issues of meaning and truth.

Deep Dive

Greenwood, Kyle, ed. *Since the Beginning: Interpreting Genesis 1 and 2 through the Ages*. Grand Rapids: Baker Academic, 2018.

    On the history of interpretation more broadly.

Johnson, Dru. *The Universal Story: Genesis 1–11*. Transformative Word. Bellingham, WA: Lexham, 2018.

    Superb analysis of text and biblical worldview.

CHAPTER 9

HOW TO START A CULT

Reading Apocalypse as Apocalypse

Here's a quiz to start us off. I'll begin with an easy question:

1. What do all the following men have in common: Barack Obama, Donald Trump, Pope John Paul II, Pope Francis, all the other popes, Emperor Nero, Henry Kissinger, Napoleon?
Answer: They are all the antichrist.[1]

2. Which popular soft-drink is secretly satanic?
Answer: Monster Energy Drink, of course. The "M" in the logo is actually three Hebrew vavs (ווו) which gives a numerical value of 6–6–6.[2]

3. What day in 2016 was the rapture most likely to take place?
Answer: 10 October 2016 was the all-time high of 189 on the Rapture Ready Index, which tracks forty-five indicators of pretribulation rapture activity across the world, from floods to occult practices.[3]

I know all this because in preparation for this chapter, I spent a lot of time on YouTube, diving down a rabbit hole populated by weird and wonderful speculation based on the books of Daniel and Revelation. Turns out you are only ever a couple of autoplay videos away from joining a sect. I learned from an "end-times survivors group" that the easiest way to identify the antichrist is to convert their name to numbers and add them up. I learnt all about the perils of microchips and barcodes, and how the world banking system is an elaborate front for the seven-headed, ten-horned empire that is about to be revealed. I even delved down

---

1. At least according to some end-times comments on Daniel and Revelation I watched on various YouTube channels.
2. In gematria (Hebrew number games), you *add* the values together, so the satanic code on the can is actually "18."
3. "The Rapture Ready Index," Rapture Ready, 4 September 2023, www.raptureready.com/rapture-ready-index.

into the comments section and nearly got into a debate with a pseudonymous user who had a whole video on Daniel 11:37 proposing a new translation of the Hebrew to finally reveal the identity of the antichrist (turns out the user didn't actually know Hebrew, and that's half the fun of YouTube). It's fair to say that my "videos you might like" algorithm will likely never recover from researching this chapter.

Books like Daniel and Revelation have prompted more wild speculation and conspiracy theories about the future than perhaps any other books in the Bible. If one of your life goals is to start your own conspiracy-theory YouTube channel, this kind of literature will give you lots of material to work with.

Given these dangers, however, you might be tempted to stay well away from these books of the Bible (or at least stick to the court stories in Daniel 1–6 and the letters in Revelation 2–3). I think a lot of Christian preachers would be, frankly, scared of tackling a sermon on Daniel 10–12.

We should avoid both these extremes because these wild books are part of how God has chosen to reveal himself to us. Daniel and Revelation offer messages that, in their own distinctive way, are relevant to us and authoritative over us today. To understand what they are saying, let's spend some time thinking about the question of genre. We will begin by describing the formal features and content that form the basis of standard definitions of the apocalypse genre. Yet modern genre theory encourages us to ask not just how apocalypses are written but also what situations they arise in (tenet 7) and what functions they perform (tenet 8).

The next section of this chapter will introduce an ongoing conversation about the social function of the apocalypse genre. To draw together what difference all this makes to our interpretation of the Bible, we will finish this chapter with a reading of Daniel 7 in which I try to sketch out something of the distinctive experience of reading an apocalypse.

INTRODUCING THE GENRE APOCALYPSE

Tim LaHaye, coauthor of the incredibly successful *Left Behind* series, has a golden rule for interpretation that drives this reading of Revelation: "Take every word at its primary, ordinary, usual, literal meaning unless the facts of the immediate text, studied in the light of related passages and axiomatic and fundamental truths, clearly indicate otherwise."[4] Adopting this as your golden rule basically rules out reading Revelation as anything other than a prediction of concrete future events in chronological sequence.

---

4. Tim LaHaye, *Revelation Unveiled* (Grand Rapids: Zondervan, 1999), 17.

But where does this golden rule come from? It is not a universally self-evident principle of theology or hermeneutics. It is a decision about the genre of the text – an assumption that we as readers bring to the text before we even start reading. To work out whether this assumption is helpful or unhelpful, we need to start coming up to speed on a genre that was all the rage in Judea around the time when Jesus was born called *apocalypse*.

To begin thinking about the "apocalypse" genre, forget every sci-fi, end-of-the-world action movie you've seen. "Apocalypse" comes from a Greek word that means something like "reveal" or "disclose." This hints at what we often find in the apocalypse genre – "*secrets*."[5] It is all about pulling back the curtain, often through dreams or visions, on the unseen spiritual realities determining human destiny. This reality is both present (in the unseen but real world of angels and demons) and future (in some kind of final judgment, whether personal or global in scale).

But hold on – I'm getting ahead of myself here. As we will see, coming up with a definition like this turns out to be much harder than we might expect. Genres are fuzzy around the edges, so it's probably better to start with a couple of prototypes (tenet 3).

The term *apocalypse* was first attached as a genre label to the New Testament book of Revelation, based on its opening line:

> The revelation [*apocalypsis*] from Jesus Christ, which God gave him to show his servants what must soon take place. He made it known by sending his angel to his servant John. (Rev 1:1)

The apocalypse genre as a whole gets its name from Revelation (even though there were Jewish apocalypses before it). That's our first prototype for thinking about the genre, and our second will be the back part of the book of Daniel (chapters 7–12). We will also want to throw in the bonus Bible books of 1 Enoch, 4 Ezra, and 2 Baruch.[6]

The fact that the genre's name refers to the Greek word for a Christian book (Revelation) hints that Jewish apocalyptic texts were not generally called "apocalypses" until later. That said, it's not hard to see how the book of Revelation

---

5. Philipp Vielhauer and Georg Strecker, "Apocalypses and Related Subjects: Introduction," in *New Testament Apocrypha*, rev. ed., ed. Wilhelm Schneemelcher, trans. R. McL. Wilson (Louisville, KY: Westminster John Knox, 1991), 549.

6. They're a great read, but only considered canonical by certain Orthodox Christian traditions so you won't find them in most Bibles. First Enoch is five separate works: the Book of Watchers (1–36), Similitudes (37–71), Astronomical Book (72–82), Book of Dreams (83–90), and the Epistle of Enoch (91–108).

(and other books that were labelled by their authors or copyists as "apocalypses") is developing something that has its origins in the books of Daniel and 1 Enoch.

This is a good illustration of where we need to be aware of the historical development aspect to genres – they are, after all, only "relatively stable" (tenet 2).[7] The apocalyptic genre seems to have developed out of the biblical prophetic and wisdom traditions, and it became quite a popular genre in the couple of centuries before and after Christ. There are a few apocalyptic-ish elements in the Old Testament, like Isaiah 24–27 and parts of Ezekiel and Zechariah, but most of the examples come from outside the Bible. Some New Testament passages apart from Revelation also flirt with the apocalypse genre, such as Jesus's teaching in Mark 13:5–31 (plus Matt 24:1–51; 25:31–46; Luke 21:5–36), the description of postresurrection events in Matthew 27:51–53 and 28:2–4, and Paul's exhortations regarding the "man of lawlessness" in 2 Thessalonians 2:1–12.[8]

Modern study of apocalyptic literature as a distinct genre goes back at least to the early 1830s.[9] Yet the apocalypse genre received little love from within biblical studies until late in the twentieth century. Many theologians had quite a dim view of it, preferring the civilized world of respectable major prophets to the chaos of angels and demons. Form criticism, the obvious home for the study of biblical genres in the nineteenth and twentieth centuries, didn't see apocalypse as a proper "genre" but as a "mixed composition." It was more interested in the pure, pithy, and preliterary genres (like myths, visions, and prayers) embedded in this literature (see chapter 1). The genre was so neglected, in fact, that in 1970, Klaus Koch published *Ratlos vor der Apokalyptik* – "Baffled by Apocalyptic: A Polemic about a Neglected Field of Biblical Studies and the Damaging Repercussions for Theology and Philosophy" – which I can only assume was a strong favorite for Title of the Year in 1970.[10]

But then in the mid-1970s came the invention of disco, psychedelic drugs, and a renewal of interest in the apocalypse genre. (These things may not all have been related.) It's an important period for genre theory and the Bible because many scholars were more influenced by literary genre theory than by home-brew form criticism. John Collins is one significant North American figure in this movement. While his views on disco are not well documented, he did lead

7. Paolo Sacchi traces their development from preexilic southern Israel onwards: *Jewish Apocalyptic and Its History*, trans. William J. Short, JSPSup 20 (Sheffield: Sheffield Academic Press, 1990), 107. For a survey of diachronic studies: Lorenzo DiTommaso, "Apocalypses and Apocalypticism in Antiquity: (Part II)," *CurBR* 5, no. 3 (2007): 367–432.

8. Thanks, Andrew Malone, for this point.

9. Wide acceptance of the genre began with Friedrich Lücke's *Versuch einer vollständigen Einleitung in die Offenbarung des Johannes* (1832). On the history of apocalypse studies: Lorenzo DiTommaso, "Apocalypses and Apocalypticism in Antiquity (Part I)," *CurBR* 5, no. 2 (2007): 235–86.

10. English translation by Margaret Kohl, SBT 2.22 (London: SCM, 1972).

a group that produced the most influential definition of apocalypse ever – in the same year that *Saturday Night Fever* was released.[11] There was little explicit discussion of theoretical questions of genre in that volume (called *Semeia* 14), but their literary approach seems to have been mainly influenced by Alastair Fowler and E. D. Hirsch, as adapted for biblical studies by Mary Gerhart and William Doty.[12] This was groovy literary genre theory at the time.

This group was interested in finding apocalyptic features across all sorts of literature, even from cultures and times that in no way could have been historically connected (I would describe it as a "synchronic" genre approach). Therefore, using this kind of nonhistorical comparative approach, we can identify all sorts of culturally unconnected texts as apocalyptic – there are Jewish apocalypses, Christian apocalypses, and Gnostic apocalypses, but also Hellenistic-era Persian apocalypses, and even Greco-Roman apocalypses. (I'm pretty sure that the *Simpsons* episode where Homer eats an insanity pepper and goes on a journey with his spirit guide would count too.) John Collins doubts that all these types of apocalypses can be traced back historically to a single source, so the similarities are just that – similarities.

Tabulating the common criteria that all these apocalypses share enabled Collins and friends to form a "comprehensive" definition that "marks the boundaries" of the genre:

☐ a *narrative framework* that introduces the revelation (usually by means of visions or an otherworldly journey, sometimes also with discourse, dialog, or a heavenly book)

---

11. This volume grew out of the "Forms and Genres" project of the Society of Biblical Literature; see John J. Collins, "Apocalypse: Towards the Morphology of a Genre," in *Society of Biblical Literature 1977 Seminar Papers*, ed. Paul J. Achtemeier (Missoula, MT: Scholars Press, 1977). It developed a definition in Paul D. Hanson, *The Dawn of Apocalyptic* (Philadelphia: Fortress, 1975). See also Phillip Vielhauer's *Geschichte der urchristlichen Literatur* (Berlin: Walter de Gruyter, 1975). On Revelation: George Eldon Ladd, "The Revelation and Jewish Apocalyptic," *EvQ* 29.2 (1957): 94–100; Elisabeth Schüssler Fiorenza, *Revelation* (Minneapolis: Fortress, 1985).

12. See William Doty, "The Concept of Genre in Literary Analysis," in *Proceedings of the Society of Biblical Literature*, 108th annual meeting, vol. 2 (1972), 413–48; Mary Gerhart, "Generic Studies: Their Renewed Importance in Religious and Literary Interpretation," *JAAR* 45.3 (1977); Mary Gerhart, "Generic Competence in Biblical Hermeneutics," *Semeia* 43 (1988); Mary Gerhart, *Genre Choices, Gender Questions* (Norman: University of Oklahoma Press, 1992), 86–87. The *Semeia* 14 group cites Alastair Fowler's 1971 article "The Life and Death of Literary Forms" (*NLH* 2:199–216) but not his 1982 major work *Kinds of Literature: An Introduction to the Theory of Genres and Modes* (Oxford: Oxford University Press, 1982). Reflecting some thirty-five years later, John J. Collins thinks it would have been good to discuss genre theory more explicitly: "The Genre Apocalypse Reconsidered," *ZAC* 20, no. 1 (2016): 22–23. The 2016 edition of *Apocalyptic Imagination* engages with Carol Newsom's genre theory and acknowledges that apocalyptic texts might have fuzzy edges and relationships with other genres: John J. Collins, *The Apocalyptic Imagination: An Introduction to Jewish Apocalyptic Literature*, 3rd ed. (Grand Rapids: Eerdmans, 2016), 10–17.

- ☐ an *otherworldly mediator* (angel) that mediates the revelation (interpreting the otherwise unintelligible vision or acting as a guide for the journey)
- ☐ a hapless *human recipient* who receives the revelation but often has no idea what it means (in Jewish apocalypses, this recipient is pseudonymously identified with a venerable religious figure from the past, like Enoch)
- ☐ a revelation that concerns a *transcendent reality*, which has two dimensions:
  - ○ *spatially*, it involves supernatural beings and activity in another dimension.
  - ○ *temporally*, it anticipates some kind of eschatological future (for example, a personal life after death, or final judgment and destruction of the wicked).[13]

The *Semeia* 14 group divided apocalypses into two different types: historical apocalypses that review history up to the present crisis (such as Daniel, and the Apocalypse of Weeks in 1 En. 93:1–10 and 91:11–17) and otherworldly journeys (such as 1 En. 1–36, and 3 Bar.). These elements all have to do with the form and content of revelation. (There are a bunch of other elements that commonly, but not always, show up in apocalypses too.)

The fact that the group was prepared to move past form criticism and consider apocalyptic as a proper genre was a great step in the right direction. From a genre theory perspective, their approach has many strengths too. They recognized that apocalyptic literature could embed other genres (such as the prayer in Dan 9), or itself show up embedded within a larger work (such as T.Levi 2–5).[14] Unlike other definitions of apocalyptic, their definition considered the recurring *content* of the revelation, and not only its *form*. This is important because without its transcendent view of reality or an eschatological worldview, an apocalypse starts to look like any old prophetic vision.

Another impressive feature of the group's definition is that it is *functional*. It goes beyond simply listing the formal features and explains how those elements function – why the presence of certain elements makes sense, given the transcendent reality that apocalypses are trying to communicate. For example, the reason an angel guide is needed is because the world is unintelligible without direct supernatural revelation. The reason for the otherworldly journey is that the course of human history is ultimately determined by a hidden world of supernatural beings.

---

13. Summarized from John J. Collins, "Introduction: Towards the Morphology of a Genre," *Semeia* 14 (1979): 1–19; Collins, *Apocalyptic Imagination*.

14. David Aune suggests that the *Martyrdom of Perpetua and Felicitas* embeds an apocalypse in 11:1–13:8: "The Apocalypse of John and the Problem of Genre," *Semeia* 36 (1986): 74.

However, the group's approach also had some limitations.[15] First, their defi-nition was all about *how* apocalypses are written (literary features and content) and not *why* they are written (the recurring social situation and function).[16] They carefully tried to separate questions about the "apocalypse genre" from related research into the religious beliefs of the people who wrote apocalypses (which they distinguished using the term "apocalyptic eschatology") and the worldview that went along with it (which they called "apocalypticism").[17] Social situation and function were explicitly regarded as secondary issues – good questions we might get to one day, perhaps after we have defined what the genre is (in the classical sense of its formal features and content).

John Collins actually had a good sense of what the social setting might be: "a loss of meaning and a sense of alienation in the present."[18] Yet he cautioned that a Greek or Roman author might produce an identical genre for quite differ-ent reasons, and so he put these social considerations to one side. (Modern genre theory sees social function at the heart of a genre, and so might query whether such a genre is "identical" at all – see tenet 7.)

Second, the goal of the group's study was still a fairly rigid classification schema. They hoped to give "precision to the traditional category of 'apocalyptic literature.'"[19] Beginning with all the works scholars call apocalyptic, they would produce a definitive list of what all true apocalypses have in common. Based on this list of compulsory criteria (plus a handful of features that sometimes show up), we'd be able to once and for all decide which works truly belong to the genre. Modern genre theory, however, advises us that it might have been better to stick with the prototypes they started with (tenet 3) and observe the relative similarities and differences between those undisputed apocalypses and other texts in the various tradition.[20]

Hold Your Four Horses

To see why this classical approach to genre theory can be unhelpful, we only need to consider Lucian's satires. Harold Attridge (a contributor to the *Semeia* 14 volume) identifies several Greco-Roman texts that would count as

---

15. See Carol A. Newsom, "Spying out the Land: A Report from Genology," in *Bakhtin and Genre Theory in Biblical Studies*, SemeiaSt 63, ed. Boer (Atlanta: Scholars Press, 2007).

16. Perhaps the baby of life-situation had been thrown out with the bathwater of form criticism.

17. This distinction was introduced by Klaus Koch and Paul Hanson: see Adela Yarbro Collins, "Apocalypse Now: The State of Apocalyptic Studies near the End of the First Decade of the Twenty-First Century," *HTR* 104, no. 4 (2011): 447.

18. Collins, "Introduction: Towards the Morphology of a Genre," 11.

19. Collins, *Apocalyptic Imagination*, 5.

20. Collins later acknowledged the pitfalls of family resemblance, suggesting that prototype theory might have "saved us some agonizing about boundary cases": Collins, "Genre Apocalypse Reconsidered," 30.

apocalypses under the group's definition. He includes one of Lucian's satires, the *Icaromenippus*, which is classed as an apocalypse type IIa (Revelatory Journey).[21] It includes an otherworldly journey, a semidivine mediator, and the revelation of philosophical truths. Tick, tick, tick; it must be an apocalypse.

But before you tick those boxes, you might want to know that the star adventurer in Lucian's otherworldly journey is a character called Menippus, based on a real third-century BC satirist of the same name. The whole thing is meant to be silly. The point of the dialog between Menippus and his friend is mostly about making fun at the expense of the "best" philosophers (at least he presumes they are the "best," judging by their sad faces, pale skin, and full beards). Lucian is the Monty Python of his day. If Lucian's satires count as apocalypses, we would have to say that Monty Python's satirical film *The Life of Brian* counts as a gospel. The relationship between *Icaromenippus* and Greco-Roman revelatory journeys (for example, the *Odyssey*, chapter 11) cannot be described as simply "belonging" to the same genre (Type IIa), no matter how many formal features they share. There *is* a relationship with the genre, but it is a complex one because what Lucian is *doing* with the genre serves a different social function – namely, it is satire.

It's an even bigger stretch to put Lucian's satires alongside the book of Daniel and claim that they belong to the same genre. They both count as apocalypses according to the *Semeia* 14 definition (even though Daniel doesn't go on an otherworldly journey at all, and the closest thing Menippus gets to an angel guide is the vaguely helpful Empedocles). But the social setting and function of the two works couldn't be more different. Daniel is providing assurance of an eschatological vindication for oppressed people; Lucian is having a laugh.

Another example of why a modern genre theory approach is helpful comes from the book of Jubilees, a second-century BC work that retells much of Genesis and Exodus.[22] It has a bit in common with other apocalypses, most obviously in that an angel mediates divine revelation to Moses. It also includes some eschatological themes – in particular, the final judgment (Jub. 1:5–19, 23–29; 23:14–31). The text provides exhortation into a typical situation of distress (in this case, probably moral distress over compromised Jewish religion). However, there is a lot in there that reads more like a retelling of Genesis and Exodus (particularly unapocalyptic is its interest in the Mosaic law). Recognizing these

---

21. Harold W. Attridge, "Greek and Latin Apocalypses," *Semeia* 14 (1979): 159.

22. See John J. Collins, "The Genre of the Book of *Jubilees*," in *A Teacher for All Generations: Essays in Honor of James C. VanderKam*, ed. Eric F. Mason et al., JSJSup 153 (Leiden: Brill, 2012), 2:737–55; Collins, "Genre Apocalypse Reconsidered"; James C. VanderKam, *Jubilees 1 & 2: A Commentary on the Book of Jubilees, Chapters 1–50*, vol. 1 of *Hermeneia* (Minneapolis: Fortress, 2018), 20.

issues, Collins originally assigned only part of Jubilees (chapter 23) to the genre of apocalypse.[23] Yet this rather awkward and artificial division reflects more on the rigidity of the classification scheme than the text itself.

Here it is helpful to take on board some tenets of modern genre theory. First, texts are promiscuous when it comes to genres (tenet 1), so it is possible that a text imports some features, thanks to its participation in the apocalyptic genre (such as the narrative frame, revelatory truth-effects, and occasional eschatological themes), but also takes part in some other genre or genres that explain other elements of its social function and content.[24] It's common, for instance, to identify Jubilees as an example of the "rewritten Scripture" or "discourse tied to a founder" genre, which would explain the retelling of Genesis and Exodus bits. Second, genres are fuzzy around the edges (tenet 3), which means there will be loads of texts that seem to straddle closely related genres like prophecy, commentary, and apocalyptic. Carol Newsom suggests that using a prototype approach to genre, we can say that the book sits further away from the central examples of Daniel and Revelation. Third, genres are only relatively stable anyway (tenet 2), which means we should expect that what we find in a mid-second-century apocalyptic work like Jubilees will be different from what we find in even roughly contemporaneous books like the Apocalypse of Weeks, and certainly in later works such as the New Testament book of Revelation.

Despite these issues, the *Semeia* 14 definition of the apocalypse genre keeps on showing up in commentaries and textbooks. I'm willing to bet that right at this moment, somewhere in the world, someone is giving a lecture on apocalyptic literature using the group's 1979 definition (you may be in one!). It's inevitable, I guess. Simple definitions like these are hard to formulate, and even harder to resist once one has been offered to you. There is a feedback loop in operation here too. As generations of scholars are raised on this definition, their understanding of the apocalyptic class is shaped by it. No wonder it seems like such a good fit!

But rather than try to come up with the perfect definition that leaves nothing out (and includes nothing that isn't meant to be there), modern genre theory invites us to leave the whole task of forming the perfect definition to one side. Let's start, instead, with the texts themselves – both prototypical and unusual – and the recurring forms and content we find (or don't find) in them.

In particular, we need to ask why someone would use such a genre in the first place. In other words, let's bring the genre to life, and consider the social situation and function of an apocalypse.

---

23. For a later position (using some modern genre theory): Collins, "Genre of the Book of *Jubilees*."

24. On John's gospel as apocalypse: Benjamin E. Reynolds, *John among the Apocalypses: Jewish Apocalyptic Tradition and the "Apocalyptic" Gospel* (Oxford: Oxford University Press, 2020).

BRINGING APOCALYPSE TO LIFE: THE SOCIAL SITUATION AND FUNCTION OF THE GENRE

The omission of social function as part of the *Semeia* 14 definition of apocalypse was deliberate and reflected a general feeling especially in North American scholarship.[25] Earlier studies of apocalypses had, under the influence of form criticism, made space for considering the life-situation (*Sitz im Leben*) of the apocalypse genre, even if they admitted that they knew little about it for sure.[26] Yet, Collins argued, the purpose or function of particular texts could vary, even within a genre, and including function would make the definition too abstract to be useful. This lack of attention to social function was lamented by some at the time, yet the genre definition in *Semeia* 14 became widely adopted and continues to be the starting point for many studies even today.

In the early 1980s, however, things started to change. More scholars became open to considering the social dimension of the apocalypse genre. A conference in Uppsala, Sweden, held in the same year as John Collins's book was published, considered apocalypses from a much broader sociological angle.[27]

In 1986, a different Society of Biblical Literature group led by another Collins – Adela Yarbro Collins – published *Semeia* 36 on early Christian apocalypticism.[28] They agreed that there were serious questions about how adequate a definition of apocalypse could be if it didn't include something of the setting that gave rise to it. The *Semeia* 36 group agreed in general that social function was an important aspect of the genre, though some had slightly different views on how to describe that function.

Reflecting back in 2011, Yarbro Collins can safely say that "most scholars would now agree that an apocalypse is an imaginative response to a specific historical and social situation."[29] Yet many remain reluctant to delve too far into the social function, worldview, or chronotope of the apocalypse genre, preferring to define the genre by its literary forms and content.[30]

---

25. Doty, "Concept of Genre," 439–42; Collins, *Apocalypse*, 359.

26. For a comparison of various proposals: E. P. Sanders, "The Genre of Palestinian Jewish Apocalypses," in David Hellholm, ed., *Apocalypticism in the Mediterranean World and the Near East: Proceedings of the International Colloquium on Apocalypticism, Uppsala, August 12–17, 1979*, 2nd ed. (Tübingen: Mohr, 1989), 448–49.

27. See especially the contributions by Lars Hartman, Elisabeth Schüssler Fiorenza, E. P. Sanders, and George W. E. Nickelsburg in *Apocalypticism*, ed. Hellholm. They acknowledged that social function may differ between early Jewish apocalypses and later Christian apocalypses: see Elisabeth Schüssler Fiorenza, "The Phenomenon of Early Christian Apocalyptic," in *Apocalypticism*, ed. Hellholm, 312–14.

28. Adela Yarbro Collins, ed., *Early Christian Apocalypticism: Genre and Social Setting*, Semeia, vol. 36 (Decatur, GA: Society of Biblical Literature, 1986).

29. Yarbro Collins, "Apocalypse Now," 457.

30. John Collins would now amend his definition with a general statement about function, though

Some might raise the question of whether we can in fact know anything about the actual historical situation of the writers or first readers of the texts. Were they really in a crisis? How can we know when the imagery is so vague? Who decides what counts as a crisis anyway? Can't a genre be reused in multiple settings for different purposes? These are helpful objections because they reveal a misunderstanding we need to clear up. When we ask about the context of culture and context of situation of a genre, we are *not* thinking (directly, at least) about the actual historical occasion that gave rise to this particular apocalyptic text. From an RGS or SFL perspective, we are interested in the typical or recurring functions that the particular genre anticipates or makes possible (see chapter 3).[31] Someone might have all sorts of secret motives for inviting me to their wedding, but the function of the "wedding invitation" genre within our context of situation and culture is nevertheless pretty straightforward. (A smart archaeologist who found a wedding invitation in three thousand years' time would probably get the gist.) In the same way, if I choose to write an apocalypse I'm choosing to invoke a particular kind of situation – be that "consolation during crisis," or something more general.

Modern genre theory is not an invitation to start speculating beyond the evidence about who wrote these texts, why, and whether they were oppressed or not. As fun as it might be to play a game of "pin the apocalyptic tail on the scribal-party donkey," we just don't have enough evidence to go off.[32] What we can (and I think should) ask about, however, is the kinds of situations and functions that the genre as a whole would generally be useful for.

On the Wrong Side of History

Yarbro Collins and the *Semeia* 36 crew refined the earlier definition of apocalypse genre by adding something about the function of the genre. In addition to its formal features, an apocalypse is typically "intended to interpret present, earthly circumstances in light of the supernatural world and of the future, and

---

he remains cautious about specifying a social setting or linking literary genre too closely with social action and worldview: see John J. Collins, "Genre, Ideology and Social Movements in Jewish Apocalypticism," in *Seers, Sibyls and Sages in Hellenistic-Roman Judaism* (Leiden: Brill, 1997), 33; Collins, "Genre of the Book of *Jubilees*," 740; Collins, "Genre Apocalypse Reconsidered," 28.

31. Situations are defined and anticipated by the genres themselves (see chapter 3). A fictional autobiography invokes the recurring situation of someone recounting their life, even though that person never existed. Likewise, apocalypse might project the situation of a group in crisis, even if the actual writers are being unreasonably melodramatic. How far we stray into historical or sociological realities depends on whether we adopt an ethnographic methodology (RGS) or a linguistic approach (SFL).

32. Apocalypses are sometimes linked to specific breakaway groups, though there is little evidence to go on. A common suggestion is the Hasidim, but they were more enthusiastic about militant resistance than Daniel seems (Dan 11:34).

to influence both the understanding and the behavior of the audience by means of divine authority."[33]

That's a good general starting place, though others have tried to be more specific. Earlier sociological studies described the setting as an experience of social upheaval and turmoil, with a resulting feeling of alienation and powerlessness.[34] H. H. Rowley described apocalypses as "keeping alive the flame of hope in dark and difficult days."[35] In Paul Hanson's definition, apocalypses function to bring about "the renewal of faith and the reordering of life" through a vision revealed to a religious community via a seer which relativizes existing realities.[36] Yarbro Collins's own earlier study described the function of apocalypse as resolution of tension caused by a perceived crisis.[37] David Hellholm would add that apocalyptic is a genre for divinely authorized exhortation or consolation of a group in crisis.[38] Thinking especially of Revelation, David Aune suggested that genre is about replicating a revelatory experience through its performance in a public (or even cultic) setting to give divine authority to the message. The shock of the whole transcendent experience is designed to change their thinking and behavior.[39] E. P. Sanders saw the heart of the apocalypse genre as literature of the oppressed, with restoration and reversal its defining themes.[40]

The exact social function of the apocalypse continues to be discussed. Stephen Cook critiques the "deprivation theory" of the social setting, using a sociological approach to focus attention on millennial groups.[41] More recently, Michael Vines offers a description of the generic setting, using Mikhail Bakhtin's idea of a chronotope: "The purpose of apocalypse would therefore seem to be to gain a God's-eye view on human history and activity."[42] Thinking particularly about the book of Revelation, David Barr puts forward the view that apocalypses function not to predict the future but "to transform the audience by their experience of the

33. Yarbro Collins, "Introduction," in *Early Christian Apocalypticism*, 7.

34. See George W. E. Nickelsburg, "Social Aspects of Palestinian Jewish Apocalypticism," in *Apocalypticism*, ed. Hellholm, 646.

35. H. H. Rowley, *The Relevance of Apocalyptic: A Study of Jewish and Christian Apocalypses from Daniel to the Revelation*, 3rd ed. (London: Lutterworth, 1963), 53.

36. Paul D. Hanson, *Old Testament Apocalyptic*, Interpreting Biblical Texts (Nashville: Abingdon, 1987), 27–28; Paul D. Hanson, *The Dawn of Apocalyptic* (Philadelphia: Fortress, 1975), 1–31.

37. Adela Yarbro Collins, *Crisis and Catharsis: The Power of the Apocalypse* (Philadelphia: Westminster, 1984), 170.

38. David Hellholm, "The Problem of Apocalyptic Genre and the Apocalypse of John," *Semeia* 36 (1986): 23. This helpfully focuses on the speech act itself rather than the hypothetical setting.

39. Aune, "Apocalypse of John," 65–96.

40. E. P. Sanders, "The Genre of Palestinian Jewish Apocalypses," in *Apocalypticism*, ed. Hellholm, 447–59.

41. Stephen L. Cook, *Prophecy and Apocalypticism: The Postexilic Social Setting* (Minneapolis: Fortress, 1995), 52. Cf. Hanson, *Dawn of Apocalyptic*, 409.

42. Michael E. Vines, "The Apocalyptic Chronotope," in *Bakhtin and Genre Theory*, ed. Boer, 113.

other reality of the apocalypse."[43] Anathea Portier-Young locates apocalypses as resistance literature – equipping and commissioning Jews to resist the violent hegemony of empire.[44] These questions of genre often blur into social-scientific discussions about the actual communities that produced these texts, and so in the late twentieth century, many attempts were made to anchor the texts in real scribal communities, be they oppressed or elite.[45]

Apocalypse strikes me as a genre for people who have found themselves on the wrong side of history, offering them meaning within their distress. I prefer the term "distress" (as in Dan 12:1 and Matt 24:29) to "crisis" or "oppression" because it speaks to what the situation feels like to those writing and receiving these kinds of texts – whether or not it looks like a crisis or oppression to onlookers.[46] That distress might be in response to violent persecution, but it could also be about cultural change, moral or religious isolation, powerlessness, or just a general malaise about the state of the world or the human condition. Imagine living at a time in which powerful empires control the world and evil is seemingly unstoppable. No human could stand against such forces, so God himself needs to show up in person and turn the world the right way up. There is no hope within this present evil age – apocalypse looks not to a salvation event within history, but to a spiritual reality above and beyond it.

The Function of the Forms

As John Collins puts it, adapting T. S. Eliot, "apocalypses are written for times when humankind cannot bear very much reality."[47] Seen in light of this social function, the reason why apocalyptic is the way it is (with its distinctive form and wild content) makes much more sense. To experience an apocalypse is to peer behind the curtain of history – to see through the pretension of unstoppable human powers and grasp reality as it truly is. But how do you describe the indescribable or communicate a reality that is beyond anything in world history? With an array of otherworldly images that speak to the imagination, of course!

Apocalyptic texts are largely organized around a narrative framework, but

---

43. David L. Barr, "Beyond Genre: The Expectations of Apocalypse," in *The Reality of Apocalypse: Rhetoric and Politics in the Book of Revelation*, ed. David L. Barr, SBL Symposium Series 39 (Leiden: Brill, 2006), 86.

44. Anathea E. Portier-Young, *Apocalypse against Empire: Theologies of Resistance in Early Judaism* (Grand Rapids: Eerdmans, 2011), 277–79.

45. For a survey, see DiTommaso, "Apocalypses and Apocalypticism in Antiquity (Part I)."

46. For example, 1 Enoch 6–11 addresses a general moral crisis that only someone with a sensitive conscience would have felt distressed by (like Lot in 2 Pet 2:7). Against models of deprivation or oppression, some argue that apocalypses were used by people in power too. This highlights the importance of (1) considering genres diachronically and (2) examining power relations negotiated through genre. See Nickelsburg, "Social Aspects," in *Apocalypticism*, ed. Hellholm, 646.

47. John J. Collins, *Apocalypse, Prophecy and Pseudepigraphy: On Jewish Apocalyptic Literature* (Grand Rapids: Eerdmans, 2015), 247.

that narrative brings together a rich feast of symbolic material. They are full of visions, dreams, hidden meaning, animal symbols, meteorology, angels, and demons. Some of the imagery seems to be drawn from Ugaritic motifs or Hellenistic propaganda, but adapted to the Bible's monotheistic worldview.

These images and symbols pile up in ways that get at the truth indirectly, with both repetition and variation. This means we expect juxtapositions and even tension between the elements. One mistake made by early critical scholars was to assume that everything should be able to be tied down to a single referent in a mathematical way, and anything contradictory must be from a competing source.[48] But that's not how the imagination works. The vision of the beasts in Daniel 7 and the warring angels in Daniel 10–12 are not different stages in an incredibly complex sequence of events, but two ways of pointing to the spiritual realities behind the same events (in the immediate context, the persecution by Antiochus IV Epiphanes). Likewise, Revelation 17:9 and 17:10 interpret the seven heads that John sees in two different ways.[49]

There are lots of numbers in apocalyptic literature, but the idea is not to take them literally, as many on YouTube are inclined to do. In Revelation 7:4–8, for example, there are 144,000 servants of God who receive seals on their foreheads. Some sects have taken this number as a literal capacity limit on the chosen few, or even as a goal (hit this number of card-carrying adherents and the Messiah will return!). Within the apocalypse genre, however, the number should be seen as symbolic, representing by multiplication (12 tribes × 12 apostles × 1000) the fullness of the remnant.[50]

Likewise, the four-kingdom schema and thousand-year periods throughout Daniel are probably literary features adapted to the Jewish context from Persian literature. They're not there so you can put a reminder in your calendar for when judgment day is due. They are symbolic, dividing up history into defined periods and giving the sense that history is determined in advance – this is a "managed universe"[51] – and so nothing that anyone does can change the ending of the story. In a Jewish context, this means that God is in charge. Justice will be done in the end (so don't worry if justice isn't being done; it just isn't the end yet).

It's sometimes said that apocalyptic is dualistic – it sees the world through the lens of a struggle between forces of good and forces of evil. What happens in earthly politics is a skirmish in this cosmic battle. You can understand why this kind of literature would be relevant during periods of extreme pressure and persecution.

48. Collins, *Apocalyptic Imagination*, 21.
49. Thanks, Andrew Malone, for this example.
50. David E. Aune, *Revelation 6–16*, WBC 52B (Dallas, TX: Word, 1998), 444.
51. Collins, *Apocalyptic Imagination*, 121.

Backwards Prophecy

Apocalypses can also convey a sense that the future is determined by looking backwards. A number of nonbiblical apocalypses retell history up until the present as if it were a revelation given long ago. The device is called *vaticina ex eventu* prophecy, and we see parallels in some Akkadian prophecies. These texts "predict" the past up until the present day before giving their real prediction (e.g., 1 En. 85–90). A related device is pseudonymity, which was used throughout the Hellenistic period, including in Jewish texts (in the case of 1 Enoch, that figure is Enoch who famously was taken away in Gen 5:24). We could think of this genre as "discourses tied to a founder."[52] It is debatable whether these techniques were meant to deceive, or to merely engage the imagination.

How does this inform the way we read biblical apocalyptic literature? While Revelation was almost certainly written by someone called John, who was known to the original audience, the book of Daniel is more controversial. It really depends when you think it was written. If (like most scholars) we date Daniel 9–12 to the second century BC, then many of the prophecies about the Hellenistic empire were actually written after they happened. This dating would explain why Daniel 11 describes the rise of Antiochus IV Epiphanes accurately (Dan 11:21–31) but then is less specific on the circumstances around his death (11:44–45). However, if (with some conservative scholars) we insist that the prophecy originated in the time the narrative is set (the Babylonian court, sixth century BC), then these are predictive prophecies.

This might sound like a strange thing to say, but either option works in terms of what the genre "prophecy" is. Biblical prophecy is much broader than just predicting the future; it's about speaking for and to God. Sometimes this is about what's coming in the future, but very often it means giving God's perspective on the past. Some prophetic literature therefore can take the form of a review, looking back on historical events the way an opinion piece might interpret events that have already been reported (except God's opinion carries a lot more weight!). In our culture, we might call these books like Samuel and Kings "history," but in the Hebrew Bible, they are actually considered "prophecy." The function of the genre is more about interpreting than recounting the past. There is no reason God couldn't have told Daniel all about what was going to happen centuries later; equally, there is no reason he couldn't use this genre of backwards prophecy in the second century BC to get his point across.

---

52. Hindy Najman, "The Idea of Biblical Genre: From Discourse to Constellation," in *Prayer and Poetry*

The revelation of this spiritual reality and future judgment is mediated by an angel who guides a perplexed human through the scary and confusing images. This is necessary because the revelation concerns things that are out of this world – although they still concern our reality, because what happens in that spiritual dimension determines what goes on here. The angel guide is uniquely able to give authority to the revelation and offer reassurance and guidance to people in distress.

Having experienced this unveiling, we are put in a position where we can reassess our current circumstances in light of present and future spiritual reality. John Collins says that the "function of the apocalyptic literature is to shape one's imaginative perception of a situation and so lay the basis for whatever course of action it exhorts."[53] This puts our problems in perspective, and while ethical teaching isn't the main game, the experience does help us clarify what's important and emboldens us to stay faithful, no matter what happens. You may be on the wrong side of history from a human perspective, but not when you take into account the bigger picture.

The Eschatological Judgment

Often some kind of eschatology has been seen as central to the apocalypse genre. Eschatology refers to the ultimate judgment – a climactic intervention when, for example, the victories of evil will finally be reversed on a global or even cosmic scale. But by the late 1980s, some scholars were criticizing John Collins's definition for overemphasizing eschatology. Eschatology is not the only thing apocalypses are interested in, and it is hard to narrow down the unique eschatological perspective of apocalypses because they vary so much and have a lot in common with other genres.[54] In response, Collins points out that eschatological judgment need not always be public, cosmic, or political. While some anticipate the end of history, other apocalypses anticipate individual judgment after death.[55]

Modern genre theory also encourages us to be a little more flexible with issues such as whether the apocalypse genre must include an eschatological element. A Western film doesn't need to have a shoot-out in a bar to be a Western, but it is certainly one of the resources available to filmmakers and audiences to place

---

in the Dead Sea Scrolls and Related Literature: Essays in Honor of Eileen Schuller on the Occasion of Her 65th Birthday, ed. Jeremy Penner, Ken M. Penner, and Cecilia Wassén, STDJ 98 (Leiden: Brill, 2011), 314.

53. Collins, Apocalyptic Imagination, 52.

54. See essays by David Aune and Martha Himmelfarb in Semeia 36. Christopher Rowland thinks revelation rather than eschatology is key to the genre: The Open Heaven: A Study of Apocalyptic in Judaism and Early Christianity (London: SPCK, 1982), 2.

55. Collins, Apocalyptic Imagination, 8, 14. See also John J. Collins, "Apocalyptic Eschatology as the Transcendence of Death," CBQ 36 (1974): 21–43.

characters within the violent clash between good and bad. Similarly, we should recognize that not every apocalypse will necessarily be eschatological (in the "end of the world" sense). However, one very obvious way to interpret present earthly circumstances in light of supernatural realities is by showing a different future.

The relationship between apocalypse and eschatology is not as straightforward, then, as we might think. Modern readers tend to assume that an apocalypse is always giving us a blow-by-blow preview of the future as it is leading up to the end of history, and sometimes it is doing just that. Yet the central function of an apocalypse is not predicting the future but understanding the present. It's likely that the series of images we read in Revelation are describing present spiritual realities in multiple ways rather than events in the distant future.[56]

The Genre Ecosystem

There is much debate around the relationships between apocalypse and other genres, and this complex relationship is something that modern genre theory is much better positioned to account for.

Texts are promiscuous when it comes to genres, which means apocalypses will have simultaneous relationships with other genres as well (tenet 1). This accounts for much of the variation we have seen between different examples of apocalypse, which classical definitions of the genre struggle to account for. *Semeia* 14 provided a detailed classificatory system or "morphology" of the genre, with the book of Revelation, for example, classed in subcategory Ib – "Apocalypses with Cosmic and/or Political Eschatology (Which Have Neither Historical Review Nor Otherworldly Journey)." Modern genre theory invites us to abandon this focus on scientific classification and instead see texts as promiscuous, participating in multiple genres within a literary and social ecosystem. This ecosystem of related genres includes oracles, speeches, letters, and testaments. Sometimes the function of an apocalypse will be best served by drawing on the genre of "otherworldly journey," but at other times an oracle reviewing history in highly symbolic terms will do the trick.[57]

The book of Revelation stands out, for instance, in framing its revelation in letter form (Rev 1:4–5), as well as a prophecy to be read aloud in a particular community (1:3 – also 10:11; 11:3–6; 19:10; 22:7–19). This explains some of the important differences between Revelation and your typical apocalypse, including that it is not pseudonymous, lacks a retelling of biblical history, features loads of direct speech from God, and has a rather underfunctioning angelic mediator.

---

56. Barr, "Beyond Genre, in *The Reality of Apocalypse*, ed. Barr, 87–89.
57. See introduction to Greg Carey and L. Gregory Bloomquist, eds., *Vision and Persuasion: Rhetorical Dimensions of Apocalyptic Discourse* (St. Louis, MO: Chalice Press, 1999), 1–17.

The letter and prophecy genres suggest the book directly concerns the situation the recipients are currently in rather than events long in their future (see chapter 12 on letters).[58]

Genres overlap and have fuzzy borders (tenet 3), and exist within systems of genres (tenet 11). The relationship between apocalypse and other genres has often been debated, with some seeing it as a class of prophecy, and others as evolving out of wisdom. The limitation of a genetic "family resemblances" approach is that it focuses on finding similarities, which are endless, whereas in the case of apocalypse, a lot can be learned by contrasting apocalypses with other related genres within the ecosystem, especially prophecy and wisdom literature.

The apocalypse genre is often described as a child of prophecy, but there are differences too.[59] The perspective on history is partly what distinguishes apocalyptic from the overlapping genre of Old Testament prophecy. Whereas the prophets saw God working within history to bring about his kingdom, by the time we get to the apocalypse genre, there is little hope of that. The world stage is the setting for a cosmic battle between light and dark; the present age is dominated by evil principalities and powers opposed to God; and our only hope is that God himself will break into history and bring about an entirely new age. In classical prophecy, our hope is within history. In apocalyptic, our hope is the end of history. While earlier prophetic texts often warned of coming judgment, this judgment was typically seen as coming within history (for example, by the action of an enemy army). In apocalyptic texts, judgment comes from outside history – if necessary, even beyond death. Apocalypses typically have much less interest in the Mosaic covenant.

Unlike straight prophecy, which has its origins in verbal communication, apocalyptic is a literary genre from the outset. Apocalypses rarely employ the kind of direct proclamations we see in prophetic oracles, and the closest we get to a heavenly journey in prophetic texts is Isaiah's brief glimpse into the heavenly throne room (Isa 6).

---

58. Thanks, Ian Paul, for many of the observations in this paragraph. On the effect of Revelation's multiple embedded genres, see his "The Genre of Revelation," in *The Apocalypse of John Among Its Critics: Questions and Controversies*, ed. Alan S. Bandy and Alexander E. Stewart (Bellingham, WA: Lexham Academic, 2023), 36–50; "Introduction to the Book of Revelation," in *The Cambridge Companion to Apocalyptic Literature*, ed. Colin McAllister, Cambridge Companions to Religion (Cambridge: Cambridge University Press, 2020). On the difficulties with Revelation's genre, see Gregory L. Linton, "Reading the Apocalypse as Apocalypse: The Limits of Genre," in *Reality of Apocalypse*, ed. Barr, 9–41. For an intertextual approach: Sean Michael Ryan, "'The Testimony of Jesus' and 'The Testimony of Enoch': An Emic Approach to the Genre of the Apocalypse," in *The Book of Revelation: Currents in British Research on the Apocalypse*, ed. Garrick V. Allen, Ian Paul, and Simon Patrick Woodman, WUNT 411 (Tübingen: Mohr Siebeck, 2015), 95–114. Michelle Fletcher describes Revelation's use of the apocalypse genre as "pastiche": *Reading Revelation as Pastiche: Imitating the Past*, LNTS 571 (New York: Bloomsbury, 2017), 182–213.

59. See Rowley, *The Relevance of Apocalyptic*, 15.

In other ways, the apocalypse genre seems to continue something of the wisdom genre.[60] It's not hard to draw a link between Daniel's dreams and the wisdom themes of the Joseph story in Genesis 37–50. Wisdom and apocalypse both seek to understand the world and act accordingly. The two genres share an interest in the whole world not just the covenantal nation of Israel. Wisdom is distinct, however, in that it is not usually received through direct divine revelation.

THE EXPERIENCE OF THE GENRE

Here's one last trivia question:

What is the date set for Christ's return?

Answer? 22 October 1844. This is the date as calculated by American preacher William Miller based on Daniel 8:14. He gained quite a following, in his day, until October 1844 rolled by and nothing (visibly) happened.[61]

How did William Miller go wrong and start his very own doomsday sect? At least part of his problem is that he got his genres muddled up. Miller had refined a method to "understand the literal meaning of figures used in prophecy."[62] He assumed that Daniel was straight "prophecy," and that all prophecy in the Bible was the same thing – "speaking the same things, observing the same rules" – and so he used his concordance to join the dots. He read in Daniel 8:14 about the 2,300 days from the decree to restore Jerusalem to the cleansing of the sanctuary, and then he imported the principle from other texts of different genres (Gen 29:27; Num 14:34; Ezek 4:6) that one day equals one year. Taking 457 BC (Ezra 7:11–13) as the decree to restore Jerusalem, therefore, this gives a date for the second coming of Christ of 1843–44.

Just about the worst thing you can do with an apocalyptic text is to try to decode it like this. I think it's telling that Paul Ricoeur describes commentary writing on apocalyptic literature as a kind of "detective game": "All the energy of some exegetes seems to be given over to a term by term and detail by detail translation: for this beast, this empire; for that horn, that petty king!"[63]

---

60. See Gerhard von Rad, *Old Testament Theology* (London: SCM, 1965), 2:306–8.

61. Ellen White, a founding figure of the Seventh-Day Adventists, kept running with this date for a spiritualized return.

62. William Miller, *Evidence from Scripture and History of the Second Coming of Christ, about the Year 1843* (Boston: Dow, 1841), 4.

63. Paul Ricoeur, foreword to André Lacocque, *The Book of Daniel*, 2nd ed. (Eugene, OR: Cascade, 2018), xix–xx. Ricoeur points out that such "univocal decipherment," while to some extent invited by the text, risks shutting down the symbolic potential: "The very fact that the discourse remains *allusive* leaves a margin of free play."

What's lost in taking up an apocalypse like a detective game? It is not just that we might arrive at the wrong date for the second coming. There is something lost even if we decode the literature correctly. Genres aren't just containers for truth; they each offer their readers a different experience (tenet 4). Imagine for a moment that Daniel's message had been sent as an email:

> Hey, future saints! Hope you're doing okay. I know it's a bit of a crisis right now, but just wanted to reassure you that every empire has its day . . . FYI, I think we decided on Babylon–Persia–Greece–Rome (wait, was Media in there as well?) . . . anyway, stay true . . . don't let them get you down. Oh, and maybe don't go all in with Maccabeus?
>
> Be well,
>
> Daniel
>
> P.S. This won't mean anything to you now, but the Messiah is due back in 2,300 years.
>
> P.P.S. If someone offers you Apple shares at $2.95, buy them.

Much clearer! But what's lost in this change of genre from apocalyptic to email?[64] If prophecy is about boiling down the imagery to find the "literal" meaning, then not much. But, of course, the apocalyptic experience is so much more than that.

Let's compare this with the experience of Daniel's first apocalyptic vision in Daniel 7. Within the narrative frame, Daniel shares his dream about four beasts:

> Daniel said: "In my vision at night I looked, and there before me were the four winds of heaven churning up the great sea. Four great beasts, each different from the others, came up out of the sea. (Dan 7:2–3)

Notice the symbolic language here of the sea and the great beasts. Read on, and we'll meet a lion with eagle's wings and the mind of a human, a bear with ribs stuck in its teeth, a leopard with four wings and four heads. The fourth beast is covered with ten horns and has iron teeth – a grotesque image of power

---

64. Some apocalyptic texts are presented as letters: see 1 Enoch 91–108.

and aggression. (We don't feel too sorry for it when another horn grows eyes and a boastful mouth and plucks three of its horns out.)

Symbolism is the primary language of apocalyptic genre because symbols allow us to express the inexpressible, to point to a reality behind the everyday world. Miller went to some lengths to decode these beasts, identifying which beast represents which nation, and he is certainly not alone in this. Read a typical commentary on this chapter, and you'll probably get a table: this means Babylon; this means Persia; the three ribs (7:5) are the three conquests; and so on.

But is that all there is to it? After all, Daniel knows a thing or two about interpreting dreams (he interpreted a very similar dream in Dan 2:36–45), and yet even he is "troubled in spirit" and "disturbed" by all that he sees and has to ask one of those standing nearby what it all means (7:15).

This makes me think that, while the animals chosen could perhaps be alluding to the various empires, maybe the reader's job is not merely to decode them. Instead, imagine coming face-to-face with these creatures. You're surrounded by darkness, and you can hear a huge storm on the sea in front of you. Then through the darkness, you see these . . . what are they? Animals? Beasts rising menacingly out of the sea. They are horrifying, all the more so because you know they are manifestations of very real evil in the world – empires that would tear you apart in a second. Such monsters shouldn't be real, and yet they are, which forces deep and painful questions to the surface. Why has God allowed such evil powers of chaos to run wild in this world? And is anyone able to stop them?

The way commentators dissect these images, we can forget to *see* them and *feel* their full weight. If we saw them, our primary response would be terror.

But then, just as suddenly, the scene dissolves. The lights come up, and we go from a nightmarish horror film filled with chaotic and uncontrollable animals to a courtroom scene with an old man sitting on a throne:

As I looked,

> thrones were set in place,
>> and the Ancient of Days took his seat.
> His clothing was as white as snow;
>> the hair of his head was white like wool.
> His throne was flaming with fire,
>> and its wheels were all ablaze.
> A river of fire was flowing,
>> coming out from before him.

> Thousands upon thousands attended him;
>> ten thousand times ten thousand stood before him.
> The court was seated,
>> and the books were opened. (Dan 7:9–10)

Here, finally, is someone who has the power to tame these monsters – to reassert justice and order to a chaotic world. One beast is killed and thrown into the fire, while the others are put on tight leashes. There is a Canaanite myth in which Baal triumphs over the sea monster Yamm – but notice here that God is not engaged in a violent struggle for supremacy against the forces of chaos. God destroys evil without even getting out of his chair.

Someone just opens the books, and justice is done. With the forces of evil put in their place, the way is cleared for a new worldwide kingdom to be established:

> In my vision at night I looked, and there before me was one like a son of man, coming with the clouds of heaven. He approached the Ancient of Days and was led into his presence. He was given authority, glory and sovereign power; all nations and peoples of every language worshiped him. His dominion is an everlasting dominion that will not pass away, and his kingdom is one that will never be destroyed. (Dan 7:13–14)

Who is this one like the son of man? Is he a human figure or a heavenly figure? What am I seeing?

Daniel is overwhelmed and confused by all this, so he asks an angel guide what it all means. Daniel the dream interpreter now needs his own vision interpreted. The angel authoritatively connects what he has seen with history. The beasts are four human kings, Daniel is told, but God's holy people will receive an everlasting kingdom. (Interestingly the explanation doesn't include whether the bear is Media or Persia.)

Daniel is especially worried about the fourth beast (toothy guy with too many horns). He also asks about the horn with the mouth and eyes that attacks the beast. This horn is especially vindictive and wages war on the people of God. The angel guide explains to Daniel what it all means. After the ten kings of the fourth kingdom will come an especially nasty king who will blaspheme God, oppress his people, and change religious observances. God's people will be subject to him for a period. But that's not the end of the story. Judgment day will come. The "court will sit" (Dan 7:26). However unprecedented and unstoppable this final king seems to be, like the others before him, his power will be taken away.

Anyone who thinks that Daniel 2 and Daniel 7 are basically saying the same thing isn't seeing what Daniel is seeing. Yeah, okay, there are four statues in Daniel 2, and they can be decoded to give you the same four kingdoms. But the different genres offer completely different experiences. In Daniel 1–6, Nebuchadnezzar's dream is interpreted as part of a narrative that is all about how faithful Jews can prosper in the court of the empire. But by Daniel 7, there is no hope of a happy ending within history. Rising to prominence within the gentile court by eating vegetables and doing a good job is no longer an option. This is literature for people on the wrong side of history. The content of the two chapters might overlap substantially, but the social setting and function of the genre are distinct, producing a very different experience for the reader.

For those living in the late second century BC, this final horn would have been an unmistakable reference to Antiochus IV Epiphanes, the Seleucid king who terrorized Judeans in 167 BC. Yet the enduring power of a vivid image like this is that – unlike an email – it continues to speak powerfully *whenever* an unstoppable evil power seems to threaten God's people. That's why decoding the image and identifying the four beasts only serve to limit the power of the passage. For those in New Testament times, the power is Rome (Rev 13). For the families of the twenty-one Coptic Orthodox men beheaded on a beach in Libya in February 2015, that monster is Daesh. These monsters are truly evil, but they are not eternal. In the end, God's kingdom will be the only one left standing. The goal of Daniel is not to predict who the Antichrist will be;[65] rather it is to put all the forces of evil in this world into perspective.

SUMMARY

Apocalypses present a particular challenge for interpretation because they are so unlike other kinds of literature we are familiar with. Understanding their typical formal features and content can help us avoid interpretations that take us down the rabbit hole of end-times speculation, obsessing over questions the texts aren't very interested in, and (even worse!) missing what the texts *are* saying. Many popular definitions of apocalypse have avoided considering social setting, but it's important to understand not only how apocalypses are written but also why someone might write one (tenets 7 and 8). While the exact social background of apocalypses is disputed, in general this is literature for people who have found

---

65. "Antichrist" doesn't appear in Daniel or Revelation: only in 1 John 2:18–23; 4:3; 2 John 7.

themselves on the wrong side of history. It speaks into their distress and offers them meaning. This function helps us better understand the experience of a text like Daniel 7, with its otherworldly images. No matter how unstoppable the forces against God and his people seem, there is a greater spiritual reality that puts those forces in perspective and calls on God's people to persevere.

Suggested Workflow for Apocalypses

History

- ☐ What can we say about the historical and cultural context that the text was likely produced in, or that the text addresses? Are there obvious (or potential) historical referents for the people, places, things, customs, or events mentioned and alluded to? What worldview is assumed? What political and spiritual questions might God's people have been asking at the time?
- ☐ How might the typical social function(s) of an apocalypse have been useful or relevant to someone in this context?
- ☐ Are there similar texts inside or outside the Bible? How do they compare and contrast with this one?
- ☐ How have communities in different times, places, and cultures understood and recontextualized this passage? Given your own tradition, what assumptions are you likely to make about the text?

Literature

- ☐ Where does the passage you are looking at fit within the surrounding text? Is it embedded or framed somehow? What is the structure of the book as a whole?
- ☐ Can you identify any specific formal features or content that is typical of the apocalypse genre?
- ☐ What images, metaphors, or symbols (numbers, names, materials, objects, animals, colors, time, etc.) are used? What ideas or feelings might they bring to mind? Where else in the Bible do similar metaphors show up? What reality or realities were they likely pointing to in the original historical setting? Do other elements in the passage give clues about which potential meanings are most relevant in this context? Are the different metaphors talking about different things, or are they offering multiple angles on the same realities?
- ☐ How does the experience offered by these formal features serve the social function of the apocalypse genre?

☐ What other genre relationships can you identify in or around this text (including embedded genres)? Why are they there, and what do they each bring to the table? What new ideas or effects emerge from combining the different genres?

Scripture

☐ What perspective on God, people, life, history, suffering, justice, the world, etc. is being assumed or developed? How might this feed into our systematic theology? In particular, what understanding of future judgment (whether for individuals or the whole world) is presented? What developments in the unfolding of God's plans for the future would be missing or less clear if this text were missing from your Bible?

☐ What other passages need to be brought into conversation with this text to give a full picture? What interpretations of this passage are ruled out by other texts of Scripture? Where and how has this text been taken up elsewhere in the Bible?

☐ What ethical stance does the text offer? How does it want God's people to respond to the circumstances around them? Are there comparable situations that God's people find themselves in today? How might the text be relevant for those situations? How *shouldn't* someone apply this apocalypse?

QUESTIONS FOR DISCUSSION AND REFLECTION

1. Why are some modern readers drawn to interpretations of Daniel and Revelation that try to uncover a secret code or predict the timeline of future events?
2. Read Revelation 1.
   - What genres does the chapter appear to participate in?
   - What situations and functions are invoked by each genre?
   - How does each genre contribute to the message and experience of the book of Revelation?
3. In one sentence, how might you explain the social setting and function of the book of Daniel (or Revelation)? What is this genre of literature *for*?
4. Revelation 18:20 seems to delight in the punishment of Rome.[66] Is this the posture Christians should have towards the impending judgment of cities

---

66. See discussion in Adela Yarbro Collins, "Persecution and Vengeance in the Book of Revelation," in *Apocalypticism*, ed. Hellholm, 729–49.

today? How would situating the book as a response to violent persecution by the rich and powerful change how we read and apply these verses?

5. What is one thing that could help people in your context better understand apocalypses (without starting a cult)?

FURTHER READING

Introductory

Collins, John J. *The Apocalyptic Imagination: An Introduction to Jewish Apocalyptic Literature*. Third edition. Grand Rapids: Eerdmans, 2016.

> Standard textbook on apocalypses.

Paul, Ian. *Revelation: An Introduction and Commentary*. Tyndale New Testament Commentaries 20. London: IVP, 2018.

> Reliable, conspiracy-theory-free guide to Revelation.

Widder, Wendy. *Daniel*. The Story of God Bible Commentary 20. Grand Rapids: Zondervan, 2016.

> Reliable, conspiracy-theory-free guide to Daniel.

Deep Dive

DiTommaso, Lorenzo. "Apocalypses and Apocalypticism in Antiquity (Part I)." *Currents in Biblical Research* 5.2 (2007): 235–86.

———. "Apocalypses and Apocalypticism in Antiquity: (Part II)." *Currents in Biblical Research* 5.3 (2007): 367–432.

> Detailed literature review of the apocalypse genre question.

Hellholm, David, ed. *Apocalypticism in the Mediterranean World and the Near East: Proceedings of the International Colloquium on Apocalypticism, Uppsala, August 12–17, 1979*. Second edition. Tübingen: Mohr, 1989.

> Older essays including social perspective on apocalypse.

McAllister, Colin, ed. *The Cambridge Companion to Apocalyptic Literature*. Cambridge: Cambridge University Press, 2020.

> Introduction to apocalyptic literature and movements in general.

Portier-Young, Anathea E. *Apocalypse against Empire: Theologies of Resistance in Early Judaism*. Grand Rapids: Eerdmans, 2011.

> On apocalypse as resistance to empire.

Yarbro Collins, Adela, ed. *Early Christian Apocalypticism: Genre and Social Setting*. Semeia 36. (1986).

> Older essays including social perspective on apocalypse.

CHAPTER 10

WISDOM

Where *Can't* It Be Found?

The first church my wife, Stephanie, and I worked in together was an amazing community in one of the least wealthy and most culturally diverse parts of southwest Sydney – the perfect place for two trainee ministers to learn a thing or two about the world. I don't just mean pastoral skills or communicating the gospel across cultures; I mean practical things. The older men of the church, though grateful we'd come to share our biblical theology with them, were concerned that my college education hadn't equipped me with the things everyone needs to know, like how to fix a dripping faucet. They took me under their wing and inducted me into their life philosophy – that licensed tradespeople should only be called once you've had a go yourself and really messed it up.

I think of them whenever the topic of biblical wisdom comes up. Wisdom is where the Bible gets most practical. The focus is everyday life, and it's not just intellectual or book smarts we're after, but also practical know-how. While there's nothing on plumbing in Proverbs, being handy with tap washers would certainly count as wisdom. The craftsmen who constructed the tabernacle and temple were given wisdom on the tools (Exod 35; 1 Kgs 7). Sailors, navigators, farmers, and governors all draw on wisdom to get the job done. To have wisdom is to have skill in living.[1] It's being able to successfully deal with reality, anticipating consequences[2] and ordering your life to hit the right goals.

While wisdom as a theme can be found throughout the Bible, there are some parts of the Bible that seem particularly focused on the topic. Bible scholars have often talked about these texts as a distinct collection and genre – "Wisdom Literature." Yet nailing down the exact limits of this category turns out to be surprisingly tricky. The category ends up being weirdly narrow, impossibly broad, or based on nothing more than circular reasoning ("Wisdom Literature includes the books scholars consider wisdom literature").[3]

1. Bruce K. Waltke, *The Book of Proverbs*, NICOT (Grand Rapids: Eerdmans, 2004), 78.
2. Ellen F. Davis, *Opening Israel's Scriptures* (New York: Oxford University Press, 2019), 451.
3. Roland Murphy defines wisdom literature not as a true form-critical category but as basically "those

Sounds like a job for modern genre theory!

Excitingly, wisdom literature is one area where scholars have already begun to apply many of our modern genre theory tenets, laying to rest the rigid boundaries of the wisdom literature genre as traditionally conceived.[4] In this chapter, we will briefly describe wisdom (the topic) and Wisdom Literature (the collection), before considering what's at stake in one leading attempt at rethinking wisdom literature (the genre) using modern genre theory. We will finish off by running another boomerang test on Judges 19 (the same passage we read as a horror film in chapter 6), but this time seeing what a tactical decision to read the passage as wisdom comes back with. While wisdom comes in lots of different shapes and sizes, there does seem to be a common social context (tenet 7) and function (tenet 8) driving the features of these various genres. Wisdom is not dead; it is alive and well, working as an ecosystem of genres.

WISDOM: WHAT IS IT GOOD FOR?

Before we talk about the Wisdom Literature collection and the wisdom genre, it's helpful to get a sense of what wisdom as a concept is. Wisdom comes up in all sorts of places in the Bible. We might use words like understanding, skill, cleverness, wit, lifehacks, prudence, moral virtue, and insight to talk about wisdom. For Joseph (Gen 37–50), wisdom includes his ability to interpret dreams, but also his prudent and competent leadership that allows him to reach the top of his industry and save many lives. Priests need to be wise at teaching the law. Prophets need to be wise at proclaiming God's will into present circumstances. We even meet groups like the "wise woman" (2 Sam 20:15–16) and semiprofessionals called "the wise" (Eccl 12:11) whose job seems to be to give advice. The opposite of wisdom is folly – a lack of discipline, a lack of experience, or even a willful perversity. Young people especially need wisdom to navigate life without falling into sin and destruction.

Wisdom is ultimately a gift from God, but the way we get wisdom is different from the way we get, say, a prophetic oracle. Prophecy is normally about direct revelation – God communicating his message to people via an authorized spokesperson. In contrast, wisdom is gathered more indirectly by

books the editors asked me to write about": *Wisdom Literature: Job, Proverbs, Ruth, Canticles, Ecclesiastes, and Esther*, FOTL 13 (Grand Rapids: Eerdmans, 1981), 3. Thanks, Joel Atwood, for this nugget.

4. See, generally, Will Kynes, ed., *The Oxford Handbook of Wisdom and the Bible*, Oxford Handbooks (New York: Oxford University Press, 2021). On "wisdom literature" as mode, not genre: Mark R. Sneed, "Is the 'Wisdom Tradition' a Tradition?," *CBQ* 73.1 (2011): 50–71. For other applications of modern genre theory to the "wisdom" genre, see, for example, Simon Chi-chung Cheung, *Wisdom Intoned: A Reappraisal of the Genre "Wisdom Psalms,"* LHBOTS 613 (London: Bloomsbury T&T Clark, 2015).

observation and experience about the usual way the world works (Prov 6:6; 24:30–34), and then handed down from person to person as tradition. It can be learnt from parents, teachers, and friends (or even be borrowed from outside of Israel). This is why texts that aim to grow someone's wisdom often have a didactic ("teaching") tone. The writer presents as a teacher, and the reader as a pupil or son. The goal is long-range formation and growth in character and capacity. Rhetorical techniques try to persuade the listener to arrive at wisdom for themselves. The vibe is less "thou shalt not do that" and more "have you considered this?"

How to Chew on a Proverb

The Skeptic's Annotated Bible (a study Bible for atheists to debate Christians) has a whole section on contradictions in the Bible. It has a field day with the book of Proverbs.

> Do not answer fools according to their folly,
>> lest you be a fool yourself. (Prov 26:4 NRSVue)

> Answer fools according to their folly,
>> lest they be wise in their own eyes. (Prov 26:5 NRSVue)

Skeptics take this direct contradiction as yet more proof that the Bible is broken, written by people so ignorant they didn't realize they'd said the exact opposite thing one verse earlier.

But what this example actually highlights is not the ignorance of the Hebrew scribes, but our lack of cultural awareness about how the genre works. This is a "saying" (sometimes called "sentence proverb" or "epigram") – the main genre Proverbs 10–29 is built from. It's a classic two-line observation about the world expressed in parallel lines, just like typical Hebrew poetry (see chapter 7).

It's important to realize that these sayings are sketches in black and white, not grey. They make general observations about how the world works, but draw them as absolutes. That's why seemingly contradictory statements can both be true. Proverbs 10:4 says that poverty is caused by laziness, whereas 13:23 says that poverty is caused by injustice. Which is it? Well, both can be true in different circumstances. The unqualified, generally true first saying (plant some seeds or you'll be hungry!) needs to be held in tension with the different perspective of the second saying (hunger is not always your fault). Part of wisdom is knowing which saying applies to this case. (It's a bit like how we need to decide whether in a given instance "many hands make light work" – or, on the contrary, "too many cooks spoil the broth.")

As general observations, sayings shouldn't be taken up as a promise or guarantee. Proverbs 22:6 says that if you train children, they will stick to the right path when they are old. Now, this is not always guaranteed. The child has their own responsibility to choose the path of wisdom. That wise parents sometimes beget foolish children will be obvious to anyone who has spent ten seconds reading the history of Israel (looking at you, Rehoboam). But as a general principle, good discipline and teaching will set them up well for life – certainly they'll be better off than if you never discipline them at all!

Sayings aren't always *dictating* how things should be, but sometimes are just *describing* the way things generally are. Proverbs 14:20 tells us that the poor get treated worse than the rich. Proverbs 27:14 tells us that if you bless your neighbor loudly in the early morning, they will take it as a curse. Do with this information what you will, but that's life.

The most important thing about the saying genre, therefore, is the role of the hearer. Genres give readers different tasks (tenet 4); they tell us what game we are playing (tenet 2). To navigate reality, you need to be able to see both sides of the coin and know about the exceptions that break the general rule. Life is, after all, messy. The contradictions between sayings are deliberate. They force you to slow down and think – is this the kind of situation where answering a fool is going to help them change (Prov 26:5), or is it the situation where I'll just be the fool for trying (26:4)? You'd be wise to consider both possibilities.

This is why I love the wisdom genre. It's not just a list of rules to follow, but an invitation to a way of life. Proverbs offers us seeds to plant and cultivate rather than fast food to consume. It invites us to sit and observe the contradictions and puzzles of life, and so to grow in our own ability to navigate life successfully.

The big personality in the wisdom space is King Solomon, who was granted a wise and discerning heart by God as a gift (1 Kgs 3). One of the more memorable demonstrations of his powers was when he mediated between two women who both claimed that the same baby was theirs. To resolve the dispute, he declares that the baby be cut in two and they can each keep half the baby. Naturally, the true mother immediately says the other woman can keep the whole baby and – *voila!* – the original Poirot has cracked the case. In addition, we are told Solomon spoke three thousand proverbs and knew all about plants, timber, animals, fish, and mosses that grow on walls. Understandably, people came from all over the world to listen to him talk mosses (1 Kgs 4:32–34).

In Solomon's case, wisdom meant shrewd insight into how humans operate, discernment in administering justice, and a keen observational eye for how the created world is put together. Ironically, however, the *other thing* that Solomon is remembered for apart from wisdom is being led by his heart into compromise and idolatry. This suggests that while there is overlap between godliness and wisdom, it's not always the same thing.

We often think of the Old Testament in terms of the main storylines – headline events like the exodus, exile, and return, and VIPs like Abraham, Moses, and David. Our mental landscape is dominated by themes like fall and redemption, covenant and promise, judgment and hope. But where does Job fit in all that? Or Ecclesiastes? Wisdom seems to sit slightly outside of salvation history. It never mentions God's specific dealings with Israel, the exodus, or the law of Moses. It's not interested in covenants or the distinction between Jew and gentile. It's about human life in its most general and universal form, beginning back in the Garden of Eden.

To say that it is more interested in the *design* than the designer is too strong, but it does seem more interested in a theology of creation than redemption. When we look at Proverbs, for instance, we find a big focus on creation. God is often described as the creator of the world, of the rich and poor, of the eye and ear, and even of wrongdoers. He delights in what he's made, and the people in it. As the original master craftsman, God's number one tool is wisdom. The earth and sky are created in wisdom (Prov 3:19–20). There is an extended monolog in Proverbs 8:22–31, where wisdom herself speaks (*hokmah*, wisdom, is a feminine noun, so it is personified as a woman). She was the first thing created and essential to the creation of the world. That's why wisdom is so powerful. The same wisdom that God used to create the world, we can use to gain general knowledge about it, as well as skills for living in it.

None of this is to say that wisdom contradicts the rest of the Old Testament, or that covenantal theology is irrelevant, or that God is absent from discussions about wisdom. Quite the opposite. God is actively involved in everything in creation – in the smallest details of everyday life. There is nothing that is outside his kingly rule. The reason there is order to be observed in the first place is that God made and sustains that order (Prov 3:19–20; 8; Job 38–41). Furthermore, many of the ethical demands of the covenant are bolted onto the created order. Proverbs 17:5 warns that whoever mocks the poor mocks their creator. Wisdom is a distinct layer, but it's all part of the same cake.

This is why, while the biblical writers happily borrow insights from foreign wisdom traditions, they bring it all under a framework that begins with "the fear of the LORD" (Prov 1:7; 2:5–6). There is such a thing as healthy fear. From high voltages to the Australian surf, if you want to keep enjoying them, then you must understand that they can destroy you in a second if you approach them the wrong way. Yet the fear of the Lord isn't just the emotional response of being afraid; the fear of the Lord has intellectual and moral depth as well. It is mentioned side by side with a knowledge of God and of his commands, as well as observance of his standards based on his character. It is knowing who God is, and who we are, and treating him accordingly. It's almost another way of saying "the religion of Israel," and especially the humble attitude that comes from the right understanding of where we stand with him. The fear of the Lord is therefore not only a starting point for wisdom, but also its fundamental principle and constant goal.

WISDOM LITERATURE

Since the nineteenth century, Bible scholars have identified three books of the Bible as a distinct category called "Wisdom Literature": Proverbs, Ecclesiastes, and Job. (Sometimes people will throw in Song of Songs, a handful of psalms, and some bonus Bible books like the Wisdom of Solomon and Ben Sira too.) Taking these three texts as our prototypes, we can start to get a picture of what the genre of wisdom literature looks like.

Formal Features

Our prototypes come in very different shapes and sizes, which suggests that we are going to need to lean more heavily on the content and social function to pin down the genre. They each offer quite different experiences and use language in very different ways. The staging structure is all over the place. Job's overall frame is a narrative; Proverbs is more of a curated playlist; Ecclesiastes alternates between first-person observations and third-person sayings.[5]

The one thing our prototypes have in common, however, is the ability to embed a broad array of primary genres – questions and riddles (Eccl 2:19; Prov 23:29–30; 30:4; Job 8:11–12), instruction (Eccl 12:12), prayers (Prov 30:7–9), praise (Prov 8; Job 12:13–25), poems (Eccl 3:1–8; Job 28), dialog (Job 3–28), sayings (Proverbs 10–29; Job 17:5; Eccl 7:1–6), royal autobiography (Eccl 1:12–18),

---

5. Inconsistent staging structure can have various causes. Some genres have flexible stages; a genre can operate as a mode, with another genre in charge of structure; the genre's normal structure can be complicated by a text's participation in another genre. (Thanks, Doug Fyfe, for the observation about Ecclesiastes.)

speeches (Prov 1:20–33; Job 38–41), numerical lists (Prov 6:16–19), and narrative (Job 1:1–5).[6] These embedded genres usually have a strong didactic function and association with wisdom in their own right. This suggests that the overall (secondary or complex) genre of our prototypical books (Proverbs, Job, and Ecclesiastes) could be described as a kind of compilation of smaller didactic genres, or an "instructional book."[7]

A Collision of Disputation and Thanksgiving

In the middle of the debate with his friends, Job breaks into what sounds like a hymn of thanksgiving and praise (Job 12:13–23). In fact, some of the lines are close to, or exactly the same as, parts of Psalm 107, which can be described as a kind of thanksgiving psalm. What is thanksgiving doing in the middle of a debate?

Some scholars have suggested that the thanksgiving psalm doesn't belong here in Job at all. Others have described it as a kind of parody of the pious psalmist. But modern genre theory suggests some more subtle possibilities. A collision between genres brings worlds together that normally belong apart – what cognitive linguistics calls "conceptual blending" (see tenet 1). Genres provide resources for making meaning (tenet 4), and the thanksgiving psalm genre preloads a whole theology of God's justice and retribution, which sits in tension with Job's experience of righteous suffering. Bringing whole genres into play like this is an efficient way of making his argument and also a good way of pursuing the didactic function of the book as a whole by forcing us to consider life in its complexity.

But the genre also brings with it a social situation of communal praise after God's acts of deliverance, and so taking up the genre places Job himself in the congregation of God's righteous people. Maybe this allows Job to reject simple theological answers to his complex questions without giving up his position in the choir and his claim to belong on the right side of God's justice.

---

6. See Markus Witte, "Literary Genres of Old Testament Wisdom," in *Handbook of Wisdom*, ed. Kynes, 361–68. On how Job's various genres serve wisdom goals by bringing their distinctive moral imaginations into dialog, see Carol A. Newsom, *The Book of Job: A Contest of Moral Imaginations* (New York: Oxford University Press, 2003).

7. Witte, "Literary Genres of Old Testament Wisdom," 360–61. Witte identifies headings, calls to attention, and recapitulations as recurring structural features of the instructional book genre. Katharine Dell takes the proverb as prototype for the overall wisdom genre: *The Solomonic Corpus of 'Wisdom' and Its Influence* (New York: Oxford University Press, 2020), 19.

Content

When it comes to content, it's no surprise that all the prototypes major on the topic of wisdom. At the risk of outrageous reductionism, we could say that Proverbs talks about how and why to get wisdom (Prov 1:1–7), Ecclesiastes stress-tests wisdom to see where it breaks down (Eccl 1:12–18), and Job pushes back on wisdom, pointing out the folly of presuming to know how God runs the world (Job 42:8).

Wisdom comes up as a theme in other places, of course (for example, Gen 37–50).[8] But the degree of emphasis on wisdom makes these books the weird kids of the Old Testament. While everyone else is talking about the covenant with Abraham and the Law given at Mount Sinai, the wisdom genre is staring out the window, wondering about what clouds are made of. The three books seem almost completely disinterested in what we might think of as the main Old Testament storyline – God's particular relationship with his people Israel. Some of the book of Proverbs, for example, seems to be borrowed from Egyptian wisdom traditions.[9]

God's Own Instruction

While scholars might be right to distinguish wisdom literature from the Mosaic law, it is interesting to compare the wisdom genre with the general (or "apod-ictic") instruction we find in the Decalogue (Exod 20). While some law genres address specific case studies (if x happens, then y is the best way forward), these "ten words" that God spoke are expressed as unconditional statements ("you will not steal"). These reveal a general principle, a bit like a saying in Proverbs. We often assume that they are designed to work like laws in a modern statute book. But consider the final word: "You shall not covet." How can a civil or criminal statute regulate matters of the heart? To me, the ethical guidance that God speaks to his "son" Israel here is not so different from the ethical guidance a father speaks to his son in Proverbs. While the grammatical forms and register of the ten words is different from the saying genre, they both belong to the same system of interrelated and overlapping genres we could call Torah – "Instruction."

---

8. On wisdom in biblical narrative: Lindsay Wilson, *Joseph, Wise and Otherwise: The Intersection of Wisdom and Covenant in Genesis 37–50* (Milton Keynes: Paternoster, 2004).

9. Notably Proverbs 22:17–23:11. See Waltke, *Book of Proverbs*, 217.

An earlier generation of scholars often took this distinctive content as evidence that wisdom literature was written by a particular movement within Israel that stood isolated from (or even in opposition to) king, prophet, and priest. Yet we have no evidence that such a cloister of renegade scribes or secretive sages ever existed – the people who copied Proverbs probably copied everything else too.[10] More likely, the distinctive content reflects not the social isolation of its writers but the specific social function of the genre.

The wisdom subject matter predicts various common words will show up: "wise," "instruction," "teaching," "fool," "know," "understand," and so on. But it's important not to reduce the wisdom genre to a checklist of vocab items. Instead, we should look for how these regularities in lexical choice relate to other aspects of the genre in a functional way – for example, family terms like "father" and "my son" are used to realize the constructed social situation of the text. Speaking of which . . .

Social Function

To understand a genre we need to ask not just "how is it written?" but, more importantly, "what is it for?" Form criticism was hunting for a concrete life situation behind every genre, and so you'll find scholars peddling all sorts of wonderful theories identifying the exact "sages" or "sapiential circles" ("wise guys") that were responsible for creating each wisdom text – even dreaming up the politics between them and other groups in society. The truth is, we just don't have anything like the information we would need to back up these imaginative portraits. Thankfully, we don't have to. Genres create the social context as well as reflect it (tenet 9). To begin to sketch out the recurring situation and social function of a genre (tenets 7 and 8), you just need to look at what the text seems to be doing. In the case of wisdom literature, it's pretty obviously a genre for *teaching* someone about something. These are the texts you use if you want to pass on or receive wisdom. The broad practical, moral, and spiritual content of this instruction and the slow-burn teaching style suggest it is specifically about guiding a person's growth in discernment, character formation, and all-round personal capacity.[11]

---

10. See Mark Sneed, "Methods, Muddles, and Modes of Literature: The Question of Influence Between Wisdom and Prophecy," in *Riddles and Revelations: Explorations into the Relationship between Wisdom and Prophecy in the Hebrew Bible*, ed. Mark J. Boda, Russell L. Meek, and William R. Osborne (London: T&T Clark, 2018), 30–44.

11. On parallels with Hellenistic cultural and educational formation, see Elisa Uusimäki, *Spiritual Formation in Hellenistic Jewish Wisdom Teaching* (Leiden: Brill, 2016).

This formative function is realized (or predicts) certain regularities in the way language is used in the text. They are geared towards instruction, and so they often prefer didactic registers – a father's exhortations to his son (Prov 1:8), the teacher's provocations to reflection (Eccl 1:1–2), or the creator's general knowledge test (Job 38:1–4).[12] This is often realized through features like imperatives, prohibitions, and words that imply a father-son audience ("you," "father," "sons"). Unlike a commandment, this is typically framed not as vertical revelation (God-to-you) but as horizontal (you-to-me) discourse designed to prompt reflection and formation.[13] Unlike most biblical literature, wisdom typically brackets out its own particular social, historical, and covenantal context in order to speak to universals of human experience.[14] The name of the man and the particular city he saved is not remembered (Eccl 9:13–15; cf. 2 Sam 20:15–22). The characters are de-identified so that observations can be generalized.

Different genres are different games, with different roles for readers to play (tenet 4). What the genre is for impacts what the reader is meant to do with it. While gothic fiction and detective novels, for example, share similar murderous content and dark settings, the task for readers of detective fiction is distinct (work out "who done it" before the mystery is revealed). Wisdom literature shares similar content to other types of literature in the Bible, but what is expected of the reader? For me, a distinctive feature of the wisdom genre experience is its slow-burn teaching style. As a reader, you are expected not simply to hear and obey, but to first go away and ponder. Gerhard von Rad, drawing on Hans-Georg Gadamer, describes the poetic form of wisdom as an "intellectual game."[15] Whether it's the deceptive simplicity of a riddle or a proverb, or the enigmatic layers of the speeches in a book like Job, wisdom texts refuse simple, single-use readings. Ellen Davis describes how proverbs force us to "ruminate slowly on one saying and then another" in order to build a "habit of slowly reconsidering what once seemed clear."[16] The case seems closed, until the next person gets up to argue their point of view (Prov 18:17). The puzzles, contradictions, and ambiguities you often find in these texts aren't bugs but features. They keep the loop open and force you to come back again and again, to keep thinking and reflecting. This serves the social function of the genre by sharpening your wisdom intuitions.

---

12. These are literary constructs, not necessarily real relationships. An RGS analysis might use ethnographic or sociological studies to understand the real relationships behind the text, but our access to such social background is limited. Instead, using SFL, we can examine how recurring situations are realized in, and constructed by, the discourse itself.

13. For a summary of social function, see Witte, "Literary Genres of Old Testament Wisdom," 358.

14. See Mark Sneed, "The Social Setting of Wisdom Literature," in *Handbook of Wisdom*, ed. Kynes, 337.

15. Gerhard von Rad, *Wisdom in Israel* (London: SCM Press, 1972), 50.

16. Davis, *Opening Israel's Scriptures*, 451.

Wisdom Psalms

A great test case for this description of wisdom literature is the debate over how many psalms, if any, should be considered part of the wisdom genre. Depending on who you ask, between three and thirty-nine psalms have been identified as "wisdom," "didactic," or (my favorite) "gnomic" psalms on form-critical criteria.[17]

Simon Chi-chung Cheung has applied a healthy dose of modern genre theory to this scholarly debate. Taking Proverbs and Ecclesiastes as his prototypes, he describes the wisdom psalms genre as a family that fuses three features: a dominant wisdom theme, an intellectual tone, and an intention to teach. This final feature he identifies within psalms, using a tool called "speech act theory," looking for clues about what the speaker is doing in the vocabulary, verb forms, and surrounding text.[18]

- Read through Psalm 37 and/or Psalm 49. What features in the psalm remind you of Proverbs or Ecclesiastes?
- Now consider Psalms 1; 19; 32; 39; 73; 111; 112; and/or 128. How is it similar and how is it different to the psalm(s) you just read?
- On a scale of 0–10, how strongly (if at all) would you say the psalms you've just read participate in the wisdom literature genre? See if you can point to particular formal features, content, and functions we've discussed so far.
- Would your verdict on these psalms change if you took Job as the prototype for wisdom literature rather than Proverbs or Ecclesiastes?

One interesting angle on this social context comes from the little we know about the context of culture and power relations (tenet 10) in which these texts were probably copied.[19] Literacy was a specialized skill in those days, about as common then as being able to write music is today. It depends a little on what period we are talking about, but in general, scribes would probably have passed on their skills in rooms at the temple or in their homes, a bit like music teachers

---

17. See appendix to Cheung, *Wisdom Intoned*.

18. Using speech act theory for genre analysis is promising, but it needs to be better at taking into account the staging structure of genres. In staged discourse, various illocutionary acts function together in sequence to enact the overall function. A complaint psalm begins by describing a situation and ends by expressing confidence in God, but the functional heart of the genre is the middle stage in which the psalmist asks for intervention.

19. The following picture is from Sneed, "Social Setting," 339–49; Mark Sneed, *The Social World of the Sages: An Introduction to Israelite and Jewish Wisdom Literature* (Minneapolis: Fortress, 2015), 147–82.

today. Scribes were typically male and perhaps employed by the rich and powerful. They were better off than peasants, but their social status was defined more by their cultural capital than by raw wealth and worldly power. Across the ancient world, scribes were trained to write curriculums that included hymns, erotica, and model letters. It's very possible that collections of proverbs might have a dual social function of honing writing skills at the same time as giving the young trainees solid life advice to write on the tablets of their hearts as well (Prov 3:3).

The likely social setting of wisdom texts is (like everything in the field) contested, so feel free to substitute your own favorite historical picture. My central point remains that social setting needs to inform our understanding of the genre of the text. At the very least, we can probably agree that the social function of wisdom literature is, broadly, didactic. We may even infer, based on the content and teaching style described above, that wisdom literature is the kind of teaching that aims for discernment, long-range character formation, and capacity building rather than rote-learning rules. It's about increasing a person's appreciation of and ability for wisdom so they can make it through the complexities of life.

Understanding what the genre is for, and what we are meant to do with it, means sometimes fighting against the natural instincts of biblical interpreters to nail down any ambiguities we find. Take Ecclesiastes 7:12's observation that "Wisdom is a shelter / as money is a shelter." I suspect we are meant to pause and wrestle with this simile. The comparison to money makes sense (in general, yes, rich people have more resources to cope with adversity), but it is a little odd as a comparison for wisdom, given that riches are often treated with caution as being ephemeral or unsatisfying (Eccl 2:8; 5:10). Pause a little longer in the verse and we might realize that the word for "shelter" here is *tseil*, which can be positive in the sense of protection but can also mean "shadow" in the fleeting and insubstantial sense. In fact, in the previous chapter, the word appears in the negative sense: "few and meaningless days they pass through like a shadow" (Eccl 6:12). Wisdom, it turns out, is like money and shadows: good – while it lasts.

THE OBITUARY

Normally biblical studies monographs are prescribed for people suffering from insomnia, but when I first read Will Kynes's *An Obituary for "Wisdom Literature,"* I couldn't sleep until I'd finished it.[20] It is one of the most exciting

---

20. Will Kynes, *An Obituary for "Wisdom Literature": The Birth, Death, and Intertextual Reintegration of a Biblical Corpus* (Oxford: Oxford University Press, 2019). See my review in *JETS* 63.4 (2020): 857–59. This chapter engages mostly with Kynes, but he isn't alone in using modern genre theory to question the wisdom literature category: see Sneed, "Is the 'Wisdom Tradition' a Tradition?"; *Social World*, 183–215.

attempts to put modern genre theory to work on problems in biblical studies. Even the title of the book plays with genres – an "obituary" invokes the recurring situation of someone who has already died, so announcing his scholarly monograph in that genre is a provocative way of saying that the whole scholarly category of "wisdom literature" needs to be laid to rest.

The obituary begins by revealing a startling family secret: wisdom literature wasn't nearly as old when it died as everyone thought it was. Kynes points out that the idea that there is such a distinct collection of texts was invented by a German scholar as recently as 1851. Before that, people obviously still studied Proverbs, Ecclesiastes, and Job, but they weren't treated as their own exclusive club. Being a new scholarly category is not in itself a problem, but it does give us pause to ask whether it is so self-evident a classification as we might have thought.

Kynes's postmortem reveals that a key cause of death was a rigid approach to genre. Wisdom literature was always assumed to have firm edges: these three (or four) texts are considered wisdom literature, whereas the rest of the canon isn't. Of course, as modern genre theorists, we will be suspicious of these kinds of hard borders (tenet 3). Proverbs, Ecclesiastes, and Job may have similar themes, but they have very different literary forms – compare Solomon's sayings to the narration of Job's testing. Any definition broad enough to cover the full diversity of what we find in these books will inevitably be so vague that a good argument could be made for almost any part of the Bible to be included in Wisdom Literature. To keep the category meaningful, scholars have (Kynes argues) effectively fallen back on circular reasoning: wisdom literature only includes those texts that scholars accept as wisdom literature. To be fair, circular reasoning is not always terminal. If genres are relatively stable conventions (tenet 2), it's fine to take as a starting point consensus about what texts belong in the genre. But it does prompt us to ask if there are better ways of understanding the genre of these texts.

Kynes effectively runs the boomerang test (see chapter 4) on the wisdom genre. First, he shows some of the drawbacks of using the wisdom literature category. The hard line around wisdom literature means that scholars have come to specialize in those texts, seldom venturing out to consider the relationship between wisdom literature and the rest of the canon.[21] Worse still, the wisdom literature genre tends to draw out the humanistic themes in texts and leave behind the connections with Israel's broader theology and history, turning ancient Israelites into post-Enlightenment thinkers (which is suspicious, given that the genre was first described by post-Enlightenment thinkers).

---

21. On the Psalms–Job silos, see Kynes, *Obituary*, 152–55.

Second, Kynes shows how reading Proverbs, Ecclesiastes, and Job in other genres highlights intertextual links we would otherwise miss. Our so-called "wisdom literature" texts can sometimes have as much – or more – in common with other genres than they do with each other. Before people talked about "wisdom literature" they might have seen Ecclesiastes as part of "Solomonic" literature (with Proverbs and Song of Songs), "skeptical" literature (with Job), "misfortune" literature (with Job and Lamentations), or the Megillot (with Song of Songs, Ruth, Lamentations, and Esther).[22] Like artworks curated for an exhibition, each grouping brings out something slightly different in the text. Preserving the strict three-text category of "wisdom literature" means we miss out on a lot.

So What Next?

Everybody agrees that the old wisdom literature category needs a rethink. The debate now is over how to think about the wisdom literature genre in light of modern genre theory. Some think the genre is still useful, so they want to keep it but make it fuzzier at the edges; a few are happy seeing basically everything in the Bible as wisdom literature; some think we should just move on and stop talking about wisdom literature altogether. Kynes's proposal is slightly different from all these options. Kynes declares wisdom literature as a classification dead, but suggests it might live on as one of many potential genre designations readers would choose to read Job, Ecclesiastes, Proverbs, or indeed any biblical text within. These genre designations are, by his definition, "selective, self-reflective, and subjective phenomena."[23] In thinking about genre this way, Kynes has picked up many of the insights, and theorists, we met in chapter 2 (especially Alistair Fowler and John Frow).

The main way Kynes talks about genres is as a constellation. Genres are made up of texts in the same way that constellations are made up of stars. You may recall that the constellation metaphor came up in chapter 2 as a metaphor for the fusion of form, content, and function in genres, but Kynes is using the metaphor in quite a different way. Consider the Orion constellation – eight main stars forming a hunter from Greek mythology. Like all constellations, it really only exists in the eye of the beholder. Physically, the three stars in Orion's Belt are nowhere near each other and only look close together from our perspective on earth. Which stars we group together isn't totally random, of course. Nobody is going to pick out a constellation involving two barely visible stars from opposite

---

22. Katharine Dell takes "Solomonic literature" as the core: *Solomonic Corpus*.
23. Kynes, *Obituary*, 12.

ends of the sky. Certain stars appear brighter and closer and therefore seem (from our shared perspective on earth) to belong together, which is why Chinese, Muslim, and Greek astronomers all had a name for the three very bright stars in a row we call "Orion's Belt." But while some cultures call these three stars "Orion's Belt" (grouping them as part of a bigger picture of a hunter), others simply call them the "three wise men." There is more than one way of dividing up the night sky.

In the same way, Kynes suggests, as readers we can connect texts together in multiple ways to form genres. These groupings are not totally arbitrary, as some texts make more sense when read together than others. But neither is there only one right way to group texts together. Reading Ecclesiastes together with Job and Proverbs, as in the traditional Wisdom Literature trio, brings out certain features. But then again, so does seeing it alongside Lamentations and Job, which explore similarly dark themes. For Kynes, there is feedback into our subjective genre designations because some text groupings are going to bring up more, or less, interesting results. On this theory of genre, therefore, "biblical wisdom literature" is still a genre, but so potentially is "biblical miserable literature," "bad bedtime reading," or "biblical literature that reminds me of a Cormac McCarthy novel."

All this takes Kynes's genre theory in more of a reader-response direction than the one I've been proposing in this book.[24] Readers take what they want from the buffet breakfast of biblical literature, and whatever ends up on their plates we call a "genre." I think we need to carefully consider three questions before we follow him on this.

First, can a genre be *any* intertextual connection I see between texts, or is there more to it? For Kynes, readers can choose to join the dots almost any way they like, and so "genre" very quickly becomes another word for "intertextuality."[25] But it's worth noting that most modern genre theorists would see genre as something more specific than that. Carolyn Miller, for example, argues that genre "cannot refer to just any category or kind of discourse," or the term becomes too broad to be useful.[26] This is reflected in the quite different way that RGS uses the constellation metaphor. Kynes's constellation is a constellation of *texts*, whereas in RGS, it's a functional relationship between elements within

---

24. Kynes clarifies that his "reception-oriented" approach is ultimately aimed at better objective appreciation of the historical texts: Kynes, "Wisdom and Wisdom Literature," in Kynes, *Handbook of Wisdom*, 10. In this case, seeing genres as social conventions and not just subjective networks is all the more critical.

25. See Michael Stead, "Intertextuality and Innerbiblical Interpretation," in *Dictionary of the Old Testament: Prophets*, ed. Gordon J. McConville and Mark Boda (Downers Grove, IL: IVP Academic, 2012), 362; Marianne Grohmann and Hyun Chul Paul Kim, eds., *Second Wave Intertextuality and the Hebrew Bible* (Atlanta: SBL Press, 2019).

26. Carolyn R. Miller, "Genre as Social Action," *QJS* 70 (May 1984): 151.

a *genre* – the forms, stylistic features, and content that together serve a social function.[27]

Second, is there more to a genre than the texts that belong to it? I guess you *could* think of genres as an intertextual network of similar texts, just as you *could* describe English grammar as an intertextual network of all the sentences that readers recognize as using English grammar – but there's a reason linguists don't think of either of them that way.[28] I have suggested instead that we see genres as stable(ish) social conventions, a bit like games (tenet 2). These conventions do give rise to similarities between texts, but they are more than that.

Finally, are these genre constellations subjective or social? To count as a genre, Carolyn Miller thinks, a group of texts needs not only similar formal features but also a truly recurring social action in pursuit of goals that are public.[29] In contrast, Will Kynes drops this aspect of social context from his application of modern genre theory. On one level, that's totally fine. Plenty of literary critics are reluctant to bring on board the full social package of SFL and RGS (chapter 3). But by taking the constellation metaphor without the social context that goes with it, genre loses the interpersonal dynamic of social convention involving writers and readers, and it becomes essentially a tool of reader response. This is a substantial point of departure from most modern genre theorists. Mikhail Bakhtin, Hans Robert Jauss, Tzvetan Todorov, John Frow, and many others make the point that even the most creative writers take up genres that already exist, even if they end up dramatically modifying them (see tenet 4).

In thinking of genres like conventions and participating in genres like playing a game, I've tried to emphasize the interpersonal dimension of genre. Like playing sport, we find ourselves involved in something bigger than ourselves. It's one thing to say that the ball is in the reader's court (tenet 12), but another to say that tennis is whatever you want it to be. To make this concrete, let's bring back my parking ticket from chapter 3. There are lots of ways I could subjectively

---

27. The lines between the "stars" are not subjective but are bound together by an "internal dynamic." They belong together because they serve the social function. See Kathleen Hall Jamieson and Karlyn Kohrs Campbell, "Form and Genre in Rhetorical Criticism," in *Form and Genre: Shaping Rhetorical Action* (Falls Church, VA: Speech Communication Association, 1978), 18, 21; John Frow, *Genre*, 2nd ed. (New York: Routledge, 2015) 71. See also Thomas O. BeeBee, *The Ideology of Genre: A Comparative Study of Generic Instability* (University Park: Pennsylvania State University Press, 1994), 282. For a different application to biblical studies: Hindy Najman, "The Idea of Biblical Genre: From Discourse to Constellation," in *Prayer and Poetry in the Dead Sea Scrolls and Related Literature: Essays in Honor of Eileen Schuller on the Occasion of Her 65th Birthday*, ed. Jeremy Penner, Ken M. Penner, and Cecilia Wassén, STDJ 98 (Leiden: Brill, 2011).

28. Kynes uses "emergence" to model this relationship between discourse and genre. SFL's model of "realization" between levels of discourse and context (chapter 3) is preferable, as it situates genre at the context of culture level and distinguishes it from intertextual relationships with similar texts at the discourse level. Looking at language systemically is also less likely to make your head spin.

29. Miller, "Genre as Social Action," 163–64.

choose to group this piece of paper with other pieces of paper like it. I could group the parking ticket together with library recall notices and poorly written novels as part of a constellation called "texts that ruin my whole day." But while "parking ticket" is a genre, "texts that ruin my whole day" is not. It may be a selective, self-reflective, and subjective grouping (tick, tick, and tick on Kynes's definition), but it lacks the conventional power of a genre.

Seeing genre as a social convention is important because it allows us to recognize the involvement of writers as well as readers (without reducing the meaning of the text to "whatever was in the author's mind"). Not every genre needs there to be coordination between the writer and the reader, of course – I enjoy a pun even when no pun was intended. But many, many genres have as their function some form of communication, and so our genre theory needs to account for the social context that makes this possible.[30] This is not to say that readers are always constrained in their genre choices – I raised the possibility of tactical or resistant readings in chapter 4. But even the most subversive readings take for granted an existing ecosystem of genres and existing social conventions (tenet 2) that none of us could invent on our own. Otherwise, there would be nothing to resist.

How Will the Dead Be Raised?

Will Kynes is obviously right about burying wisdom literature as a strict category. Modern genre theory reminds us that texts are promiscuous (tenet 1) and the borders between genres are fuzzy and overlapping (tenet 3). Even if we still think that the wisdom literature genre is a useful circle to draw about certain texts, we should use a few different colored highlighters rather than one big, thick permanent marker. However, Kynes's proposal that wisdom literature be reborn as a subjective constellation in the sky needs some careful thought. Should genre *really* be reconceived as simply one grouping of texts that readers can use to bring out interesting features of the texts? For the reasons given above, I think genres are more than intertextuality. As conventions that function within a social context to provide resources to writers and readers, they cannot be described in purely reader-response terms.

Having clarified our theory, however, there is still the massive open question about how useful it is to talk about wisdom literature as a genre. If our goal is to coordinate as much as possible with the conventions of its ancient social contexts,[31]

---

30. On the function of Scripture, see Jeannine K. Brown, *Scripture as Communication: Introducing Biblical Hermeneutics*, 2nd ed. (Grand Rapids: Baker Academic, 2021), 112–13.

31. I say contexts (plural) because biblical texts have notoriously complex histories (from oral tradition to editorial shaping to later canonical reception). *Which* social contexts are most relevant to interpretation is a bigger hermeneutical question that I'm happy to dodge right now.

then Kynes may well be right that wisdom literature has outlived its usefulness. If wisdom literature does exist as a meaningful genre, we should find it in more down-to-earth places – as a social convention, existing at the level of context of culture and context of situation. It may be one of several genres that a text promiscuously participates in, but it will be realized in identifiable recurring forms and situations. It's tricky, though, because with ancient texts we only have access to the context of culture through the texts themselves. Coming to a resolution will require not just solid genre theory but careful literary and historical analysis (and lots of boomerang testing).

The Wisdom Ecosystem

In assessing how the wisdom literature genre holds up, I suggest we start with the primary genres that all our wisdom literature prototypes are made up of. We can probably agree that, under the general wisdom banner, there are certain definite recurring forms and social functions we can meaningfully talk about as genres. Nobody is suggesting that proverbs, parables, dialogs, songs, riddles, and didactic stories aren't a thing.[32] These genres work quite differently from each other, but they all seem to anticipate a similar context of situation and function – gaining wisdom of one sort or another (Prov 1:2). What do we call this overarching group of wisdom genres then? Modern genre theory recognizes that genres don't live alone but function in systems of related genres within the context of culture (tenet 11). The riddle is taken up by an answer; the saying is gathered in a collection; and the didactic story calls for reflection followed by action. Zooming out, the books of Proverbs, Ecclesiastes, and Job bring these and other genres into dialog for our instruction. Given that these genres use language in quite different ways as they perform this function, it seems unwieldy to talk about them as participating in one *genre* of wisdom literature (though we could). Perhaps it is best to think of wisdom literature as *an ecosystem of genres that work within a similar context of situation.*[33] The old wisdom literature category lives on, not as a single genre, but as an ecosystem of related wisdom genres.

I'll leave this ongoing research with the professionals. For now, let's keep wisdom literature alive as a genre and see how well it accounts for the features of a biblical text taken from outside the traditional "Wisdom Literature" corpus.

---

32. Though how we understand these genres is a live issue: see Jacqueline Vayntrub, *Beyond Orality: Biblical Poetry on Its Own Terms*, The Ancient World (London: Routledge, 2019).

33. This works better than trying to squeeze quite diverse texts into a single genre based on "family resemblances" (cf. Dell, *Solomonic Corpus*, 30–31) or a shared wisdom mode (cf. Sneed, "Is the 'Wisdom Tradition' a Tradition?"). It also keeps different levels distinct. A two-line proverb is not the same thing as the book of Job, though they might be part of the same genre ecosystem.

ANOTHER TACTICAL READING OF JUDGES 19

We've already tried out a tactical reading of Judges 19 as a horror film to some success (see chapter 6). There we applied the boomerang test (chapter 4) as our best method for trying out a genre on a text – give the text a go, and if it comes back to us with a coherent reading, it is good evidence that our genre guess was not too far off. But what comes back when we try out that same text as wisdom literature?[34]

The Staging Structure

Wisdom literature is often written as poetry, but it can also take the form of didactic narratives, such as the story of Job 1. The staging structure of Judges 19 begins as a narrative.[35] An *orientation* gives us some context (v. 1); the young woman's departure introduces a *complication* (v. 2); and this is followed by a *quest* (vv. 3–21) that seems set to bring about the resolution of her return. However, no such resolution comes, and instead there is an *incident* in Gibeah (vv. 22–29) and finally an *evaluation* stage:

> Everyone who saw it was saying to one another, "Such a thing has never been seen or done, not since the day the Israelites came up out of Egypt. Just imagine! We must do something! So speak up!" (Judg 19:30)

Who is the "everyone who saw" referring to? This chorus of commentators seem to come out of nowhere, and the explicit moral commentary they provide is unusual for a narrative. An incident stage followed by evaluation stage is, however, a very normal way to finish an exemplum (a genre for evaluating characters' actions, which we discussed back in chapter 5). So the staging structure starts off as a narrative, but that story about an unhappy marriage is never resolved, and instead the chapter becomes an exemplum – a didactic genre for providing clear moral judgments on an incident.

The words of that final chorus are wisdom-heavy too. Wisdom is typically based on observation, so accordingly it is "every seer" of these events who is meant to respond in this way (including us). The imperatives that follow sound a

---

34. For a more technical reading, see my "Judges 19 as Wisdom: Sitting with the Wise in Ambivalence and Discontinuity," in *Honoring the Wise: Wisdom in Scripture, Ministry, and Life; Celebrating Lindsay Wilson's Thirty Years at Ridley*, Australian College of Theology Monograph Series (Eugene, OR: Wipf & Stock, 2022), 15–27.

35. Judges 19 is embedded within a complex text (Judges) with its own genre and function and has a sequel in chapters 20–21. We know nothing about any earlier versions, but for this test, I'll take Judges 19 as having its own integrity and genre.

lot like Proverbs 31:9 and its call to "speak up and judge fairly; defend the rights of the poor and needy."

Seems pretty on-brand for wisdom literature already.

The Orientation Stage

Orientations bear a lot of weight when it comes to establishing the genre of a story, so it is worth looking closely at how the story is introduced:

> In those days Israel had no king.
> Now [there was a man,] a Levite who lived in a remote area in the hill country of Ephraim [and he] took [a woman,] a concubine from Bethlehem in Judah. (Judg 19:1)[36]

Taking up the story as wisdom literature makes sense of some of the odd features of this introduction. This is the only story in the book of Judges (and one of few in the Old Testament) where nobody seems to have a name.[37] We are simply told there was "a man" from Ephraim and "a woman" from Bethlehem. Later we meet a servant, a father, an old man, and a mob – all de-identified. And while the geographical setting is foregrounded throughout, the historical context is quite vague. We are not told immediately how these events fit in with the other stories in Judges.[38] This vagueness about who and when fits awkwardly with a historical recount genre but is perfect for a didactic narrative whose function is to help us draw general moral lessons, using de-identified examples.

The wisdom function also helps explain the first sentence: "In those days Israel had no king." Kingship is not a feature of this chapter, so why is it mentioned here? A common answer is that Judges is a sort of historical propaganda justifying the need for a king, but the problem with this is that they already have a perfect king – God! – and as the story goes on, Israel's kings often make things worse, not better. I think the wisdom literature genre is a much better explanation for why the story starts with a nod to kingship. Kingship is strongly associated with the wisdom literature setting and function. Part of wisdom is wise statecraft, as well as understanding what good governance looks like. In that light, the story functions to help hone our understanding of how a nation should work by showing us a situation in which no king was around and things

---

36. The brackets resupply words smoothed by the NIV translation.
37. See Adele Reinhartz, *Why Ask My Name? Anonymity and Identity in Biblical Narrative* (New York: Oxford University Press, 1998), 126, 188.
38. Judges 20:28 implies these chapters involved the first generation after Joshua, before the events of Judges 3–16.

went badly wrong. But would things have turned out any different under a king? Unlike propaganda, the wisdom literature genre suggests we are left to sit with the tensions here. Kingship is no silver bullet, as the rest of the story of Israel will show.

The other thing about that phrase is that in Judges 17:6 and 21:25, the absence of a king is explicitly linked to personal moral accountability: "In those days there was no king in Israel; a man did what was right in his own eyes" (my translation). Proverbs is full of examples of men who do "what is right in their own eyes" – and normally not in a good way. We are set up to read Judges 19 as a proverbial example of what that ethical autonomy looks like when it goes wrong: "There was no king. A man, a Levite . . . took a concubine. . . ." (my translation). The proverbial foolish man doing what is right in his own eyes will be played convincingly in this story by a certain Levite from Ephraim.

Wisdom Themes and Motifs

Seeing Judges 19 through the wisdom literature lens spotlights several themes and symbols. The man who speaks to the wife's heart is a glimpse of an ideal straight out of Song of Songs (Song 5:4). Hospitality is an important aspect of acting rightly in the world (Job 31:32). The incident happens after dark on a journey planned by a fool, which leads to death – a literal take on a recurring motif in Proverbs (Prov 4:19; 12:15; 14:12; 16:25). Relationships at home are a classic setting for wisdom instruction (1:8). Wisdom means anticipating consequences and making successful plans, neither of which the Levite seems able to do. He leaves abruptly on a long journey without enough time to get home, runs into the most predictable of all dangers for a traveler (nightfall!), and ignores the street-smart suggestion of his servant. The sayings in Proverbs are often a study in contrasts, placing the wise and foolish, righteous and the wicked, side by side. Judges 19 is similarly a study in contrasts between Gibeah and Jebus, Israelite and Canaanite, hostility and hospitality, husband and stranger.

The wisdom lens also brings out an important absence that reflects the wisdom worldview (tenet 9). In wisdom literature, humans make choices and events are left to play out, with God's agency in the background. The story in Judges 19 is almost identical to what happens in Sodom in Genesis 19 – until we get to verse 25, that is. At that point in the Genesis story, God intervenes and blinds the would-be rapists. But in this version of the story in Judges, God remains painfully silent.

In terms of distinctive wisdom words and phrases, a number of them jump out. The mob of people who surround the house are described as "sons of worthlessness" (Judg 19:22, my translation), a terrifying incarnation of the worthless man of Proverbs (Prov 6:12; 16:27; 19:28). They are exhorted by the old man not to act "so wickedly," or do this "folly" (Judg 19:23, my translation). He sounds like a father figure exhorting young men against evil (Prov 4:16; 17:4; 24:8, 19) and foolishness (17:7, 21; 30:32) – until, of course, he suggests that they do to his daughter and the young woman that "which is good in your eyes" (Judg 19:24, my translation).

Perhaps the most interesting potential wisdom figure, however, is the young woman herself. In wisdom literature, wisdom is often embodied as a woman, and the young woman is a poignant symbol of Lady Wisdom cast aside by foolish men.[39] Lady Wisdom announces:

> For those who find me find life
> and receive favor from the Lord.
> But those who fail to find me harm themselves;
> all who hate me love death. (Prov 8:35–36)

In this story, the Levite seeks after the young woman, taking the path to wisdom, but he ultimately abandons her in the town square. Unlike Joseph, whose wisdom brings life to his family in Genesis, the Levite's path of folly and wickedness leads to nothing but escalating violence and death in the following chapters. The final image of the young woman reaching for the threshold of the house (Judg 19:26–27) is haunting – wisdom cries out in the public square, but here in Gibeah, nobody listens (Prov 1:20–21; 8:3).

Wisdom Function: Wrestling with the Ambivalence and Discontinuities

The most crucial thing about the wisdom literature genre, however, is the formative social function. It aims to guide a person as they grow in spiritual discernment, character, and all-round personal capacity. Its slow-burn teaching style invites us to receive and reflect, and then re-receive and re-reflect, rather than giving us the answers.[40] This function does a great job of explaining why there are so many finely balanced ambiguities and discontinuities in the Judges 19 story, and what we are meant to do with them as readers.

The young woman's character is far from simple. Her marital status as *pilegesh* (a wife of secondary status?), the exact nature of the breakdown of

---

39. See Nicholas Ansell, "This Is Her Body: Judges 19 as Call to Discernment," in *Tamar's Tears: Evangelical Engagements with Feminist Old Testament Hermeneutics*, ed. Andrew Sloane (Eugene, OR: Wipf & Stock, 2012), 65–103.

40. Thanks, Joel Atwood, for helping sharpen this description of social function.

relationship (was she unfaithful, or did she leave him?), and the father's motives throughout (why does he take the young woman back in if she is an adulteress? And what's going on with his extreme hospitality? Does he trust the Levite or not?) have all troubled commentators. They have usually tried to resolve these ambiguities one way or the other, either casting her as an immoral woman who got what she deserved in the end, or exonerating her and trying to salvage her reputation and make her a perfectly innocent victim. This is necessary for them in order to get a clean, tidy moral out of the story. But wisdom literature often requires us to sit in complex situations for a while and consider things from multiple angles. On the one hand, maybe she was unfaithful to her husband; on the other hand, was his betrayal not infinitely worse?

The horrific negotiations at the door of the house in Gibeah present us with many gaps and inconsistencies. The mob demands to rape the Levite, and the host offers the young woman and his own daughter instead. The mob refuses, but then "he" (the Levite or the old man?) pushes the young woman out and the men rape her. The whole thing is simply awful. It's also confusing. Why does the mob reject the offer of two women but then seem to be satisfied by the young woman? There's been no mention of the man having a virgin daughter, though there is a male servant who has been very quiet since they arrived in the town. Every explanation you can come up with runs aground at some point – and maybe that's the point. This is a story we are meant to observe, take with us, and think over. We need to sit with the ambivalence and discontinuities a bit, because life is complex and people are never one-dimensional.

WISDOM LITERATURE, OR JUST SPARKLING WISDOM THEMES?

We have now applied two different tactical uptakes for Judges 19 through the boomerang test – horror film (see chapter 6) and wisdom literature. Both, I think, make better sense of the difficulties in the story than traditional assumptions about the genre of the passage. Whatever Judges 19 is, it seems to work more like a horror film or wisdom story than a heroic saga or fairy tale.

Personally, I find that the staging structure and social function encourage me towards seeing this as a kind of didactic story. But I'll leave you to work out whether you think the tactical uptake of Judges 19 as wisdom literature was successful. You might decide that Judges 19 is a plain old biblical narrative, even if it does have some interesting points of connection with wisdom themes. Or you might demote wisdom literature here to a "mode" – a narrative with a hint of proverb or didactic story about it.

SUMMARY

Modern genre theory has already begun to transform the study of wisdom literature. The classical wisdom literature category no doubt needs to be laid to rest. Rather than put a hard border around a collection of books called Wisdom Literature, we need to recognize that texts have promiscuous relationships with many genres (tenet 1), and that these genres will be overlapping and fuzzy around the edges (tenet 3). While quite diverse in terms of staging structure and use of language, the wisdom literature prototypes do seem to share recurring formal features and content (tenet 6), but they can especially be distinguished by the role the reader is invited to play (tenet 4), which serves its social function (tenet 8). When interpreting wisdom literature, we need to pay attention not just to how it is written but also to what it is for. The broad content of this instruction and the slow-burn teaching style suggest it is a genre for formation – aiming to grow a person's spiritual discernment, character, and all-round personal capacity.

Rather than follow Will Kynes in seeing genre as a subjective tool for reader-response, it is best to see genres as conventions (tenet 2) that involve both readers and writers (tenet 5). The fact that smaller genres like "saying" and "riddle" exist and have similar themes and social function seems beyond doubt. It also seems clear that certain "instructional books" – like Proverbs, Ecclesiastes, and Job – might have a particular interest in those themes and be designed to pull together genres for instructional ends.

But how should we think of the overarching category for all this? Genres do not exist in isolation (tenet 11), so perhaps it is best to see wisdom literature as living on not as one wisdom genre but as an ecosystem of related wisdom genres. Running the boomerang test (chapter 4) on a tactical uptake of Judges 19 as didactic story does seem to make sense of the ambivalences and discontinuities that have otherwise puzzled commentators, suggesting that it might function well within the recurring social situation of wisdom literature.

Suggested Workflow for Wisdom Literature

History

☐ What (if anything) can we say about the historical context that the text was likely produced in or that the text addresses? What worldview and values are being assumed?

☐ How does the text go about the typical function of wisdom literature (slow-burn character formation)? What role is being expected of the reader?

- ☐ Are there similar texts inside or outside the Bible? How do they compare and contrast with this one?
- ☐ How have communities in different times, places, and cultures approached this passage? Given your own tradition, what assumptions are you likely to make about the text?

Literature

- ☐ What primary or complex genre(s) *within* the wisdom literature genre ecosystem are we dealing with in this text – proverb, saying, riddle, poem, narrative, compilation, instructional book, etc.?
- ☐ What genres *outside* the typical wisdom literature genre ecosystem can you identify in or around this text (including embedded genres)? What do they each bring to the table? What new ideas or effects emerge from combining the different genres?
- ☐ Where does the passage you are looking at fit within the surrounding text? Is it embedded or framed somehow? What is the structure of the book as a whole?
- ☐ What typical wisdom terms, relationships, motifs, etc. are used?
- ☐ What puzzles, contradictions, or ambiguities force us to keep thinking?
- ☐ What formal features (such as staging structure) would you expect to find in this genre, and how are they realized in this text? How does the experience offered by these formal features serve the social function of the wisdom genre?

Scripture

- ☐ What general observations about reality are being presented here?
- ☐ What posture does this text take towards other texts in the wisdom tradition, or Scripture more broadly? Is it endorsing, collating, applying, qualifying, or complicating them?
- ☐ Where and how has this text been taken up elsewhere in the Bible? What other Bible passages need to be brought into conversation with this text to give a full picture? What interpretations of this passage are ruled out by other texts of Scripture?
- ☐ What connections and tensions (if any) can you see between this text and the themes and theology of the Bible as a whole – salvation history, creation, ethics, anthropology, our view of God, retribution, providence, etc.? What would be missing or less clear if this text were missing from your Bible?

☐ What ethical concerns are raised, and what insights are offered? How might they be relevant to situations that God's people find themselves in today? How *shouldn't* someone apply this text?

QUESTIONS FOR DISCUSSION OR REFLECTION

1. What is lost, and what is gained, by reading Judges 19 as wisdom literature?
2. Do you think it is better perhaps to ditch the whole category of wisdom literature and just focus on the more recognizable genres like proverb, riddle, and didactic story? If so, how might we describe the overall (secondary or complex) genre of Proverbs, Job, and Ecclesiastes? If not, why not?
3. How important is it to you that meaning be more than a subjective experience by the reader? (How might your answer change, depending on the genre you are reading?)

FURTHER READING

Introductory

Firth, David G., and Lindsay Wilson, eds. *Exploring Old Testament Wisdom: Literature and Themes*. London: Apollos, 2016.
    Survey of wisdom themes.
Longman, Tremper, III. *The Fear of the Lord Is Wisdom: A Theological Introduction to Wisdom in Israel*. Grand Rapids: Baker Academic, 2017.
    Introduction to wisdom.
Murphy, Roland E. *The Tree of Life: An Exploration of Biblical Wisdom Literature*. Third edition. Grand Rapids: Eerdmans, 2002.
    Classic on wisdom literature.

Deep Dive

Cheung, Simon Chi-chung. *Wisdom Intoned: A Reappraisal of the Genre "Wisdom Psalms."* Library of Hebrew Bible/Old Testament Studies 613. London: Bloomsbury T&T Clark, 2015.
    Clarifies how we identify wisdom psalms.
Dell, Katharine J. *The Solomonic Corpus of "Wisdom" and Its Influence*. Oxford: Oxford University Press, 2020.
    Argues for a Solomonic organizing principle.
Kynes, Will. *An Obituary for "Wisdom Literature": The Birth, Death, and Intertextual Reintegration of a Biblical Corpus*. Oxford: Oxford University Press, 2019.
    Redefines the wisdom genre as a subjective constellation.

————, ed. *The Oxford Handbook of Wisdom and the Bible.* Oxford Handbooks. New York: Oxford University Press, 2021.

Collection of essays summarizing various conversations.

Sneed, Mark R., ed. *Is There a Wisdom Tradition? New Prospects in Israelite Wisdom Studies.* Ancient Israel and Its Literature 23. Atlanta: SBL Press, 2015.

Explores the social context of wisdom.

CHAPTER 11

MORE THAN BIOGRAPHY

What Is a Gospel?

I once stumbled upon a long online discussion in which devoted Taylor Swift fans ("Swifties") were debating whether her albums should be categorized as country music, pop music, or country-pop music. I couldn't tell which side won the debate, but I do remember thinking, *Wow, Swifties sure feel strongly about this*, and then, *This reminds me of New Testament scholars debating the genre of the Gospels*, followed immediately by, *This would be a great illustration to use if ever I write a book on modern genre theory*. So here we are.

The debate is about whether Matthew, Mark, Luke, and John should be considered as (A) a unique genre, (B) Greco-Roman biographies, or (C) something else. It's a great case study for how our modern genre theory tenets and the boomerang test help us when deciding the genre of a thing, especially when that thing is from long ago. This chapter begins by evaluating the three options, before showing how our modern genre theory tenets might help break the deadlock. But we don't want to leave it at simply identifying the genre. The final part of this chapter sketches out what difference genre might make for how we interpret the Gospels.

Let's start by getting up to speed with the debate.[1]

THE DEBATE SO FAR

Option A: The Gospels Are Their Own Unique Genre

A banana is a banana; a gospel is a gospel. For a long time, the Gospels were seen as unique – *sui generis*. The earliest gospel writer (say, Mark) produced something with no direct literary parallel in Greco-Roman literature, and so a new genre was born. Mark might have drawn on existing forms and content

---

1. For an overview: Judith A. Diehl, "What Is a 'Gospel'? Recent Studies in the Gospel Genre," *CurBR* 9, no. 2 (2011): 176; Steve Walton, "What Are the Gospels? Richard Burridge's Impact on Scholarly Understanding of the Genre of the Gospels," *CurBR* 14, no. 1 (2015): 81–93; Michal Beth Dinkler, "What Is a Genre? Contemporary Genre Theory and the Gospels," in *Modern and Ancient Literary Criticism of the Gospels: Continuing the Debate on Gospel Genre(s)*, ed. Robert Matthew Calhoun, David P. Moessner, and Tobias Nicklas, WUNT 451 (Tübingen: Mohr Siebeck, 2020), 77–96.

from oral tradition, but those secret herbs and spices were combined according to a new recipe to meet the demands of a new situation.

To many today, the claim that the Gospels are *sui generis* sounds extraordinary: "from a literary point of view, it is a nonsense."[2] Even if Mark *could* have invented his own literary conventions from scratch all on his own (which seems pretty tricky), there'd be little point inventing a genre that nobody else knew what to do with.

But then why did smart people like Karl Schmidt, Martin Dibelius, and Rudolf Bultmann accept this seemingly impossible conclusion? As form critics, they had some hard-coded assumptions about genre that make more sense of the *sui generis* claim.[3]

First, they drew a firm line between *high literature* and *folk literature*.[4] High literature is what serious authors sit down to produce, and in doing so, they consciously adopt literary genres like history or biography. Folk literature is more of a team sport – oral traditions in multiple versions that have more to do with the life of a community than the personality of a single "author." (Think of it as the difference between J. R. R. Tolkien's *The Lord of the Rings* and the children's story "The Boy Who Cried Wolf.") If the Gospels are considered collections of folk literature, with no one author, then there's no point looking for parallels with literary genres like biography.

Second, form critics are interested in the *pithy, pure,* and *preliterary* texts behind the written biblical documents (see chapter 1). Folk literature obviously has its own folk genres, and so we find early Christian genres preserved *in* the Gospels: "In the beginning was the sermon," wrote Dibelius.[5] But if the Gospel books themselves evolved as overgrown sermons, then questions about their literary genre as a book aren't relevant; we won't find much editorial shaping, and certainly no use of Greco-Roman genres.

Third, Hermann Gunkel's home-brew genre theory defined genres by their situation and content, not just formal features (see chapter 1). The Gospels began as early Christian sermons about Jesus. If Jesus and his message are unique, then so is the genre.[6]

---

2. Richard A. Burridge, *What Are the Gospels? A Comparison with Graeco-Roman Biography*, 2nd ed. (Grand Rapids: Eerdmans, 2004), 12.

3. See Rudolf Bultmann, *The History of the Synoptic Tradition*, trans. John Marsh (Oxford: Basil Blackwell, 1963), 368; Martin Dibelius, *From Tradition to Gospel*, trans. Bertram Lee Woolf (Cambridge: Clarke, 1971), 3–8.

4. See Zachary K. Dawson, "The Problem of Gospel Genres: Unmasking a Flawed Consensus and Providing a Fresh Way Forward with Systemic Functional Linguistics Genre Theory," *BAGL* 8 (2019): 37.

5. Martin Dibelius, "Die alttestamentlichen Motive in der Leidensgeschichte," in *Botschaft und Geschichte: Gesammelte Aufsätze von Martin Dibelius*, ed. Erster Band (Tübingen: Mohr Siebeck, 1953), 242.

6. However, the gospels are more than sermon transcripts. See Helmut Koester, *Ancient Christian*

Finally, the *sui generis* label was required because of the classical genre theory assumption that each text needs a single genre designation. *Sui generis* doesn't mean "without any influence or precedent"; it's almost an error code for classifying texts with *too many* genre influences to pick just one. New genres *are* new, but they are also built on earlier genres (tenet 2). In the 1960s, Miles Davis invented a new genre of "jazz fusion," but as the name implies, he drew on preexisting genres: bebop, rock, and funk. Similarly, we might recognize "gospel" as something new (*sui generis*) but also recognize its roots in earlier genres (perhaps not high literary genres, but certainly oral genres like the sermon and "folk biography").

The *sui generis* view isn't as silly as it sounds at first. In studying the Gospels, the argument goes, let's approach them first and foremost as something distinct – *gospel*. Loveday Alexander offers a recent definition like this: "A gospel is a loose-knit, episodic narrative relating the words and deeds of a Galilean prophet called Jesus, culminating in his trial and death and ending with varied reports of his resurrection."[7]

It's a reasonable place to start – a gospel is a gospel. But option A is less popular these days. As form criticism gave way to redaction criticism and more literary approaches, the hunt was on for a genre that would account for the literary shape of the Gospels as a whole. People started looking for similarities with Greco-Roman genres, which brings us to option B.

Option B: Richard Burridge and the Biography

A *bios* is the Greek name for a genre that focuses on a single extraordinary "life" – often a great political leader or influential philosopher. It's where we get "*bio*graphy."[8] By the standards of modern biographies of sports stars and politicians, the Gospels are a bit odd. They don't tell us the date when Jesus was born, for example, or who his friends were at school. (I once read a modern biography that forgot to include the subject's birthday, but it's certainly an outlier in its genre.) But genres are only relatively stable (tenet 2), so how do they compare with *ancient* Greco-Roman biographies?

Gospels: Their History and Development (Philadelphia: Trinity, 1990), 24–43; Francis Watson, *What Is a Gospel?* (Grand Rapids: Eerdmans, 2022), chapter 1.

7. Loveday Alexander, "What Is a Gospel?," in *The Cambridge Companion to the Gospels*, ed. Stephen C. Barton, 2nd ed., Cambridge Companions to Religion (Cambridge: Cambridge University Press, 2021), 13. See also Scot McKnight, "Matthew as 'Gospel,'" in *Jesus, Matthew's Gospel and Early Christianity: Studies in Memory of Graham N. Stanton*, ed. D. M. Gurtner, J. Willitts, and R. A. Burridge, LNTS 435 (London: T&T Clark, 2011), 59–75; Ryder Wishart, "The Polarizing Gospel Genre and Register" (PhD thesis, McMaster Divinity College, 2022), 306.

8. I'm using "biographies" throughout, even though genres change (tenet 2) and ancient *bioi* aren't the same as modern biographies. Please don't call the genre police.

Enter Richard Burridge. He wasn't the first to argue that the Gospels are examples of Greco-Roman biographies,[9] but his doctoral thesis (published in 1992) is what convinced most people.[10] (By revolutionizing gospels scholarship with his PhD, he also gave every graduate student since a massive inferiority complex.)

Burridge compared the Gospels with ten Greco-Roman biographies, looking for similarities on eighteen criteria (including opening features like titles, external features like length and structure, and internal features like characterization).[11] He put the most weight on the genre's subject, which he determined by using statistics on who gets the most airplay and verbs. Finding similarities between the Gospels and these ten examples, especially in their focus on a single person as subject, he concluded that the Gospels were Greco-Roman biographies.

Biographies and histories overlap. A history tends to focus on a major event or period and brings up individuals only when they are relevant to that larger story. In a biography, however, the camera stays focused on the individual and mentions events that are relevant to their life. If the Gospels are biographies, we expect them to mostly paint a portrait of their subject – Jesus. That's not to say that the Gospels are *un*historical, but the goal is not to write the definitive history of Late Second Temple Judaism or of Judean politics in AD 30–33. Each story will be chosen and arranged for what it contributes to our understanding of this person.

So the Gospels are Greco-Roman biographies. Several scholars have continued to refine our understanding of the Gospels along these lines, including Helen Bond, Mike Bird, and Craig Keener.[12] With this debate settled, everyone went back to their tents to work on other things.

Not So Fast . . .

Scholarly consensus has a short shelf life.[13] In the thirty years since, several scholars have critiqued Richard Burridge's theory, method, and conclusions. This is where things get interesting for us in terms of genre theory.

---

9. First were Ernest Rénan (1863) and Clyde Votaw (1915); then Charles Talbert and Philip Shuler built the consensus: see David E. Aune, "Greco-Roman Biography," in *Greco-Roman Literature and the New Testament*, ed. David E. Aune, SBLSBS 21 (Atlanta, GA: Scholars Press, 1988), 107–26.

10. Richard A. Burridge, *What Are the Gospels? A Comparison with Graeco-Roman Biography*, 25th anniversary ed. (Waco, TX: Baylor University Press, 2018).

11. Burridge lists nineteen criteria but drops one (meter). Thanks, Ryder Wishart, for this observation.

12. Helen K. Bond, *The First Biography of Jesus: Genre and Meaning in Mark's Gospel* (Grand Rapids: Eerdmans, 2020); Michael F. Bird, *The Gospel of the Lord: How the Early Church Wrote the Story of Jesus* (Grand Rapids: Eerdmans, 2014); Craig S. Keener, *Christobiography: Memory, History, and the Reliability of the Gospels* (Grand Rapids: Eerdmans, 2019).

13. Few PhDs are awarded for agreeing with everything said already.

First, some criticize Burridge's genre theory for being dated and for mixing up incompatible approaches (hang around SFL people and you'll quickly learn they find mixing theories about as appealing as sashimi ice cream with extra BBQ sauce).[14] Burridge leans heavily on Alastair Fowler, looking for family resemblances between the gospels and Greco-Roman biographies.[15] I explained in chapter 2 why we now avoid using family resemblances.[16] (You could probably find "resemblances" between any random group of ten texts.) Yet he also assumes that texts "belong" to a "class," whereas texts have complex relationships with multiple genres (tenet 1).

The second criticism has to do with method. Burridge only really compares the gospels to one potential genre (his ten examples were all biographies) and mostly looks for similarities (not differences).[17] It's like arguing that Louis Armstrong played country music because, like many country music stars, he came from the southern USA and often wrote songs about humans. The *differences* between country music and New Orleans jazz need to be considered too. This method means Burridge doesn't take seriously enough alternative possibilities (especially Jewish genres).[18]

The third criticism is that Burridge pays too little attention to social situation and function.[19] I could point out any number of "family resemblances" between a gospel and Arthur Conan Doyle's *The Adventures of Sherlock Holmes* – they are about the same length; they are participant-driven narratives; the subject of each story is the predominant subject of its main verbs; they contain themes of truth and justice; they highlight the extraordinary abilities of a central enigmatic

---

14. See Elizabeth E. Shively, "A Critique of Richard Burridge's Genre Theory: From One-Dimensional to a Multi-Dimensional Approach to Gospel Genre," in *Modern and Ancient Literary Criticism of the Gospels: Continuing the Debate on Gospel Genre(s)*, ed. Robert Matthew Calhoun, David P. Moessner, and Tobias Nicklas, WUNT 451 (Tübingen: Mohr Siebeck, 2020), 101, 107; Dawson, "Problem of Gospel Genres," 50.

15. Burridge, *What Are the Gospels?*, 31–47. While the updated 2018 edition makes reference to John Frow's work, the genre theory driving the methodology is still essentially that of Fowler, plus E. D. Hirsch, René Wellek, Austin Warren, Northrop Frye, and Jonathan Culler. Their major works were all published between 1957 and 1976. It may be a stretch to call this "modern" genre theory in 2018.

16. With family resemblances, where do you draw the line between siblings, weird cousins, and strangers? Are the differences between the Gospel of John and the Synoptic Gospels greater than that between Mark and the Gospel of Thomas? What about the book of Mormon? (Thanks, Mike Bird, for highlighting this issue. I owe you a coffee.)

17. See Adela Yarbro Collins, "Genre and the Gospels," *JR* 75 (1995): 239–46; Shively, "Critique," 100–104; Andrew W. Pitts, *History, Biography, and the Genre of Luke-Acts: An Exploration of Literary Divergence in Greek Narrative Discourse* (Leiden: Brill, 2019); Andrew Pitts, "The Fowler Fallacy: Biography, History, and the Genre of Luke-Acts," *JBL* 139, no. 2 (2020): 341–59; Wishart, "Polarizing Gospel Genre," 69–86. In later work, Burridge somewhat addresses this criticism.

18. See Dinkler, "What Is a Genre?," in *Modern and Ancient Literary Criticism of the Gospels*, ed. Calhoun, Moessner, and Nicklas; Yarbro Collins, "Gospels."

19. Dawson, "Problem of Gospel Genres"; Wishart, "Polarizing Gospel Genre."

figure; the plot revolves around the death of an innocent victim – but no matter how many formal or thematic features I point to, nobody is going to believe me when I say that Mark is detective fiction.

Burridge does consider occasion and purpose in broad terms, concluding that biographies can be written to fulfil a wide range of social purposes. But is a gospel's function more specific? Modern genre theory gives us tools to explore the function of the genre in its social context (whether focusing on the texts using SFL or on the culture using RGS: see chapter 3). Depending on what we find, "biography" alone may not be an adequate description of the gospel genre. We need to ask not just how gospels are written but what they are for (tenet 8).

These criticisms don't invalidate Burridge's observations about the similarities between gospels and ancient biographies, but they do urge more cautious conclusions. Gospels may be similar to biographies in many ways, but that doesn't rule out participation in other genres as well.

Option C: Something Else

Alongside biography, the other main contender for the genre of the Gospels is history. This is especially popular when talking about Luke. Luke and Acts are normally taken to be a two-part work by the same author. But unlike the Gospels, Acts doesn't focus on a single individual; it explains the spread of the gospel during the early years of the church. One good solution is to take Acts as "collected biography,"[20] but another is to say that Acts is actually history, not biography.[21]

This presents a unique conundrum for classical genre theory if we think the other Gospels are biographies – either Luke–Acts changes genre at the halfway mark, or Luke is a different genre from the other Gospels. Neither conclusion sits easily with classical genre theory. If our goal is to identify the one true genre for each text, and if Luke is meant to be taken together with Acts, then scholars are going to keep going around in circles on this one forever.

The Gospels have also been compared to Hebrew Bible texts (including historical narratives, prophetic literature, and apocalypse), as well as to Jewish commentaries/midrash, biographies of righteous people, apologetic historiography, and novels.[22] Comparisons are also sometimes made to other Greco-Roman

---

20. Sean A. Adams, *The Genre of Acts and Collected Biography* (New York: Cambridge University Press, 2013).

21. See David E. Aune, *The New Testament in Its Literary Environment*, LEC 8 (Philadelphia: Westminster, 1987), 77; Pitts, *History*, 168.

22. On Mark as Jewish novel: Michael E. Vines, *The Problem of Markan Genre: The Gospel of Mark and*

literary genres, including "aretalogy" (a kind of wild story about spiritual men who lived long ago), encomium (a more specific type of Greco-Roman biography that praises a person's character and words), succession narrative (introducing an influential figure and establishing his rightful successors), miracle story, novel, epic, and even theatrical tragedy.

The debate shows little signs of fizzling out. There is merit to almost all of these suggestions, in addition to options A and B as we saw above. Fueling the squabble is a fundamental confusion about genre theory – what genres are and do, and how we should approach diagnosing them. The claim that the Gospels are unique seems simultaneously self-evident (when you examine what is distinctive about them) and absurd (when you examine their similarities to earlier genres). Even amongst those using formal features to diagnose the genre, there is significant disagreement about how to tally the results. Some look to where the majority of features fall, while others look to specific elements like introductions and staging structures as decisive. Who shall deliver us from this theoretical dead end?

SOUNDS LIKE A CASE FOR MODERN GENRE THEORY

Whether it is fans deciding what genre Taylor Swift belongs to or New Testament scholars debating what genre the Gospels belong to, modern genre theory can help by re-examining what "belonging to" a genre means.

Texts Are Promiscuous

It's often observed that strong cases can be made for all three genre options, and none totally fit the evidence.[23] People say this like it's a bad thing – and it is indeed frustrating if your goal is to find a single class for each text. But modern genre theory accepts that texts have complex relationships with multiple genres (tenet 1).[24] It's a good thing! In Taylor Swift's case, straddling the country-pop divide has made her very rich. Likewise, it's entirely possible (likely, even) that a complex literary text such as Luke-Acts will draw on the resources of multiple

---

the *Jewish Novel* (Atlanta: SBL Press, 2002); Christopher C. Fuller, "Matthew's Genealogy as Eschatological Satire: Bakhtin Meets Form Criticism," in *Bakhtin and Genre Theory in Biblical Studies*, ed. Roland Boer (Atlanta: SBL Press, 2007), 119–32; David E. Aune, "Genre Theory and Genre-Function of Mark and Matthew," in *Mark and Matthew I: Comparative Readings: Understanding the Earliest Gospels in Their First-Century Settings*, ed. Eve-Marie Becker and Anders Runesson, WUNT 271 (Tübingen: Mohr Siebeck, 2011), 145–76; Brian Larsen, *Archetypes and the Fourth Gospel: Literature and Theology in Conversation*, (London: T&T Clark, 2018).

23. See, for example, Pitts, *History*, 3.

24. Alan Bale applies this principle in *Genre and Narrative Coherence in the Acts of the Apostles*, LNTS 514 (London: T&T Clark, 2015), 70–93.

genres to achieve its purpose. This is why the metaphor of "family resemblance" is so misleading. *Family* implies (unless you're part of a weird polygamous cult) simple genetic relationships with clear lines and one spot each on a family tree. Genres aren't like that.

That's not to say that every genre option discussed above is equally as helpful. It ultimately comes down to the boomerang test (chapter 4): What happens when we read a gospel as unique folk literature, or a biography, or as something else?[25] Clearing the hurdles of classical genre theory, I hope more work can be done in evaluating the payoffs for reading the Gospels in these various kinds of ways.

Even if we keep the consensus opinion that the Gospels are closest to Greco-Roman biographies, I expect we'll find other genre-based resources at play as well. Luke may be Greco-Roman biography like the other Gospels, for example, but it also makes sense in light of Acts to consider the influence of historical genres.

The most obvious genre influence alongside Greco-Roman biography is Hebrew narrative, which influences the form as well as the content of the Gospels.[26] Luke's gospel, for example, frames the narrative with a reference to the king of Judea (1:5) and stories about people other than Jesus (Zechariah, Elizabeth, John, and Mary). Introducing multiple individuals within a time period is sometimes taken as a sign we are dealing with history, not biography. But ask any Old Testament writer, "How do you introduce a super-important figure in Hebrew narrative?" and they'll describe exactly this kind of opening: the context of the current king of Judea, the type-scene of the childless couple, the angelic announcement, the embedded genealogy, and the song of praise.[27] This means everybody is a bit right: the Gospels are a new genre (option A) that takes the form of Greco-Roman biographies (option B) and combines it in new ways with genres from the Hebrew Bible (option C).

Fuzzy around the Edges

The fact that genres are fuzzy around the edges (tenet 3) explains why the debate over gospel genre goes back and forth. Very few people think the Gospels are novels, whereas we can debate all day about whether the Gospels are biography or history. Why? Because biographies and histories are close, and the edges between them are not always easy to define.[28] Rather than tallying loose

---

25. For example, the folk literature genre pays off by explaining the existence of multiple versions and different arrangements of the same tradition: see Alexander, "What Is a Gospel?," 23.

26. N. T. Wright sees the gospels as a "unique combination of Hellenistic biography and Jewish history": *People of God* (London: SPCK, 1992), 434. Cf. Bond, *First Biography of Jesus*, 29.

27. See Genesis 11–21; 25; 29–30; Judges 13; 1 Samuel 1–2.

28. See Adams, *Genre of Acts*, 247.

family resemblances, we should describe the similarity of each gospel to certain prototypes (tenet 3).[29]

Historical and Cultural Perspective

Seen in a historical perspective, genres are only ever relatively stable (tenet 2). This avoids the squabble over whether gospel is a *sui generis* class or a part of Greco-Roman literary culture. It's always both. Sure, the Beatles were geniuses, and they changed music forever, but they didn't invent from scratch guitars, rock and roll, or the idea of a love song.

Genres don't live alone but function in sets within a context of culture (tenet 11). We should remember that New Testament texts belong to at least three overlapping and at times competing genre sets: Greco-Roman, Hellenized Jewish, and biblical literature. Within these overlapping sets, power dynamics are at play (tenet 10). Sean Adams suggests that writers may have modified the biography genre to bring it in line with features of classier historical genre features, trying to raise the social standing of the work by using the social prestige that the historical genre implies.[30]

What about Readers?

The ball is in the reader's court (tenet 12), so receiving the four gospels as part of the canon has implications for their genre. By reading Luke as part of the canon of Scripture, Luke becomes the third gospel, a voice alongside Matthew, Mark, and John. It is natural that this brings out the biographical features of the text. But when scholars see Luke as part of a two-volume work with Acts, this might bring historical genres into play too. For example, Jesus's ministry is framed as the beginning of the story of the early church.

More fundamentally, even if Mark had copied the biography form exactly, his gospel would still be something that no other ancient life of a statesman or poet claims to be – Scripture. The role that readers expect the text to play is fundamentally changed, as is its intertextual network, authority, power relations, and truth effects.

Without modern genre theory, the debate over the gospel genre can go on forever because all three options are onto something. Rather than quarrelling over which genre the Gospels belong to, we should ask different questions: What genres do the Gospels participate in? And what difference does it make? Let's move on to that second question now.

---

29. See Elizabeth E. Shively, "Recognizing Penguins: Audience Expectation, Cognitive Genre Theory, and the Ending of Mark's Gospel," *CBQ* 80, no. 2 (2018).
30. Adams, *Genre of Acts*, 253.

WHAT DIFFERENCE DOES A GOSPEL GENRE MAKE?

For many scholars, argues Helen Bond, the answer to the second question is this: "not a whole lot." Commentaries devote an introductory section to this debate, but from then on, they "often seem strangely unaffected by whatever genre the scholar has assigned to the work"; the "payoff," she laments, is "disappointingly meager."[31]

We aren't going to fix this overnight. But calling a ceasefire in the debate over rigid genre categories will (I hope) give more space for gospels scholars to start addressing this question. Bond herself, in *The First Biography of Jesus*, explores the interpretive payoffs for taking up Mark as a biography. Modern genre theory calls for more of this kind of boomerang testing. For now, let's sketch out some observations about the gospel experience.

Genres Function within a Recurring Social Situation

The form critics were wrong about lots of things, but they were right to ask about the social setting of the Gospels. Understanding the gospel genre means looking not just at how it is written but also at what it is for (tenet 7). I could write a biography of legendary Australian spin bowler Shane Warne that met almost all of Burridge's formal criteria for what a gospel is – from preface to structure to themes and, yes, even content (sports writers love borrowing religious language). But there is no community of "Warney worshippers" to be discipled. There are no heresies around his bowling technique to be confronted. A biography celebrating the legendary deeds of a sporting hero can't be a gospel because that's not what a gospel is for.

The formal features and content of the gospel genre are important to study, but the function they serve within their social context is underexplored. If I were a New Testament scholar working on the Gospels, I'd be asking about the recurring function within the context of the early church – things like discipleship, generational change, identity formation, and worship.[32] It's telling that one of the earliest explicit references to the Gospels comes from Justin Martyr, when he describes them being read in Sunday gatherings.[33] The concrete purposes and audiences of the four gospels will no doubt differ, but it should be possible to identify the conventional and recurring functions that genre offers them to pursue those purposes – not why someone *did* write this text, but why someone *would* typically use this genre.

---

31. Bond, *First Biography of Jesus*, 2.
32. These questions are raised in Larry Hurtado, "Gospel (Genre)," in *Dictionary of Jesus and the Gospels*, ed. Joel B. Green et al. (Downers Grove, IL: InterVarsity, 1992), 276–82. Cf. the 2013 edition entry.
33. Justin Martyr, *First Apology*, chapter 67.

Why Would Someone Do a Gospel?

Scholars have begun exploring the social function of the gospel genre:

- Stanley Porter uses register analysis to describe the context of situation and context of culture of Mark's gospel: a literate culture, a community already convinced of Jesus's identity, before tension with Rome or Jewish leaders.[34]
- Sean Adams thinks the collected biography genre of Acts serves the social situation and the needs of the early Christian community, functioning to define the authentic movement and identify the second generation of leaders.[35]
- Zach Dawson analyzes the social function of the Lord's Prayer in Matthew 6:7–13, concluding that the Sermon on the Mount (and perhaps therefore Matthew as a whole) is a genre for discipleship.[36]
- Ryder Wishart analyzes the register of each genre embedded in the Gospels (as implied by the narrative context) and uses those statistics to predict that the gospel genre as a whole calls readers to take the right side in an existing conflict, using vilification, warning, instruction, and persuasion.[37]
- Helen Bond thinks Mark adapted the typical social functions of Greco-Roman biography, along with its form, to articulate shared values, form group identity, and address the needs of the early Christian community.[38]

Forming Christians

Let's assume the gospels are biographies for a moment. What does that suggest about their function? Unlike most modern historiography, ancient biographies often present an exemplary figure's character, celebrating their virtues and perhaps even putting them forward as a model to be emulated. Helen Bond observes how Greco-Roman biographies often depicted the death of a philosopher in accordance with his teaching as a paradigm of integrity for others to follow. In taking up the biography's social function, she argues, Mark is reworking earlier traditional material about Jesus's life, ministry, and teaching, bringing it together with accounts of his death and resurrection to forge "a distinctive

---

34. Stanley E. Porter, "Register in the Greek of the New Testament: Application with Reference to Mark's Gospel," in *Rethinking Contexts, Rereading Texts: Contributions from the Social Sciences to Biblical Interpretation*, ed. M. Daniel Carroll R., JSOTSup 299 (Sheffield: Sheffield Academic, 2000), 209–29.

35. See Adams, *Genre of Acts*, 248.

36. Dawson, "Problem of Gospel Genres."

37. Wishart, "Polarizing Gospel," 308.

38. See Bond, *First Biography of Jesus*.

Christian identity based on the countercultural way of life (and death) of its founding figure."[39]

This function might explain features like Mark's abrupt ending.[40] The earliest manuscripts we have end abruptly at Mark 16:8, where the witnesses to the resurrection walk away "trembling and bewildered," saying "nothing to anyone, because they were afraid." Some manuscripts resolve the cliffhanger by adding one or two bonus endings, which are probably not original. (Most agree that when Jesus returns, we'll still be debating how Mark originally ended.)

If the genre's function is satisfying historical curiosity, then, yes, verse 8 is a strange place to end the story. But if the function of the genre is the formation of Christian identity around the exemplary life of Jesus, the ending works brilliantly. Films that give the prequel to a known story often leave the ending unresolved. Think the *Alien* prequel *Prometheus* (2012), or Peter Jackson's *Hobbit* movies (2012–2014) as prequels to *Lord of the Rings*.

A similar experience is created by the abrupt ending of Mark. As Christians, we have already received testimony of Jesus's post-resurrection appearances to Peter, the Twelve, James, Paul, and the five hundred others (1 Cor 15:3–8). If Bond is right, then the biography genre is about taking the *next* step of Christian formation and discipleship, which requires going *back* before the well-known resurrection story to examine the crucial but (at the time) less familiar prequel of Christ's life and death itself. Given this social situation and function, the abruptness is a feature, not a bug. We know the gospel story didn't end in fear and confusion at the tomb, or we wouldn't have heard about it. But by leaving us hanging, perhaps the ending puts us in the shoes of those first witnesses, laying down a challenge – *Over to you! You have heard the same good news. If Mary, Mary, and Salome had remained silent in fear and uncertainty, nobody would know about it. Will the gospel end with you?*

This function of formation has implications for how we read the various genres embedded within the gospels too. It's not only the red-letter words of Jesus that are vital to our formation; the stories about people he helped and the people who opposed him are there to teach us too. The cast of characters provide memorable examples of responses to Jesus, both positive and negative: Will we go away sad because we have many possessions (Luke 18:23), or will we give half our possessions to the poor like Zacchaeus in the next chapter (19:8)? Richard Burridge points out that sometimes these genres balance each other out. The high standard in Jesus's teaching is met by the gracious welcoming of sinners in the narratives.[41]

---

39. Bond, *First Biography of Jesus*, 5.
40. See Bond, *First Biography of Jesus*, 249–52.
41. Richard A. Burridge, *Imitating Jesus: An Inclusive Approach to New Testament Ethics* (Grand Rapids: Eerdmans, 2007).

The Focus on Jesus

In biographies, we expect the camera to stay focused on the primary subject throughout. In this respect, the gospels pass the boomerang test. Jesus is the consistent thread that ties everything together. Various secondary and tertiary characters come in and out of frame, usually for a single episode, and these interactions each serve to reveal something about Jesus. I would love to know what happens to the rich man in the end (Mark 10:22), but he quickly exits stage left, leaving us with the question, "Who then can be saved?" (Mark 10:26).

This means the other characters need only be roughly sketched. Don't expect a comprehensive and nuanced depiction of the Pharisees, for instance. They are there, not to refine our insights into first-century politics and polemics, but as a foil to reveal Jesus's characteristic teaching and personality.

Staging Structure

Genres pursue their function in stages (see chapter 3). The writers could have introduced Jesus and his teaching under thematic headings ("1.3: Riches, warnings against; 1.4: Eschatology"), but I'm glad they went with *ancient rhetorically-shaped narratives that claim to be reliable records of recent events.*[42] The episodes are mostly self-contained, but together they build up to the death and resurrection of Jesus. (Jesus's itinerant ministry makes geography a convenient staging device too – the slow journey towards Jerusalem in Luke, for example.)

The arrangement of the episodes often serves the gospel function by building connections between themes and juxtaposing events and characters. Consider the classic "Markan sandwich" of Mark 11:12–21, which takes place over three days. Jesus is hailed as a king as he enters Jerusalem on the way to looking around the temple (11:1–11); the next day, on the way to the temple, he curses a fig tree (11:12–14), clears the temple, and makes enemies with his teaching (11:15–18); on day three, they pass the same fig tree, which has withered (11:20–25). On its own, the fig tree story could be taken as a demonstration of Jesus's power or a lesson on prayer. But Mark's sandwich forces us to read it side by side with the clearing of the temple. This juxtaposition then helps us understand the tearing of the curtain later in Mark 15:38 as an act of God's judgment. At this point, an unnamed centurion appears, declaring, "Surely this man was the Son of God" (v. 39), echoing the words of God at Jesus's baptism in Mark 1:11 when the

---

42. Dinkler, "What Is a Genre?," in *Modern and Ancient Literary Criticism of the Gospels*, ed. Calhoun, Moessner, and Nicklas, 92, emphasis in original.

heavens were torn open.[43] All this shows Christian disciples how to think about and respond to the destruction of the rest of the temple when it comes in AD 69.

The genre's function may require episodes to be arranged out of strict chronological order. Generally, gospels start at the beginning of Jesus's life and end after his death, but in the middle, the writers seem free to use the sequence of events as a teaching tool. In John, clearing the temple is almost the first thing Jesus does (John 2). But in the other gospels, it's one of the last things he does before his arrest (Mark 11; Matthew 21; Luke 19). Assuming that the genre's function is recounting events in strict chronological order, it seems to many scholars that someone has messed up. Either John got the timeline wrong or the temple incident did happen twice – in which case, the temple guards really should have been on the lookout for Jesus the second time. But there is another possibility. Strict chronology is not the only way to stage an episodic narrative. If the genre's function is character formation (rather than to satisfy historical interest), the scenes may be arranged in a more strategic way, helping us understand aspects of Jesus's character and ministry through comparison and contrast.

A Portable Passage

John 7:53–8:11 is the story of a woman who is accused of adultery and brought before Jesus, who refuses to condemn her. The passage sometimes appears in different places in early manuscripts:

- after John 7:52 (as in the NIV)
- after John 7:36
- after John 21:25
- after Luke 21:38
- after Luke 24:53

Greco-Roman biographies often used juxtaposition as a means of character formation.[44] Consider how placing this story in each location in John might affect its meaning. Who or what is being juxtaposed? What point is being made about Jesus, or about discipleship in general?

---

43. See Ben Witherington III, *The Gospel of Mark: A Socio-Rhetorical Commentary* (Grand Rapids: Eerdmans, 2001), 400.

44. See Bond, *First Biography of Jesus*, 175.

Embedded Genres

Gospel is a complex genre, meaning it can swallow other genres whole (see tenet 1). The primary frame is narrative, but it has many other genres embedded within it. Reading the Gospels requires us to be aware of the distinct literary forms and functions those embedded genres bring into play. If, for example, the story of the rich man and Lazarus is a parable (Luke 16:19–31), we shouldn't build our understanding of the afterlife on it.[45]

Stepping back, it's also important to consider how the social function of the embedded genre is filtered through the social function of the complex genre. Jesus says, "Your will be done," twice in Matthew – once during the Sermon on the Mount (Matt 6:10) and once in Gethsemane (26:42). Both passages are prayers – a genre for communicating commitment and dependence in the recurring situation of talking to God.[46] But the first prayer is embedded within a sermon, a genre for giving instruction ("this, then, is how you should pray": 6:9). Being embedded in a teaching genre transposes the social function of the prayer from communicating with God to instructing Jesus's disciples.

We need to pay attention to these levels or we'll often miss the point of an embedded story. The famous parable of the lost son in Luke 15 is embedded within a conflict narrative. Sinners are gathering to hear Jesus, and the teachers of the law don't like it. Jesus gives his rejoinder in the form of parables – the lost sheep, the lost coin, and then the lost son. The lost son parable ends with a dispute between the father and older son about the prodigal brother being welcomed home. This dispute mirrors the dispute between the Pharisees and Jesus over his welcome of the sinners and tax collectors. In response to the older son's complaint, the father makes a rejoinder, and the whole thing ends, like many parables, with a classic pithy saying that points us to the deeper meaning of the story: "We had to celebrate and be glad, because this brother of yours was dead and is alive again; he was lost and is found." We're now six layers deep into the genre onion, and each embedded genre projects its own situation and function.

But being embedded changes what each genre does. Read alone as a story about a lost son, the point is that God welcomes us back. But embedded in the dispute story, it becomes a pointy rejoinder to Jesus's opponents; it's a story about how far they, like the older son, are from God's mercy. Notice how the father's rejoinder to the son parallels Jesus's own rejoinder two layers up in the genre onion. Embedded here, the function of parable is not only communicating general spiritual truths but also pointedly challenging his opponents.

---

45. V. Philips Long, *The Art of Biblical History*, Foundations of Contemporary Interpretation 5 (Leicester, England: Apollos, 1994), 41.

46. This example is from Dawson, "Problem of Gospel Genres," 69.

Gospel					(Luke 1–24)
	Dispute story				(Luke 15)
		Rejoinder			(Luke 15:11b–32)
			= Parable/ story		(Luke 15:11b–32)
				Dispute	(Luke 15:29–32)
				Rejoinder	(Luke 15:31–32)
				Pithy saying	(Luke 15:33)

This complex interaction between genres is why we should read the text in its context several times before diving down into the detail of a passage. Along with focusing on identifying the different genres (parable, narrative, speech) and their formal features, we do well to pay attention to their distinct social situations and functions.

Truth Effects

Different genres have different functions that call for different ways to get at the truth (tenet 9). How much poetic license should someone be allowed in telling a true story? My pastor is fine with preachers skipping irrelevant details or conflating minor characters in illustrations from real life, but he would not be happy if I told a story that happened to someone else as though it had happened to me. Such rules are decided by convention and depend hugely on genre.

A few scholars think the gospels are fictional,[47] while others allow for a degree of embellishment[48] or unverifiable anecdotes[49] that nevertheless depict the character truly. Personally, I have no doubt that the gospel genre aims to depict real people and events truthfully. The social function of calling Christians to costly discipleship depends on it, and the name-dropping of identifiable people and events make little sense otherwise.[50] Even so, Craig Blomberg rightly cautions that it is the standards of the day that are relevant, not the standards of

---

47. Dennis R. MacDonald, *Mythologizing Jesus: From Jewish Teacher to Epic Hero* (Lanham, MA: Rowman & Littlefield, 2015), 142. Michal Beth Dinkler rightly critiques the essentialist genre binary of "fact" versus "fiction": "What Is a Genre?," in *Modern and Ancient Literary Criticism of the Gospels*, ed. Calhoun, Moessner, and Nicklas, 85.

48. Andrew T. Lincoln, "'We Know That His Testimony Is True': Johannine Truth Claims and Historicity," in *John, Jesus, and History*, vol. 1, ed. Paul N. Anderson, Felix Just, and Tom Thatcher, SBL SymS 44 (Atlanta: Society of Biblical Literature, 2007), 179–98.

49. Bond, *First Biography of Jesus*, 70.

50. See Bond, *First Biography of Jesus*, 221.

"scientific precision or exact quotation that our modern society relishes."[51] If the function of the genre is to convey an accurate picture of Jesus and his teaching rather than satisfying historical curiosity, we should grant the writers a little more poetic license in laying things out for us than we would a modern historian.

Resources

Genres supply writers and readers with resources for making meaning (tenet 4). In painting their picture of Jesus, the gospel writers use a variety of genre-based themes and archetypes. Many of these resources are imported via the biblical narrative genre. Settings are also loaded with symbolic potential. Leland Ryken observes how archetypal plots, characters, and motifs tie the gospel episodes together – journeys, conflicts, the sea, nighttime, traitors, refusing to take part in festivities.[52] Grant Osborne observes how many key scenes in Luke's gospel take place in banquet settings, using eating as a symbol of social and spiritual fellowship (Luke 5; 9; 15; 19; 22; 24).[53]

The Other Good Samaritan

In John 4:3–26, Jesus has an extended conversation with a Samaritan. Read the passage a few times and then consider these questions:

- In chapter 5, we discussed a genre-based resource called the "type-scene." Read Genesis 24, noting any similarities. In what ways does the interaction between Jesus and the Samaritan woman draw on a betrothal type-scene?[54] How might this influence how you interpret the interaction?
- Compare John 4 to John 2:13–25. How would you describe the tone of the dialog in each chapter? (Perhaps use a register analysis of field, tenor, and mode.) How would Jesus's words in verse 22 change if they were said during a hostile debate?

51. Craig L. Blomberg, *Jesus and the Gospels: An Introduction and Survey*, 3rd ed. (Nashville: B&H Academic, 2022), 220, 320. See also Craig S. Keener and Edward T. Wright, eds., *Biographies and Jesus: What Does It Mean for the Gospels to Be Biographies?* (Lexington, KY: Emeth, 2016); Keener, *Christobiography*, 14, 24.

52. See Leland Ryken, *Jesus the Hero: A Guided Literary History of the Bible* (Wooster, OH: Weaver, 2016), 17.

53. Grant R. Osborne, *The Hermeneutical Spiral: A Comprehensive Introduction to Biblical Interpretation*, 2nd ed. (Downers Grove, IL: InterVarsity, 2006), 209.

54. For criticism of Alter's type-scene suggestion, see Andrew E. Arterbury, "Breaking the Betrothal Bonds: Hospitality in John 4," *CBQ* 72.1 (2010): 63–83. Rather than replaying or parodying the ancestral betrothal stories, the type-scene is best considered a shared genre resource.

- People often assume that Jesus is commenting on the woman's shady past in verses 17–18. How might taking the story as a particular genre (conflict story, miracle story, discipleship story) affect how we read Jesus's words there?
- How does the interaction with the Samaritan serve the function of instructing Christian disciples?

The Scripture Genre

Genres function in systems within a context of culture (tenet 11) and the genre ball is in the reader's court (tenet 12). This means there is a genre that all the gospels participate in that is so obvious we almost never talk about it. The church has received the four canonical Gospels as Scripture (see chapter 4).[55] The Gospels are more than biographies of an inspiring historical figure. The Scripture genre introduces functions that cannot be explained by the biography or history genres:

- The recurring situation of reading short passages publicly in worship emphasizes the episodic structure, and the function of forming disciples.
- Canonical texts function in communities as an authoritative ruler against which beliefs and behaviors are measured.
- Reading a gospel as Scripture invites readers to take on a particular role as disciples – to find their own place within the story, and to imitate Christ both in his teaching and in his example.
- The Scripture genre pre-loads an additional set of resources for writers and readers to play with: imagery, intertextual associations, typologies, and thematic resources inherited from the Hebrew Bible.

What Are the Bonus Gospels?

The original gospels (OGs) inspired a whole genre of "bonus gospels" (BGs) – as featured in Dan Brown's novels, and often no more historically reliable.[56] There are dozens that we know about. The Gospel of Peter seems to supplement Matthew. The Gospel of Thomas collects various "sayings" of Jesus to paint an alternative picture to the OGs.

---

55. Whether the gospel writers believed they were writing Scripture or continuing the storyline of the Hebrew Bible is a separate question.

56. See Bird, *Gospel of the Lord*, 218–27.

Scholars debate whether OGs and BGs can be distinguished by their genre. Francis Watson argues that any genre definition must include BGs like the Gospel of Thomas, which uses the same "sayings" genre we find throughout the OGs.[57] Simon Gathercole argues that the theological content of the OGs distinguishes them from the BGs.[58] Modern genre theory injects the following observations into this debate:

- Texts have complex relationships with multiple genre prototypes (tenets 1 and 3). The Gospel of Peter is closer to the OG prototypes than the Gospel of Thomas, which shares the sayings format but lacks the apostolic teaching and includes more gnostic flavors.
- Genres are only relatively stable (tenet 2). Later BGs may have developed the genre beyond the original formal features and function of the OG prototypes.
- Genre is about power (tenet 10). Some BGs explicitly call themselves "gospels," invoking authority and prestige for texts that might have little in common with the OGs. (I found a *Gospel of the Flying Spaghetti Monster* on Amazon.com.)
- Genres imply a distinctive content and theology (tenet 9). Within all-purpose "Jesus literature," Mike Bird distinguishes the genre of "kerygmatic biography," which includes the canonical gospels and Gospel of Peter, but not the Gospel of Thomas (which has Jesus's sayings but not the narrative frame) and the Gospel of the Egyptians (which focuses on Seth, not Jesus).
- Genre is about social context and function (tenets 7 and 8), and the ball is in the reader's court (tenet 12). I find it helpful to compare BGs to the fan fiction genre. Fan fiction mirrors the internal features of an original story – characters, plot forms, and style (prompting uptake by copyright lawyers using the genre of "cease-and-desist letter"). The difference between *Harry Potter* and Potter fanfic is social context. Fanfic is by definition an unauthorized work shared within a community of people who love Harry Potter but aren't J. K. Rowling. In a similar way, OGs and BGs might be distinguished by their apostolic authority and reception (or rejection) by a particular religious community.

---

57. Francis Watson, *What Is a Gospel?* (Grand Rapids: Eerdmans, 2022), chapter 1. Cf. Burridge, *What Are the Gospels?*, 243.

58. Simon Gathercole, *The Gospel and the Gospels: Christian Proclamation and Early Jesus Books* (Grand Rapids: Eerdmans, 2022), 15.

SUMMARY

We began with the impasse over whether the gospels are unique (option A), *or* belong to the Greco-Roman biography genre (option B), *or* some other genre like history (option C). Modern genre theory suggests that each "or" in this sentence is misleading. Texts don't "belong" to genres but have complex relationships with multiple genres (tenet 1). Genres are fuzzy around the edges and organized around prototypes, so we can avoid the impossible task of drawing a firm line between history and biography (tenet 3). The boomerang test may well confirm that there is something to all three options.

Having declared a ceasefire in the debate over genre, we can move on to exploring what difference genre makes. We should ask not just about how a text is written but also about what it's for (tenet 8). Like biographies, the focus is on Jesus and the example of his life and teaching. The gospel narratives (and not just the red-letter bits) are meant to form disciples. The staging structure is driven by this function, not necessarily by a strict historical chronology. The interaction between onion layers of embedded genres makes a big difference as to what a passage means. The truth effects imply a realism you could stake your life on, but the degree of poetic license should be dictated by the genre of the text, not by our modern standards for biographies. The story is told making full use of a range of themes and archetypes inherited through Jewish genes. Genre is about readers as well as writers (tenets 5 and 12), which means the reception of a gospel as Scripture needs to be considered.

Gospel is a distinct, new genre, but like all new genres, it's built out of older genres. It's quite like a Greco-Roman biography, but in its own way – pulling on resources from other genres, including the Hebrew Bible, and meeting the recurring needs of the emerging Christian community.

Suggested Workflow for Interpreting Gospel Texts

History

☐ Identify where this passage fits within the structure of the Gospel as a whole and try to understand its context. If the passage contains embedded genres, what are their probable functions and recurring social situations as framed by the gospel narrative? How does this passage contribute to the function of the gospel genre as a whole?

☐ What can we say about the historical and cultural context that the passage is set in and written from? Are there references to particular people, customs, festivals, institutions, geography, or events? If so, what is the potential significance of these?

□ How have communities in different times, places, and cultures approached this text? Given your own tradition, what assumptions are you likely to make about the passage?

Literature

□ What other genre relationships can you identify in or around this text (including embedded genres)? Why are they there, and what do they each bring to the table? What new ideas or effects emerge from combining the different genres? Refer to the workflows for those genres as appropriate.

□ Why is this passage placed here in the gospel? What comparisons or contrasts might be drawn? If there are parallel passages in other gospels, think about what is distinctive about the way the passage is being presented here.

□ What resources of the gospel genre does the writer draw on? What quotations, ideas, allusions, or symbols are drawn from other parts of the Bible (including the Old Testament)?

Scripture

□ What do we understand better about the identity, life, ministry, and death of Jesus thanks to this passage?

□ How does the passage expect disciples of Jesus to respond? Are there characters who particularly provide a model (positive or negative) for discipleship? How *shouldn't* we respond to this text?

□ What themes running through the gospel are developed in this passage? How does the passage contribute to our broader systematic theology or our understanding of salvation history?

□ What other Bible passages need to be brought into conversation with this text to give a full picture? What interpretations of this passage are ruled out by other texts of Scripture?

□ What would be missing from Christianity if this passage had not been passed down for us?

QUESTIONS FOR DISCUSSION AND REFLECTION

1. Read Acts 1. What "staging structure" can you see at work here? Is it more like a biography or a history?
2. If someone were to ask you after church, "What is a gospel?" what would you have said to them before reading this chapter? What about now?

3. Read Mark 10:9. What are the embedded genres around this verse, and what situations are implied? How might the genres' social purposes influence how you read this passage?

FURTHER READING

Introductory

Burridge, Richard A. "Gospel: Genre." Pages 335–42 in *Dictionary of Jesus and the Gospels*. Edited by Joel B. Green, Jeannine K. Brown, and Nicholas Perrin. Second edition. Downers Grove, IL: IVP Academic, 2013.

Summary of the biography position.

Ryken, Leland. *Jesus the Hero: A Guided Literary Study of the Gospels*. Reading the Bible as Literature. Bellingham, WA: Lexham, 2016.

Creative suggestions for interpreting the genre.

Deep Dive

Adams, Sean A. *Greek Genres and Jewish Authors: Negotiating Literary Culture in the Greco-Roman Era*. Waco, TX: Baylor University Press, 2020.

Explores influence of Greek genres on minority Jewish culture; see especially chapter 8 on biographies.

Bond, Helen. *The First Biography of Jesus: Genre and Meaning in Mark's Gospel*. Grand Rapids: Eerdmans, 2020.

What difference it makes to take Mark as biography.

Calhoun, Robert Matthew, David P. Moessner, and Tobias Nicklas, eds. *Modern and Ancient Literary Criticism of the Gospels: Continuing the Debate on Gospel Genre(s)*. Wissenschaftliche Untersuchungen zum Neuen Testament 451. Tübingen: Mohr Siebeck, 2020.

Stimulating essays using modern genre theory to address the gospel genre question.

Dawson, Zachary K. "The Problem of Gospel Genres: Unmasking a Flawed Consensus and Providing a Fresh Way Forward with Systemic Functional Linguistics Genre Theory." *Biblical and Ancient Greek Linguistics* 8 (2019): 33–77.

Illustrates the potential of an SFL approach.

Diehl, Judith A. "What Is a 'Gospel'"? Recent Studies in the Gospel Genre." *Currents in Biblical Research* 9.2 (2011): 171–99.

Overview of the debate so far.

CHAPTER 12

YOU'RE SO VAIN

You Probably Think This Letter Is to You

Let's play a game. I'm about to give you two randomly selected phrases taken from somewhere in the New Testament. I'm not going to tell you where they are from (and no cheating!). They have similar content – both are about how God has fulfilled his promises in Christ. They are even attributed to the same apostle – Paul. But each is from a different genre. One is taken from the opening of a letter, and the other is taken from a speech. Can you guess which is which?

> A: "by the will of God, in keeping with the promise of life that is in Christ Jesus . . ."
> B: "What God promised our ancestors he has fulfilled for us, their children . . ."

Okay, lock in your guess. Which one is from the letter genre and which one is from the narrative genre? Now check the footnote to this sentence for the answer.[1] Did you get it right?

I thought so. From just these few words, most people can successfully guess which genre is which. The chain of prepositional phrases ("by . . . in . . .") and use of nouns rather than verbs to describe events ("the promise" in the first example versus "God promised" in the second) is perfect for the salutation part of a letter but would be a very strange way of standing up and telling a story.

Apart from an idea for the worst board game ever, what was the point of this grammatical guessing game? By correctly identifying which sentence belongs in which genre, you have just demonstrated one of the important insights that SFL makes about the predictable relationships between situation, genre, stages, and grammar (see chapter 3). We use genres to get things done in recurring social situations (like sending a letter). These genres usually have stages we go through

---

1. Example A is from the salutation of a letter (2 Tim 1:1), and B is from Paul's speech in Pisidian Antioch (Acts 13:32–33).

to achieve that purpose (a letter begins with a salutation, thus establishing the interpersonal relationships). These stages are realized in the choices we make at every level, right down to grammar (in a salutation you're more likely to see past events described using noun phrases than verbs). In other words, long strings of prepositions and nouns (like example A) are more likely to show up in the opening stage of a letter than a speech in a narrative (example B).

It's particularly important that Bible interpreters think carefully about the implications of modern genre theory for reading letters – not least because there are so many letters in the Bible! By my rough count, well over a third of the New Testament word count is epistolary in genre. The New Testament contains twenty books that are framed as letters (the thirteen Pauline epistles, plus the seven catholic epistles and Hebrews).[2] Then there are letters embedded in Acts (for example, the letter from the Jerusalem council in Acts 15:22–29) and Revelation (the spicy letters to the seven churches in Rev 2–3). The Old Testament also contains some fun examples of letters embedded in narrative (for example, the nasty letter sent to Artaxerxes by the enemies of Judah in Ezra 4:11–17), though in this chapter we will focus mainly on the New Testament epistles (especially Paul's letters).

This chapter begins with the basics, looking at the staging structure typically seen in New Testament epistles and the way that letters can both be embedded within narratives and themselves embed other genres. Then we will clarify how the experience of reading a letter as an occasional and situational piece of literature affects how we understand and apply a letter as Scripture today. Finally, I'm going to put out there an exciting and controversial implication of SFL – if genres are about recurring social situations, then can the social situation of a text be recoverable from the discourse itself?

HOW TO WRITE AN (ANCIENT) LETTER

I've been using the terms "letter" and "epistle" quite loosely.[3] But modern genre theory's historical perspective reminds us that those genres are only relatively stable conventions (tenet 2). We need to be more specific about what the letter genre meant in the literary environment they were developed in: What did writing a letter involve in the cultural context (or, more accurately, contexts) of the New Testament?

The social practice of letter writing probably evolved out of messengers who

---

2. Hebrews and 1 John don't begin in the expected way with a salutation, but they otherwise follow the epistolary staging.

3. Adolph Deissmann's old distinction between letter and epistle is probably unhelpful: see Introduction to Stanley E. Porter and Sean A. Adams, eds., *Paul and the Ancient Letter Form*, Pauline Studies 6 (Leiden: Brill, 2010), 1.

memorized a message and delivered it orally. If you were a Persian emperor, you might have had the option of using a proto-postal system, but if plebs like you or I wanted to send a letter to a loved one, we would have to find someone who was going the right way and get them to take the letter with them by hand. This is an important clue as to social function. A letter in the ancient world was "a substitute for personal presence."[4]

In general, a letter is the genre you use when you need to maintain relationships, make requests, or share information with physically distanced people. As a result, there is considerable overlap between the letter genre and everyday spoken genres – genres that might include "instructing your employee," "reassuring your mum," or "teaching a class." That's a good starting point for letters in general, but, of course, different types of letters perform more specific functions and address particular recurring social situations.

There were various reasons for writing a letter in the ancient world. Most letters, particularly early on, belong in the "boring but important" category of official government or military correspondence.[5] Rulers would make edicts and proclamations, and administrators would write to the head office seeking instructions on particular questions. Personal letters, by contrast, are about maintaining (or establishing) a relationship between sender and recipient. Friends and family members would write to stay in touch and check on each other's well-being. Business letters are part of everyday life. A brother might advise his brother that olive oil is too expensive right now to buy.[6] Religious people might write prayers and letters to the dead. Letters could let you perform various recurring actions – praising or blaming, advising or asking, thanking or threatening.[7]

Some kinds of letters, however, seem to have had a broader goal. For example, scholars and philosophers would sometimes share their thoughts and findings for posterity in letter format. These are often called "literary letters" because they use the familiar letter form but seem aimed at an audience well beyond the initial recipients.

Below is a table of some of the types of Greco-Roman letters scholars have identified. Of course, letter genres aren't fixed in stone (tenet 2) and will often overlap (tenet 3).[8]

---

4. Stanley K. Stowers, "Social Typification and the Classification of Ancient Letters," in *The Social World of Formative Christianity and Judaism: Essays in Tribute to Howard Clark Kee*, ed. Jacob Neusner et al. (Philadelphia: Fortress, 1988), 81. The letter "fictionalizes" this presence as if I am talking to you, but I'm not really.

5. Aune, *New Testament in Its Literary Environment*, 158–82; John L. White, "The Greek Documentary Letter Tradition Third Century B.C.E. to Third Century C.E.," *Semeia* 22 (1981): 89–106. Whether private or official letters came first is debated.

6. See, for example, p.mich.mchl.25, https://papyri.info/ddbdp/p.mich.mchl;;25.

7. Stowers, "Social Typification," 86.

8. For an introduction to the genres in this table, see White, "Greek Documentary Letter Tradition";

Personal letters	• Letters between family members • Letters to friends • Letter from soldiers back home • Birth announcements • Travelogs
Business letters	• Letters of introduction / commendation • Applications for rental or purchase • Transactional letters (price check, payment arrangements, invoice, receipt, demand for payment) • Letters of petition
Official correspondence	• Administrative letters • Questions and answers to the emperor • Letters between kings • Military correspondence • Edicts and proclamations • Birth or death notices • Census registrations • Circular letters
Religious, philosophical, and literary letters	• Treatises or letter essays • Divination reports • Astrological observations • Historical letters • Letters to god(s) • Letters to the dead • Curses • Prayers

Each of these genres within the broader letter-like genre family is slightly different, matching particular recurring forms with particular recurring social situations. For example, the power dynamic in a letter of petition is very different from that in a personal letter, and this is reflected in the respective register variables of those texts (see chapter 3). You might remind a recipient that they are remiss in their duties with "just as I wrote formerly . . ." or "I am astonished that . . . ," but only if they are at or below your social standing – don't try that out on the emperor!

Thinking about Paul's letters, for example, he often strikes quite a warmly personal tone, so he's not writing official letters. But then again, they don't work

Jeffrey A. D. Weima, "Letters, Greco-Roman," in *Dictionary of New Testament Background* (Downers Grove, IL: IVP Academic, 2000), 640–44; Leland Ryken, *Letters of Grace and Beauty: A Guided Literary Study of New Testament Epistles* (Wooster, OH: Weaver, 2016). See also E. Randolph Richards, "Letters, Letter Forms," in *Dictionary of Paul and His Letters*, ed. Scot McKnight, Lynn H. Cohick, and Nijay K. Gupta, 2nd ed. (Downers Grove, IL: IVP Academic, 2023), 639.

exactly like personal letters either. While some are written to his fellow workers (like 1 and 2 Timothy), others are addressed to whole communities (and Romans to Christians he hadn't visited yet). Paul anticipates that his letters will be used in gatherings for teaching and even shared among the churches as a kind of circular letter.[9] Even those letters addressed to an individual may have served a semipublic function: Paul may have meant for his instructions to Timothy to be overheard by the churches to establish the authority of his delegate.[10] Paul's letters are also much longer than your typical personal letter. His extensive treatment of theological topics is a little bit like the literary letters of the philosophers, and yet he also addresses very particular situations and people, giving rebukes, encouragement, and even advice regarding complex situations and questions.

Style Guide

As for what the formal conventions of letter writing involved, there are a couple of ways to explore this. One place to start would be to look at the "how to write a letter" guides produced by ancient rhetorical schools. By the time of Paul, you could pick up a handbook written by Pseudo-Demetrius or Pseudo-Libanius to learn about the twenty-one or forty-one kinds of letters – from consoling to congratulatory to censorious.[11] But the problem with such handbooks is that writers seldom stick to the rules they were taught in school. (I just started a sentence with a conjunction, and I'm about to brazenly split an infinitive – *Strunk & White* recommends neither.)

A better way to find out how to write a letter in the first century is to look at the many examples of letters that have survived and notice their common features. In the early twentieth century, Adolph Deissmann got very excited about the discovery of a stack of Greek papyri letters in Egypt, and since then, New Testament scholars have benefited greatly from comparisons to ancient Greek letters.[12] I often begin my hermeneutics class on letters with a letter by a young soldier called Apollinarius to his mother in the second century AD, reassuring her that he has arrived safely, and, yes, mum, I'm doing just fine:

---

9. See David A. Smith, *The Epistles for All Christians: Epistolary Literature, Circulation, and the Gospels for All Christians*, BibInt 186 (Leiden: Brill, 2020), 37–46. Thanks, Katya Covrett, for this.

10. See Luke Timothy Johnson, *The First and Second Letters to Timothy*, AB 35A (New York: Doubleday, 2001), 139–42.

11. See Jeffrey T. Reed, "The Epistle," in *Handbook of Classical Rhetoric in the Hellenistic Period 330 BC–AD 400*, ed. Stanley E. Porter (Boston: Brill, 2001), 174. Their actual use probably depended on education level: Stowers, "Social Typification," 85–87.

12. See Porter and Adams, *Paul and the Ancient Letter Form*, 1–7; White, "Greek Documentary Letter Tradition." The University of Michigan's Advanced Papyrological Information System lets you search an amazing database of Papyri letters: https://quod.lib.umich.edu/a/apis?page=index. Put "letter" in under "Type of Text" and have fun!

Opening Stage

Apollinarius to Taesis, his mother and lady [*the normal respectful way to address your mum*], many greetings. Before all else I pray for your health. I myself am well, and I make obeisance on your behalf before the gods of this place.

Body Stage

I wish you to know, mother, that I arrived in Rome in good health on the 25th of the month Pachon and was assigned to Misenum. But I have not yet learned my century [*i.e., regiment*], for I had not gone to Misenum when I wrote you this letter. I beg you then, mother, take care of yourself, and do not worry about me, for I have come into a fine place. Please write to me about your welfare and that of my brothers and all your kinsfolk. And for my part, if I find someone [*to carry a letter*], I will write to you; I will not delay to write to you.

Closing Stage

I salute my brothers often, and Apollinarius and his children, and Karalas and his children. I salute Ptolemaios, and Ptolemais and her children, and Heraklous and her children. I salute all your friends, each by name. I pray for your health.

[On the Back]

Deliver to Karanis, to Taesis, from Apollinarius, her son, of Misenum.[13]

I love this letter because of how relatable the context of situation is. Maybe you've sent or received a similar letter in the "homesick letter back home" genre. The recurring formal features of the letter genre all serve the recurring social function of keeping in touch with someone despite physical absence, particularly (in this personal letter genre) reassuring a loved one of your well-being and asking them to write. Apollinarius is writing to his mum, but he still follows the standard way of sending a letter within the Greco-Roman context of culture.

Staging Structure

Following the staging structure of the letter genre is what enables Apollinarius to get this social function done (tenet 8). I've split the letter above into paragraphs to help show the three stages that make the letter work. In the *opening*, he says who the letter is from and who it is to and provides a standard greeting and health wish. In the *body*, he shares the information the recipient

---

13. "Letter from Apollinarius to his Mother, Taesis" (P.Mich.inv. 4528), University of Michigan Library Digital Collections, https://quod.lib.umich.edu/a/apis/x-2221/4528v.tif-2.

needs to know – that he has arrived in good health. Here he makes his requests too – look after yourself, don't worry about me, and please write again. The *closing* is, like the opening, less about information and more about maintaining relational ties despite physical distance – he sends greetings to family and friends by name and prays again for her health.[14]

The New Testament writers seem to stick pretty closely to this staging structure. However, there are some differences that have caused commotion amongst biblical scholars working with a strict classical approach to genres. For example, while Greco-Roman letters tended to have three sections, when it comes to New Testament letters, many scholars have found four or five (depending on how you cut the sandwich).

Modern genre theory helps us here. Viewed historically, genres are only relatively stable (tenet 2) and part of a context of culture (tenet 7), so it is no surprise to find New Testament authors adapting the Greco-Roman genre to suit the needs and content of their Jewish and Christian subcultures (as well as their particular recurring situational needs). Furthermore, the stages of the letter genre are not stylistic rules to be obeyed, but moving parts that serve a function, and so the purpose of the writer on a given occasion may call for some variation.

Rather than debate whether New Testament epistles have a three-, four-, or five-part structure, I suggest it's better to lose the rigid genre analysis and break out some flexible SFL terminology for analyzing staging structures. SFL analyses often distinguish between the nearly compulsory **stages** of a text (opening, body, closing) and the smaller optional functional units within those stages, which are often called **phases**. You can decide whether you take or leave that jargon, but either way, modern genre theory's functional approach recognizes that within the three stages of a letter we regularly find other functional units.

Opening Stage (or Salutation, Greeting)

Just as the header of an email gives you the "to" and "from" fields, the opening of a letter establishes who the people involved in the communication are and what their relationship is. This reflects the letter's social function of maintaining contact between physically distanced people.

The *prescript* is the first name mentioned (e.g., "Apollinarius") and tells us the name of the person who is writing the letter. Paul's letters often expand this prescript substantially, using it, for example, to establish his apostolic credentials or to flag some of the major themes of the letter that will be discussed (see Rom 1:1–6; Gal 1:1–2; Titus 1:1–3).

---

14. See Reed, "Epistle," in *Handbook of Classical Rhetoric*, ed. Porter, 179–82.

The *adscript* is the second name, and it tells us who the recipient of the letter is (e.g., "to Taesis, his mother and lady"). Again, Paul sometimes expands this to flesh out their relationship in theological terms (see Rom 1:7; 1 Cor 1:2; Phlm 1–2).

Just as you wouldn't normally launch straight into an email without saying something friendly ("Heya, Andy! Hope the family is well . . ."), so a letter usually, but not always, begins with a *greeting*. In a typical letter like Apollinarius's letter to his mum, the word to use is "greetings" (*chairein*), and we see that in James 1:1 and Acts 15:23. However, Paul seems to favor "grace and peace" (*charis kai eirene*). This might be a deliberate combination of Greek and Hebrew ideas, or perhaps a catchy little phrase to sum up in two words what it means to be a follower of Jesus.[15]

New Testament writers distinguish themselves from the typical Greco-Roman letter writers by often, but not always, including a *thanksgiving phase* towards the end of the opening stage.[16] Where Apollinarius inserts his best wishes for his mother's health here, or a soldier might thank the gods for ensuring their safe arrival at port, Paul usually finds something distinctively Christian to thank God for – the faith of the Romans (Rom 1:8), the Philippians' partnership in the gospel (Phil 1:3), or simply the grace of God to the Corinthians (1 Cor 1:4–9).[17] Leaning into his participation in a Jewish context of culture, sometimes Paul uses a eulogy formula, where in invoking the Old Testament praise genre, he blesses God for who he is and what he has done (2 Cor 1:3; Eph 1:3). This makes it all the more interesting that Paul skips the thanksgiving phase and launches straight in with criticism for the Galatians (Gal 1:6–9).[18] Far from being simply formulaic, choices made in the opening stage contribute significantly to the message, tone, and ultimate impact of the letter.

Body Stage

The body stage is where the primary payload of the missive is found. The bulk of what the writer wants to communicate or request appears here. Here's another second-century Greek letter from a child to their parent:

---

15. Sean A. Adams, "Paul's Letter Opening and Greek Epistolography," in *Paul and the Ancient Letter Form*, ed. Porter and Adams, 45–48. 2 John 3 adds "mercy."

16. See Peter Arzt, "The 'Epistolary Introductory Thanksgiving' in the Papyri and in Paul," *NovT* 36.1 (1994): 29–46; Jeffrey T. Reed, "Are Paul's Thanksgivings 'Epistolary,'" *JSNT* 18.61 (1996): 87–99; Robert E. Van Voorst, "Why Is There No Thanksgiving Period in Galatians?" An Assessment of an Exegetical Commonplace," *JBL* 129.1 (2010): 153–72.

17. 3 John 2 has a more traditional Greco-Roman health wish.

18. For more examples of how a functional approach to staging structures can help in the analysis of New Testament epistles, see Stanley Porter, "A Functional Letter Perspective," in *Paul and the Ancient Letter Form*, ed. Porter and Adams, 20–31.

Trapbos to Herakles his [or her] father, very many greetings. Before all else I pray for your health. I have caused unpleasantness for my overseers, and I want to get away from them. If you can come, come at once. For if I do not get away from them, they will give me a hiding every day. Give salutations to all in the house.[19]

I love this as an example of the genre because Trapbos gets straight to the point – you get a sense that the opening and closing were scrawled in a hurry! The real point of the letter is the body section, which gives the required information (I've messed up!) and the request (come help!).

In longer letters, typically a variety of topics will be addressed. In 1 Corinthians, Paul has a list of issues he needs to raise (sex, virgins, food sacrificed to idols, spiritual gifts, and collections). These changes of topic are often flagged by the phrase "now concerning . . ." (1 Cor 7:1, 25; 8:1; 12:1; 16:1) or by what's called a disclosure formula – "I want you to know that . . ." We saw Apollinarius introduce the topic of his well-being with, "I want you to know . . ." and this kind of formula also shows up in New Testament letters (for example, 1 Cor 12:3; 15:1; 2 Cor 8:1; Gal 1:11; Phil 1:12; Col 2:1; 1 Thess 2:1), as well as the corresponding double negative, "I don't want you to be unaware" (Rom 1:13; 11:25; 1 Cor 10:1–2; 12:1; 2 Cor 1:8; 1 Thess 4:13). A closing subject matter change is sometimes signposted with "Finally, brothers and sisters" (2 Cor 13:11; Eph 6:10; Phil 3:1; 4:8; 1 Thess 4:1; 2 Thess 3:1).

Information Flow Formulas

Several other epistolary formulas have been identified that can help regulate the information flow in the body stage:[20]

- *thanksgiving* formula – "We give thanks" (1 Thess 1:2)
- *petition* formula – "I urge you to . . ." (1 Cor 1:10; Phlm 8)
- *joy* formula – "I rejoiced that . . ." (Phil 4:10)
- *astonishment* formula – "I am astonished that . . ." (Gal 1:6)
- *reiteration* formula – "I say again . . ." (Gal 1:9)
- *report* formula – "I hear that" (1 Cor 5:1–2; 11:18; 2 Thess 3:11)

---

19. "P.Mich.inv. 1637; Verso." University of Michigan Library Digital Collections, https://quod.lib.umich.edu/a/apis/x-1494/1637v.tif.

20. This list is compiled using Stanley Porter, "A Functional Letter Perspective," in Porter and Adams, *Paul and the Ancient Letter Form*, 16; John Lee White, "Introductory Formulae in the Body of the Pauline Letter," *JBL* 90.1 (1971): 91–97.

- *affirmation* formula – "Indeed . . ." (1 Cor 15:31)
- *quotation* formula – "Here is a trustworthy saying" (2 Tim 2:11)
- *blessing and doxology* formula – "Praise be . . ." (2 Cor 1:3)
- *greetings* formula – "Give my greetings . . ." (Col 4:15)
- *travelog* formula – "I wanted to visit . . ." (2 Cor 1:16)

This conveyor belt of content is not random, nor are the New Testament epistles a jumble sale of carelessly edited fragments (as is sometimes argued). But nor should we expect a letter to be structured the way you were taught to write an essay or deliver a sermon – with a single logical flow developing one big idea.[21] That's not how a letter is structured. The letter genre allows for a rather wide-ranging and free-flowing discussion of a variety of topics, all brought together because they are useful for and relevant to the situation the letter is addressing.

The relational dynamic of a letter situation informs the register and therefore the kind of language used in a letter, and this is much more noticeable in the body than in the more standard opening and closing formulas. On the whole, a New Testament epistle is on the informal end of the spectrum, but there is markedly more distance in Paul's tone when writing to Rome than Corinth – probably because he did not establish the church in Rome, and his relationship is not as clearly paternal. Paul can often be warm and sincere, but he can also serve up some searing sarcasm when the need arises: "We are fools for Christ, but you are so wise in Christ!" (1 Cor 4:10). (Ouch, Paul, that stings!)

Before we get to the closing, some scholars want to add an additional section off the back of the body called the *parenesis*. This is where the writer tells us what to do, attempting to influence how we think, feel, or act (Eph 4:1–6:20; 1 Thess 5:12–22; Heb 13:1–19). Of course, exhorting Christians to conform their behavior to their identity in Christ is about as close as you can get to the generic purpose of an apostolic letter, so we find parenesis throughout the letters. Once more, with a dash of modern genre theory, we can avoid the fairly fruitless debate about whether parenesis is a separate section to the body or a subsection of the body.[22] Using SFL terminology, it's probably best to see this parenesis as an optional phase that can occur as often as necessary within the body stage of the letter.

Language can be used in different ways to give instructions, and we might link these choices to the register variables of the situation or the writer's rhetorical

---

21. See Ryken, *Letters of Grace and Beauty*, 83–84.
22. See the discussion in Young Chul Whang, "Paul's Letter Paraenesis," in *Paul and the Ancient Letter Form*, ed. Porter and Adams, 266–68.

strategy. The most direct types of commands lean on the interpersonal authority of the speaker over the addressee: "I appeal to you" (Rom 12:1; 15:30; Phil 4:2; 1 Cor 1:10; 2 Cor 10:1; 1 Thess 4:1; Phlm 9–10) or "command you" (1 Cor 7:10; 2 Thess 3:6; 1 Tim 1:18; 6:13–14). A more indirect way of doing that is to say, "I am confident that . . ." (2 Cor 7:16; Gal 5:10; 2 Thess 3:4; Phlm 21). A friendly reminder of the interpersonal dynamic that supports this instruction is often standing close by (1 Cor 14:37; Phil 4:1–3; 1 Thess 2:3–6; 2 Thess 3:12–13). Paul can also lean on the positive reinforcement of contributing to his joy (Phil 2:2; Phlm 7) or negatively in expressing his astonishment (Gal 1:6).

Closing Stage

It is hard to know how to sign off in an email. The choices here can make a big difference to how the message goes down with its recipient. While often neglected as mere formality, the same is true for the closing of an ancient letter. In ancient letters, as in emails, a good closing reaffirms the interpersonal dynamic of the situation, often including a farewell ("sincerely") or health wish ("be well!").

Paul usually begins his closing stages with a *benediction phase*, wishing something for the recipient by using a peace-based formula ("the God of peace will be with you": Phil 4:9), and he always includes a grace-based one at, or almost at, the very end ("the grace of the Lord Jesus Christ be with your spirit": Phil 4:23). A *doxology phase* is similar but contains praise directed towards God (e.g., Heb 13:21). Sometimes the recipients are addressed once more in what is called a *hortatory phase* ("brothers and sisters, pray for us": 1 Thess 5:25). Often there is a *greeting phase* ("say hi to . . ."), with a list of people to greet (sometimes with a "kiss of love": 1 Pet 5:14) or who send their greeting. Sometimes you'll also see an *autograph stage*, giving information about the production of the letter – the sender's name written in their own hand (Phlm 19), or, in an official letter, perhaps the name of the person who wrote the letter down (if the sender cannot write). Closing stages can also include expressions of joy, commendations, or other final remarks.

As with the opening stage, the content of the closing stage is important and shouldn't be skipped over like the legal boilerplate at the end of corporate emails. The greetings phase in Romans, for example, is unusually long and offers extensive commendation of the individuals listed. This probably reflects the apostle's situation. Having never visited the Roman churches, the greetings serve to establish his apostolic credentials by name-dropping people who can vouch for him.[23]

---

23. Jeffrey A. D. Weima, *Neglected Endings: The Significance of the Pauline Letter Closings*, JSOTSup 101 (Sheffield: JSOT Press, 1994), 116, 225–28.

Promiscuous Letters

We expect, thanks to modern genre theory, that texts will be promiscuous when it comes to genres (tenet 1). Straight away, therefore, we can side-step arguments about which New Testament epistles should be classed as letters and which ones are really just homilies and should never have been taken as letters.[24] Let go of classical genre theory and its rigid categories, and these kinds of sharp genre divisions just don't stand up.

New Testament letters resemble Greco-Roman letter genres in some ways, but that doesn't explain everything about them. While they are often quite like personal letters in tone, New Testament letters tend to be on the longer end of the spectrum compared to your average letter between friends or family members. The length and subject matter of New Testament epistles suggest they may be participating in other genres as well – perhaps sermon, or even philosophical treatise.

In recognizing their Greco-Roman background in the letter genre, we should not ignore the fundamental ways in which the New Testament epistles take part in a Jewish literary and theological context as well. While in formal features Paul's letters resemble Apollinarius's letter to his mum, in terms of their social function and register, they are much more like Jeremiah's letter to the exiles in Babylon (Jer 29:4–28) – an authoritative message from God's chosen spokesperson to a particular community, dripping with Old Testament allusions and theology.[25]

The way a New Testament writer adapts common letter formulas often reflects this participation in a Jewish context of culture, as well as the specific purpose or key themes of the letter itself. Instead of a standard Greco-Roman health wish, New Testament writers tend to close off their letter (or section of a letter) with a doxology, calling for God to be praised (Rom 11:36; 16:25–27; 1 Tim 1:17) or a benediction that blesses God (2 Cor 1:3). The language of these is more formal and liturgical – a bit like an Old Testament psalm.

Embedded Genres

The staging structure of the letter genre also easily allows writers to embed other genres within their letter:

---

24. For an argument that 1 John, James, Hebrews, and Jude are homilies, not letters, see Ben Witherington III, *Letters and Homilies for Hellenized Christians: A Socio-Rhetorical Commentary on Titus, 1–2 Timothy and 1–3 John* (Downers Grove, IL: IVP Academic, 2006), 1:43. Thanks, Andrew Bailey, for suggesting how genre theory might be relevant to this debate.

25. See Roy Ciampa and Brian S. Rosner, "The Structure and Argument of 1 Corinthians: A Biblical/Jewish Approach," *NTS* 52.2 (2006): 205–18.

- In setting out how Christians are to live as children of God, New Testament writers often provide ethical guidance on relationships between wife and husband, parent and child, and slave and master (Eph 5:22–6:9; Col 3:18–4:1; perhaps also 1 Tim 2–6; Titus 2:1–10; 1 Pet 2:11–3:7). These are called the *household codes*, and parallels are often suggested with Hellenistic household management traditions (while earlier scholarship tended to look to Aristotelian, Stoic, and Jewish sources).

- Lists of *virtues* and *vices* are a simple way of collecting ethical material, and there are many such lists in the New Testament (for example, Gal 5:16–21; Col 3:5–14; 1 Tim 1:9–11; 2 Tim 2:22).

- Precious gospel traditions are rehearsed in *Christ hymns* (Phil 2:6–11; Col 1:15–20; 1 Tim 3:16), *sayings* (1 Tim 1:15; 2 Tim 2:11–13), and *narratives* (1 Cor 10:1–10).

- Paul has an outburst of *praise* of God in Romans 11:33–36, which is outside the normal staging structure but the most appropriate response to the mysteries of God's will. Abstract qualities and human behavior – such as love (1 Cor 13) and faith (Heb 11) – are commended, using the *encomium* genre.

- Paul includes *autobiographical* stories about his own conversion and ministry (2 Cor 11:32–33; Gal 2:1–14). The social function of a letter also lends itself to information about travels (past and planned) in the form of *travelog* (Rom 15:23–29; 1 Cor 16:1–11).

- Paul *prays* often, which, though addressed to God, changes to a more didactic or exhortative register by being embedded in the letter (Col 1:9–14; 1 Thess 3:11–13).

- Many have found illustrations of *midrashic exegesis* – for example, in Paul's allegorical treatment of Hagar's story (Gal 4:21–31). Old Testament quotations in general bring their genre with them – for example, the *wisdom* flavor that comes with a quote from Proverbs (Rom 12:20; Heb 12:5–6; 1 Pet 4:8).[26]

- *Policies* and *procedures* for pastoral ministry are included in 1 Timothy and Titus, where Paul gives instructions for appointment to leadership, care for widows, and right behavior.

- Depending on how low-level you want to look at things, there are also any number of micro-genres that letter writers put to work at times: *instruction*, *request*, *rebuke*, *encouragement*, *defense*, and so on.

---

26. Embedded proverbs may give a wisdom flavor to the surrounding text as well: Adam Ch'ng, "Assimilating Genre: Identifying Hebrews 12:4–14 as Proverbial Wisdom" (Master's Thesis, Ridley College, 2018).

Style

This variety of embedded genres in the New Testament epistles means we will come across quite different registers at different points – for example, a doxology is going to be much less chatty than a travelog.

Even at a global level, letter writers make choices about how to use language, and the fact that the New Testament epistles participate in both the personal letter genre and more literary genres gives lots of freedom. For example, we might compare the almost comically conversational Paul of 1 Corinthians 1:16–17 with him in full rhetorical flight in 1 Corinthians 15:35–16:4 or 2 Corinthians 11:21–30.

Rhetoric

That texts are promiscuous when it comes to genre relationships may have significant implications for the discussion about the relationship between Greco-Roman rhetoric and the New Testament epistles.[27] On the one hand, numerous scholars have applied classical rhetorical categories fruitfully to analyze New Testament epistles, and there are many points at which (especially in the body stage) the style and function of the letters bear a striking similarity to tools of the trade of classical rhetoricians. On the other hand, classical rhetoric was generally geared towards oral performance more than towards written letters. And it has proven quite difficult to nail down a single pure rhetorical genre for each epistle and to match the staging structure of ancient rhetorical forms with what we see in the New Testament epistles.

Modern genre theory allows us to recognize that the New Testament epistles participate in classical rhetorical genres through some of their functional and stylistic features, while also recognizing that their participation in the letter genres is more determinative of the staging structure. The rhetorical genres are a natural fit with the social function of a letter from apostle to church. They assist in the moral formation of the recipients by supplying the resources and role of the moral philosopher.[28]

For example, while Romans does not present itself as a philosophical speech, it does have the distinct flavor of the "diatribe" genre about it.[29] In a diatribe, the philosopher would often introduce an imaginary interlocutor who becomes a

---

27. See Anders Eriksson, *Traditions as Rhetorical Proof: Pauline Argumentation in I Corinthians*, ConBNT 29 (Stockholm: Almquist & Wiksell, 1998), 280–83; Stanley E. Porter, "Saul of Tarsus and His Letters," in *Handbook*, ed. Porter, 533–85; Reed, "Epistle," in *Handbook*, ed. Porter, 191.

28. Johnson, *First and Second Letters to Timothy*, 92.

29. See Stanley K. Stowers, "The Diatribe," in *Greco-Roman Literature and the New Testament*, ed. David E. Aune, SBLSBS 21 (Atlanta, GA: Scholars Press, 1988), 71–83; Stanley E. Porter, "The Argument of Romans 5: Can a Rhetorical Question Make a Difference?," *JBL* 110.4 (1991): 655.

dialog partner (or sometimes more like a punching bag) for the argument being made. The Stoic philosopher Epictetus, for example, introduces a hypothetical objection with "but some will say . . ." before shutting down the idea.[30] Paul will also often introduce an idea just to shoot it down – such as the famous "What shall we say, then? Shall we go on sinning so that grace may increase?" in Romans 6:1–2. His answer to this rhetorical question is made clear in a standard way: "By no means!"

Identifying the diatribe genre is important because it brings with it a particular interpersonal setup. It immediately invokes a pedagogical relationship between teacher and student.[31] Paul carries on just such a conversation from chapters 1 to 14 of Romans.[32] For example, in Romans 2, he introduces a Jewish voice, and in Romans 11, he introduces a gentile voice. Paul's argument proceeds by showing how both interlocutors are mistaken. The objections are thus a crucial structuring device.

Appreciating these techniques as part of a particular genre is important in interpreting the tone of Paul's letters. Otherwise we might think that such fierce-sounding rhetoric must mean he was engaged in nasty polemic with actual people, or we might spend a lifetime trying to identify the various factions within the Roman church, when in fact Paul is using the imaginary dialog simply as a teaching tool.[33]

HOW TO RECEIVE A LETTER: APPLICATION AND SITUATION

In 1972, Carly Simon released a song with some of the most delightfully paradoxical lyrics of all time. "You're So Vain" describes an insufferably self-absorbed man in a scarf. The chorus addresses him directly, accusing him of arrogantly assuming that he is the subject of the song. There are endless theories about who the song is about, but the truth is that nobody really knows. Of course, it would be arrogant for any man to think that Simon had written the song about him. But then again, if he did think that, then in another sense the song really would be speaking directly to him. Let's call it the "Carly Simon paradox." This may be a stretch, but the Carly Simon paradox reminds me of the issue we face when applying the letters we find in the Bible. In one sense, it would be arrogant to

30. Epictetus, *Discourses* II.8, http://data.perseus.org/citations/urn:cts:greekLit:tlg0557.tlg001.perseus-engl:2.8.

31. See Stowers, "Diatribe," in *Greco-Roman Literature*, ed. Aune, 73.

32. See Stowers, "Diatribe," in *Greco-Roman Literature*, ed. Aune, 80–83. Other examples are 1 Corinthians 6:12–20; 15:29–35.

33. See Stanley K. Stowers, *The Diatribe and Paul's Letter to the Romans*, SBLDS 57 (Chico, CA: Scholars Press, 1981), 152–54.

think that Paul or Peter or any of the New Testament writers are writing directly about us and our situation – after all, it's not all about us! But at the same time, what they have written into those situations most certainly speaks *to us*. It is this tension I want to explore now.

We saw above how, in general, letters function to establish and maintain relationships and share information between physically distanced people. This social function has an important implication for how we understand and apply the letters within the New Testament. Unlike a psalm, which we saw addresses general human experience at an emotional level, a letter is tethered much more closely to the speaking situation within which it arose. For example, consider this verse in isolation:

> When you come, bring the cloak that I left with Carpus at Troas, and my scrolls, especially the parchments. (2 Tim 4:13)

This is part of the canonical book of 2 Timothy, which is traditionally attributed to Saint Paul. Christians believe that it is God's word to us. The word "bring" is a command. Yet Christians today are so lax in obeying this command! Do we not take the word of God seriously?

While I wouldn't be surprised if there are Christians somewhere in the world who, to this day, carry around cloaks and scrolls in obedience to this command, most of us see this as a command that is specific to the particular historical occasion involving Paul and Timothy when the letter was written. (Presumably Paul, since being promoted to glory, doesn't need his cloak anymore.)

There's a tension here though, isn't there? We're not so vain as to assume that Paul's letter to Timothy is written primarily about us. At the same time, the social function of Paul's letters is not private. While warmly personal at times, Paul seems to have anticipated that the letters would be read and treasured by multiple churches, as well as likely to be used in gatherings for the instruction of believers (hence the relatively large size for a Greco-Roman letter and the big-picture theological topics).[34] Letters address particular situations but anticipate potentially quite broad secondary audiences as well. Furthermore, whatever their original social function, the letters have been received as part of the canon and so participate in the social function of the Scripture genre as well (see chapter 4). We take up this letter to Timothy as Scripture, believing it has enduring relevance and authority in our own contemporary situations.

Extremely specific instructions like 2 Timothy 4:13 remind us to pause and

---

34. See Smith, *Epistles for All Christians*, 37–46, 59–63.

consider our assumptions about how the genre of New Testament epistle works and how we go about applying what we read to our own context. The enduring truths we find in it have been expressed into a very specific situation. We begin, therefore, by trying to first understand the **occasion** that the letter was addressing.[35] (The occasion addressed by a *text* is more specific than the general recurring situations anticipated by the *genre*, though the two are related.) It's no accident that since the second century, commentary writers have tried to explain the circumstances of the letter and why it was written.[36] This kind of information really helps when interpreting a letter! The same words spoken into a different situation can produce very different meanings.[37]

But reconstructing the occasion can be tricky because we don't have all the information. As Brian Rosner and Roy Ciampa put it, "Reading Paul's letters is like listening to one end of a telephone conversation; unfortunately we are left to guess what the party on the other end of the line is saying."[38] In fact, even Paul's original recipients missed what he was saying sometimes – for example, when he told the Corinthians in an earlier letter not to associate with immoral people, they took this to mean people outside the church, whereas he was thinking specifically of the situation where someone calls themselves Christian but lives immorally (1 Cor 5:9–10). This isn't reason to give up hope of understanding a letter's context, but it is reason to be honest about what we don't know and humble about our conclusions.

Here we should also pay attention to the **embedded genres** of a letter. While the genre of the letter as a whole is usually tethered to the immediate situation, the same is not always true of the embedded genre. The content of a Christ hymn is likely to be the same, no matter to whom the letter is written, and will be as relevant to us today as to its original recipients. The qualities mentioned in a vice or virtue list are much more likely to be applicable to us than the commands in a travelog.

Once we have a reasonable idea about the situation being spoken into, it's time to step back for a moment and see how this letter relates to other relevant teaching on related topics. When a doctor gives you a diagnosis for your ailment, you are not suddenly equipped to go out and practice medicine on other people with similar symptoms. While your doctor is (hopefully) drawing on real

---

35. On the occasional nature of Pauline correspondence and its implications for theology and rhetoric, see Johnson, *First and Second Letters to Timothy*, 93–94.

36. See Johnson, *First and Second Letters to Timothy*, 13.

37. The pastoral epistles sound similar but don't say the same thing: Johnson, *First and Second Letters to Timothy*, 94.

38. Roy E. Ciampa and Brian S. Rosner, *The First Letter to the Corinthians*, PNTC (Grand Rapids: Eerdmans, 2010), 46.

medical knowledge as it applies to your case, what they tell you in a five-minute consultation cannot replace what you would learn in your pursuit of a medical degree. Similarly, letters address particular occasions with what is relevant in that context, so they don't always say everything that can be said on a given topic.

Finally, having formed a working understanding of the teaching as it relates to the specific situation addressed in the letter, we can ask about what similar situations we find in our own context. Our lives are different from the lives of those who lived in first-century Corinth, to be sure, but our common humanity, Christian faith, and traditions mean that it's not totally foreign. People are still people. With a little imagination, it's possible to find similar situations in our world – and to hear the apostolic voice with the same urgency and conviction as the original audience.

Applying 2 John to Our Situation

A good example of the importance of this process is the letter of 2 John.[39] Addressing his letter to "the lady," the "elder" (traditionally identified as John) exhorts her and her children to continue to walk in love and to watch out for deceivers who have abandoned the teaching of Christ. The opening and closing reflect the expected function of maintaining the relationship despite absence – for example, in the wish to visit and talk face-to-face (v. 12). The sender's title implies the authority of seniority and a degree of responsibility over the church, if not in a formal role. The tone is warm and respectful but with a clear sense that he writes with apostolic authority anchored in the teachings of Jesus (for example, v. 5: "dear lady, I am not writing you a new command").

Into this context, the writer delivers the following direct command:

> If anyone comes to you and does not bring this teaching, do not take them into your house or welcome them. Anyone who welcomes them shares in their wicked work. (2 John 10–11)

The implication is clear: Christians are forbidden to show hospitality to anyone who fails to acknowledge the incarnation of Jesus (v. 7).

How should that apply today? Should Christians exclude their skeptical uncles from family dinners, or issue a test on Nicaean orthodoxy before allowing a plumber to enter your house?

Surely not! But the easy way out of saying, "Well, that was a specific situation so it isn't applicable anymore" doesn't work for me either. After all, almost

---

39. See Witherington III, *Letters and Homilies*, 1:563–82.

everything in the New Testament is written into a specific context. Instead, we need to explore the context of the command a little more.

The first thing to note is that this letter is probably meant to instruct and command a whole church, not just a single individual (the recipients include "her children" in v. 1, and the plural "you" in v. 12). In that corporate context, to take a false teacher "into your house" might imply welcoming that person into the church, not just into a private home. The second important piece of context is that to welcome a visiting preacher means more than just an act of neighborly love to a stranger; it's about supporting an itinerant preaching ministry.[40] The third piece of context is that hospitality in general is something that Christians are indeed to practice. It's unlikely that the elder is wanting to contradict Jesus (Luke 10) and Paul (Rom 12:13) on this point.

Putting all this together, the command has little relevance to whether Christians should invite their Muslim neighbors for afternoon tea. A morally comparable situation would be whether Christians should support the ministries of people who have been shown to be false teachers or otherwise threaten the integrity of the church. The elder might urge us to think carefully about whose books we endorse, which speakers we promote, and what ministries are propped up by the royalties from our worship music.

NEXT STEPS: CAN WE RECOVER THE SITUATION FROM THE GENRE?

Let's return to one of the examples we started this chapter with:

> B: "What God promised our ancestors he has fulfilled for us, their children . . ."

You may have guessed something about the *context* of that speech – that the speaker is probably addressing fellow Israelites because he uses the pronouns "our" and "us." This points to a further exciting implication of the SFL account of genre. If genre stages predict certain choices in the discourse itself, then sometimes it will be possible to reverse engineer the context from the text. Can we make an educated guess at the recurring situation anticipated by the genre based on an analysis of such semantic choices in the text? If we are able to match up recurring forms with recurring social situations in this way, it may even be

---

40. See William R. G. Loader, *The Johannine Epistles*, Epworth Commentaries (London: Epworth, 1992), 96; Robert W. Yarbrough, *1–3 John*, BECNT (Grand Rapids: Baker Academic, 2008), 351–52; Karen H. Jobes, *1, 2, and 3 John*, ZECNT (Grand Rapids: Zondervan, 2014), 271–74.

possible to use the text to recover something about the text's context of situation or even context of culture.

Consider two more examples of the simple genres we find embedded in the New Testament – Paul's defense speech before Agrippa (Acts 26) and his letter to the Romans (which comes a couple of pages later in New Testament canonical order). There is much in these two genres that SFL would have a productive and enjoyable field day with. As we just saw, in SFL each genre has a distinct staging structure. Accordingly, Paul's defense begins by respectfully addressing the king (Acts 26:1–3) before recounting his autobiography (26:4–11) as background for his "road to Damascus" experience and commissioning by Christ to preach the gospel (26:12–18), before giving a defense of himself and his message against the charge of being an agitator (26:19–23). In contrast, Romans opens using the expected epistolary stages of salutation (Rom 1:1–7) followed by a thanksgiving (1:8–10).

Both the autobiographical recount stage of the defense and the salutation stage of the letter give Paul an opportunity to describe how he was commissioned by Christ as an apostle, yet the register variables reflect very different situations. In one, Paul is pleading for his life before a powerful king; in the other, he is writing to introduce himself to the Roman church as an authoritative apostle of Christ. We might notice how the positioning of the subjects establishes a different affinity and power dynamic with King Agrippa (whom Paul addresses three times in the vocative, "O King Agrippa," interrupting the narrative and positioning the king as an observer of the events) compared to the Romans (whom he situates as participants in the events with *"you also* are among those Gentiles" and "God *our* father").

It doesn't just stop at staging, however. SFL predicts that the genre's staging structure and register configuration will affect every level of the discourse. SFL researchers like to pay attention to the choices that language users make from the menu of options available to them. For example, when do speakers describe events as simple processes (one verb after another), and when do they turn events into things (by hiding a verb inside a noun)?[41] We find a similar pattern here as we did in the first example. When recounting his calling in his defense, Paul uses several verbs to narrate the action (Jesus is "saying" directly to Paul, "I am sending you" [Acts 26:14, 17]) whereas in the salutation, the road-to-Damascus process is grammatically distilled into an adjective and noun pair ("called to be an apostle," Rom 1:1). This shift in language usage is not proof that we are

---

41. This nominalization often appears in scientific or historical genres: see J. R. Martin, "Making History: Grammar for Interpretation," in *Re/Reading the Past*, ed. Martin and Wodak, 19–57.

dealing with a different Paul, however. The choice of a noun over a verb partly reflects the register (written letter to a congregation versus verbal defense) and partly reflects the stage of the genre he is in (vv. 1–7 of the letter is mostly full of nouns rather than verbs, which is typical of a letter opening).

Stanley Porter has used this kind of analysis to make some educated guesses about the social situation and function that the letter to the Romans as a whole is addressing – writing to Christians in Rome whom Paul holds in high regard and admiration; introducing not just himself but pointing to Jesus and establishing his identity as the fulfilment of Scripture and the Son of God (as against the rhetoric of the growing Roman emperor cult); announcing the good news of grace and peace, which is his mission to bring to all nations.[42]

.SFL shows us how genre and register predict choices right down to whether we use a verb or a noun. This means we don't always need to know the context in advance – sometimes we may be able to reconstruct it from the grammar. This suggests a fascinating new direction for future New Testament research – maybe by you!

SUMMARY

Genres change over time (tenet 2), and ancient letters are not the same as modern ones, so we began this chapter by looking at some prototypes of ancient letters (tenet 3). We observed some typical formal features, including their distinctive staging structure, formulas for regulating the flow of information, and use of embedded genres. Letters participate in multiple genres (tenet 1), so we also expect to find a range of Old Testament resources and rhetorical conventions at play.

All this helps us keep up with what a letter writer is doing – the experiences, roles, and resources they are drawing on (tenet 4), as well as the choices they are making. However, to understand the letter genre, we need to ask what it is for, not just how it is written (tenets 7 and 8). Letters are generally used for maintaining relationships and sharing information between physically distant people, and so they are a bit like everyday spoken genres in that their function is tied closely to the situation they address. Like personal letters, New Testament letters are typically addressed to specific congregations and individuals. This close link between the text and situation is why it is important to understand as much as possible about the occasion of the letter. Yet biblical letters were also

---

42. Stanley E. Porter, *The Letter to the Romans: A Linguistic and Literary Commentary*, New Testament Monographs 37 (Sheffield: Sheffield Phoenix, 2015), 41–49.

intended to be shared and read more broadly for the instruction of Christians in other places, and their inclusion in the canon and participation in the Scripture genre invite us to apply them to our own context. This presents something of a paradox. While it would be vain to assume that these ancient letters are written directly to us in our situation, to read them as Scripture is to assume that they continue to function as God's word for us. We looked at how this process of applying an occasional letter to our context might work, using the example of 2 John.

The situation anticipated by a letter is realized in thousands of little decisions, right down to the level of grammar and syntax. This suggests some next steps for genre research. By studying these decisions, we might be able to recover something of the social context of the letter.

Suggested Workflow for Interpreting Letters

History

- ☐ Can you identify people, places, customs, institutions, social conditions, or events in the text? What do these suggest about the historical and cultural context of the letter? What worldview is assumed?
- ☐ Who is the letter from and to, and what do we know (or can we infer) about their relationship? What type of letter is it most like? How would you characterize the register?
- ☐ How have communities in different times, places, and cultures approached the passage? Given your own tradition, what assumptions are you likely to make about the letter?

Literature

- ☐ How would you describe the style and tone of the letter? What poetic or rhetorical techniques are used to get things done?
- ☐ Break up the text into stages (opening, body, closing) and phases. How do these meet, or depart from, our expectations of a Greco-Roman letter? How is it similar to or different from other letters in the New Testament?
- ☐ What topics are dealt with in the letter? What key terms are used? Are there structural markers that help regulate the information flow?
- ☐ What other genre relationships can you identify in or around this text (including embedded genres)? Why are they there, and what do they each contribute? What new ideas or effects emerge from combining the different genres?

Scripture

- □ Are there important biblical cross-references? Are there allusions to biblical people, events, ideas, principles, or passages? Are there Old Testament quotations or allusions?
- □ What connections can you see between this letter and the themes and storyline of the Bible as a whole? What is being assumed, corrected, reapplied, or highlighted?
- □ How does the passage contribute to our systematic theology? What is said, and what is left out? What would be missing from our understanding of key topics (God, humanity, Christ, salvation, and so on) if this passage were missing from our Bibles? What other passages need to be brought into the conversation to give us the full picture?
- □ What moral instruction or general teaching is given to the recipients? How is our situation similar to that of the original audience? How is it different? What teachings or principles are applied here that might be relevant to us? What new story or identity are we invited to take on for ourselves? What spiritual struggles can you relate to?
- □ How have you personally been challenged by the text and its implications? What do you find hard to understand or accept? How *shouldn't* we apply this letter?

QUESTIONS FOR DISCUSSION AND REFLECTION

1. Choose two (or more) of the following books: Romans, Galatians, Ephesians, 1 Timothy, 2 Corinthians, Philemon, Hebrews, James, and Revelation. Which ancient letter genres mentioned on page 228 do you think they are most similar to? Are there other genres that these letters (or parts of them) seem to participate in as well?
2. Most letters are addressed to specific groups or individuals, but some anticipate that they will be circulated more broadly. Can you think of any New Testament letters that speak directly to all Christians everywhere? How does this affect their social function? What might it mean for how we apply them to our situation?
3. A pastor prays at church wearing a Melbourne Football Club hat. What might 1 Corinthians 11:4 say into this situation?
4. Read 2 Corinthians 1:1–2:11. What can you infer from the register about the situation of that letter?

FURTHER READING

Introductory

Richards, E. Randolph. "Letters, Letter Forms." Pages 639–46 in *Dictionary of Paul and His Letters*. Edited by Scot McKnight, Lynn H. Cohick, and Nijay K. Gupta. Second edition. Downers Grove, IL: IVP Academic, 2023.
>Overview of the forms and cultural background of New Testament letters.

Ryken, Leland. *Letters of Grace and Beauty: A Guided Literary Study of New Testament Epistles*. Wooster, OH: Weaver, 2016.
>Principles and examples for interpreting the literary forms of New Testament epistles.

Weima, Jeffrey A. D. "Letters, Greco-Roman." Pages 640–44 in *Dictionary of New Testament Background*. Downers Grove, IL: IVP Academic, 2000.
>Overview of the ancient letter genres.

Deep Dive

Johnson, Luke Timothy. *The First and Second Letters to Timothy*. Anchor Yale Bible. New Haven, CT: Yale University Press, 2001.
>Demonstrates how situation and occasion should be taken into account in interpreting New Testament letters.

Porter, Stanley E., ed. *Handbook of Classical Rhetoric in the Hellenistic Period 330 BC–AD 400*. Boston: Brill, 2001.
>Collection of essays on rhetorical forms including chapters on rhetoric in New Testament epistles.

Porter, Stanley E., and Sean A. Adams, eds. *Paul and the Ancient Letter Form*. Pauline Studies 6. Leiden: Brill, 2010.
>Collection of essays approaching the stages of the ancient letter genre from a broadly SFL perspective.

PLAYING WITH GENRE

> In a theatre, it happened that a fire started offstage. The clown came
> out to tell the audience. They thought it was a joke and applauded. He
> told them again, and they became still more hilarious. This is the way,
> I suppose, that the world will be destroyed – amid the universal hilarity
> of wits and wags who think it is all a joke.
>
> Søren Kierkegaard, *Either/Or I* (1843)

It's bad enough when we get the genre wrong – dangerous even, if we mistake
a fire alarm for a comedy sketch. But *imagine if genre didn't exist at all*. Okay,
we'd still have language. And we would still have the need to communicate our
thoughts and make things happen in the world around us. Our elders would
still have a lifetime of experiences to share. Our poets and preachers would still
be brimming with creativity and urgent insight. Our friends would still feel our
absence and long for some way to keep in touch. But our ability to achieve these
goals through language would be subject to frustration at every turn.

Just think what it would be like. Every sentence a typical sentence, all
discourse longer than a sentence a law unto itself, nothing taken for granted.
Each time we spoke or wrote, we would have to work out from scratch how
to get things done with words. We'd all be like toddlers pointing to their food
for the first time and saying, "More." It takes a genius like John Milton to
find new ways of using existing genres; to produce literature in such a world
would be humanly impossible. We rightly marvel at cathedrals whose feats of
engineering took generations of skilled workers to design and build, each generation building on the engineering feats of the last. Genres deserve, likewise,
to be counted amongst the most impressive and enduring accomplishments of
human culture.

Genre deserves our careful study. And thankfully, over the past half century,
genre theory has been through a happy renaissance, as scholars in the fields of
literature, linguistics, and rhetoric have put their minds to work towards understanding this important and elusive aspect of language and culture. Biblical

scholars should be right at the forefront of this research, given the myriad biblical genres that greet us as we open the Bible. And yet, with some notable exceptions, we have chosen to muddle along with our own home-brew form criticism. Worse still, dissatisfied with the rigid categories and stubborn essentialism in Hermann Gunkel's genre theory, some have filed away genre as just one hyphenated fad on the way to more urgent redaction-, historical-, or reception-critical questions. Scholars skim over questions of genre with all the bluster of someone who wants to understand chess without learning the rules.

The Bible deserves better. I hope it's clear by now that form criticism needs to die (chapter 1). Yet the study of recurring forms and situations must absolutely go on, only this time underwritten by a theory of genre that's fit for purpose. The good thing about being so far behind is that we don't have to reinvent the wheel ourselves. We can easily get up to speed by plundering the Egyptians and seeing what's been going on in secular literary theory, linguistics, and social science. Turns out they've been busy. In chapter 2, I tried to give you a tasting plate of modern genre theory tenets, packed up and ready to go in a convenient takeaway box:

1. Texts don't belong to any one genre but are *promiscuous*, participating in complex relationships with multiple genres.
2. Genres are *relatively stable conventions*, like games we play with words.
3. Genres are fuzzy around the edges but have solid *prototypes* at their core.
4. Genres are about much more than merely sorting texts onto predefined shelves; they are functional. Each genre invites us to play a different *reading-game*, offering different *experiences*, inviting us to take up different hermeneutical *roles*, setting particular *goals*, and furnishing us with a treasury of *resources* to play with as we make meaning together.
5. These experiences, roles, and resources are about *readers* as much as *writers*.
6. Genres can regulate all sorts of things about a text, including *formal features*, distinctive *content*, and situational dynamics in the *social context*.

The limitations of form criticism have led some biblical scholars to give up on considering social context in genre. But Gunkel was onto something, however imperfectly form criticism pursued the idea. Chapter 3 offered some insights into how the social context relates to genre, courtesy of SFL and RGS:

7. Genres are recurring responses to recurring social situations.
8. As social action, genres are used for getting something done.
9. Genres both reflect and help create the world we experience.
10. Part of that social context is the power dynamic – genre is always working for someone.
11. Genres don't live alone but function in genre ecosystems within a context of culture.

The Bible, with its gloriously rich diversity of ancient genres, needs this kind of flexible and contextually aware approach to genre. Our access to the historical and cultural context of biblical genres is, like all ancient literature, limited. I am optimistic, however, and don't propose resigning ourselves to the echoes of our own subjectivity. Conventions are resilient things, and some genres work better with the biblical text than others. Central to my approach is the boomerang test (chapter 4), an invitation to pick up biblical texts, give them a throw as a particular genre, and see what comes back. While I can't tell you what payoffs to look for, things like coherence between the elements of a text and an assumption that the ancient writers weren't morons will go a long way.

At the very least, some self-awareness about what we are doing when we make a genre designation is essential, and so I distinguish between the kind of tacit genre designations we make when reading a text from our own culture and the more tactical decisions we must make when trying to understand texts from a foreign culture.

These tactical uptakes may be aimed compliantly at coordination with the writer, or they may be on a spectrum towards creative or even resistant readings. Either way, let's play around with genre a bit and see what we discover.

12. Texts don't read themselves, so the ball is always in the reader's court. Genre uptake is usually *tacit*, but as readers, we can also choose to make more *tactical* decisions about genre. Our goal in doing so might be somewhere on a spectrum from coordination to resistance.

As the twentieth-century philosopher Mike Tyson once said, everyone's got a plan until they get punched in the mouth. Likewise, anyone can have a theory – the test is what happens when we get hit by a real live text. In the spirit of testing these tenets, in the second part of the book, we dived headlong into actual examples from some of the main genres in the Bible – narratives, poetry, apocalypses, wisdom literature, gospels, and letters. We explored some of the potential payoffs of a historical perspective (tenets 1 to 6) for biblical studies. Moving away from seeing genres as rigid classifications helped us break through some intractable debates, like whether Genesis 1 is poetry or narrative (it's a spectrum, chapter 8), whether wisdom literature is a genre (it's a system of genres, chapter 10), and whether gospels are histories or biographies (yes, and yes, chapter 11). We've also been reminded that readers of the Bible are met, not by one homogenous set of conventions, but are invited to participate in all kinds of diverse experiences, roles, and resources. We can be drawn into the gaps of a great story (chapter 5), struck by the collision of images in poetry (chapter 7), confronted and comforted by apocalyptic images (chapter 9), or introduced to an apostle who is not physically present (chapter 12).

Of course, the fact that genres invoke different conventions in different contexts creates problems too. Whether it's narratives about slavery or apocalyptic visions, we've also seen how our disagreements about what a text means so often begin as tacit decisions about genre by readers. Highlighting the reader's active role in genre might sound like we are sliding into subjectivism, but I've argued that putting a genre decision through the boomerang test can actually help us see which readings are more, or less, coordinated with the writer – as with my tactical decision in chapter 6 to read Judges 19 as horror film, which I think helps us better understand that troubling story.

Studying genres as historical creatures pushes us to examine them in their social context as well. Embracing tenets 7–12, and seeing situation and function as fundamental parts of genre, will probably be an even bigger leap for biblical studies than tenets 1–6. Yet already the payoffs are promising. A recurring social situation helps us appreciate why an apocalypse is the way it is (chapter 9); slow-burn character formation is the function that binds the wisdom genre ecosystem together (chapter 10); the situational nature of a letter directs how we go about applying the text to our own context.

I hope it's clear by now that I am not at all arguing for a new technique called "genre criticism," as if to replace "form criticism" in the buffet of methodological approaches. Genre is not a scholarly approach we can put on or take off at will; it is part of how language works. The only choice we have is how well we want to understand it. Do we fall back on our automatic assumptions about the genre, or do we think carefully about how different conventions produce very different experiences of the text? It seems almost too obvious to say, but our conceptions of genre (whether tacit or tactical) have a huge impact on how we interpret the

Bible. Whether it's narrative, poetry, apocalyptic, wisdom, gospel, or letter, our disagreements about what the Bible *means* often boil down to different assumptions about what the biblical text's genre is — what reading-game we are playing.

We've covered a lot of biblical terrain in this book. Along the way, I've tried to sketch some potential applications for these modern genre tools, and I hope my amateurish suggestions will provoke actual specialists to see what modern genre theory can do for their research. I'm convinced that biblical studies has a lot to learn about genre from secular literary criticism, linguistics, and rhetorical studies right now. One day I would love to see us return the favor, contributing our own new insights and well-tested approaches to modern genre theory.

ACKNOWLEDGMENTS

Writing a little book on genre and the Bible has been more fun than I ever could have imagined. I am grateful to two communities that have shaped my thinking. The first is the Sydney University English department – my doctoral supervisor Liam who got me hooked on genre, and professors John Frow and Jim Martin for their insights and generosity.

The second is the biblical studies community, especially my amazing colleagues and students at Ridley College Melbourne. Thanks especially to principal Brian Rosner and the board for valuing research. I'm grateful for my friends at Moore College Sydney and in the SBLAAR (Society for Beer Lovers and Assorted Academic Research). Thanks go out to Walter Moberly and Stanley Porter for their encouragement and thought-provoking feedback on my thesis. I've learned so much through conversations about genre with Ryder Wishart, Andrew Myers, Adam Ch'ng, Andrew Bailey, and Dave Schreiner. Thanks, Katya Covrett, for encouraging and developing this project. I'm grateful to the Zondervan Academic team for bringing this book into being. A hearty high five and heartfelt thanks to my comrades in genre, Brandon Hurlbert and Tim Escott.

In this book, I really wanted to point to real-life examples of how modern genre theory might be useful across all kinds of biblical literature, but, of course, writing on everything from apocalypse to epistle meant taking on a 100 percent risk that I would say something silly about an academic specialty I have no business writing about. I am especially grateful to the phalanx of nerdy friends who have so graciously escorted my amateur incursions into their field by reading drafts of chapters: Andrew Malone, Mike Bird, Brian Rosner, Brandon Hurlbert, Andrew Shead, Joel Atwood, Doug Fyfe, John Anthony Dunne, Tim Escott, Con Campbell, and Kit Barker. Thank you to my dad, Stephen Judd, and my sister, Stephanie Kate Judd, for their judicious feedback on the whole manuscript. I'm grateful for Dirk Buursma's cheerfully punctilious copyediting powers. All errors that remain in this book are, naturally, intended as satire.

I hope you enjoy the genre theory ride as much as I have. Most importantly, I hope you're more excited and better equipped than ever to play along with the great book of genres.

GLOSSARY

Chronotope: Mikhail Bakhtin's term for the way a setting brings together time, space, and certain values.

Classical genre theory: broad term for older approaches to genre, which tend to classify texts into mostly fixed categories. Usually *synchronic* rather than *diachronic* in their approach.

Cline: a scale or spectrum that maps how closely a text realizes a certain parameter of a genre prototype.

Complex genre: a genre that can *embed* other genres. (Sometimes called a "secondary genre".)

Conceptual blending: from cognitive linguistics, describing what happens when two different mental sets are brought together – for example, in a metaphor or a text with multiple genres.

Convention: patterns of behavior we all observe because things go better if we do.

Context of culture: the broadest level of context that SFL is interested in. It includes all the genres available to us as language users in, for example, twenty-first century Australia.

Context of situation: the specific context in which language is used, which SFL models using *register* analysis. A genre is born when a recurring context of situation hooks up with a recurring way of using language.

Coordination: when the strategic decisions made by each player align, producing positive payoffs for both. Borrowed from game theory.

Diachronic: looking at how genres develop through time, seeing how they relate to their historical and social setting. (The opposite of *synchronic*.)

Embed, embedded genre: a genre that is introduced as a section within a complex genre – for example, a novel might embed a letter in one of its chapters.

Essentialist: treating genres as hardwired eternal rules, like the laws of geometry.

Etiology: a simple story genre for explaining why something is the way it is.

Exemplum: a simple story genre for describing and then evaluating someone's character or behavior, normally so we can imitate or avoid their moral example. Examples include "The Boy Who Cried Wolf," the Good Samaritan parable, and gossip about a colleague.

Family resemblance: a scientific-sounding way of talking about similarities between texts.

Field: the *register variable* that has to do with what's happening – the kinds of activities and topics.

Formal features: features (or "regularities") of a genre relating to the form or shape of the text as opposed to their content or function – the way poems rhyme, for example. (Not "formal" in the sense of how casual or "formal" the language is!) We might also use the terms "literary" or "internal" features.

Form criticism: a method (that needs to die) pioneered by Hermann Gunkel for investigating the forms and social setting of preliterary genres behind the biblical text.

Genre: relatively stable conventions that writers and readers use to make meaning in certain contexts but not others.

Genre theory: our working understanding of what genre is and how genres work.

Life-situation: technical term used in *form criticism* for the recurring situation within which the original preliterary genre was developed. Translation of the German *Sitz im Leben*, literally "seat in life." Compare with *situation*.

Mode (1): a genre but in stealth mode – for example, in a *gothic* novel, the mode (gothic) doesn't govern the text as a whole or supply a staging structure, but it lends a more subtle (creepy) flavor.

Mode (2): the *register variable* to do with how language is being used – is this a conversation with few words and lots of gestures, or a long novel?

Modern genre theory: broad term for more recent *genre theories*, which typically approach genres *diachronically*, placing them within their historical (tenets 1 to 6) and social (tenets 7 to 12) context.

Occasion: the specific circumstances that prompted a particular text to be created. Occasion relates to the actual historical context of an individual text, whereas *situation* is the general recurring context anticipated by the genre as a whole.

Phase: recurring elements that (sometimes) happen in a *stage*.

Plain meaning of the text: originally meant "non-allegorical" interpretations; now usually means "what I thought the text meant before I thought about it much."

Prototype, prototype theory: a way of thinking about a class of things centered around clear examples. From cognitive linguistics.

Reading-game: a way of thinking about genres. Like games, genres are conventions that writers and readers take part in to make meaning together.

Realization, realized: when general patterns actually show up in a specific concrete instance – for example, the country music genre predicts regularities in instrumentation, which may actually be realized in the song you're listening to, or not. Helpful for describing the relationship between higher and lower levels of analysis if you're trying not to be too prescriptive – how genres shape a specific text, how genre stages predict register variables, or how register variables show up in semantic patterns.

Register, register variables: a way of describing the social context of a text using three variables: *field*, *tenor*, and *mode*.

Rhetorical genre studies (RGS): a way of studying the social context of genres developed within rhetorical studies.

Romanticism: a European literary movement (roughly nineteenth century) that loved nature, hated rules, and sought to unleash the authentic genius of the individual artist.

Situation: the recurring social context in which genres get things done. Whether actual or anticipated, situations are partly assumed by and partly constructed by the genre. (Situation should not be confused with the actual historical circumstances that produced a given text, which we refer to as the *occasion*.)

Sitz im Leben: see *life-situation*.

Stage: an expected element in the *staging structure* of a genre, which works towards its function.

Staging structure, staged: the sequence of *stages* (and *phases*) we expect to go through in a given genre to achieve its function – how you tell a story (orientation, complication, quest, resolution, ending) or write an essay (abstract, title, introduction, body paragraphs, conclusion, bibliography).

Structuralist, structuralism: looking at things (words, ideas, categories, forms, genres) not as things but in light of the relationships between them. The goal is to understand the fundamental structures that human brains use to make sense of the world.

Structure: in biblical studies this can mean anything (from sentence structure to chiastic structure of an oracle to the arrangement of the canon). See *staging structure*.

Sydney School: see *Systemic functional linguistics*.

Synchronic: studying genres without taking history into account (the opposite of *diachronic*). Looks at systems of meaning available to speakers, examining the logical or psychological relationships that form a genre.

Systemic functional linguistics (SFL): a way of studying genres in their social context developed in linguistics.

Tacit: a normal reading or genre *uptake* made without thinking about it too much. The implicit goal is usually coordination between writer and reader.

Tactical: a reading or genre *uptake* that consciously responds to a text in a way that's not expected, for our own purposes. Our purposes can be somewhere on a spectrum from compliance (Shakespeare wants us to feel sympathy for Romeo and Juliet, so we do) to resistance (we expose Shakespeare's hegemonic cultural ideology by using feminist, womanist, queer, post-colonial, or Marxist readings).

Tenor: the *register* variable that tells you about who is typically involved in speaking or writing, including things like the relative power dynamic (is this a conversation between equals, or do my words make clear that I am the boss of you?) and affinity/solidarity (are we best buddies, or strangers?).

Text: something we try to understand as a meaningful whole – for example, a spoken promise, a written novel, an abstract work of art.

Truth effects: the kind of truth offered by a text. A fictional detective novel, a true-crime podcast and a police report offer different truth effects, because they purport to connect with different parts of reality, in different ways, for different purposes.

Uptake: the genre we use to respond to another genre – for example, a proposal is the expected uptake of a call for papers.

SCRIPTURE INDEX

SUBJECT INDEX

Note: References to subjects of a chapter are indicated in **boldface**.

AUTHOR INDEX